New Orleans

New Orleans

A Concise History of an Exceptional City

CHARLES D. CHAMBERLAIN

LOUISIANA STATE UNIVERSITY PRESS
BATON ROUGE

Published by Louisiana State University Press
lsupress.org

LSU Press Paperback Original
Manufactured in the United States of America
First printing

DESIGNER: Michelle A. Neustrom
TYPEFACE: MillerText
PRINTER AND BINDER: Sheridan Books, Inc.

Front cover photo Adobe Stock/James; back cover photos courtesy Historic New Orleans Collection.

Cataloging-in-Publication Data are available from the Library of Congress.

ISBN 978-0-8071-8487-5 (pbk.: alk. paper) — ISBN 978-0-8071-8534-6 (pdf) — ISBN 978-0-8071-8533-9 (epub)

To the guardians of the flame

Contents

Illustrations

Preface

THIS BOOK IS INTENDED to provide a readable, concise history of New Orleans. The city has inspired a voluminous literature on its rich history and culture, and many historical interpretations provide excellent in-depth scholarly examinations of specific time periods, events, neighborhoods, environment, and inhabitants. Clearly, with a city so tied to its past, a great need exists for exploring deeply the roots and evolution of the environment, the people, and cultures, as well as their destruction and resilience.

One often hears the lament that no accessible historical account exists that is also scholarly and comprehensive in covering the city's more than three centuries of history. This book aims to provide an all-embracing but short history that is not only trustworthy in terms of scholarship but also entertaining and relevant. As a tour guide, history professor, and museum professional, I often envision the readers as tourists or guides, educators and students of many ages, and casual readers who may be curious about the broad outlines of the city's history.

For this reason, some readers with local historical expertise may find the narrative and interpretation oversimplified. As a short history of New Orleans, this book does not explore the minutia of various topics. Instead, the work is intended to serve as an introduction and guide to scholarly history books and to archival-based sources that provide more detail. In many cases, the citations refer to a published work on a specific topic that can satisfy a reader's deeper interests. Thus, this book is intended not only to cover the comprehensive history but also to provide suggestions for deep dives.

Each chapter of this book also includes a list of relevant historical sites and a carefully selected recipe to make history come to life through site visits and culinary pursuits, encouraging readers to experience the city firsthand. New Orleans's history is one to be appreciated by living and often imbibing. Therefore, in the spirit of New Orleans, this short history encourages readers to explore and experience the city through narrative, *terroir*, and cuisine.

Acknowledgments

THE LIST OF PERSONS to whom I am indebted is immense, given the broad span of my career. I have learned from a large number of researchers, archivists, scholars, tour guides, culture bearers, and residents who have graciously shared their knowledge and expertise over the years in classes and conversations. Some of them have passed, while others live.

First, I would like to thank all the staff and researchers at the Hogan Jazz Archives and the Amistad Research Center, where my career began in the early 1990s. Hogan Archive curators Richard Allen and Bruce Raeburn, along with staff members Alma Williams, Dirk Van Teurenhaut, Tola Mosadomi, Angie Milner, and Lynn Abbott, laid the groundwork for my understanding of the social complexity that underlies the city's rich music history. I gained an appreciation for the city's rich musical-social history through friendships with Thomas Brothers, Jack Stewart, Wade Barnes, Andrea DuPlessis, Jason Barry, Tad Jones, Al Jackson, Matt Hampsey, Ben Schenk, William Kenney, John McCusker, Bjorn Barnheim, Fatima Shaik, Matt Sakakeeny, Evan Christopher, Lars Edegran, Barry Martyn, Yoshio and Keiko Toyama, David Kunian, Earl Turbinton, and Emily Epstein Landau. Similarly, the staff and researchers at the Amistad Research Center, including Ulysses S. Ricard Jr., Anne Harvey, Clarence Jones, Rebecca Hankins, Lester Sullivan, Barbara Guillory, Elise Cain, and Greg Osborn, patiently and graciously shared their experiences and knowledge of the city's rich Afro-Creole and African American cultures, thereby opening a door to understanding more fully the city's joyful and tragic histories.

Through the Tulane University graduate studies program, I also became acquainted with scholars with whom I have maintained professional relations and friendships. Tulane faculty—Sylvia Frey, John Blassingame, Clarence Mohr, Joe Caldwell, Roseanne Adderley, Richard Greenleaf, Rachel Devlin, Jim Boyden, Linda Pollock, Cora Presley, Bill Malone, and Larry Powell—all encouraged my development as a student of history. Many provided valuable writing advice that I attempt to share with my students. I still value my friendships with colleagues in graduate school whose research reveals a profound understanding of New Orleans history, from the colonial period to the modern era. These scholars include Walter Hickel, Jamie Carson, Leslie Parr, Bobbie Malone, Kenneth Hoffman, Kent Germany, Katy Coyle, Mark Souther, Guillaume Aubert, David Simonelli, Jeff Turner, and Emily Clark.

My ten years as historian at the Louisiana State Museum (LSM) provided greater exposure to the city and state's beautifully rich tapestry of cultures, stories, and experiences. I remain grateful to my former curatorial colleagues Alecia Long, Karen Leathem, Sam Rykels, Patrick Burns, Jeff Rubin and Michael Leathem, Larry Lovell and Ariana Ganak, Kacey Hill and Tom Riley, Aimée St. Amant Spangenberg, Kacey Godso Bolton, Jonathan Foret, Ryan Shaw, Christina Barrois, Shelby Doris, Polly Rolman-Smith, Gabriella Hernandez, Whitney Stone, Wayne Phillips, Janel Davis, Jane Irvin, Gaynelle Brady, and Cassandra Erb for their friendship and guidance in developing a number of well-received exhibits. Let me extend a special acknowledgment to Tamra Carboni for giving me the opportunity to work at the LSM; this experience laid the broad foundation for learning and absorbing all the layers of New Orleans history.

I gained immense knowledge from and formed friendships with advisory scholars as together we helped develop many LSM exhibits. In my work with the state museum in Natchitoches, I appreciate the contributions of Pete Gregory, Dusty Fuqua, Melinda Reliford, Eliza and Jack Brittain, Doug Ireland, Sandra Haynie Prudhomme, Rene and Kathy Prudhomme, Janet and Tracey Colson, Tommy Whitehead, Morgan Lasyone, Mary Linn Wernet, Carolyn Harrington, Sharon and Coley Gahagan, Bobby DeBlieux, as well as Chiefs Rufus Davis, Johnny Procell, and Laura Gates. Earl Robicheaux of Berwick graciously shared his love of birds and soundscapes of the back bayous of the Atchafalaya Basin. Judy Boudreaux and Clarence Becknell Sr. helped curate the marvelous Zulu Centennial exhibit. Richard Campanella was a gracious adviser to the Living with Hurricanes exhibit (and this book as well), and Kim Marie Vaz and Millisia White shone beautifully in creating the Baby Dolls exhibition. Glen Pitre and Michelle Benoit continue to inspire through their colorful and compelling visual storytelling. Chuck Siler, Grayhawk Perkins, Adela Gautier, Sybil Kein, Ina Fandrich, Willie "Tee" Turbinton, the Roots of Music educators (Derrick Tabb, Lawrence Rawlins Sr., Allen Dejan, and Edward Lee), and, above all, Cherice Harrison-Nelson shared their experiences and knowledge at the many educational outreach programs sponsored by the LSM system.

Additionally, I greatly treasure my bonds with LSM staff members Linda Keelin, "Lulu Bell" and "Brewstie," Gilbert Harrison, Kirby Aubert, Maya Hansell, Bobby Roy, Stacy Banks (and the Sudan Social and Pleasure Club), and their extended families who joyously shared their love of the city's culinary, celebratory, and family traditions in the trying years of post-Katrina recovery, when we celebrated Memorial Days at the lakefront, on the riverfront, and under the bridge.

During my years as a professor at the University of New Orleans, I have appreciated the support of my colleagues Jim Mokhiber, Michael Mizell-Nelson, Raphael Cassimere Jr., Andrea Mosterman, John Fitzmorris, Bobby Dupont, Kathryn Dungy, Marc Landry, Gunther Bischoff, Molly Mitchell, and Connie Atkinson of the Midlo Center, as well as Laine Kaplan-Levinson, then at WWNO, and students Jessica Dauterive, Derek Wood, Winston Ho, Daniel Lamplugh and Laura Guccione, Dana Logsdon, Tim Wilson and Cara Harrison Daniels, and Kathryn O'Dwyer. For enriching the field trips of my public history classes, I am indebted to and grateful for the time and effort of curators Ibrahima Seck of the Whitney Plantation and Slavery Museum, Leona Tate of the Lower Ninth Ward Living Museum, Ronald Lewis of the House of Dance and Feathers, Sylvester Francis of the Backstreet Cultural Museum, Liz Williams of the Southern Food and Beverage Museum, and the extended Harrison family at the Donald Harrison Sr. Museum.

Additionally, my years serving the Friends of the Cabildo (FOC) gave me a deep appreciation of the work provided by this organization. Jason Strada deserves immense credit for continually promoting lectures and walking tours related to New Orleans history. Bob Freeland, Bill Hyland, and Robbie Cangelosi Jr. also deserve praise for their selfless sharing of knowledge. They continually uncovered new layers of understanding related to New Orleans's Spanish, Latin American, and architectural history. Additionally,

FOC supporter Michael Messier-LeMoyne deepened my understanding of New Orleans's continuing family and cultural connections to French-speaking Canada and France.

Above all, I must thank all the deceased and living culture bearers I have known over the years, many of whom continue practicing the traditions that define New Orleans as an exceptional city with African and Caribbean roots. I treasure my friendships (past and present) with Black Masking Indians (especially Chiefs Rod Sylvas and Brian Harrison Nelson), the Northside Skull and Bones Gang (Chiefs Al Morris and Bruce Barnes, Royce Osborn, and Harambee), the Baby Doll Ladies and Dancers, educator-drummer Luther Gray, and dancer Jamilah Peters-Muhammed, as well as all brass band musicians and purveyors of New Orleans sounds.

And lastly, I thank my family for their profound love and support, as well as their appreciation for the special place that New Orleans will always hold in our lives. I am eternally grateful to my wife Vivian and my daughter Lene for their sharing of French culture and family, and my son Josh and daughter Jenny for passing a good time at (and tolerating) countless music festivals, second lines, and special cultural events.

New Orleans

Introduction

Is New Orleans Exceptional?

NEW ORLEANS IS OFTEN set apart from all other communities in the United States and even maintains an outsized character within the larger world. Since La Nouvelle Orléans's official founding by France in 1718, the historic town has earned a reputation as a place that embodies sin and decadence, exhibits Old World architectural charm, and offers extraordinarily mouth-watering Creole cuisine. Even before the United States acquired the Louisiana Territory in 1803, New Orleans was already renowned for permitting public African dances on Sundays and staging celebratory musical parades, and the locale was known internationally for its port that sat astride the great Mississippi River, as if with arms open to the world. All these attributes drew visitors to the Crescent City even before the mass tourism of the twentieth century.

Building on these characteristics in the post–World War I era, promoters branded New Orleans as "America's Most Interesting City." As the larger metro area experienced suburbanization in the post–World War II years, New Orleans continued to trumpet its unique characteristics. Even as late as the 1990s, a road sign on Interstate 10 at the Orleans-Jefferson Parish line welcomed visitors to the city with a superfluous boast of "most interesting." Given New Orleans's historical reputation for debauchery, colorful architecture, raucous jazz music, world-renowned gastronomy, intriguing spiritualism, and a penchant for merriment and Carnival parades, the sign seemed appropriate to many residents, who appreciated the celebratory culture despite some of the city's day-to-day dysfunction.

For this reason, present-day New Orleanians sometimes characterize neighboring Jefferson Parish, the West Bank, or the North Shore of Lake

Pontchartrain as epitomizing stereotypical bland suburbia with shopping centers and houses that all look the same. Some locals even joke that they are "going to America" when traveling to Metairie on a shopping errand. Conversely, some inhabitants of surrounding parishes look down on New Orleans as a wild, "un-American" place of decadence, particularly in the French Quarter and on Bourbon Street, and as a city where crime is rampant and potholes fill the streets. This mutual distrust and disdain partly stem from political differences: New Orleans stands out as a liberal bastion amidst more conservative suburban enclaves that emerged in the years after World War II, especially from the 1950s to the 2000s.

Side by side, the two geographical cultures of the "wild" city and the "conventional" suburbs help define New Orleans's historic and distinctive reputation, even within Louisiana. Yet, the great majority of suburban residents are native-born Louisianians who share much in common culturally with native New Orleanians. And these suburban areas today house a great diversity of ethnicities, religions, economic conditions, and traditions. The truth is that the suburbs, as an extension of New Orleans, also embrace the culture of reverence for culinary traditions and the revelry and spectacle of year-round parades and festivals, while "passing a good time" with family and friends at social events on the lake or in the backyard of a relative's home.

Even within New Orleans, one hears the same division applied to the uptown and downtown areas. Residents of the historically Creole neighborhoods below Canal Street may deride those living in the historically English-speaking area upriver for being staid and privileged, despite the reality of the diverse uptown culture and economic levels. Like the perceived New Orleans–suburban dichotomy, downtowners might claim that the more conservative and wealthier uptown area does not uphold the same rich cultural street and Creole food traditions for which New Orleans is known internationally. And in a city that maintained very strong neighborhood identities before the 2010s, the terms "frozen cup" (uptown) and "huck-a-buck" (downtown) referring to a homemade frozen treat, could signify on which side of the city one was raised. Similarly, the historic Afro-Creole Mardi Gras Indian and second-line costuming traditions embody different styles of imagery and design depending on whether the artisan lives uptown or downtown.

In recent years, a slogan emerged to "Keep New Orleans Funky," implying that the city's distinct Afro-Creole and artistic-bohemian culture is threatened by suburbanization, chain restaurants, big box stores, gentrification, and mass tourism. In fact, New Orleans East, which was developed in the 1960s and 1970s, sought to create from its inception a modern suburban lifestyle with some of those features. But tourists are never directed to visit the East, in part because the older historic neighborhoods such as the Vieux Carré (French Quarter), the Garden District, the Tremé, the Marigny, and the Bywater exude colorful architecture and exotic European-Latin-Caribbean-inspired culture that differentiates New Orleans from cookie-cutter suburbs and other American cities.

But is New Orleans truly exceptional? And, if so, based on what criteria? Although residents are often proud to claim the exceptionalist mantle, critics tire of the claim. Indeed, since the nineteenth century, New Orleans has evolved into an American city in its language, infrastructure, economy, and politics. Today, the process of gentrification and the increasing number of non-natives living in the city help weaken the city's historic Creole traditions, unique dialects, and older neighborhood identities. The presence of national chain stores, hotels, coffee shops, and restaurants also reflects the encroaching prevalence of national economic trends.

Nevertheless, within the United States, the city stands out in terms of its Creole history, cuisine, musical and Carnival traditions, and its deep Catholic roots. New Orleans is known internationally for having distinct indigenous food customs that include gumbo, jambalaya, red beans and rice, po-boys, muffulettas, Creole tomatoes, beignets, and king cake, to name just a handful of local and tourist favorites. In the broad category of American music, New Orleans is deemed the birthplace of jazz, one of the birthplaces of rock 'n' roll and funk, and home to a one-of-a-kind brass band performance tradition, as well as the modern hip-hop subgenre of bounce. And all these native music styles are driven by city residents' love for dancing, communal socializing, and forgetting one's troubles and cares.

New Orleans is also the only place in the United States where the Carnival season still follows a three-centuries-long historical thread of social rituals and is celebrated for up to four continuous weeks. Although the southern Gulf Coast from Pensacola to Galveston can be considered America's "Carnival Belt," New Orleans stands out as its glittery, blinged-out, oversized buckle. Northern and western cities such as Seattle and Philadelphia may have tried, unsuccessfully, to initiate their own Mardi Gras celebrations, but New Orleans pulls off these massive public events with decades of practice and professionalism.

New Orleans may take the title of the Carnival capital in the United States. But the Crescent City is but one of many places and cultures that celebrate the season in the larger Atlantic Creole world. Today the festival is an essential celebration in Rio de Janeiro, Cádiz, Veracruz, Mindelo, Nice, Cartagena, Venice, Santo Domingo, and Luanda, to name just a few places. This feast associated with gluttony and debauchery has roots in the Catholic celebration held immediately preceding the Lenten season of sacrifice and austerity. The culture of New Orleans (and south Louisiana generally) reflects the region's long history with the Catholic faith and therefore remains connected to other strongly spiritual Catholic Creole regional cultures of the Atlantic Basin.

New Orleans is promoted not only as an American city with Old World charm but also as the northernmost Caribbean community. During the French colonial period, the city and surrounding area received the designation of L'Île d'Orléans, the Isle of Orleans. The historic name reflected its location on an elevated landmass surrounded by water on all sides: Lake Pontchartrain to the north and Lake Borgne to the east, the Mississippi River to the west, and the Barataria marshes and lakes to the south.

And at the same time, the Île moniker conveys the location's similarity and historic relationship to the Caribbean islands. On many levels New Orleans maintains strong cultural and social similarities with tropical regions to the south. In fact, Caribbean cultures reflect the process of "creolization" that unites Atlantic Basin (and some Indian Ocean) colonial communities and cultures. Therefore, although New Orleans may be exceptional in the United States, the city is but one of many Creole communities that inhabit the larger Atlantic world.

New Orleans in the Atlantic Creole World

In New Orleans today, tourists and even locals use the term *Creole* to describe local cuisine (Creole gumbo), architecture (Creole cottage), people, and culture (the distinct French Catholic Carnival traditions) that contrast sharply with the Anglo-American culture of the rest of the United States.

But for both tourists and locals, the term is not always clearly defined. Is Creole a culture? An ethnic designation? Or a term that helps differentiate New Orleans from other regions of the United States?

In fact, *Creole* is quite difficult to explain, because the word's meaning has evolved over hundreds of years and in many different locations throughout the Atlantic world. In the Caribbean, Latin America, coastal Africa, and Louisiana, the term is often associated with an aspect of culture that is local, distinct, and rooted in the adaptation and blending of Atlantic cultures—Indigenous, European, African, and Asian. In some areas, such as Brazil and southwestern Louisiana, the word is also associated strongly with African cultures: as an ethnic designation for both persons of African ancestry and those who have European and sometimes Indigenous and Asian ancestry.

The word *Creole* originated in the first generation of Portuguese and Spanish Atlantic colonies to describe someone born in the Americas; hence, the reference was used to designate "American" in the Atlantic world, regardless of race and ethnicity. The term derived from the verbs *criar* (Portugese), *crear* (Spanish), and *créer* (French), meaning "create," "raise," and "breed," respectively. These words evolved into the adjectives-nouns *crioulo* (Portuguese), *criollo* (Spanish), and *créole* (French).[1]

In New Orleans, the word *Creole* is often used to designate the local Catholic French African traditions, as distinct from the more Protestant Anglo-American culture. But, in fact, former English colonies in the Caribbean, such as Barbados, the Bahamas, and Belize, as well as residents of the coast of South Carolina, also describe their cultures as Creole. In these English-speaking Creole locales, the dialects, cuisine, and the historic layers of colonial residents define their culture. Therefore, the term *English Creole* also recognizes the creation of a new distinct local culture that maintains historic ties to the larger Atlantic world.

Since the 1990s, modern scholars of Creole studies including Jean Bernabé, Eduard Glissant, Stuart Hall, and Michelle Martineau have used the verb "creolize" to describe this creation process. As related to New Orleans history, Shannon Dawdy uses the noun "creolization" to designate the end result of creating a new native society based on the local experiences of its diverse inhabitants. In her study of French colonial New Orleans, Dawdy clarifies that the term *Creole* should not be associated with ethnic identity but with culture and local identity—regardless of ethnicity.[2]

Similarly, colonial African historian Gwendolyn Midlo Hall claimed that the first generations of Afro-Creole people in Louisiana engaged in the same creation process. The late scholar argued that Africans in colonial Louisiana drew from a variety of cultures to create a Creole language, religion, music, and foodways specific to the lower Mississippi Valley. As Midlo Hall explained, "Conditions prevailing during the earliest stage of colonization molded a creole or Afro-American slave culture through a process of blending and adaptation of cultural materials brought by the slaves who were first introduced."[3] One could add to this idea that African people in south Louisiana incorporated Indigenous and European cultural elements into their Afro-Creole culture.

Therefore, the process of creolization applies certainly to New Orleans and south Louisiana's distinct Catholic cultures but also to any other location in the Atlantic colonial world in which European, African, Indigenous, and Asian peoples created a new and distinct society. The term *Creole* is found not only in the Americas but also on the west coast of Africa in places such as the Cape Verde Islands, where new communities and societies were created after the 1400s. *Creole* is also applied as far away as the Spanish Philippine islands of Mindanao and Luzon in the South Pacific and the former French colonies of Mauritius and Réunion in the southern Indian Ocean. Because of these islands' strong cultural connections to the Atlantic Basin, their residents use *criollo* and *créole* to convey their culinary traditions, music, language, and cultural identity.

During the nineteenth and early twentieth centuries in New Orleans (and in Catholic Louisiana generally), the term *Creole* morphed into various and contested definitions. When the first Americans began to arrive in New Orleans after the Louisiana Purchase in 1803, the native French- and Spanish-speaking Catholic residents viewed their culture and lifestyle as being very different from that of the new immigrants. Hence. the term "Creole" was applied to the *ancienne population,* or those Indigenous "Latin" inhabitants. These cultural differences were certainly based on the historic evolution of national identities and the disdain for one another that French and Spanish Catholics and English Protestants brought from Europe to the Americas.[4]

During the 1800s, those persons of French, Spanish, African, or Indigenous ancestry who were born and raised in La Nouvelle Orléans (and La

Louisiane) identified with their distinct local Creole mores, rather than with the customs of the Anglo-American immigrants. From the Louisiana Purchase in 1803 to the Civil War, this cultural clash was manifested in differences in language, religion, dance, theater, politics, commerce, and settlement within the city. The residential areas of New Orleans downriver from Canal Street (downtown) were largely French speaking and Catholic. The English-speaking Americans generally settled in the newer neighborhoods being subdivided from Creole plantations on the upriver (uptown) side of Canal Street.

And in the era of formal racial segregation after the American Civil War, persons who identified as French Creole—that is, as white—attempted to claim the word as their own. Their racial and cultural designation excluded any French-speaking Catholics of mixed African-European-Indigenous ancestry, whom racial conservatives labeled as "mulatto." Nevertheless, Creoles of color still claimed the term to proudly describe their culture and identity, seeing it as an act of cultural resistance toward the racial hierarchy promoted by both Creole and American white supremacists.[5]

For Afro-Creoles or Creoles of color living in New Orleans during the late nineteenth and early twentieth centuries, the term *Creole* also applied to the local French dialect, an Africanized "pidgin" French language, with characteristics similar to what was spoken in the former colonial Afro-Creole communities of Haiti, Guadeloupe, Martinique, French Guyana, and Cape Verde. The Creole dialect is all but gone today in New Orleans but is evident in a few terms that still linger in the city: *cayoudle* (mutt, mixed breed), *cowan* (turtle), and in New Orleans's traditional Black Masking Indian (aka Mardi Gras Indian) shouts such as "Two way pocky way" (*get out of the way!*).

During the twentieth century, however, French Creole identity largely diminished in the white community while remaining strong among Creoles of color. As in the larger Atlantic Basin, the term *Creole* in New Orleans came to describe local cuisine, customs, language, and native-born people, many of whom still actively identify as Creole today. A considerable portion of African Americans today in the New Orleans metro area still proudly proclaim their Creole identity as part of their heritage, family history, and culture.[6] Yet the term is applied most often to local architecture (Creole cottages), locally grown food such as Creole tomatoes, and, of course, Creole gumbo and cuisine. The common use of Creole to describe local foods still resonates for locals, who value food not just for nourishment but also for socializing and sharing their family and community heritage.

Food as Metaphor: History, Culture, and Tradition

Food is central to the life, culture, and heritage of New Orleans and Catholic south Louisiana. The culinary heritage in New Orleans plays a similar role to that of other internationally famous gastronomic traditions, where food is an important part of one's cultural identity. In France, to give an example relevant to New Orleans's history, one can spend an entire dinner discussing the merits of certain cheeses, of which the nation boasts more than 240 varieties. In the French Mediterranean city of Marseille, locals debate competing recipes for bouillabaisse, a hearty fish stew from the coast.[7]

Similarly, one can go to a dinner in New Orleans and easily have a long discussion on different gumbo recipes and how long to cook a roux or whether to include tomatoes in a recipe for jambalaya. And when tourists ask locals about the best place to find a good gumbo, the common response is "my mee maw's kitchen." Underlying the amusing nature of this claim is the association of food with family, comfort, heritage, and social life—and the reality that gumbo from a restaurant only occasionally meets the standards of locals.

In New Orleans, residents often socialize together while eating local (Creole) foods, drinking (often alcohol) together, and listening to music (and often dancing) in a communal friendly setting such as a backyard, on a public street, at a park, or on the lakefront or bayou. In this context, the crawfish boil is the ultimate social food event. As the steaming spicy crustaceans are poured out onto a long table covered with newspapers, the guests gather around to eat the crawfish, share some beers, and have a good laugh while listening to celebratory music. Food defines the New Orleans experience, as reflected in New Orleans's international reputation for its distinct foodways. Although the city is one of the smaller big cities in the United States (#53 as of 2024), it remains one of the top U.S. tourist destinations internationally.

This book integrates the centrality of food into the telling of the city's past. Cuisine reflects the different layers of immigration and creolization that have unfolded for more than 300 years since before the city's official founding in 1718. Because cuisine remains central to New Orleans's traditional and current identity, each chapter relates the history of a popular dish that is relevant to the time period of the city as a continental trading site, international maritime river port, and cultural crossroads.

Chapter 1 focuses on how the original Indigenous settlement site emerged as an important continental trade center and crossroads. The Choctaw name for the site where New Orleans was founded means "the place of many languages." Located near the mouth of the Mississippi River Basin and in the central Gulf Coast of North America, the site existed at the intersection of two very important trading routes both before and after the arrival of Europeans and enslaved Africans. The chapter uses corn maque choux, a local corn stew, as a metaphor for the legacy of Native cuisine. Indigenous peoples throughout the Americas cultivated corn and relied on the crop for much of their diet well before colonial settlement. Therefore, corn is the ultimate symbol of American Indian food customs that continue to be a large part of the heritage of New Orleans. Corn (*tanchi*) also reflects the importance of the city's location as an important Native trade site, where food products such as bear meat, bear oil, fish, and filé (ground sassafras) were bartered and exchanged.

The establishment of the first European permanent settlement on the lower Mississippi River is the subject of Chapter 2. The French crown under King Louis XIV claimed the Mississippi River and all its tributaries as La Louisiane in 1682 and then established the capital town of La Nouvelle Orléans in 1718. The population of this diverse but small international port, in the location of today's Vieux Carré, never surpassed 2,500 residents during the forty-five years of French colonial rule. The small size of the settlement reflected the challenges that France faced in recruiting settlers to the far-flung outpost. In this chapter, jambalaya is used as a metaphor for the importance and prevalence of rice, with roots in Senegal (*riz jollof*), Spain (*paella*), and France (*riz de Camargue*). The dish reflects the food customs that early immigrants (both voluntary and forced) shared in their diets.

The third chapter covers the period from 1763 to 1803 when Spain administered the colony as part of its vast empire in the Americas from Cape Horn (Cabo des Hornos), South America, to the headwaters of the Mississippi River. During this period, the small port town of Nueva Orleans grew to more than eight thousand people, in part because of the expansion of slavery to fuel a growing tobacco export market in Louisiana. Most enslaved arrivals came from the Congo region of Central Africa, and their culture left an imprint on the colony's music, religion, language, and foodways. Enslaved Africans often worked as cooks, so that the evolving Creole cuisine reflected the African propensity to add red pepper to the cooking pots. In this chapter, stuffed peppers (*pimientos rellenos*) are the iconic New Orleans dish common to Spain, France, North Africa, and throughout the Mediterranean Basin.

After the United States bought the Louisiana Territory for $15 million, the booming port city began bursting at the seams, attracting American immigrants and their enslaved workers from the Atlantic Coast, as well as immigrants fleeing the Haitian Revolution, the Irish potato famine, and political upheavals in Germany and France during the mid-1800s. By 1840, the city was one of the nation's slave trade centers and had reached a population of more than 83,000, making it the third-largest city in the United States. The metropolis doubled in size to reach 170,000 inhabitants by 1860. In chapter 4, the dish Creole court-bouillon reflects the creolization of older French traditions, as local cooks adapted to the warm flavors and fresh seafood available in the waters surrounding their city.

New Orleans continued to be the economic center of the American South after the Civil War and Reconstruction. And as a major port of entry to the United States, the city attracted a new wave of immigrants from the Mediterranean Basin (Sicilian, Croatian, Greek, and Lebanese Maronite), and others from Eastern Europe (Ashkenazi Jews) and the China Sea Basin of Asia (Filipino and Cantonese). Chapter 5 explores the postwar industrialization of the city and its continued importance as a Latin American port. The section also examines New Orleans's rise as an American tourist center fueled in part by its Creole past, all against the backdrop of formal legal racial segregation and resistance. The local seafood dish of grilled oysters is featured, representing the strong influence of these social, economic, and cultural developments and the process of creolization in the Gilded Age.

In the decades following World War I, New Orleans's sensational musical export gave rise to the city's nickname "the Birthplace of Jazz," the subject of chapter 6. As part of this social and cultural development, the city's native son Louis Armstrong became perhaps the best-known entertainer across the globe. In this era of formalized racial segregation, the city's older neighborhood residential patterns continued despite the legal racial hierarchy. During this new automobile age, the city continued to develop as a tourist destination, and the "French Quarter," as the Vieux Carré became known, emerged as a bohemian community with a taste of the Old World for domestic transplants and visitors. Fittingly, Louis Armstrong's favorite meal, red beans and rice, one of New Orleans's celebrated dishes, reflects the history of working people and the city's African and Latin American culinary heritages.

In the five decades after World War II, as discussed in chapter 7, the city attempted to accrue modern amenities—a new airport, an interstate highway, a new city hall, and a bridge across the Mississippi—all the while dismantling the archaic system of racial segregation and promoting its historic Latin-European charm for tourists. During this rock 'n' roll era, New Orleans produced many great artists such as Fats Domino, Little Richard, and Allen Toussaint. These soulful entertainers inspired a generation of British Invasion artists, who themselves romanticized New Orleans's music legacy. After 1965, the city gradually embraced a new post–civil rights social and political tourist environment, in which all the major national hotel chains built new high-rise lodgings in the city, and the boosters promoted New Orleans as "America's Most Interesting City."

In this post-segregation period, New Orleans also welcomed a new wave of Catholic immigrants from Vietnam and Honduras, along with Palestinian and Pakistani families seeking a new life in the United States. Reflecting the new "Vietnamese Creole" culture, the locally beloved and spicy grilled pork banh mi sandwich serves as the metaphorical food: it showcases the culinary heritage of France (flaky pistolette bread) and Vietnam (grilled pork), while adding a layer of sliced carrots and cucumbers topped with spicy garden-fresh jalapeño peppers.

Modern New Orleans presents itself as a city that rebounded from the tragedy of Hurricane Katrina, as explored in chapter 8. The powerful wind, rain, and tidal event was followed by the failure of several levees and an inundation of half the city that sits below sea level. The storm and the flood made international news with images of residents being rescued from their rooftops. New Orleans's gradual recovery and federal reinvestment enhancing the city's flood protection reflected the resilient spirit of a community that endured devastating fires, springtime Mississippi River floods, yellow fever epidemics, and waves of racial violence over its more than three-hundred-year history.

And with the new era of mass tourism fed by short-term rentals and travel advice apps, the city underwent a new wave of development and gentrification of older neighborhoods such as the Bywater, the Tremé, and the Lower Garden District. Rising costs of living provided a test to the city's livability in the new age. In this post-Katrina era, the Asian-inspired soup yakamein, originally found in corner stores in older African American neighborhoods, came to new prominence at festivals and cooking contests, along with the New Orleans fast-paced bounce hip-hop genre known for twerk dancing. Together these two cultural gems became a symbol of the gentrification of the city's previously overlooked food and music cultures.

Still an Exceptional City?

The debate over New Orleans's exceptionalism reflects the dual identities of a city that was born in the context of the colonial Atlantic Creole world but that came of age firmly within the United States. The history of the city in the following pages follows both threads.

From the beginning, the city maintained a reputation as a community trying to reconcile desire and piety. From the earliest years of the colony, the debaucherous comportment of its residents contrasted and coexisted with the piousness of devout Catholics, Muslims, and Afro-Creole spiritualists. As a reflection of this dualistic behavior, up until the 2000s, most historic New Orleans neighborhoods supported more churches than bars, despite the city's reputation for hedonism.

New Orleans is also marked by a resiliency that may not be unique but that reflects the residents' commitment to place. The city has overcome many strong hurricanes, engineered an existence amidst the environmental challenges of river flooding and tropical deluges, rebuilt anew following sweeping fires, survived two military assaults in wartime, and endured numerous epidemics that fractured society. Like other international ports around the world, New Orleans has absorbed immigrants from across the globe, often integrating their cultures into the city's creolized layers of culture. Therefore, in many aspects, the city may have more in common with

London, Shanghai, Buenos Aires, and Cape Town than its neighboring U.S. communities.

But given these broad universal attributes ascribed to the city, the question remains how New Orleans continues to stand out in the age of globalization. The city's renowned Creole food culture still draws tourists; the city is still renowned as one of the great food meccas of the United States and the world. These foods are often so distinct (and the residents so particular) that many locals feel lost and hungry when they eat in places outside New Orleans. After Katrina, when many residents found themselves stranded in Houston, Atlanta, or Denver, they lamented how they could not buy proper po-boy "French" bread, specific brands of red beans, or smoked sausage. Nor could they form an impromptu second-line street parade or carry open containers of alcohol on the street.

Despite all the challenges posed by Katrina and threats to the city's way of life and culture, many of New Orleans's customs prevail. One sees old Creole cottages and shotgun houses painted in bright pinks, purples, turquoise, peach, and yellow colors associated with the tropical colors of the Caribbean. In the city and surrounding suburbs, one can still detect the soft drawl of locals that remains different from the twangy drawl of other southern regions and mystifies tourists who think the dialect sounds like a Brooklyn or Boston accent. And greetings of "where y'at babeh" still resound among some residents of New Orleans and the surrounding parishes.

Certainly, the cultural layers of Catholic immigrants make New Orleans a distinct American port city but one with ties to its historical trade partners and homelands. People from the Choctaw nation, Normandy, Senegal, Alsace, Andalusia, the Congo, Cuba, Bavaria, Ghana, New York, Haiti, Lancashire, Mexico, Ireland, Sicily, the Philippines, Croatia, South Vietnam, Palestine, and coastal Honduras all shape the city in a myriad of ways. And for many locals and tourists, the resulting Latin-Afro-Creole culture of the city remains one of the great touchstones of attraction, pleasure, and desire.

One of New Orleans's strongest connections to the Afro-Caribbean-Creole world is the tradition of celebrating in the streets on Sunday with dance and music. Every Sunday between Labor Day and Memorial Day, thirty-plus African American Social Aid and Pleasure Clubs host their own second-line parades open to anyone who cares to join in the festivities. Club members dress in elaborate matching costumes and wield handcrafted accessories such as umbrellas, baskets, or fans. The walking-dancing street parade is powered by funky brass bands, playing a mashed-up repertoire from old traditional hymns to the latest pop or R&B hit. This moving mass of dancers-strutters may be followed by a whole subculture of urban cowboys on horses, ATV and dirt-bike gangs, and low-rider bike clubs, along with countless food trucks, smoky barbeque trailers, mobile alcohol vendors dispensing from their pickup truck bed, or a child's wagon toting an icy cooler filled with beer. Nowhere else in the United States does this phenomenon occur.

At Carnival time, New Orleans still embraces its French and Spanish Catholic traditions. On Mardi Gras Day, St. Charles Avenue and Canal Street are filled with revelers watching the large Rex and Zulu parades, while the backstreets are witness to colorful Afro-Creole Indian beaded suits, menacing Skull and Bone skeletons, and sassy Baby Doll ladies.[8] The African American costuming traditions have deep ties to the larger African diaspora found in the Caribbean and Atlantic Basin, where Afro-Latin cultures remain integral to Carnival celebrations. Although Hurricane Katrina stoked fears among many residents that the floodwaters would wash away Creole street traditions, culture bearers remained even more committed to their customs, especially when they encountered life without their celebrations while in exodus.

Since Katrina, New Orleans has changed considerably in many ways. Many older neighborhoods have been gentrified. The city's culture bearers have trouble making ends meet, given the higher costs of living and of elaborate costume supplies. Nevertheless, its unique customs still make the New Orleans an incomparable city within the United States, while the Creole port city remains part of the larger Atlantic world stretching from the Caribbean and the east coast of Latin America to the western coasts of Africa and Europe. The city is American in its language, economy, and politics but remains Creole in its culture and way of life for many remaining residents. The locale, historically known as L'Île d'Orléans, therefore exists as an extraordinary American city in an Atlantic Creole world.

1

Bulbancha

An Indigenous American Crossroads, Pre-1718

PIERRE LE MOYNE, Sieur d'Iberville, provided the first written account of the future site of New Orleans. In 1699, the French commandant who was raised in Quebec led an expedition to thoroughly explore the lower Mississippi River and establish formal relations with Indigenous nations. Hearing about a possible settlement from his Bayou Goula guides, Iberville wrote in his journal, "I went and looked at a spot where the Quinipissa once had a village." On December 19, 1699, the day Iberville encountered the abandoned Quinipissa village (*lukuli*), he noted, "Here I found that the land did not become inundated, or did so very little." He further observed how "trees have grown back in the fields as big as two feet around," indicating that the cleared farmlands had remained untilled for a decade or so.[1] Nearly two decades later, in 1718, Jean-Baptiste Le Moyne, Sieur de Bienville, and Pierre's younger brother would establish the new settlement of La Nouvelle Orléans at this site on the banks of the Mississippi.

Indigenous activists in New Orleans reminded the public of this precolonial history in 2018, the year celebrated as the three hundredth anniversary of New Orleans's founding as the new capital of the French colony La Louisiane. To counter the city's heralding of French colonial history, a group of Indigenous historians promoted the claim that "Bulbancha is still a place."[2]

The term *Bulbancha,* also spelled "Balbancha," is included in Cyrus Byington's *Dictionary of the Choctaw Language,* published in 1915. Byington's entry for New Orleans is listed simply as "Balbancha." This word of Choctaw origin translates as "place of foreign languages."[3] Early Europeans recognized that the term applied broadly to the lower Mississippi River and Pontchartrain Basin. The settlement at Bulbancha was located at the intersection of Indigenous trade and transportation routes, where the Mississippi River and the Gulf of Mexico converged. More than three centuries later, New Orleans continues to be a major trade crossroads for the North American continent and a "place of foreign languages."[4]

But if the site existed as a settlement or seasonal trade crossroads, why did Iberville only find the remnants of a Quinipissa village when he arrived in 1699? The French Quebec-born commandant kept a detailed log, published today as *Iberville's Gulf Journals,* that is a rich source documenting Native settlements and cultures at that time. Perhaps his observation that the land had not been flooded reveals why the location was founded as a farming village earlier in the seventeenth century.

All the Ground Here Becomes Inundated

Iberville's focus on inundation, or the lack thereof, was of paramount importance to his quest for a permanent colonial settlement site. In this wetland environment, topography likely determined the locations of both seasonal and permanent Indigenous communities on the Mississippi. As Iberville noted, his expedition encountered the first small village of the Quinipissa about six miles upriver from the site of New Orleans at Cannes Brulés (present-day Rivertown in Kenner). There Iberville observed a small redoubt made of river canes that contained about ten huts made of thatched palmetto. At that time, this bamboo-like cane (*Arundinaria gigantea*) grew in impenetrable canebrake forests along the banks of rivers and creeks of the lower Mississippi Valley, providing essential material for making baskets, tools, and shelters. The site's name (translated as "Burned Canes") reflected how the Quinipissa used fire to clear a section of the canebrake for their settlement in the narrow slice of elevated ridge along the river and close to the lake.[5]

The next village that Iberville's party encountered, that of the Bayou Goula people, was located almost fifty miles upriver from the site of New Orleans. The contemporary river hamlet of Bayou Goula remains in that location on the west bank of the Mississippi near Baton Rouge.[6] The absence of large settlements in the flood-prone region between New Orleans and Baton Rouge might have led the expedition to believe that the environment and topography of the lower Mississippi indeed played a role in the Quinipissa's abandonment of the Bulbancha site.

In this first expedition in 1699–1700, Iberville hoped to gain important insight into the environment and topography of the lower river that would help him determine where the French might establish their permanent settlement. While at the Cannes Bruleés site on March 7, 1699, the commandant observed, "All of the ground here becomes inundated a foot deep as far back as half a league in the woods where I went." This entry presents Iberville's first account of the deltaic topography of the lower Mississippi, in which the rivers and bayous had built up natural sedimentary elevated ridges. These crests provided high ground in a vast wetland largely defined by swamps (flooded freshwater forests) and marshes (flooded brackish-water grasslands).[7]

Iberville's observation of the natural ridge along the lower river at Cannes Bruleés was an important acknowledgment of the environmental challenges that existed (and still exist) in south Louisiana. In this deltaic waterscape, geology likely played a very important role in determining settlement locations and, in the case of Bulbancha, possible seasonal abandonments.

The Mississippi River has had a 5,000-year history of creating at least six successive river deltas. Geologists have now determined the locations of the six deltas and assigned them names and rough dates. As the Ice Age ended, the river began to build its first delta mouth, known as Sale-Cypremort Delta, around 4600 BP (before the present), far to the west of New Orleans around the present-day Atchafalaya Basin.

In this evolving deltaic process, the river deposits sediment along its banks, creating a natural ridge or high ground. After one thousand years or so of sediment deposition, the Mississippi seeks a new course: the river finds a new natural flow that has less land resistance. The old delta and its course are then abandoned and erode, while the river creates a completely new delta.

Over the next four thousand years (4600–500 BP), the river built and abandoned four succeeding deltas: the Teche (3500–2800 BP), the St. Bernard (2800–1000 BP), the Lafourche (1000–300 BP), and the Plaquemine (750–500 BP). The present-day delta is the Balize (500 BP). In its cyclical process, the river would naturally abandon the Balize and move its dominant current to the Atchafalaya River Basin. But that riparian shift will not happen because the U.S. Army Corps of Engineers' Old River Complex north of Baton Rouge ensures that the current Balize "birdfoot" course is maintained, given its economic importance for shipping between Baton Rouge and New Orleans.[8]

As Indigenous people moved into the lower Mississippi Valley after the Ice Age, the natural ridges along the bayous and rivers provided elevated locations for settlement above the surrounding inundated swamps and marshes of the low wetlands. And as the Louisiana Division of Archaeology has documented, remains of Indigenous settlements can be found along the many river and bayou ridges, as well as on the shores of brackish-water lakes, such as Lake Pontchartrain, around New Orleans.[9]

In these settlements, the remains of middens—piles of discarded oyster and clam shells—indicate the historic presence of Indigenous peoples. André Pénicaut, a member of the Iberville expedition, noted in 1699 that at the Rigolets channel east of New Orleans, "Both sides of this entrance are covered with shells in such great quantities they form banks."[10] Because of their historical importance and the threat of looting, the locations of these middens are closely guarded today. Nonetheless, one can easily encounter such piles along the shores of many lakes and bayous in the immediate New Orleans area.

But the question remains: Why did the Quinipissa abandon their established settlement at Bulbancha by the 1690s? The answer may involve conflicts between local Indigenous nations, or the practice of settling impermanently in one location. Yet an equally plausible cause is the river's annual cycle: each spring the snowmelt from the Rocky Mountains and sometimes excessive rains upriver would cause the river to swell and overflow the sediment ridges, thereby inundating the lower river and surrounding wetlands with freshwater. And every so often, a severe flood, perhaps a destructive Mississippi River flood or a hurricane tidal surge from Lake Pontchartrain, created too much insecurity, instability, and stress to justify a long-term settlement.

Historically, the annual "spring melt" floods helped create and support a freshwater environment, in which forests of cypress trees thrived in the swamps and massive live oaks and swamp maples grew along the elevated ridges. Before the French, Spanish, and Americans built levees, the river overflowed its banks every spring, making settlement precarious for Indigenous people along the lower Mississippi. Perhaps that is why the Bayou

Goula village that Iberville's expedition encountered was located far upriver from the site of Bulbancha, where nondeltaic upland ridges and hills first emerge along the river's banks.

So, after encountering the abandoned village and farmlands at Bulbancha in December 1699, Iberville instructed his younger brother Bienville to go to the Bayou Goula and "ask them about places on the lower part of the river that are [not] subject to overflow." In scouting a location for their colonial capital and port, the Frenchmen relied on the experience and wisdom of the Bayou Goula Indigenous people to guide them in their search.[11]

Plusiers Nations

In 1735 French royal engineer Alexandre de Batz painted a remarkable scene of a Native American market at the site of New Orleans, which he titled *Desseins de Sauvages du Plusiers Nations, Nv. Orleans, 1735* (Drawing of Savages from Several Nations, New Orleans, 1735; fig. 1). The colorful illustration depicts a variety of women, men, and children from several nations gathered on the banks of the Mississippi River at a market selling domesticated dogs and geese, *huille d'ourse* (bear oil), *suif* (tallow—perhaps bison), and *plat côté* (ribs—perhaps bison or deer). In the painting, de Batz identifies people from the Attakapas and Illinois nations, as well as a *Renarde Sauvagese Esclave* (female Fox Indian slave) and a *negre* (African) of undetermined status.

De Batz's depiction is important because it shows New Orleans as a trade crossroads for the Indigenous nations of the Mississippi Valley and Gulf Coast. At that time, the Illinois Confederation and Miskwaki (Fox) peoples lived in the upper Mississippi River and Great Lakes region, and the Ishak (Attakapas) people resided on the coast and prairies of present-day southwestern Louisiana. The presence of a young Black boy in the image indicates that African people, likely maroons (formerly enslaved captives from English or Spanish settlements), lived in the region along with native peoples before French settlement. The Black child's presence in the image foreshadowed a complex relationship between Indigenous and African peoples in the early colony.

De Batz's painting exemplifies the definition of Bulbancha as "the place of many languages." Indeed, the artist placed the word *Balbancha* at the

FIG. 1. This illustration depicts Bulbancha as an important trade crossroads for people of different nations speaking multiple languages. Alexandre de Batz, *Desseins de Sauvages du Plusiers Nations, Nv. Orleans, 1735,* Peabody Museum of Archaeology and Ethnology, Harvard University, 60741527.

bottom of the painting in reference to the site's location along the "Missyssipy" or "Fleuve St. Louis." This seasonal marketplace likely existed before the French arrived, attracting traders of goods from throughout the larger region. Since the end of the Ice Age, the Mississippi River and all its tributaries, as well as the inland bayous and marshes of the Gulf Coast, had served as major trade routes, similar to today's interstates and highways. In the seasonal cycle of Indigenous trade networks, Bulbancha probably served as a regional market in the autumn or early spring, when the area was less prone to flooding and wild game was plentiful.

Generally, the territories and settlements of Indigenous nations in the region changed frequently because of seasonal migrations, population pressures, epidemics, warfare, and environmental factors. At the time of French settlement, several smaller nations, known as *petites nations,* resided in what is today the New Orleans metro area. Larger nations such as the Choctaw and the Chickasaw lived farther upriver.

Antoine-Simon Le Page du Pratz, an early French settler, observed the frequent migrations of Indigenous people and their subsequent resettlements. Living among the Natchez nation in the 1720s, the Frenchman heard from them how quickly the Choctaw appeared in their midst. In his firsthand account *La Histoire de la Louisiane,* du Pratz claimed that the Natchez informed him how a "nation arrived so suddenly, and passed so rapidly through the territories of others." When he inquired "whence came the Chatkas [Choctaw]?" the Natchez answered, "They sprung out of the ground; by which they meant to express their great surprise at seeing them appear so suddenly."

Yet, despite their "great numbers," the Choctaw were "little inclined to war, [and] did not inspire [the Natchez] with the fury of conquest." Like many Indigenous peoples pushed farther west by pressures from English colonial settlements, these nations "at length arrived in an uninhabited country which nobody disputed with them." There the new arrivals lived "without any disputes with their neighbours; who on the other hand have never dared to try whether they were brave or not."[12]

On his arrival in 1699, Iberville had noted the presence of numerous *petites nations* in the areas around present-day New Orleans. He first encountered the Annocchy (Biloxi), who lived farther east along the present-day Mississippi coast, and then the Bayou Goula, who lived along the lower river with the Quinipissa, whom Iberville determined might have been the same nation.[13] Additionally, the Chawasha and the Washa resided in the marshes and swamps near present-day New Orleans, whereas the Acolapissa lived on the north shore of Lake Pontchartrain.

Upriver from the Bayou Goula lived the Houma, who dwelled at a village north of present-day Baton Rouge in the Tunica Hills, named for the neighboring Tunica nation that eventually pushed the Houma farther south. In 1699 Iberville observed a *baton rouge* (*iti humma*) or red stick, after which the present-day capital city was named: it served as a marker on the bluffs of the Mississippi River identifying the border between the Houma and Bayou Goula territories. Gradually over the following 150 years, the Houma moved to the elevated regions along the river (near the present-day Houmas House and Cabahanoce [Cabahannosé/Cabanocey] Plantations), and then farther south to the lowland marshes of present-day Terrebonne Parish, from which the town of Houma takes its name. Their frequent migrations reflect the constant pressure that many Indigenous peoples experienced in eighteenth- and nineteenth-century Louisiana, as they settled in isolated areas to avoid conflicts with more powerful tribes and aggressive white settlers as well.[14]

To the west of the Mississippi River lived the Chitimacha in the region of the Atchafalaya River Basin. They had originally resided on the ridges and swamps of the lower Mississippi. But when France declared war on the nation early on, they sought refuge in the swamps to the west, where their present-day federally recognized reservation is located in Charenton along the banks of Bayou Teche.

In the eighteenth century, the Ishak (Attakapas) lived along the prairies and coastal wetlands stretching from present-day Bayou Teche to the Texas border. Based on de Batz's illustration of the locale from 1735, which shows an "Attakapas" male sporting facial tattoos and holding a calumet (peace) pipe, the Ishak traveled to the area of Bulbancha to trade with other nations. Along the lower Red River, the Avogel (Avoyelles) resided on lands near present-day Marksville and Alexandria, known in colonial times as Les Rapides for the rocky falls on the lower river. Although a small group, they were important regional traders of flint from the surrounding upland hills to the Indigenous peoples of the Gulf Coast. To their east, the Natchez nation resided in a large settlement near the site of the present-day town named for them along the Mississippi River.[15]

Farther north along the Mississippi and Red Rivers, several larger, more powerful nations maintained a dominating presence, sometimes forcing the dislocation of smaller nations as population pressures from the east pushed native peoples westward. The Caddo Confederacy were the major traders in present-day northwest Louisiana, while the powerful Chickasaw and Choctaw ruled the areas of present-day northern and southern Mississippi, respectively. The Choctaw became important trading partners with the French in the colonial period, and the Mobilian trade language, based largely on Choctaw, became the regional trade language (*lingua franca*) of the lower Mississippi Valley and central Gulf Coast.

Using the Mississippi River and its tributaries as major interregional trading and transportation routes, the nations of the lower Mississippi traded goods in a vast region from the Great Lakes westward to the Rocky Mountains, along the Atlantic coast, and south to the Caribbean Basin. For example, the red Catlinite "pipestone" used for calumet bowls along the Gulf Coast originated in the upper Mississippi River basin of present-day Minnesota (Pipestone National Monument). Other products such as salt and flint came from the Red River Valley of present-day central and north Louisiana; the sediment-based land of the Mississippi River delta around Bulbancha did not provide natural stone for tools and weapons. Given these continental trade networks and the highly mobile nature of Indigenous people, many of the *petites* and *grandes nations* of the area adopted and shared similar religious practices, greeting customs, diplomatic rituals, trade languages, and foodways.

A large number of Indigenous earthworks that date from circa 6000 BP to 1000 BP exist throughout the Mississippi and Ohio Valleys, as well as the American southeast. In Louisiana, historic earthworks line the elevated ridges of the Mississippi and Red Rivers and smaller bayous. Archaeologists have determined that ancient peoples constructed these mounds and large earthworks for religious purposes. At Poverty Point in northeast Louisiana, the mounds reflect a religious orientation eastward toward worship of the rising sun. This belief system continued into the colonial period. While living at the Natchez village in 1704, André Pénicaut observed how the Natchez continuously maintained in their temple a fire representing "the sun, which they worship."[16]

These earthworks exist as some of the most significant antiquities in the present-day United States, equivalent to the stone pyramids in Mexico and Central America. However, most Americans remain completely unaware of their presence or importance. Although the Louisiana Division of Archaeology prefers not to promote the location of these mounds for preservation purposes, numerous earthworks are open to public view at Pottery Hill in Mandeville, the campus of Louisiana State University, the Louisiana State Capitol Park, Marksville State Park, the Emerald Mounds in Natchez, and Poverty Point State Park near Lake Providence, which is a UNESCO World Heritage Site.

Relevant Historic Sites

Bayou Road, New Orleans: The route of the original Indigenous portage trail extending from Gentilly Ave. to Gov. Nicholls St.

Bayou St. John, Moss at Bell St., New Orleans: The "Old Portage" historic marker is placed at the location of the original Indigenous portage connecting the bayou and the river.

City Park Lagoon, north of City Park Ave. between North Carrollton Ave. and Marconi Dr.: The lagoon is the only remnant of the original Bayou Metairie distributary channel. The large live oaks along the ridge form one of the city's grandest groves of ancient trees, thought to be more than five hundred years old.

French Market, New Orleans: The likely site of Quinipissa Village, as mentioned by Iberville, and a seasonal regional Indigenous market, as illustrated by Alexandre de Batz.

Jean Lafitte National Park and Preserve, Barataria Unit, 6588 Barataria Blvd., Marrero: The Bayou Coquille Trail is named for the clam-shell (*coquille*) midden piles marking settlement sites of Indigenous people.

Fontainebleau State Park, 62883 LA-1089, Mandeville: This park has a Native Peoples historic marker, as well as several identified earthworks, including one at the nearby Northlake Nature Center.

Pottery Hill, Monroe at Colbert St., Mandeville: Pottery Hill historic marker and earthwork.

Bayou Lacombe Museum, 61115 S. St. Mary St., Lacombe: This museum interprets the history of Lacombe, an historic Choctaw-Creole community in St. Tammany Parish.

Emerald (Natchez) Mounds, Emerald Mound Rd., Natchez, Mississippi: This large earthwork complex is just outside Natchez, near the site of the former Natchez village documented by Pénicaut and du Pratz.

Bayou Belt

The shared diplomatic customs among the nations of the Mississippi Valley and Gulf Coast are evident in Iberville's *Gulf Journals*. The French Canadian commandant noted his first encounter with a group of Biloxi in six canoes at the future site of La Nouvelle Orléans in March 1699. Having been raised in Quebec and the surrounding Great Lakes–St. Lawrence River Valley, Iberville's intimate familiarity with native diplomatic customs enabled him to establish an initial trust and communicate effectively with the Indigenous peoples of the lower Mississippi Valley.

During this first encounter with people at the river crescent, Iberville greeted a native man and tried to communicate with him; Iberville wrote, "We rubbed each other after their manner, about which I have already spoken. They told me he was Annocchy [Biloxi] and that the Bayogoula and the

Annocchy I had seen at the Annocchy's Bay [Biloxi Bay, Mississippi], near the ships, to whom I had given presents and a calumet of peace, were back at the village of the Bayogoula."[17]

Iberville understood the rubbing custom to indicate friendship on meeting. But sharing the *calumet de paix* (peace pipe) was a more common diplomatic custom among Indigenous people throughout the Mississippi Valley and Gulf Coast. This ritual of peace originated in the Great Lakes region and subsequently spread down the Mississippi River to the Gulf of Mexico. Iberville described sharing a peace pipe with the Mobile, the Annocchy, the Bayou Goula, the Houma, the Quinipissa, and the Natchez peoples. Le Page du Pratz also described the practice among the Natchez in the 1720s, and Pénicaut noted the diplomatic ritual among several nations throughout the Lower Mississippi and Red River Valleys.[18]

Furthermore, Iberville's ability to understand native languages in the lower Mississippi Valley region indicated his and his brother Bienville's knowledge of Iroquois and Algonquin language families of the Great Lakes. Although these northern languages derived from a different linguistic family than the Muscogean and Siouan languages of the lower Mississippi, enough similarities existed, likely because of common trade languages, that the Canadians could communicate effectively. As Iberville wrote about the Bayou Goula, "I understand many of the words, which I have taken down in writing the first time I saw them; at least my brother did." Of his brother Bienville, Iberville wrote, "He was making himself understood fairly well, having applied himself to the task with my [Bayou Goula] guide.[19]

Pénicaut also documented the ability of the French Canadian expedition's members to communicate successfully. On their arrival at present-day Biloxi Bay, the Frenchman noted how some of the soldiers established a peaceful interaction through sign language. Additionally, he observed how "they spoke to them in the Iroquois language, as most of our soldiers were, by nation, Canadians who had often had dealings with the Iroquois."[20]

In the southeast region of North America, the Mobilian dialect was the predominant trade language. Essentially a pidgin version of the Muscogean language family (Choctaw, Chickasaw, and Muscogee), Mobilian developed in part to enable trade and diplomacy both before and after the arrival of Europeans and Africans.[21]

The Mobilian word *bayou* is integral to geography in the region. The term is a variation of the Choctaw word *bok* or *bogue,* which describes a small river or creek. The word *bayou* is used in this way throughout a broad triangular-shaped region encompassing the lower Mississippi Valley and extending along the Gulf Coast from western Florida to southeast Texas. The extensive use of the word reflects the Mobilian language's influence on the region (the nation's "Bayou Belt") in which New Orleans is at the geographical center.

In present-day New Orleans, the term is applied to Bayou St. John, which originates in the Faubourg St. John neighborhood in Mid-City and flows to Lake Pontchartrain. The word also applied to two local distributaries: Bayou Metairie, which ran west along present-day City Park Avenue and Metairie Road, and Bayou Sauvage, which flowed east along the path of present-day Gentilly Boulevard, Old Gentilly Road, and Chef Menteur Highway east of Village de L'Est. The original Choctaw term is also commonly used in the surrounding suburbs. For example, on the north shore of Lake Pontchartrain in St. Tammany Parish, the bayou known as Bogue Falaya is Choctaw for "long (*falaya*) creek (*bok*)," whereas nearby Bogue Chitto is Choctaw for "large creek." The nearby Washington Parish town of Bogalusa is named for the local creek Bogue Lusa (Black Bayou).[22]

Bayou Road, named for the historic Indigenous portage and first documented by Iberville, is the oldest historic trail in New Orleans. Based on Bayou Goula conversations about local geography, Iberville in December 1699 investigated this portage trail that served as a shortcut connecting Lake Pontchartrain—via Bayou St. John—to the Mississippi River. The present-day Bayou Road follows the same route as the portage trail, snaking across Faubourg St. John and the Tremé neighborhoods in contrast to the surrounding grid of the orderly nineteenth-century streets (fig. 2). Bayou Road in the Tremé was originally named Grand Chemin de Bayou (Large Trail of the Bayou) and is today's Governor Nicholls Street, which leads to the back of the present-day Lower Vieux Carré.[23]

The portage, as mentioned, provided an important shortcut for Indigenous people traveling by pirogue between Lake Pontchartrain and the Mississippi River. The French Quarter exists at the intersection of the two major transportation routes of inland lakes and the river. Depending on one's direction of travel, using the portage enabled one going upstream to avoid the strong currents of the river, and the trail allowed those headed downstream to take advantage of the river's powerful current.

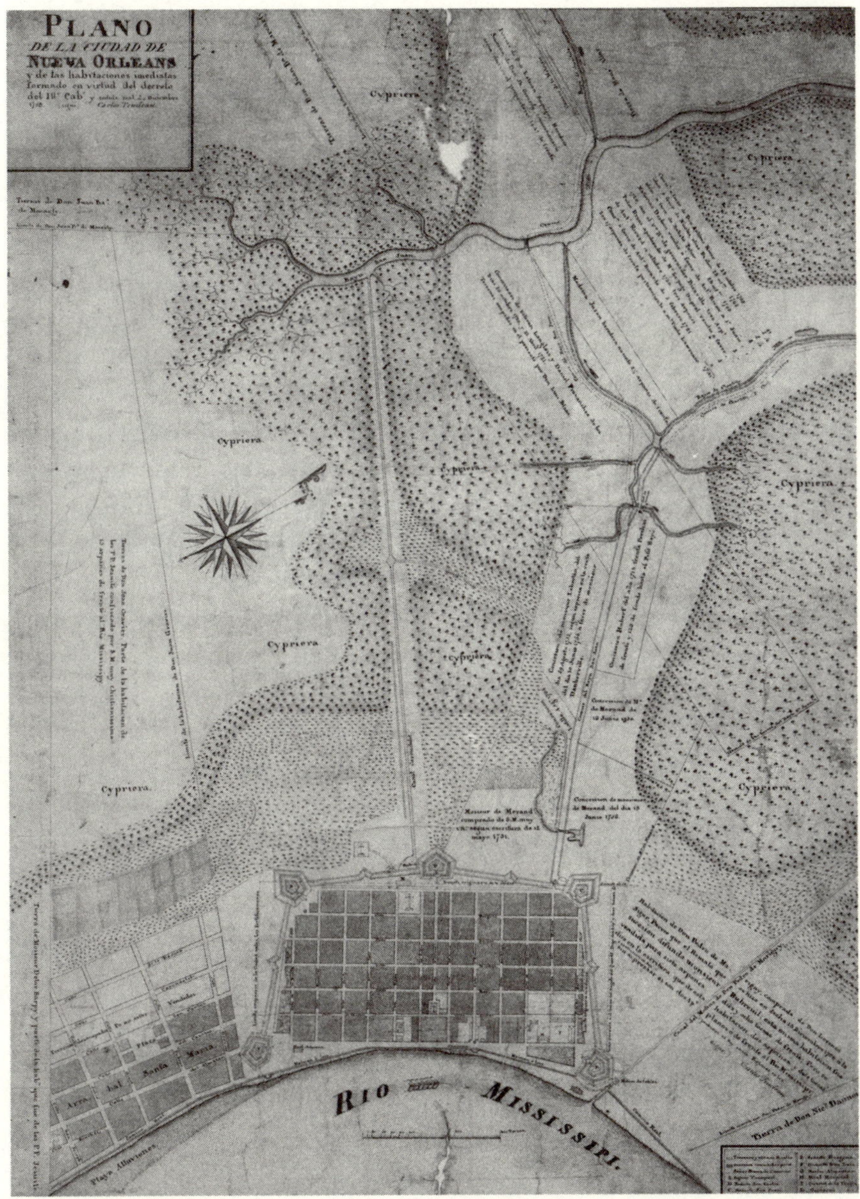

FIG. 2. This map of Nueva Orleans shows the historic Indigenous portage trail (*center right*) connecting Bayou St. John and Bayou Sauvage to the back of the Vieux Carré and the Mississippi River. Carlos Trudeau, *Plano de la Ciudad de Nueva Orleans y las Habitationes Imediatas,* 1798, Historic New Orleans Collection, 11552.5.

At a time when the present-day Faubourg St. John and Tremé neighborhoods were still swamps, Iberville described the historic trail as a slight elevated path: "I went to the portage, which I found to be one league long [3.4 miles], and about half the distance being full of water and mud up to the knee." After the path reached the natural sediment ridge of the Mississippi, Iberville noted, "The other half [is] fairly good, part of it being a country of canes and fine woods, suitable to live in."

Iberville and his crew successfully carried three canoes from Bayou St. John to the site of the present-day French Quarter on the banks of the Mississippi. As noted earlier, he observed the site of the abandoned Quinipissa village and farmlands where new trees had grown "as big as two feet around." Given Louisiana's warm subtropical climate, one might surmise that the fast-growing pioneer tree species—perhaps swamp red maple (*Acer rubrum*) or black willow (*Salix nigra*)—could have been ten to fifteen years old, indicating the time span since the Quinipissa abandoned the site.[24]

As Iberville's account illustrates, the importance of canoes for transportation in the lower Mississippi Valley and Gulf Coast cannot be overstated. In this region largely dominated by wetlands and open water, the bayous and rivers provided the most efficient routes for transportation and commerce. Although the French Canadian explorers imported "bark canoes" from the Great Lakes region, the dugout canoe—the pirogue—was the main form of transportation in this region. Indeed, the same form of watercraft can be found among Indigenous peoples throughout coastal Latin America, as well as West and Central Africa—thereby serving as a shared cultural touchstone for peoples from these regions who came to Louisiana.

The pirogue, a flat-bottomed canoe in Cajun Louisiana, is of Indigenous origin. Pénicaut described the process for creating these canoes: a felled cypress tree is burned and carved with oyster shells to create the long boats, which sometimes reached twenty-five feet in length.[25] The Carib nation, after whom the Caribbean Sea is named, called such dugout canoes *piraua*, a term adopted by the Spanish (*piragua*) and the French (*pirogue*) in the region. Hence, the word *pirogue*, like *bayou*, is another Indigenous word used commonly and also uniquely in the lower Mississippi Valley and central Gulf Coast of the United States.

Because the Mississippi River served as a central transportation and trade route, the Indigenous people of the lower Mississippi Valley and the future site of New Orleans shared many of the diplomatic practices and language terms of the diverse *petites* and *grandes nations*. In their world, vast trade networks stretched southward from the Caribbean and Latin American east coast, northward up the Mississippi River to the Great Lakes, westward to the Rocky Mountains, and eastward to the entire southeastern section of North America.

Foodways: Pan-American Indigenous Traditions

The foods of Indigenous peoples in the Mississippi Valley, as well as in the larger southeast portion of North America, continue to have a strong imprint on the cuisine of New Orleans and the region. These foodways have not only survived but also shape the daily diets of many people.

The *petites* and *grandes nations* were largely prolific farmers, but they also were hunter-gatherers in the region that had an abundance of game and seafood year-round. Iberville always made a point of describing the foods he either observed or were provided to him by the chiefs of the settlements he encountered. When he arrived in the region of present-day Ocean Springs, Mississippi, Iberville noted the presence of turkey, partridge [likely quail], hares "like the ones in France," and "rather good oysters." The Annocchy [Biloxi] fed the French settlers corn, plums, wild turkey, bison meat, and bear meat.[26] Black bear and turkey still exist in parts of Louisiana, but at Iberville's time bison roamed the forests and prairies of the Gulf Coast. Black bears were so common that Indigenous people in the region often traded bear meat and oil as commodities. And at the Bayou Goula village, Iberville noted the existence of domesticated "cocks and hens."[27]

The wetland environment also supplied a prolific amount of freshwater and salt-water fish and shellfish. Pénicaut provided a detailed description of the fish diet of the Acolapissa at their village on the north shore of Lake Pontchartrain. He also described their method of fishing: "They pulled up their nets from the lake filled with fish of all sizes. These nets actually are no more than fishing lines, numerous other little lines are tied a foot apart." On the end of each line was a baited hook. As he remarked, "With this method they do not fail to catch fish weighing more than fifteen or twenty pounds."[28]

This long-line and branch-line method of fishing is known today as a trotline and still is used in much of the American Southeast. Similarly, the tradition of noodling, or hand fishing, is also a legacy of Indigenous fishing practices throughout the region. In this latter method, a person wades into a bayou or small river and searches by hand for a catfish under the embankment or a submerged object. When found, the person grabs the fish by the mouth and pulls it up onto the bank. And although "noodling" in the American South is often credited to Indigenous peoples, the practice relevant to southern Louisiana had earlier been used in France and West Africa.

Indigenous cooking methods are also part of Indigenous people's culinary legacy in modern Louisiana. Pénicaut described the method by which the Acolapissa cooked the fish they caught from Lake Pontchartrain: "Each person takes some fish home, and after it is cooked and seasoned [fried] with bear fat . . . they begin to eat it, each in front of his door in the shade of the peach tree."[29]

And even though bear fat (*nita nia*) and bear oil (*nita bila*) are not commonly used for cooking today, the method of frying has changed little. New Orleans is well known for fried food, and this culinary practice was also part of West African and European immigrant cultures in the colony. Often, Indigenous people cooked a meal in one pot, a process that is still common in Louisiana today with dishes such as Cajun or creole gumbo, jambalaya, court-bouillon, and red or white beans. Pénicaut made a point of remarking how the Acolapissa are "rather cleanly with their food: they have an individual pot for each thing that they cook—that is, the meat pot is never used for fish." Noting the versatility of bear fat for lard and dressing, Pénicaut also observed, "They eat it with salad, use it in making pastry, in frying, and usually in everything they cook."[30]

Iberville, Le Page du Pratz, and Pénicaut documented the vegetables, fruits, and nuts consumed by Indigenous peoples. Iberville noted the presence of apples, peaches, and plums among the Bayou Goula. Le Page du Pratz wrote detailed descriptions of the native garden crops and wild plants eaten by the Natchez; he noted the importance of beans of various colors, indigenous potatoes, cushaw (winter squash), and melons, as well as small currant grapes, large muscadine grapes, persimmons, plums, papaws, wild apples, whortle-berries, black mulberries, walnuts, and hickory.[31]

Likewise, Pénicaut observed that local fruits included "peaches in season that are even bigger than those in France, and sweeter; strawberries, plums, and a grape that is a bit sour and not so big as the grapes in France." The pecan was perhaps the most common and essential indigenous nut that grew in the region stretching from northern Mexico to Virginia. Other common nuts used to make variations of porridge, bread, and pudding were hickory and acorns. Pénicaut observed the making of the traditional Choctaw dish of *bahpo* (nut pudding): "They pound [nuts] into flour, using it with water to make a pap for their children, and mixing it with corn meal to make *sagamité* or bread."[32]

Corn (*tanchi*) is perhaps the most important agricultural staple that shaped Indigenous foodways and still is a prominent part of contemporary cuisine in New Orleans and the broader American Southeast. Throughout the Americas, Indigenous peoples raised corn, often planted with beans (*tobi*), as staples of their diet.[33] Corn is the most frequently mentioned food staple in the accounts of Iberville, Pénicaut, and Le Page du Pratz. When visiting the Houma, who were prolific farmers, Iberville noted, "The corn fields are in little valleys and on hills in the vicinity." Bienville observed that the Chaouachas on the Gulf Coast east of New Orleans produced corn to trade for anything they needed from the French.[34]

As the principal food for the Indigenous people of the lower Mississippi Valley, corn served as the basis for a wide variety of dishes. In the 1750s, French Louisiana settler Jean-François-Benjamin Dumont de Montigny observed forty-two distinct corn dishes. Likewise, Cyrus Byington included in his *Choctaw Dictionary* more than forty words for corn and foods using corn, including corn bread (*tanchi paska atoba, tanchi paska*), sweet corn (*tanchi shikoa*), corn dough (*tansh yammaska*), cornmeal (*tanch pushi, tanchi pushi*), parched corn (*onush alwasha*), and hominy (*tanfula*).[35]

Certainly, parched corn (*onush alwasha*)—corn kernels (*nihi*) that are dried and roasted—was one of the most common foods consumed for travel and transport. Corn prepared as hominy (*tanfula*) was boiled and mixed with lye ash to preserve its vitamin content. In essence, the dish developed in Indigenous cultures as a nutritional cooking method to prevent pellagra. Europeans and Africans quickly adopted hominy as an important part of their diet in New Orleans.

A variation of *tanfula* evolved into grits, a corn-based dish (*tansh lakchi*). The process of making grits involved grinding or milling the dried hominy and then sifting it through a screen. The fine grit powder was used as cornmeal, and the coarser bits were used to make the hominy porridge that is commonly eaten today. Le Page du Pratz provided perhaps the first description of the process in his account of living among the Natchez in the 1720s, concluding that the meal was "a very nutritional food and is an excellent provision for travelers."[36]

Grits are still commonly used in southern American cooking and are often associated culturally as a food eaten by poorer southern people. Yet grits are now served in fine restaurants, just as local or regional meals of working people have become part of haute cuisine internationally. Tourists now order grits and shrimp at noted New Orleans restaurants, illustrating the recent gentrification of this Indigenous dish in southern cuisine.

But the most commonly mentioned corn dish in the colonial-era journals is *sagamité,* with a Choctaw variation being *tanchi okchi* (corn broth).[37] Coming from French Canada, Iberville and Bienville were familiar with the corn dish, which in its variations can range from a cornbread or paste to more of a porridge with a variety of meats, fruits, and vegetables added depending on the season.

Iberville mentions eating variations of the dish throughout his travels in the lower Mississippi Valley and Gulf Coast. Like the calumet and Mobilian trade language, the corn stew found common ground across the Mississippi Valley and Great Lakes regions, where it remains an important aspect of the Indigenous culinary heritage. In his first encounter with the Annocchy, Iberville ate *sagamité* with plums.[38] Other variations include corn with beans, squash, peppers, nuts, and other seasonal fruits and vegetables, as well as various meats such as bear and venison and seafood like crab, oysters, or shrimp.

The southern Louisiana dish corn maque choux is the contemporary Louisiana variation of *sagamité.* The two dishes share similar ingredients—a corn broth base and a mixture of whatever meats and vegetable are available. And like *sagamité,* corn maque choux is often thought of as a soup but can also be a main dish, similar to succotash, another Indigenous American variation of the corn-bean one-pot meal.

Corn maque choux is considered by many Louisianians to be a "Cajun dish"; that is, a dish cooked historically in the rural areas of south Louisiana. But in fact, like many Cajun foods, its origins are complex, and its ingredients were and are readily available. As they did with rice, French-speaking farmers, ranchers, and fishers adapted corn to their diet in Louisiana and then added ingredients available from their gardens, farms, and harvested game or seafood. Early European immigrants to rural Louisiana relied on Indian corn and rice of African origins to serve as the basis for many meals and to stretch meats and vegetables to feed their families.

Although not often acknowledged, all corn dishes across the Americas, including Louisiana, have their origins in Indigenous cuisine. For this reason, this south Louisiana dish is used to represent this period of Indigenous culture and history and corn's strong influence on the cuisine of the rural areas surrounding New Orleans. Like many Cajun-Creole dishes such as gumbo or jambalaya, the ingredients of corn maque choux vary depending on the season or location. For example, the addition of crab or shrimp may be more common on the coastal bayous, whereas farther inland pork, especially andouille sausage or tasso ham, may be added more often. And just as one can differentiate Cajun (rural) from Creole (urban) jambalaya based on the use of tomatoes, the same may be said of corn maque choux.

Corn Maque Choux

The bacon, sausage, ham, and garlic in this recipe were introduced by Europeans. Otherwise, the ingredients are mostly indigenous to the region. Therefore, a variation without those ingredients will create a flavor more historically appropriate to the pre-Colombian diet. A vegetarian version can be made by using vegetable oil to sauté the vegetables and eliminating the sausage, ham, and shrimp.

Serves 6

10 ears of fresh corn (or 5 cups of corn with corn milk)
10 bacon slices crumbled and with drippings
½ cup finely diced andouille sausage and/or tasso ham
3 cups peeled and deveined shrimp
2 cups chicken or vegetable stock
½ cup finely chopped garlic
2 cups chopped white or yellow onion
1 cup chopped celery
1 cup chopped green and red bell peppers
1 diced jalapeño pepper
4 diced large fresh tomatoes
1 bundle of chopped green onions
salt, black, and red pepper—to taste

1. Slice the whole corn kernels from the cob.
2. In a large cast-iron pot (3–4 quarts), sauté the bacon until cooked.
3. Add the sausage or ham, the garlic, onion, celery, peppers, and corn and cook until tender (10 minutes).

4. Add the chicken (or vegetable) stock and tomatoes and cook for 10 minutes; then add the shrimp and cook for 5–10 minutes.

5. Season according to taste.

6. Serve in a bowl garnished with the green onions.

Continental Crossroads

The lower Mississippi Valley that Iberville encountered in 1699 was a continually changing land and waterscape in which Indigenous people traded, temporarily settled, and interacted with one another, sometimes peacefully and other times not. Iberville's decision to build New Orleans on the site of an abandoned Quinipissa village reflects the fluid nature of settlement on the lower Mississippi River and surrounding region. Even though the site was occupied and then abandoned by the Quinipissa around the 1680s, the location remained a crossroads of trade.

The portage shortcut between Bayou St. John (Bayou Choupique) and the Mississippi River illustrates the importance of the site as an intersection of two major transportation routes: the Mississippi (Malbanchya) River and the brackish inland lakes. The presence of clam shells in midden piles throughout the area also speaks to the abundance of food resources for migrating people, who were attracted to the large variety of wild game and the prevalence of freshwater fish and brackish seafood. As archaeologist Tristan Kidder reminds us, the clam-shell midden piles along the bayou ridges (St. John, Sauvage, and Metairie) and the lakefront are one of the clearest (but often overlooked) reminders both of Indigenous peoples' habitation in the region well before the arrival of Africans and Europeans and of the locale's bounty that sustained a population in the precolonial era.[39]

For any native person seeking a central location in which to trade with others from across the larger region—the Gulf Coast and Caribbean Basin, Mississippi River, Great Lakes, or southeastern North America—the future site of New Orleans existed as an important crossroads (*hina abanabli*). The Choctaw-language term *balbaha,* meaning those who talk in a foreign language, is the basis for the term *balbancha.* The word therefore reflects the Indigenous recognition of the site's attraction to people of different nations, both Indigenous and not. When the French established a settlement on the site in the winter of 1718, this feature would remain and continue to grow in importance as diverse peoples with new languages settled from all across the Atlantic Basin. Within North America, the site was a central juncture within a larger transcontinental trade network. New Orleans would soon emerge as one of the many diverse colonial communities in the burgeoning Atlantic Creole world.

Today, the Indigenous presence remains at the site of Bulbancha, albeit not on the same level as other modern U.S. cities with large Native populations such as Albuquerque, Denver, Minneapolis, Phoenix, and Seattle. After the French settled in the region, members of the Choctaw and other nations continued to live, work, and trade in La Nouvelle Orléans and the surrounding area, despite disease, racist violence, and wars with the Chitimacha, Natchez, Washa, and Chawasha peoples.

Into the American period after 1803, the Choctaw maintained an important presence on the banks of Bayou St. John, and observers often noted their presence selling filé and other products at the French Market, remote areas back-of-town, and along the lakeshore. In the early nineteenth century, Native persons (in conjunction with Afro-Creoles) often played publicly the rough game of raquette (*isht aboli*), the forerunner of modern lacrosse, and which historically served as a ritual for settling conflicts between clans, settlements, and nations. The matches were played in open fields back-of-town of the Tremé , as well as the Plaine Labarre along Metairie Ridge in East Jefferson Parish, and remained a popular spectacle into the 1890s.[40]

During the mid-twentieth century, Chitimacha women in St. Mary Parish and Choctaw artisans in St. Tammany Parish were renowned for weaving and selling beautifully designed river cane (*Arundinaria gigantea*) baskets, which are important Indigenous artifacts in the collection of the Louisiana State Museum. Creole Choctaw maintain communities on the North Shore around Bayou Lacombe, and contemporary Creole Indigenous scholars such as Dr. Jeffrey Darensbourg, tour guide Lola Jean Darling, storyteller and educator Greyhawk Perkins, and artist-activist Monique Verdin continue to remind the world of their historical and contemporary presence at the site of Bulbancha.[41]

Despite the United States' attempts to move Indigenous communities from the American Southeast to Indian Territory (present-day Oklahoma) during the 1830s, groups of native peoples remained in rural southern Louisiana, where they sought refuge in isolated forests, swamps, and marshes. Often they maintained their traditions and lived relatively undisturbed, while also adapting to the dominant cultures, languages, religions, and economies of their non-Indigenous neighbors.

Today, the United States confers federal recognition on those nations that have maintained their original language and meet other criteria. The Chitimacha, the Tunica-Biloxi, the Coushatta, and the Jena Band of Choctaw exist as four sovereign tribes in Louisiana, and the Mississippi Band of Choctaw are recognized near Philadelphia, Mississippi. Other nations, such as the Houma, have not been able to gain federal recognition, in part because their language is largely forgotten and unused. Yet the present-day French- and English-speaking members of the Houma nation continue to live and work, hunt, fish, and maintain their cultures in the marshes, small towns, and suburbs south of New Orleans.

The historic legacy and presence of Indigenous peoples in the New Orleans area are also evident in annual pow-wow festivals, hosted by most regional tribes as celebrations of community pride, dancing, culinary traditions, folkways, and crafts. At the same time, however, climate change and rising sea levels pose a challenge to the existence of coastal Indigenous communities. The residents of the Isle de Jean Charles in Terrebonne Parish, because of increasingly powerful hurricane tides and environmental vulnerability, are now relocating to more elevated areas to the north. Ironically, these people who sought sanctuary from racist persecution in the isolated marshes during the nineteenth century now find themselves enacting a reverse northward migration seeking refuge from rising seas.[42]

In many ways, the experience of these coastal inhabitants reflects the reality of environmental challenges in communities—including New Orleans—in the risk-prone region of the lower Mississippi Valley and surrounding wetlands. This theme of cultural survival and environmental threat is one of the constant threads of history that connect New Orleans's past and present. When the French established a permanent settlement in 1718 on the crescent bend of the lower Mississippi, these newcomers first put their faith in the idea that humans could engineer a permanent and sustainable community in the face of river floods and hurricanes in the region.

2

La Nouvelle Orléans

A Créole *Village, 1718–1766*

FRENCH CARPENTER André Pénicaut provided one of the earliest accounts of the building of the French settlement of La Nouvelle Orléans on the banks of the Mississippi River in the winter of 1718. He arrived with the first French expedition to La Louisiane in 1699, and nineteen years later, he witnessed the founding of the permanent settlement on the crescent bend in the Mississippi River. Recounting Bienville's decision to establish what he hoped to be a long-lasting town on the lower river, Pénicaut wrote that progress toward that end was frustratingly slow: "This year only some living quarters were built and two large warehouses in which to store the munitions and food supplies which M. de l'Epinet sent over."[1]

From its humble beginnings as a French village as described by Pénicaut, La Nouvelle Orléans remained a rather unimpressive settlement during the sixty-eight years that France held the colony of La Louisiane. The original footprint of the city established by French royal engineer Adrien de Pauger is still evident in today's Vieux Carré rectangular grid. Yet, during this period of French colonial rule, the small settlement only grew to an underwhelming population of 2,524 persons by 1763. By today's standards a settlement of fewer than five thousand people qualifies as a village. Despite France's efforts, the colonial capital La Nouvelle Orléans failed to attract many settlers willing to move to the colony.

In their colonization efforts, the French government contracted a private company, the Company of the Indies, to manage the process of recruiting settlers, providing enslaved workers, and establishing a permanent capital town on the lower river. The company had such difficulty convincing French families to settle and invest that officials resorted to sending *forçats* (convicts), who were usually state prisoners, to live and work there. Historian Shannon Dawdy refers to this process as "colonization by abduction."[2]

The settlement thus had a challenging start during the French colonial period, reflecting a half-hearted effort by the French government to establish a viable colony and capital port city. Nevertheless, during this period, the foundations of the modern French Quarter were laid.

It Did Not Have the Appearance of a City

After Iberville's expedition of 1699–1700, France failed to establish a viable colonial settlement on the lower Mississippi River until Bienville's founding of La Nouvelle Orléans in 1718. During that intervening period, very small and underproductive settlements were established at Biloxi (1699), Mobile (1702), and Natchitoches (1714). This slow pace of development, as well as the small number of settlers recruited to France's initial colonial capitals, Biloxi and Mobile, on the Mississippi–Alabama Gulf Coast, reflected the French crown's general lack of interest in investing resources in Louisiana until 1712.

France's efforts under King Louis XIV to finally colonize Louisiana relied on a private company to settle the lower Mississippi Valley. In 1712, the crown issued a contract to Antoine Crozat, marquis du Châtel, the proprietor of la Compagnie de la Louisiane (Company of Louisiana), granting him exclusive trading and commercial privileges. The Toulouse-born Crozat served as the financier to "the Sun King" Louis XIV in the monarch's last three years. The marquis used his close relations with the crown to obtain the charter, through which he hoped to gain even greater wealth through the commercial venture.

Part of the crown's slow pace of development in Louisiana arose from the multiple responsibilities that the Secrétaire d'État de la Marine (secretary of state of the navy) had in addition to overseeing France's colonies. Under the Bourbon crown in this period, the secretary oversaw France's navy, ports, and arsenals—as well as the administration of France's many colonies in Canada and Louisiana, the Caribbean, coastal West Africa, and southern Asia. The secretary's duties also included guardianship of the numerous commercial private monopolies that established and ran enterprises in each colony. For example, by the early 1700s, the French colonial commercial empire relied on the Compagnie du Sénégal in West Africa, the Compagnie français des Indes Occidentales in the West Indies, and the Compagnie de la Louisiane in Louisiana.

Under Louis XIV in 1699, the secretary of state of the navy was Jean-Frédéric Phélypeaux, who also held the titles of marquis de Phélypeaux, compte de Maurepas, and compte de Pontchartrain. The latter two titles referred to Phélypeaux's family lands west of Paris. The names of Maurepas and Pontchartrain are familiar to modern New Orleanians as the two large lakes west and north of the city, which were titled to the secretary by Iberville in 1699. As a reflection of Bourbon noble nepotism, Jean-Frédéric's son, Jérôme Phélypeaux de Pontchartrain, succeeded him and held the post until 1715. Hence, the compte de Pontchartrain awarded the contract to the Company of Louisiana and its proprietor Antoine Crozat.

As the settlement of Louisiana finally gained momentum in 1712, Crozat appointed Gascony native Antoine Laumet (de La Mothe), Sieur de Cadillac, as governor of the colony. The founder of Le Detroit (Detroit) in La Nouvelle France (Canada), Cadillac unfortunately lacked tact or diplomacy, especially in his relations with Indigenous peoples. During his brief tenure in Louisiana, Cadillac accomplished little. Indeed, throughout Crozat's five years under contract, the Company of Louisiana failed in its mission both because of the financier's lack of support for the venture and his unpopularity among the earliest settlers who struggled to survive along the present-day Gulf Coast of Mississippi and Alabama.

Meanwhile, on King Louis XIV's death in 1715, his great-grandson Louis XV inherited the crown. Because the new king was then only five years old, his reign was managed by Philippe II, the duc d'Orléans, who installed himself in the Palais-Royal in Paris. The duke remained the boy's regent until 1723.

The post-Crozat phase of settlement began in 1717, when Philippe transferred the monopoly for settling La Louisiane to the newly formed La Compagnie d'Occident (Company of the West), under the ownership of Scottish financier John Law. A gambler by nature, Law had emerged as a leading economic theorist who had the ear of the regent. In approving Law's new contract, Philippe II finally provided some momentum and financial support to establish a more permanent centralized settlement on the lower Mississippi River at a distance from the shores of the Gulf Coast around Biloxi and Mobile.

Law's newly established proprietary company eventually grew into a complex conglomerate that assumed the name of the Company of the Indies

(Compagnie des Indes) in 1719 but was also known as the Company of the Mississippi—or colloquially as the Mississippi Bubble. During the 1710s, the innovative financier from Edinburgh made a name for himself in international finance by pioneering the idea of modern capital investment. In 1716 Law helped establish the Banque Générale (General Bank), which was succeeded by the Banque Royale (Royal Bank) in 1718. These successive banks essentially pioneered the use of paper money and provided capital for the colonial venture and the bankrupt French treasury. In this case, individuals could buy shares in the Company of the West/Indies and then realize gains in their value as the company prospered (theoretically).

Unfortunately, the novel idea known as "the System" eventually earned Law (and Louisiana) a terrible reputation throughout Europe. Initially, share owners had invested eagerly in the colonial venture, but the company's inability to earn a cash profit led to a run on the Banque Royale in 1719. After the plan morphed into a failed pyramid scheme known as the Mississippi Bubble, a financial panic swept the continent. The bubble burst, causing financial loss and misery for the conned investors.[3]

Regardless of the venture's ultimate failure, under the twenty-five-year contract Law's company maintained exclusive trading rights in La Louisiane and had the power to appoint a colonial governor and officers and issue land grants to investors. During the contracted period, the company retained the responsibility of transporting six thousand settlers and three thousand enslaved persons to the colony.

In 1718, under the direction of Commandant Bienville in Louisiana, Law's company finally established the first permanent settlement on the lower Mississippi River at La Nouvelle Orléans—named for Law's benefactor, the duc d'Orléans.[4] In his profile of Bienville, historian Lawrence Powell characterizes the French Canadian founder as dogged and headstrong, canny and cunning, full of sangfroid and savvy. Bienville served as acting commandant of the colony following the death of his older brother Iberville from yellow fever in Havana in 1706. Importantly, Bienville had much experience with Indigenous peoples in Canada and used his natural diplomatic skills to cultivate relations with the Natchez and Choctaw nations in the fledgling colony.[5]

In establishing a French presence in Louisiana, Bienville encouraged the Canadian model in which *coureurs de bois* (fur trappers) intermarried with Indigenous women to form economic, social, and political alliances with the French colonizers.[6] As stated earlier, he was well versed in Indigenous languages, customs, and cultural practices. As a symbol of his diplomatic acumen, Bienville sported serpent tattoos that symbolized the strong alliance France maintained with the Choctaw in Louisiana. Similarly, Bienville's Canadian relative Louis Juchereau de St. Denis, who was the founder of Natchitoches, also had on his legs colorful serpent tattoos applied by Caddo allies.[7]

During the winter of 1718, Bienville chose the location of the new settlement likely because of its strategic importance for both defense and trade. Geographer Richard Campanella has explained the considerations that led Bienville to choose the site at La Nouvelle Orléans, rather than Natchez or Bayou Manchac just downriver from Baton Rouge. Those two upriver sites were much farther from the coast and therefore less amenable for security and commerce.

In contrast, La Nouvelle Orléans's proximity to the Gulf of Mexico provided more protection against any foreign incursions, and the backdoor access to Lake Pontchartrain via Bayou St. John made the location accessible to shipping and trade vessels. Unfortunately, the wetlands surrounding the slightly elevated ridge at La Nouvelle Orléans provided environmental challenges to French royal engineers. Guided by hubris, idealism, and naiveté, they sought to protect the small settlement from river flooding in its early years. They had yet to discover the site's vulnerability to hurricane winds and tidal surge, until 1722 when the first major storm destroyed most of the original settlement structures.[8]

Pénicaut provided a glimpse into how the process of construction and settlement unfolded at the site of La Nouvelle Orléans. As the carpenter noted, in the winter of 1718 the newly appointed governor, Jean-Michel de Lépinay (l'Épinet), sent "eighty salt smugglers" and a "great many carpenters" to construct the first buildings. The smugglers, who had been imprisoned for their crimes, accompanied Lépinay on the voyage from France; their presence reflected the difficulties the Company of the Indies faced in recruiting immigrants.[9] That autumn, these men constructed the first living quarters and warehouses on the site. The Breton-born Lépinay, who struggled to establish respect while governing in the shadow of Bienville, was soon reassigned to a post in the French island colony of Grenada. Bienville once again served as acting governor and commandant of the colony, a position he held until 1725.

When he took over, Bienville ordered the construction work at La Nouvelle Orléans to proceed, along with the settlement of its new residents. According to Pénicaut, Bienville "sent many soldiers and workmen there to speed up the construction." The commandant also instructed the site supervisor Mr. Pailloux to "have two main buildings constructed for barracks, big enough to quarter a thousand troops each." Apparently, Bienville anticipated the arrival of a "great many" troops, along with "a number of families" who were to receive concessions. And as Pénicaut documented, two ships—the *La Duchesse des Noailles* and *La Marie* brought five hundred officers, soldiers, and settlers that year.[10]

Pénicaut's description of the rough "man-camp" site is corroborated by the first illustration of the settlement, an inset in Breton explorer Jean-Baptiste Bernard de La Harpe's and de Beauvilliers's map of La Louisiane from 1720 (fig. 3). The image, labeled *Veue de la Nouvelle Orléans,* shows an unimpressive collection of six buildings of various sizes and two ships in the nearby river. As described by Pénicaut, there existed three small cabins—perhaps the officers' quarters—and three long buildings, perhaps the soldiers' quarters and warehouses.[11]

FIG. 3. This first illustration of La Nouvelle Orléans may be the product of the artists' imagination, but the scene reflects the earliest descriptions of a small settlement along the river consisting of military barracks and several smaller structures. Inset of map by Bernard de la Harpe and de Beauvilliers, *Veue de la Nouvelle Orléans,* 1720, Library of Congress, 2021668639.

If La Harpe's illustration intended to inspire French settlers to move to Louisiana, it did not succeed. Indeed, Marie-Madeleine Hachard, who arrived with the first Ursuline nuns in 1727, admitted, "Before our arrival we were given a very bad view of the city." The nuns had been informed that New Orleans "did not have the appearance of a city until the year 1723" when officials "worked as much as they could to find laborers." And even as Hachard refers to La Nouvelle Orléans as a *ville* (city or town), the population of fewer than one thousand people at the time qualified the settlement only as a small village.[12]

The French crown likely hoped for other, more positive images of La Nouvelle Orléans from these early years to promote the colony and village port as a destination for intrepid settlers and small farmers from Europe. The monarchy also aimed to publicize the potential investment opportunity for aspiring planters among the French nobility and French Canadian gentry. The accuracy of France's depiction of the new settlement is open to question. But given that the French crown wanted to create a plantation export market in Louisiana on the same basis as their very profitable slave-based Caribbean colony of Saint Dominque, their portrayal of the new settlement of La Nouvelle Orléans in maps and illustrations was probably intended to appeal especially to aspiring planters.

For example, the *Carte du cours du fleuve St. Louis,* published around 1730, portrays the lower Mississippi River from present-day St. John the Baptist Parish downriver to Plaquemines Parish and the Gulf of Mexico (fig. 4). The map shows clearly the area of the *enceinte* (enclosure) of the new town grid at of La Nouvelle Orléans laid out in 1721. But most interesting is the map's depiction of concessions along the river above and below the village.[13]

A large parcel of land upriver from the French Quarter and present-day Algiers Point is designated as the concession claimed by Bienville. Listed as Terrain a Mr. de Bienville (Land of Bienville), the large claims reflected the commandant's self-dealings as the settlement's founder. Lawrence Powell has made clear how the Le Moyne family viewed their colonial service to the crown as an opportunity for gaining land, wealth, and titles.[14] Bienville's father Charles Le Moyne served as a Norman soldier in La Nouvelle France (Canada). For his service, Le Moyne received a seigneurial grant comprising prime lands around Montreal, of which he was a founder. In gaining the

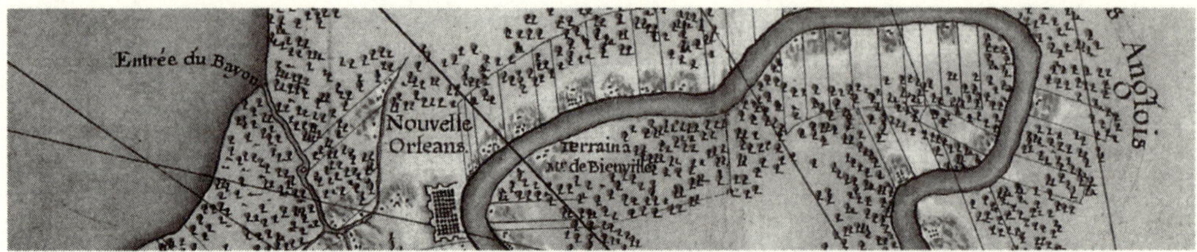

FIG. 4. The rectangular long-lot delineation of the French colonial settlement on the natural river ridge is evident in this early map, likely intended to encourage settlement along the river near the new capital port. *Carte du cours du fleuve St. Louis* (1732?), Library of Congress, G4042.M5 1732.C3.

large land concession, Le Moyne also earned the formal noble title of Sieur de Longueil et de Châteauguay.

Bienville viewed his founding of La Nouvelle Orléans as a similar opportunity. After initially claiming the large parcel comprising the present-day Central Business District (CBD) and Lower Garden District, in 1726 he sold the twenty-arpent (a French measure of land equal to 191 feet) riverfront tract directly to the Jesuits, who used enslaved labor to develop the land into a profitable cattle *vacherie* (ranch) and indigo plantation with a dye factory and tannery. Bienville maintained ownership of a portion of his original West Bank property, where he built a house. But in a dispute with authorities, he forfeited much of this claim, including the twenty-six-arpent parcel that became the Company of the West's (the King's) plantation.[15]

The *Carte du cours du fleuve St. Louis* also depicts the river lined with abutting land concessions meant to convey the rapid subdivision and development that followed the founding of La Nouvelle Orléans.[16] The map seems to be aimed at a wealthy audience in France and Canada who would want to be granted a concession in a colony allegedly bustling with economic activity and developing plantations. In reality, Bienville did not allocate the first concessions in the area as quickly and uniformly as shown on the map.

Nevertheless, the map's depiction of the long-lot plantation concessions along the Mississippi illustrates the land-grant pattern that defines the lower Mississippi River even today. Because the waterway existed as the main transportation and trade route, all concessions were essentially rectangular "long lots" (plantations), with the short end fronting the river as an access point. The plantations then stretched away from the high ground and terminated where the natural ridge gave way to swampy or marshy wetlands.

Louisiana inherited this land allocation process from New France, in which seigneurial concessions to wealthy French families of nobility were laid out along major routes such as a river or roads. The long-lot system also defines the distinct shape of plantations in Louisiana and is quite different from the later, very rigid American township and range grid system of allotment in most of the United States. Even today, the French long-lot system is easily seen when one looks at a satellite image or flies over the lands along the lower river between Baton Rouge and the river's mouth.

In 1721 Bienville commissioned newly arrived royal engineers Pierre Le Blond de La Tour and Adrien de Pauger to design a formal plan for the new settlement. In the pursuit of Enlightenment-era order, Pauger laid out the distinctive grid that defines the modern Vieux Carré and differed sharply from the original haphazard settlement built between 1718 and 1721.

Pauger's design placed the colonial port's social and political focus on the riverfront and centered the town around the Place d'Armes green space (now Jackson Square). This placement meant that the main town square greeted visitors who arrived by boat on the river. Importantly, Pauger located the St. Louis Church (later designated a cathedral) prominently at the rear center of the square, thereby emphasizing the centrality of the state-sanctioned Catholic Church. The primary house of worship was flanked to its left by the *corps de garde* (military headquarters) and the presbytère (clergy rectory) to its right. Thus, the design also underscored the prominence of the military in the colonial settlement.

The original plan, at four streets deep and eleven streets wide, was a smaller footprint than the current Vieux Carré, which was enlarged by the Spanish in the 1760s. The orderly grid contrasted with those of older European settlements, towns, and cities with their narrow, winding medieval streets. In doing so, Shannon Dawdy argues, Pauger created a new urban design that applied the reason of order associated with the Enlightenment, reflecting the modern vision of French civilization conquering the wild, natural environment.[17]

Pauger named the streets after members of the Bourbon family associated with Louis XIV and associates of the crown: Chartres, Roial (Royal), Bourbon, Conti, Toulouse, Orléans, and du Maine. Toulouse and du Maine were named for Louis XIV's two legitimated sons Louis-Alexandre de Bourbon, compte de Toulouse, and Louis-Auguste de Bourbon, duc du Maine, whom the late king had fathered with his favorite mistress Madame de Montespan. Pauger separated the family-themed streets with those named after Catholic saints: St. Louis, St. Pierre, St. Anne, and St. Philippe. He named Bienville Street for his boss and city founder, of course. The remaining streets eventually took their names from important landmarks: l'Arcenal (Arsenal) became Ursulines. In the later Spanish era, Hospital (later Gov. Nicholls) and Barracks received their names from the original King's Hospital and the Spanish Quartel (military barracks), respectively.[18]

Even though Pauger had already designed the grid, the first detailed painting of La Nouvelle Orléans does not convey the orderly arrangement of the new settlement. Royal engineer Jean-Pierre Lassus's *Vue et Perspective de la Nouvelle Orléans*, painted in 1726, shows a collection of buildings on the Mississippi River in a space carved out of the surrounding dense swamp and forest. Viewed from the perspective of the West Bank, one can make out the St. Louis Church in the center of the image. However, the square shape of the Place d'Armes is not evident. Instead, the painting shows the rather random placement of about one hundred buildings of different sizes ranging from small cabins to larger two-story homes or offices.[19]

Was Lassus's image intended to inspire settlement in and development of the new town? The engineer's depiction of La Nouvelle Orléans completely surrounded by swamp contrasted to the maps of the time, which depicted recent land concessions and implied a quickly developing agricultural port and capital. In the foreground, however, Lassus depicted enslaved persons clearing trees on what was the King's Plantation (present-day Algiers), emphasizing the colony's dependence on Indigenous and African slave labor.

Also in the foreground, Lassus painted a large skiff with four lines of rowers headed upriver. On the rear of the boat there appears to be a small, enclosed cabin or tent and a large white banner with gold emblems—perhaps intended to depict the French Bourbon flag, with (what appears to be) the *fleur de lys*—hoisted on the stern. Hence, if Lassus intended the image to encourage French gentry and settlers to immigrate, his depiction of the enslaved labor and the servants rowing a person of prestige would certainly reassure potential investors who hoped to maintain a lifestyle of luxury and comfort in Louisiana.

Yet, the colony would struggle to recruit settlers and investors throughout the French period. Just as the development of La Nouvelle Orléans was getting underway, John Law's Company of the Indies (the Mississippi Company) failed spectacularly in 1719. The colony did not produce the quick profits that Law predicted, and his reputation was permanently ruined. Law subsequently fled France for Venice, where he died in 1729. Despite the debacle, the Company of the Indies continued in Louisiana under a restructuring of its debt and with a new director until 1731.

In the wake of Law's failure, Bienville in the role of governor-commandant continued developing the colony and the port-capital of La Nouvelle Orléans. He issued concessions to noble Frenchmen such as Dijon native Claude Joseph Villars Dubreuil and associates from Canada, including the four Chauvin brothers and François Trudeau, all of whom received concessions of enslaved workers and land directly upriver from New Orleans. Lawrence Powell depicts Bienville's concessions as an example of nepotism and insider dealings. But regardless of the method, the governor-commandant remained determined to make Louisiana succeed as an agricultural export colony reliant on slave labor, in which New Orleans served as the capital, port, and population center.[20]

Le Village Diversifié

Despite the small population of La Nouvelle Orléans during the French colonial era, the tiny community developed a diverse population exhibiting many of the demographics that define the city today. From its inception, the settlement included a mix of French or French Canadian elites; *engagés* (indentured servants); *forçats* (convicts); soldiers, sailors, and *voyageurs* (Indian traders); Jesuit and Capuchin priests and Ursuline nuns; enslaved Africans from different kingdom states such as the Kaarta, Bissau, the Asante Empire, Dahomey, Benin, and the Kongo; and Indigenous people from the Choctaw nation and other *petites nations* such as the Chitimacha, Chawasha, and Washa, who were sometimes enslaved.

Among the concessionaires, many families of French nobility assumed title of the land but hired managers to run the plantations. Pénicaut mentioned these families when he recounted the end of his time in Louisiana. The French carpenter then was suffering from blindness and wrote his memoirs to prove his service to the early colony and thereby receive a pension for his disability from the count of Toulouse (Crozat). Perhaps mentioning the many concessionaires was the carpenter's way to gain support from wealthy families. Nevertheless, Pénicaut's list indicates the expanse of land grants provided by Bienville, stretching from the coast upriver from La Nouvelle Orléans to Natchez and to the Red River Valley around Natchitoches.[21]

Among the concessionaires, Claude Joseph Villars Dubreuil descended from French nobility, although the neighboring Chauvin brothers (Jacques, Joseph, Nicolas, and Louis) did not. Nevertheless, Dubreuil and the Chauvins received contiguous concessions at the site of a former Indigenous settlement known as Chapitoulas, which is the area between present-day Harahan and Ochsner Hospital in Jefferson Parish. Receiving several hundred enslaved persons as part of their generous grant, by the mid-1720s the industrious men had developed their lands to raise cattle, rice, indigo, sugar, and tobacco; they also constructed a sawmill and indigo factory. Both the Chauvins and Dubreuil are also credited with building the first private levee and drainage canals in the area and eventually emerged as Creole aristocracy in the French period. Dubreuil is known for having fathered a number of children with an enslaved Senegalese woman, Marie Anne.[22]

The question then remains: What families of nobility working for the crown in the 1720s made the drastic move to the village on the banks of the Mississippi River? In an effort to maintain more class diversity, the crown avoided recruiting only wealthy French families, as they did in Canada through the seigneurial land concessions.[23] But in fact, most of the employees of the crown who served as engineers, officers, or bureaucrats descended from families of French nobility—as revealed by the titled prefix de/du [of] (place name-land holding), which was a badge of status in France.

In the early list of royal governors and commandants, one sees, for example, Antoine de La Mothe Cadillac, Jean-Michel de Lépinay, and Pierre Dugué de Boisbriand, Étienne de Périer, and several others. In the church the young Jesuit missionary Nicolas-Ignace de Beaubois came with the Ursuline nuns, and early engineers included Adrien de Pauger, Jean-Pierre de Lassus, and Alexandre de Batz. But most of these persons of nobility served their time in Louisiana and then moved on to other French colonies or back to France if and when they were able. Jean-Baptiste Le Moyne, as the Sieur de Bienville, received the formal title from his father, who himself acquired a noble title in Quebec for his service to the crown, and not from his family lineage.

Most of the French immigrants who came to La Nouvelle Orléans during these early years were soldiers, *engagés*, or *forçats*. Therefore, many of the earliest arrivals in the colony were either desperate to leave France or were coerced into doing so. Many of the women were falsely imprisoned by the crown specifically to provide settlers to the new colony. Their lives and experiences in La Nouvelle Orléans are often undocumented, and they were left voiceless. But opportunities in Louisiana did enable some upward mobility.[24]

One of the most interesting examples of social mobility in La Nouvelle Orléans is provided by Madame Elizabeth Real Pascal Marin. In the male-dominated colony, she arrived as an indentured servant from Bordeaux in the early 1720s; she later married a sea captain, raising her social status. At the end of her life in the 1770s, Madame Marin's succession (estate) documents reveal that she, in fact, had lived as a wealthy woman by the standards of the day. She was able to take advantage of the opportunities offered by the French-colonial American (Louisiana) experience to a French person of little means to establish a new life and obtain social status and economic mobility.[25]

Madame Marin's house at 632 Dumaine Street is today known as Madame John's Legacy, a property of the Louisiana State Museum. The home's current name is taken from a fictional character in local-color writer George Washington Cable's 1874 short story, "Tite Poulette," which used the site as its setting. Importantly, this structure is the only existing French colonial-style residence remaining in the Vieux Carré. Archaeological evidence from the courtyard of the home recovered in the late twentieth century reveals a great deal about the material life of residents in this period. The diverse origins of trade goods reflect New Orleans connections to international markets, as do the succession papers at New Orleans Notarial Archives.[26]

Madame John's Legacy (Chez Marin) is a French colonial-era residence that exemplifies the Creole architectural style from that period. The ground-level floor is raised eight feet not only to reflect the social status of the family but also to elevate the residence well above any street flooding from heavy rains. This "raised basement" design also provided storage on the ground floor (a New Orleans basement) and exposed the upper levels to cool breezes during the hotter months.

The home is also characterized as a West Indies cottage, reflecting the adaptation of French design to the warmer climate of the Caribbean and Gulf Coast. The covered galleries in the front and back provide living spaces protected from the rain and sun. These spaces also make possible the quintessential New Orleans pastime of sitting on the porch (balcony, stoop, or gallery) overlooking the street. Additional Creole architectural characteristics include the arched windows, the interior fireplaces extending into the living spaces, and the lack of hallways. These attributes distinguished Creole homes from more English-influenced Atlantic homes, which often featured interior hallways and chimneys located on the exterior ends of the building.

The location of Chez Marin also reflects the residential and economic development of the village at that time. The home was built in the "front of town," on Dumaine between Chartres and Royal Streets, its location signaling the wealthier status of the inhabitants. The area close to the river housed most of the important government and church buildings (St. Louis Church and Capuchin Presbytère, Government House, and the Ursuline Convent) and the homes of well-to-do residents. In contrast, the "back-of-town" was less prestigious and abutted the swampy area just beyond the village.

Originally, Pauger envisioned a social arrangement in which enslaved people would live in cabins outside the grid and free whites would inhabit the town. However, that planned arrangement soon evolved into the racially and ethnically diverse residential pattern that continues to define New Orleans. In the French period, the urban enslaved toiled as cooks, personal servants, valets, gardeners, drovers, skilled artisans, livery stable hands, and boatmen. Because the owners of enslaved domestic workers expected their workforce to be on call and close at hand 24/7, the workers often lived on their owners' properties. Thus, the town's population reflected the diversity of the colony.[27]

Most of the white residents, who made up around 50 percent of the new settlement's population, did not own slaves. They worked as artisans, in water and land transportation, in the military, or in commerce, including trading with Indigenous peoples. The non-elite whites included *engagés,* former *forçats* and *galèriens* (galley slaves), soldiers, and *voyageurs,* the last group based on the French Canadian model. A small number of free persons of color also lived and worked in the town. Native peoples such as the Choctaw provided important foods, oils, and game to the residents.

The European farmers recruited by the Company of the Indies to settle in the lands upriver came from diverse German-speaking regions of western Europe. They arrived from present-day Alsace, France; the adjacent Rhine Valley in present-day western Germany; and northern Switzerland. In French Louisiana, these farmers settled in the upriver region that became referred to as le Quartier des Allemands, or "Neighborhood of the Germans." Today, the upriver parishes of St. Charles, St. John the Baptist, and St. James are known as "the German Coast." But the colloquial name refers specifically to the settlers' German language and not their diverse regional or national origins.[28]

During this period, French immigrants arrived mostly from the northern Atlantic provinces such as Normandy, Brittany, and Picardy and the west Atlantic provinces Poitou-Charente, Aquitaine, and Gascony. Many of the noble families came from Paris and the Bourbon-Orléans region of the middle Loire Valley. Occasionally some families and settlers came from the eastern provinces of Alsace, Lorraine, and Savoie or the Mediterranean provinces of Provence and Languedoc-Roussillon (Occitanie). But overall, the western maritime provinces had the strongest connections to the early colony: they were part of the Atlantic Creole world in which the western French ports of La Rochelle, Nantes, Le Havre, and Bordeaux had strong economic connections to French West Africa, the Caribbean, and Canada.[29]

Enslaved Africans and their Afro-Creole descendants comprised around one-third of the town's population during the French period. In fact, their minority status was the opposite demographic of that outside the town and in the rest of Louisiana, where enslaved people comprised around 60 to 70 percent of the population. In the area surrounding the town, enslaved people labored in the fields and lived in crudely constructed cabins on plantations. Two of the largest ones were the Governor's (later Jesuit) Plantation just upriver from the town and the King's Plantation on the West Bank opposite the French Quarter, where lived the largest concentration of African people in the lower river region. But in La Nouvelle Orléans, even though enslaved workers were a minority, the phenomenon of urban slavery shaped the village's social fabric, with class and race emerging as important social constraints.

Nearly all enslaved peoples' lives remain obscure in the French period, but what we know about the man Louis Congo provides a glimpse into their existence. His surname reflects the practice of naming African people after their country of origin, which in this case would be the Kongo Kingdom. He arrived initially as an enslaved person but was given his freedom in exchange for agreeing to serve as the town's executioner (*bourreau*), which Congo did from 1725 to 1737.

This agreement provided Congo a parcel of land along the Chemin du Bayou (Bayou Road) just outside the town, where he lived with his wife. As executioner, Congo also received an allotment of wine and money for performing floggings and hangings. But his position made him the target of both Indian and African maroons (runaways) who attacked him on two occasions. As an emancipated and independent man, Congo remains a fascinating and unusual figure in New Orleans's earliest history.[30]

The French crown's decision to use Louis Congo as executioner perhaps was part of its efforts to divide and thus more easily rule the white, Black, and Native American inhabitants. Having a Black man serve in that position, in which he had to punish or execute whites, Blacks, and Indians, made a public statement. The attacks on Congo during this period speak to this resentment. Bienville also used Indigenous men to hunt marooned Africans, and Governor Périer employed Africans to attack targeted Indigenous groups in the late 1720s to prevent the development of a political alliance between the Indigenous and African peoples. Périer sought to deter incidents like the Bambara Conspiracy of 1731, in which members of the enslaved West African Bambara tribe around Natchez allegedly plotted with local Indigenous peoples to overthrow the French.[31]

But despite the French divide-and-rule policy, African and Indigenous peoples did form relationships, as evident in the census, in which there was a category—*grif* or *griffe*—designating a person of mixed African and Indigenous ancestry. Certainly, maroons (self-emancipated Africans) formed social and trading relations with Indigenous people in the environs of La Nouvelle Orléans, as they did throughout Latin America and the Caribbean. Iberville even noted how African maroons, who likely were from Spanish Texas, lived in Louisiana before the French expedition of 1699. That year, Iberville related how a Nouadache man reported the existence of African maroons at a settlement called Connessi: "At this settlement, there are only

Negroes with their families. He reports them to be rather numerous and leads us to believe that the Negroes at this settlement did not welcome any white Spaniard."[32]

The African connection with Native peoples is most evident today in the Afro-Creole costuming tradition known as the Mardi Gras Indians, or Black Masking Indians of New Orleans. In this distinct masking culture associated with Mardi Gras Day and St. Joseph's Night (March 19), Afro-Creoles dress in costumes decorated with feathers and beadwork depicting the imagery of resistance. The members of the various "gangs" or tribes perform a specific repertoire of songs that often speak to the historic spiritual and social connections between the two groups. For example, the reverent prayer song "Indian Red" honors all the positions within the tribe (Chief, Queen, Wildman, Spyboy, Flagboy, and so on); other songs such as "Shallow Water" are songs of resistance, referring to evading captors by crossing through water.

Indeed, musical artist and Wild Tchoupitoulas member Cyril Neville acknowledged how "a deep bond between American Indians and African Americans became a sacred secret in parts of Louisiana," because "both peoples were oppressed and slaughtered, both estranged from a system of belief . . . that ran counter to the established culture." During the era of racial segregation in the late nineteenth and early twentieth centuries, the first tribes were more formally organized. The Creole Wild West, considered to be the oldest group still in existence, was formed in 1885. Local legend claims that the gang was inspired by the Indigenous members of Buffalo Bill's Wild West show on tour in New Orleans at that time. Today, the highly respected costuming tradition encompasses more than sixty groups, and the art form has evolved into one that speaks more to African than Native American culture. But their customs and rituals are rooted in the historic relations between Indigenous and African peoples in the environs of New Orleans.[33]

Indigenous slaves also existed in the French period, many of whom were captured in France's war against *petites nations* such as the Chitimacha or the Natchez.[34] For example, the Frenchman Antoine-Simon Le Page du Pratz purchased an enslaved Chitimacha woman on his arrival at La Nouvelle Orléans in 1718. The French had waged war against the Chitimacha in the 1710s, and the unnamed woman served as Le Page du Pratz's domestic servant and perhaps his concubine. He wrote, "A few days after my arrival, I bought an Indian female slave of one of the inhabitants, in order to have a person to dress our victuals (vittles)." Although he did not understand the Chitimacha language, he soon realized that she understood French and could communicate with him.

Their relationship seemed to be complex, with the woman protecting her enslaver, at one point killing an alligator next to their camp on Bayou St. John. Later, when she overheard Le Page du Pratz's conversation with another man about escaping the "unwholesome air" around New Orleans and moving to Natchez, she supported the idea. Indicating that she was in communication with the Chitimacha who had earlier sought refuge in Natchez, she claimed, "They tell me the country is very fine, they live well in it, and to a good old age."[35]

The class and ethnic diversity within the small grid of the town was a source of concern to the city's elite. As Shannon Dawdy has argued, the Superior Council, on which sat local planters and elites, frequently attempted to regulate the sale of alcohol, issuing "redundant ordinances" during 1725, 1746, 1751, and 1763, "attempting to control the number of taverns and discourage the mixing of slaves, soldiers, free people in these establishments."

Other Superior Council laws attempted to curb informal socializing among working people. In 1751 the council ordered all taverns closed on Sundays, on holy days during worship, and at 9 p.m. every evening. To deter socializing among the races, the law also required there to be separate taverns for soldiers, which were not allowed to "give drinks to the inhabitants, *voyageurs,* sailors, Indians, or Negroes." Likewise, in 1763, attorney general Nicolas Chauvin de La Freniere complained that the "rear of the city is infested with numbers of men without occupations . . . who adulterate the liquors they sell and expose the slaves to violent maladies."[36] These laws and court cases give a sense that in French colonial New Orleans, those in the back-of-town exhibited unruly behavior and excessive alcohol consumption not that different from that seen on today's Bourbon Street.

At the other end of the spectrum from the rowdy back-of-town taverns, the Ursuline nuns maintained a cloistered existence at their convent in the lower French Quarter, the most pastoral and calm part of the village. The Company of the Indies and Governor Périer recruited the Ursulines Order from Normandy, France, to La Nouvelle Orléans in 1727. Their contract required them to take charge of the King's Hospital (located on the present-day Ursuline and Decatur Streets) and to provide education to young females in the region. Their legacy of charity, healthcare, and education remains strong. Today, the Ursulines School in uptown New Orleans continues as the oldest existing all-girls school in the United States.[37]

The Ursuline experience in the late 1720s is well documented by Marie-Madeleine Hachard, who arrived as a twenty-three-year-old Norman nun. Her letters to her father were published by him in 1728. Despite her cloistered existence, Hachard's observations provide an interesting portrait of morality, French culture and identity, race relations and enslavement, and the education of women in the young settlement.[38]

The letters reveal how her cultural identity was shaped by her provincial Norman background, rather than as a French national.[39] The Ursulines arrived from Rouen at a time when France was a kingdom state comprising fifteen very different provinces. As she writes to her father, "The savages of Louisiana have so much respect for the Normans" and their legacy of the Crusades and the conquest of England. She added pridefully how "they regard this province [Normandy] higher than the others." One must wonder, how much these northern French biases shaped early New Orleans culture.

In her letters, Marie Hachard acknowledged the challenges that the Ursulines faced in providing an example and thereby correcting the bawdy behavior of the sailors, *voyageurs,* and the enslaved. One of Hachard's most famous lines is this: "In the end, the devil has a great empire here, but this does not take away from us the hope of destroying him, with God's love." She described how in April 1728, a Sunday Catholic mass attracted a congregation of around 200 persons in a village of more than 900. The relatively small size of the congregation reflects the complex relationship between the strongly pious and the more raucous inhabitants in La Nouvelle Orléans, one that still exists today.

Hachard's account of the Ursulines' school reveals a great deal about the nature of race relations and education during the 1720s in La Nouvelle Orléans. On the one hand, she expresses great pride that at their fledgling school "our little community grows from day to day." But at the same time, her comments reveal the nuns' assumptions about race, servitude, and cultural differences. She writes, "We have twenty boarders . . . a great number of day students, female black, and savages who come for two hours a day for instruction." The Ursuline nuns welcomed a class of ethnically diverse girls but expected the African students also to work as enslaved servants: "A few days ago, they gave us two black boarders aged six and seventeen to instruct in our religion, and they will remain here to serve us."[40]

When the nuns arrived in 1727, they lived initially at the Kolly Townhouse (Bienville's former residence), which housed their convent on the lower-lakeside corner of Bienville and Chartres streets. After seven years, they moved to a cloistered parcel of land in the calmer section of the lower village, where the Old Ursuline Convent exists today at 1112 Chartres Street. The original royal land grant comprised a large parcel between present-day Decatur, Royal, Ursulines, and Governor Nicholls Streets. The grounds included large gardens, and the convent housed rooms for the nuns and boarders, classrooms, and the infirmary.[41]

The Old Ursuline Convent is one of the most significant structures in New Orleans, in part because the structure is the oldest existing building in the lower Mississippi Valley. Additionally, the three-story convent represents the only French colonial building to survive the fires of 1788 and 1794. The original building was designed in 1733 by city architect and royal engineer Ignace François Broutin, a native of the Nord-Pas-de-Calais region of northern France. But because of Broutin's *colombage* (*briquette entre pouteaux*) design in which timbers were exposed to the elements, the original building deteriorated rapidly and had to be demolished in the 1740s.

The current convent was rebuilt by Claude Joseph Villars Dubreuil in 1753 based on Broutin's original design. Importantly, the new building used exterior stucco to protect the timbers and bricks from the powerful New Orleans rain and sun. Broutin's original plan for exposed timbers was based on the prevalent building style in Normandy and other northern French provinces, but the Louisiana climate required greater exterior protection of the structure. The use of stucco to cover the *colombage* set the standard for colonial architecture and design, as seen in buildings in the French Quarter from the Spanish colonial era and early American period that still stand today.

The Old Ursuline Convent reflects the neoclassical (French Baroque) training of Broutin and is similar to a modest chateau in the Loire Valley (or northern France generally) from the period. Noteworthy design features include the four-pitched hipped roof with the slight flanges that are typical of roof lines from Normandy of the late seventeenth and early eighteenth centuries. One finds this same four-pitch roof design in many of the oldest Creole West Indies–style homes in the lower Mississippi Valley, such as the original Government House (burned in 1828), Madame John's Legacy, and the Pitot House in New Orleans, as well as the main houses of the upriver Laura and Destrehan Plantations. The chimneys are also on the interior of the building, a French design trait, and the window frames include a shallow arch at the top. The convent's large winding cypress staircase is believed to have been salvaged from the original building.[42]

The Ursuline presence in La Nouvelle Orléans brought a certain sophistication to the small village during the French colonial period. Their convent must have been an impressive sight in the town, which was made up mostly of small residences. The Ursulines nuns' provision of both education and healthcare in the early settlement was quite remarkable: they laid the foundation for making the colonial capital a more livable town.

Relevant Historic Sites

French Quarter: The original village and grid designed by Pauger in 1721. The engineer named the streets after persons associated with the Bourbon crown of Louis XIV, as well as the duc d'Orléans.

Jackson Square, bound by Decatur, St. Peter, Chartres, and St. Anne: The original Place d'Armes in Pauger's design is at the front and center of the village.

St. Louis Cathedral, 615 Pere Antoine Alley: The site at the center of the square (Place d'Armes) is the location of the original St. Louis Church that burned in the 1788 fire.

Madame John's Legacy, 632 Dumaine: This French colonial-style residence, with a French West Indies cottage design, is a property of the Louisiana State Museum.

Old Ursuline Convent, 1112 Chartres St.: Completed in 1753, the convent is the oldest building in the lower Mississippi Valley. Now a museum, the building is open for visits and tours.

Bayou Road, New Orleans: The oldest street/trail in the city connecting the French colonial settlement to Bayou St. John, as well as the Bayou Metairie and Bayou Sauvage ridges.

Gentilly Boulevard, New Orleans: The original path of the Bayou Sauvage ridge is the site of land concessions and small plantations in the French colonial period and stretched toward the east.

Code Noir

The first ships of enslaved Africans (*l'Aurore* and *le Duce du Maine*) arrived in La Nouvelle Orléans in 1719, one year after the founding of the settlement. During the French colonial period, more than six thousand Africans were brought forcibly to the city by ship after suffering the horrific Middle Passage across the Atlantic Ocean. However, the history of enslaved people in New Orleans during the French period has only been thoroughly documented in recent years. Historians such as the late Gwendolyn Midlo Hall, Thomas Ingersoll, Daniel Usner, Sophie White, and Ibrahima Seck have illuminated the experiences of these forced migrants and their descendants, their agency and survival in an extremely harsh labor and social caste system, and their contributions to the local and regional cultures.[43]

The city of New Orleans and the tourism industry long ignored the history of slavery, in part because the subject matter is difficult and uncomfortable for many people to discuss or address. White people often feel an awkward sense of guilt or denial, while African Americans express bitterness and resentment toward enslavement, as well as exasperation that tourism often focuses on the history of slavery, instead of freedom struggles and social and economic accomplishments.

But since the 2010s, local guides, historic homes, nearby plantations, and New Orleans government have made strides in acknowledging the humanity of enslaved people in the metro area's history. In 2018, the city created a self-guided tour app to local historic sites associated with slavery within the city (New Orleans Slave Trade Marker Tour), and a state historical marker interpreting the "Transatlantic Slave Trade to Louisiana" now stands on the Moonwalk along the river in front of Jackson Square. From the colonial era until today, the legacy of enslaved Africans and Afro-Creoles remains essential to New Orleans's identity and cultural distinction within the United States.

In 2014, the Whitney Plantation (Habitation Haydel) upriver in Wallace, Louisiana, began offering a tour experience that interprets slavery on the site in a sensitive, unromanticized, and straightforward manner. To humanize and personalize the existence of people originally designated as chattel property, curator Ibrahima Seck and historian Gwendolyn Midlo Hall created two large memorials that contain the names of enslaved persons from plantation records and 107,000 enslaved individuals in Louisiana before 1820, documented in colonial and early American archives. Other nearby plantations including Oak Alley, Laura, Evergreen, and San Francisco (closed in 2022), have also made efforts to interpret the lives of enslaved persons and freed persons in a way that underscores the humanity of their experiences in an extremely harsh work and social environment.

Initially in La Louisiane, the Company of the West oversaw the importation of enslaved persons into the colony. The French crown gave the company an exclusive monopoly for the slave trade in both Louisiana and in Senegal, where it operated a headquarters at the mouth of the Senegal River in Fort St. Louis, a depot for *captifs* (captives) at Gorée Island, and a trading post at Fort St. Joseph on the upper river near the present-day border of Mali. The forced immigration of thousands from far western Africa reflected Bienville's belief that the colony would succeed only with enslaved African labor supporting its agricultural export economy. At that time, Saint-Domingue (present-day Haiti) existed as France's most productive and profitable colony in the Caribbean. The plantation economy provided the kingdom state with wealth generated by the international export and trade of sugar, which was enabled by a workforce of enslaved people who comprised more than 60 percent of the island's population.[44]

Louisiana's fledgling economy was also modeled on La Nouvelle France. In the inland rivers and bayous, French *coureurs de bois* established relations with or married (*à la façon du pays*) Indigenous women and developed a seasonal market based on the deer-hide market. At the same time, the creation of a plantation economy along the Mississippi and Red Rivers relied on enslaved Africans for labor, overseen by a white French or Canadian minority of slave owners and planters. In this system, the population center of La Nouvelle Orléans served as the *entrepôt* (trading center) port town that exported the commodities of indigo, furs, tobacco, and naval store products (tar, turpentine, and pitch) to France and the Atlantic market.[45]

Unlike Saint-Domingue, Louisiana was not able to grow and process sugar profitably until the 1790s, when the Spanish ran the colony. Nevertheless, enslaved workers provided a key part of the colonial labor force in Louisiana during the French era.[46] In New Orleans, urban slavery shaped its economy, politics, and society, with enslaved people living in the town and serving as domestics, gardeners, in skilled construction trades, and tending to livestock and liveries.

In 1724, Louisiana adopted the French Code Noir (Black Code), which was first applied in 1684 to Saint-Domingue and other French colonies where slavery existed. Given the increasing population of enslaved persons after 1719, the colony needed a set of laws that regulated the institution of slavery, as well as the lives of enslaved people, free persons of color, and slave owners associated with the system. As with many laws, the Code Noir's enactment was a legal reaction to social conditions that elites, planters, and authorities sought to control.[47]

The Code comprised fifty-four articles, of which Articles II–V strongly influenced the culture of New Orleans. The differences between the French Code Noir (along with the Spanish Code O'Reilly) and the English-Atlantic slave laws also help define New Orleans's cultural identity in the United States today in terms of the retention of African culture and the creation of Afro-Creole spiritual beliefs that align the city more with the Caribbean Atlantic-Creole world.

In contrast to the Negro Act of 1740 passed in the English Carolina colonies that enabled owners to exercise complete control over the lives of enslaved people, the Noir Code's mix of laws partially recognized the humanity of enslaved people and their owners' Christian obligations to provide them moral protection—while curbing the rights of the enslaved and creating a social caste system defined by race and status. The set of laws also codified the status of the Catholic Church as the only state-sanctioned religion. For example, Article 1, which "Decrees the expulsion of Jews from the Colony," had nothing to do with the institution of slavery but was an expression of historic Christian intolerance of other religions and Europeans' general distrust of Jews at the time.

Enforcement of the Code Noir was always arbitrary, as is shown in accounts of New Orleans in the colonial period. Despite Article 1, Sephardic Jewish slave merchants such as the Monsantos from Portugal and Holland arrived in Louisiana in the late French colonial period and thereafter became integrated into New Orleans's elite society. One of the women in the family (Madame Angélica Monsanto) was even married in St. Louis Cathedral by the Spanish Capuchin pastor Pere Antonio (Pere Antoine).

The arbitrary enforcement of the Code Noir is even more true of Articles II and III. The former "makes it imperative on masters to impart religious instruction to their slaves," a reference to Christian indoctrination in the

Catholic Church. Article III "Permits the exercise of the Roman Catholic creed only. Every other mode of worship is prohibited."

Together these two articles theoretically enforced state-sanctioned Catholic control. Yet, enslaved people were often not prevented from practicing an illicit worship of African religions, including Islam and other traditional animism, which emphasized a reverence towards ancestors and spirits. For example, Le Page du Pratz observed the continuation of traditional African spiritual practices while he served as manager of the King's Plantation on the West Bank in 1728. He commented how enslaved people "are very superstitious" and attached to their "*gris gris,*" a talisman in traditional African beliefs and in western African Islam. In addition, the manager admitted that on Sundays "they are not Christians," but that "they are capable of becoming Christians." In the end, du Pratz declined to enforce Article III.[48]

In this context, the public show of faith to the Catholic creed, mandated by the Code Noir, led to the development of a syncretic Catholic-African religion. Afro-Creole beliefs blended Catholic worship traditions (votive offerings to saints) with West African animist spirits associated with the Fon, Yoruba, Edo, and Ewe peoples from the Bight of Benin region. Conveniently, the new syncretic Afro-Creole spiritual belief system shared the Catholic belief that one must communicate with God (Supreme Deity) through the spirits/saints using prayers and offerings, unlike the Protestant faiths that allowed one to pray to God directly.

Hence, in the syncretic Afro-Creole religions, an African animist deity or spirit (an Orisha in Haitian Voodoo, Cuban Santeria, and Brazilian Candomblé) is often associated with a specific Catholic saint that shares the spirit's domain of influence. For example, Chango, the charming dancer and drummer, is represented by Santa Barbara. Elluga, the trickster owner of the crossroads, takes on the form of Saint Anthony. And Ogun/Oshun, the mighty warrior blacksmith, is represented by Saint Peter.

New Orleans is often touted in tourist clichés and popular media as a city of Haitian-style "voodoo." But, in fact, New Orleans and its rural surroundings developed their own distinct Afro-Creole religious beliefs in the colonial period. Within the Afro-Creole Atlantic world, the same process occurred in Cuba and Puerto Rico with Santeria, in Brazil with Candomblé, in Haiti with Voodoo, and in many other Atlantic-Creole societies within the African diaspora. And in this context, one could be a devout Catholic and also practice the related syncretic variation in private (and sometimes in public).

This religious development reflects the general advancement of Afro-Creole culture, as argued by Gwendolyn Midlo Hall in her history of Africans in colonial Louisiana. In this dynamic process, more than six thousand enslaved Africans of many different cultures, religions, and kingdoms arrived in Louisiana during the period of French slave importation from 1719 to 1743. They and their children and grandchildren formed a new Afro-Creole culture that reflected the specific circumstances of life in New Orleans and south Louisiana.[49]

Code Noir Articles V and XIII also had a long-lasting influence on the music and dance culture of New Orleans. Article V stated, "Sundays and holidays are to be strictly observed. All negroes found at work on these days are to be confiscated." English slave codes did not include a "blue law" or "Sunday as a day of rest" article, but the Code Noir reflected the French Catholic enforcement of this Christian idea. Thus, Afro-Creole culture in French (and many Spanish) colonies, such as Louisiana, developed distinctly from that of the English colonies, especially on the Atlantic Coast.

Article V, when tied to New Orleans's weak enforcement of Article XIII, created a social experience in colonial French La Nouvelle Orléans that continues today, in which Sundays offer a time to socialize and gather in a public place to engage in music, dancing, religious worship, and celebration. Part of Article XIII states, "We forbid slaves belonging to different masters to gather in crowds either by day or by night, under the pretext of a wedding, or for any other cause, either at the dwelling or on the grounds of one of their masters, or elsewhere." The failure to enforce Article XIII fostered a social practice that still connects the city to Afro-Latin Caribbean cultures.

Le Page du Pratz, as manager of the King's Plantation on the West Bank, writes the clearest account of how this cultural and social phenomenon developed in the area of La Nouvelle Orléans during the 1720s. He witnessed the large Sunday gatherings known as Calinda, in which Africans played music and danced throughout the day. He noted, "Nothing is more dreaded than to see the negroes assemble on Sundays, since, under the pretense of the Calinda, or the dance, they sometimes get together to the number of three to four hundred, and make kind of a Sabbath."[50]

Le Page du Pratz's observation is important for several reasons. He seemed resigned to the existence of the Calinda, which reflected his reluctance as a plantation manager to enforce Article XIII of the Code Noir. At the same time, he admitted a repugnance for the practice, a feeling expressed by many white observers of the Calinda throughout the colonial period. Additionally, his description of the crowd numbering 300 to 400 persons documents the immense size of these religious gatherings, which exceeded the Catholic mass of 200 persons noted by Ursuline nun Marie Hachard around the same time. Lastly, his reference to the Calinda is telling, because the term (with spelling variations) was also applied to African dances in other French Caribbean colonies at the time.

In this process of Afro-Creolization, enslaved peoples from many different Atlantic African environments, religions, and cultures, and who spoke different languages and dialects, all gathered to dance to live music and, in the process, express some form of religion. Midlo Hall documented how in the French colonial period, the largest group of enslaved people came from the Senegambia region of far-west Africa. Enslaved people also were taken from the Bight of Benin and the Congo/Angola region of central Africa.

But several of the settlers who kept journals, including Pénicaut, remarked on the presence of Senegalese. And Le Page du Pratz referred to the Wolof people, whom he called the Dilauf, citing their loyalty and aptitude for leadership. Part of his bias may have stemmed from some Europeans' belief that West African Muslims were superior to animists from the region. Despite this praise, Le Page du Pratz mostly expressed very ignorant and racist observations about all the Africans he supervised.[51]

More specifically, at the Calinda, Islamic people from the inland savannahs and deserts of the Mali Empire and Guinea mixed with the coastal animist forest people of the Bantu-speaking Akan and Benin regions, as well as Christians from the Kingdom of Kongo. Cultural, religious, and linguistic differences may have created some distrust or aversion that was perhaps manifested in a social hierarchy or separatism within the community of enslaved workers. But music and dance also provided an opportunity to develop new traditions distinct to New Orleans and south Louisiana, especially in the succeeding Creole generations.

The Code Noir's lack of oversight of music as a form of expression or resistance enabled the development of an Afro-Creole musical and dance culture that reinforced New Orleans's historic connections to the Afro-Caribbean-Latin American Creole world. In contrast, within the English Carolinas, Article XXXVI of the Negro Act of 1740 strictly forbade the playing of any "drums, horns, or other loud instruments which may call together or give notice" any "wicked designs or purposes."

The process of African creolization applied not only to music and dance but also to cuisine, language, folklore, and agricultural practices. The Afro-Creole dialect of French Creole developed in this context in a similar fashion within present-day Haiti, Martinique, Cape Verde, Senegal, Mali, Côte d'Ivoire, Congo, Mauritius, and Le Reunion. And, as historian Ibrahima Seck has made clear, the Afro-Creole folklore of south Louisiana, popularized through the "Br'er Rabbit" folktales published by Joel Chandler Harris in the late nineteenth century, has its origins in West African folklore.[52]

For many Africans originally from coastal marshes and the Senegambia, Niger, and Congo river deltas, the wetland environment of the lower Mississippi Valley would have appeared familiar. The use of dugout canoes among Indigenous peoples in the Americas was and is still found in the rivers of West and Central Africa. The African boating technique of poling—pushing the boat along with a pole leveraged on the bayou or river bottom—is a practice often associated with Cajuns. Hank Williams's classic song "Jambalaya" includes the famous line, "Me gotta go pole the pirogue down the bayou." In fact, the technique of poling a shallow draft boat has global roots and can be traced to navigating the rivers and marshes of Ancient Egypt, Indigenous America, southern Asia, and Europe.

Overall, the relative liberalism of the French Code Noir, compared to the more rigid English slave laws, and the general lack of their enforcement in the New Orleans area allowed for the strong cultural survival of African dancing, music performance, and religious practices. These combined elements connected New Orleans culturally more to the French and Spanish colonies of the Caribbean and eastern Latin American than the rest of North America, perhaps with the exception of the isolated Gullah-Geechee cultures of the Atlantic Sea Islands off the coasts of Georgia and South Carolina. Overall, the legacy of this cultural retention defines New Orleans's differences today from the rest of the United States.

Foodways: Creolizing of Indigenous and African Foods

As the community of La Nouvelle Orléans developed in the 1720s, foodways became central to the creolization process and development of the town's distinct food traditions. Europeans and Africans adapted to Indigenous American foods and introduced foods from both Europe and Africa to the new colony. This adaptation occurred similarly in other locales across the Americas. New Orleans cuisine's use of African rice, indigenous American corn, a variety of beans (red and white), and spicy peppers clearly has much in common with the food traditions of the Caribbean and Latin America, as well as the larger Atlantic Basin that experienced the Columbian Exchange in the sixteenth and seventeenth centuries.

Similarly, within the United States, New Orleans and south Louisiana also share an Afro-Indigenous culinary heritage of rice, corn, and seafood cuisine with the low-country region of the Gulf and Atlantic Coasts that stretches from Texas to Maryland. And the liberal use of spicy peppers in a *piquant/picante* cuisine places New Orleans clearly at the eastern end of the national "Pepper Belt" that extends from Louisiana westward to Texas, New Mexico, and southern California. But among these southern regions of the United States, New Orleans cuisine is unique because of the city's historic importance and more than 150 years of culinary tourism that has promoted distinctive dishes such as gumbo, red beans and rice, *calas* (rice fritters) and jambalaya.

In this creolization process of the eighteenth century, the new immigrants (voluntary and forced) relied on Indigenous foods, especially corn, which was plentiful and grew easily in the region. To survive in their new land, Europeans and Africans depended on the foods that were the most accessible and available. Native peoples provided much of that food on which the inhabitants of the new settlement subsisted. Supplies from France were not consistent, and other European crops such as wheat did not grow well in the climate.

So, as a continuation of the Indigenous exchanges that existed before the arrival of non-Indigenous peoples, the *petites* and *grandes nations* traders brought to New Orleans food products including wild game, fish, fowl (geese, duck, and turkey), deer and bison, and most importantly, corn. In 1718, Pénicaut observed the importance of Indigenous traders in providing food for the new settlement, when he wrote, "All these nations are highly industrious and all are quite helpful in furnishing food to the French, to the troops as well as to the people of the concessions."[53]

As explored in the first chapter, many of the first French settlers in

Louisiana commented on the ubiquitous presence of corn and corn-based dishes, especially *sagamité*. Pénicaut observed that in the fall of 1719, the commissary-general in New Orleans, Monsieur Hubert, "bought a great supply of corn from the savages and had had it stored in the warehouses."[54]

And as La Nouvelle Orléans continued to grow into the 1720s, corn remained a staple for the residents of the village, as attested by the Ursuline nun Marie Hachard. In her letters to her father in Normandy, Hachard continued to be very positive about life in her new home, despite the challenges of survival in those years. She noted, "The luxury of this city makes no distinctions of persons; all are of equal magnificence. Most of them, along with their family, are reduced to living on nothing but *sagamité,* which is kind of a gruel."[55]

But beyond the corn-based diet that provided sustenance, Hachard also documented the general variety of foods and the early consumption of alcohol—even by the nuns—perhaps as a substitute for freshwater from the river, cisterns, and the bayou. Writing to her Norman father, Hachard explained that the most common meal was "rice with milk and *sagamité,* which one makes with Indian flour ground with a mortar. . . . The people of Louisiana find this food very good." She later added, "We drink beer. Our most common food is rice with milk, little wild beans, meat and fish. . . . We buy the meat such as venison . . . this meat is better than the beef that you eat in Rouen." She also noted their consumption of wild ducks, geese, large fish, watermelons, French melons, potatoes, peaches, berries, preserves, and oranges.[56]

As Hachard mentioned, rice along with maize soon became food staples, providing a base on which to stretch their meats and vegetables. Le Page du Pratz substantiated this claim when discussing the diets of enslaved workers at the King's Plantation around 1730. In his section on providing food for the plantation, he advised, "For the better subsistence of your negroes," one should "every week to give them a small quantity of salt and of herbs of your garden, to give a better relish to their Couscou, which is a dish made of the meal of rice or maiz [*sic*] soaked in broth."[57]

Le Page du Pratz's "couscou" referred to the North African semolina-wheat dish of couscous, which is still common today in northwest Africa (the Maghreb) and France. But in Louisiana, the dish, as he described it, was a mixture of rice and corn. Ibrahima Seck in his history of Whitney

Plantation identified a number of foods from Senegal, such as couscous (*thiéré*), that are common in the lower Mississippi Valley, reflecting the influence of Senegalese culinary culture on New Orleans's and south Louisiana's food heritage. Even today, in rural parts of south Louisiana the sweet corn cereal dish of "coush coush" is a creolized variation of the original North African dish.[58]

South Louisiana, and the southern United States generally, adopted many African foods imported through the slave trade that now define the region's food culture. These foods include okra, black-eyed peas, kidney beans, watermelon, and yams (which are from a family different from the American sweet potato). Le Page du Pratz noted all these foods in his listing of crops grown in Louisiana during the 1720s.[59]

But rice is perhaps the biggest legacy of Senegambian foodways specific to New Orleans and south Louisiana. Given the wetland environment and the difficulty of growing wheat, the Company of the Indies sought to import enslaved persons from the Senegambia region who were experienced and had knowledge of rice cultivation.[60]

In the 1720s, French settlers such as Le Page du Pratz and Marie Hachard were clearly familiar with rice. During the eighth century, the Moors introduced rice to the Spanish Mediterranean city of Valencia, considered the birthplace of paella. By the Middle Ages, the crop was grown in the southern French Camargue region of the Rhone River delta, where there developed red and black varieties of *riz de camargue*. In Italy, rice cultivation is traced to the marshy regions of Tuscany in the sixteenth century, and grain later expanded broadly into the lush Po Valley to the north.

But rice was historically and remains an essential staple food in Senegal and West Africa. The crop is still raised today in two varieties: delta rice (wetland) and valley rice (dry land). In Senegal, both varieties predate the colonial era and figure in the cosmology of the Diola people of the Casamance River Valley, where rice is considered historically sacred. In the French colonial era, Louisiana supported both varieties.[61]

Le Page du Pratz commented on the importance of rice to the colony of Louisiana in the 1720s. The Frenchman claimed that the grain "was brought from Carolina" and that the dry variety could be raised without requiring flooded fields. Rice historians believe that the Carolina variety actually originated in Asia but came to West Africa through pre-European trade networks.[62] Le Page du Pratz may have been mistaken about the Carolina origin, because rice imported from West Africa during this time was referred to as the Carolina variety. And as Gwendolyn Midlo Hall clarified, in the 1720s the Company of the Indies specifically requested French slave traders in Senegal to purchase several Senegalese persons "who knew how to cultivate rice and three or four barrels of rice for seeding."[63]

In Senegal, several common dishes are based on rice, and many others are accompanied by rice on the side. Thieboudienne, the national one-pot dish of Senegal, is prepared with rice, tomatoes and garden vegetables, fish/meat, and spices. A variation is *riz jolof* (wolof rice), which many people in New Orleans could easily mistake for local jambalaya.

Le Page du Pratz observed the method that the enslaved people of the King's Plantation used to prepare their rice: "They eat their rice as they do in France, but [it is] boiled much thicker, and with much less cookery"—a reference to the one-pot method that still characterizes most of south Louisiana's traditional cuisine.[64]

Le Page du Pratz continued, "Although it is not inferior in goodness to ours [French rice]: they only wash it in warm water, taken out of the same pot you are to boil it in, then throw it in all at once, and boil it till it bursts, and so it is dressed without any further trouble." "Dressed" rice likely refers to the addition of herbs or salt and red pepper. Du Pratz's comments indicate his familiarity with the rice cooked on the plantation and how it differed from his preconceived notions of French rice.[65]

This cooking method also undoubtedly reflected the meager provisions available even to the plantation manager's kitchen in the fledgling colony. But more importantly, the account documents how Africans served as cooks in wealthy French colonial homes, thereby influencing the food preparation and ultimately the food heritage of the city and surrounding areas.

A LOVE OF RED PEPPER

Could African cooks have been the source of south Louisiana's predilection for peppers and spices? One cannot be certain about the origins of south Louisiana's love of red chili peppers, but they are not part of the culinary heritage of either France or Spain—even though the mild Espelette pepper is grown in the western Pyrenees region and is used in French (*pimente d'Espelette*) and Spanish (*pimiento de Gernika*) cuisine. The cuisine of the Italian province of Calabria is known for the use of spicy red peppers, but accounts of spicy food in Louisiana preceded the large-scale immigration to New Orleans from that southern Italian region in the late nineteenth century.

The warm capsicums are indigenous to the Americas, and the "bird's eye" chili pepper (*chili pequin/chili petin*) is native to Mexico and grows wild in Louisiana and Texas. Often the seed is deposited randomly by birds in their droppings and grows into a large bush. In the Columbian Exchange between America and the European and African continents, the hot red pepper from the Americas became widely used in African cooking. When Africans were forcefully imported to the Americas in the seventeenth and eighteenth centuries, the use of red pepper likely appeared in the kitchens of Louisiana where they served as the cooks.

French colonial prefect Pierre Clément de Laussat provided perhaps the first reference to the warm spicy undercurrents of cuisine in the New Orleans area during his residence in 1803. In describing a meal prepared by one of the enslaved chefs in his host Michel Bernard Cantrelle's kitchen in St. James Parish, Laussat proclaimed: "How much pepper! What highly seasoned food! But especially how much pepper! Real fire, this food of Louisiana!" Hence, the prevalence of Afro-Creole cooks in the colonial kitchens would lead one to deduce that at least by the end of the colonial era, New Orleans–area cuisine had developed a distinctly African orientation and piquant flavoring.[66]

Given the cultural significance of rice to Senegal and West Africa, southern France, and Louisiana, what are the origins of Louisiana jambalaya? Many present-day residents of New Orleans compare the dish to Spanish paella, the rice-based dish that originated in Valencia, the rice-growing capital of Spain. Indeed, paella is similar to jambalaya in its use of rice as a base and the addition of spices, vegetables, seafood, and/or meats. And even though paella may be part of the culinary traditions of the French rice-growing region of Camargue, cooks from the Rhone Delta were not documented among the French settlers in New Orleans during the colonial period.

The presence of West African cooks in New Orleans's colonial kitchens makes it more likely that jambalaya evolved from the Senegalese *thiéboudiènne*. The dish is often identified with the Senegal River delta city of St. Louis, and its name in Wolof means rice (*tiep*) with fish (*jen*). Other variations include *tiep yappa* (rice with meat) and *tiep ganaar* (rice with chicken).

The ingredients for *thiéboudiènne* often depend on the availability of seasonal produce, coastal seafood and fish, and inland meats such as beef or chicken. Seasonal garden vegetables that can be added to the dish include onions, tomatoes, carrots, cabbage, eggplant, as well as cassava root and red pepper. The dish is common throughout Senegal; in nearby countries such as Mauritania, Guinea, Guinea Bissau, and Mali; and in those farther east including Côte d'Ivoire, Ghana, Nigeria, and Cameroon.

Similarities exist between *thiéboudiènne* and jambalaya in the cooking methods used and the dishes' social importance. In Senegal, the dish is often presented at social gatherings, in a way very similar to how jambalaya is eaten at family or neighborhood dinners. And the one-pot method of cooking *thiéboudiènne* is also the traditional way that jambalaya is prepared throughout southeast Louisiana. Additionally, both the West African dish and jambalaya are cooked by first sautéing the onions, garlic, and other vegetables and then adding the rice and some broth until the liquid cooks off and the rice expands.

The one-pot method is known as *benachin* in the Wolof language of western Senegal. The simple process is perhaps one of the most obvious legacies of African cooking traditions in south Louisiana. Yet, this cooking method was also likely imported from rural French *paysans,* who maintained a single pot cooking over a fire in their homes throughout the day, especially in the colder months. In traditional French cuisine, examples of this culinary tradition include the simple chicken and vegetables dish *poulet au pot* from Gascony and the slow-cooked *daube* beef stew from Provence and Languedoc.

The one-pot tradition defines many dishes in New Orleans and southern Louisiana, including gumbo, corn maque choux, red or white beans, and, of course, jambalaya. Many of these dishes have African or Indigenous origins or are a creolized version with French or Spanish influences: their existence speaks to the celebrated reputation of Louisiana's cuisine with its deep roots in the French colonial era.

Chicken and Andouille Sausage Jambalaya

In south Louisiana, jambalaya is found in both urban Creole and rural Cajun kitchens. The dish could feed a family or a large social gathering because the use of rice enabled the cook to stretch the meat and seasonings in a filling and flavorful way. The recipe begins with the base of the "holy trinity"—onions, celery, and bell pepper—together with garlic, which is sometimes called "the pope" (the shape of the bulb being similar to a bishop's miter). This base is used in cooking many traditional foods in New Orleans and the surrounding areas.

Although pork sausage would not be used for rice dishes in predominantly Muslim Senegal, the use of smoked pork in south Louisiana cooking is common. Andouille sausage is a smoked pork sausage associated with the German Coast upriver from New Orleans. The River Parish variety is very different from French andouille, which is a fatty pork sausage made from odiferous pig colon. New Orleans–area residents, if they are able, travel to the town of LaPlace to buy authentic smoked Andouille from local butcher shops such as Jacob's and Bailey's that specialize in the sausage. Certainly, one can choose not to use pork in this recipe.

Jambalaya in New Orleans is often cooked with tomatoes or tomato sauce to give it a reddish color; in rural areas, cooks do not add tomatoes, giving the dish a light-brown color from the *gratons* (the layer of grease from the sautéed sausage, onions, garlic, and peppers). This recipe includes tomatoes as an option.

Serves 6

Holy Trinity + Garlic
- **1 cup chopped onions**
- **1 cup chopped celery**
- **1 cup chopped bell pepper**
- **2–4 tablespoons minced garlic (depending on one's taste)**

3 tablespoons butter
½ pound chopped andouille sausage (or tasso ham)
6 chicken thighs (dicing is optional)
1 teaspoon salt
1 teaspoon black pepper
½ teaspoon white pepper
½ teaspoon cayenne pepper
2 cups long-grain rice
2 cups diced tomatoes (optional)
2 cups chicken stock, warmed
½ cup tomato sauce (optional)
1 teaspoon fresh thyme
For garnish: 1 bunch chopped green onions

1. In a cast-iron pot (preferably), melt the butter. Sauté sausage and chicken in butter over medium heat until browned (10–15 minutes).

2. Add onions, celery, bell pepper, garlic, and salt and pepper seasonings. Sauté, stirring frequently, until the onions are transparent (10 minutes) and have absorbed the *gratons* from the meat.

3. Add the rice (and optional tomatoes). Continue to sauté and stir until the rice has also absorbed the *gratons*.

4. Add the warm chicken stock (and optional tomato sauce) and thyme. Stir thoroughly and simmer until the stock is cooked off, and the rice bursts. Avoid stirring the mixture while simmering to prevent the rice from sticking and clumping.

5. Serve with chopped onions sprinkled on top.

Le Mélange

Throughout the French colonial period, La Nouvelle Orléans struggled to attract residents. In the 1710s and 1720s, Bienville certainly hoped that awarding colonial land concessions and allocating enslaved laborers to the concessionaires would create a successful agricultural export economy. Bienville aspired for Louisiana to achieve the prominence of Saint-Domingue in the French colonial empire. But by 1731, the Company of the Indies had resigned its monopoly, and the colony officially returned to royal administration.

The last years of the Company of the Indies were marked by the governorship of Etienne Boucher de Périer. Born in the northwestern French port city of Le Havre, the governor has a mixed legacy. He improved the levees and recruited the Ursuline nuns to New Orleans, but his disastrous lack of diplomatic skills led to the 1729 uprising by the Natchez against the French. Beginning in 1716, several hundred colonists had established a farming community among the Natchez near their Grand Village, where the newcomers attempted to raise tobacco and citrus while relying on the labor of enslaved Africans. Le Page du Pratz was one of the early settlers and wrote extensively about his experiences there.[67]

But relations between the French settlers and the Natchez deteriorated as the Natives resented the increasing intrusions on their land, ways of life, and overall autonomy. On his arrival, Périer had taken the Natchez's most productive lands for his own tobacco concession. When the disreputable Fort Rosalie commandant Sieur de Chépart ordered the seizure of the lands, the Natchez men fomented an uprising to drive out the French and reestablish their precolonial way of life. According to Le Page du Pratz, Chief Great Sun rallied his people in a speech where the leader allegedly proclaimed, "We march like slaves, as we will soon be, since we are already treated as such." Asking his people, "Why do we wait?" Great Sun concluded, "Is not death preferable to slavery?"

In this uprising known as the Natchez Revolt or War, the male tribal members organized a surprise attack in which they killed more than two hundred French soldiers and settlers and took as prisoners more than two hundred women and enslaved African workers. The revolt led to the flight of the Natchez from their home as they sought refuge among the Natchitoches, Chickasaw, and other nearby Indigenous settlements. Following a French campaign of retribution in 1731, many of the captured survivors were shipped to Saint-Domingue where they were sold into slavery—a bitter ending to this tragedy. Most of the surviving French families fled to the capital New Orleans, which underwent a brief population surge in those years.[68]

By 1732, the crown renamed Bienville governor once again (his fourth term) to repair diplomatic relations with Indigenous nations. Bienville held the post until 1743, overseeing a period of general stability but one in which the economy remained stagnant. Under the rule of the French crown monopoly, the local restrictive mercantilist economy was largely sustained by illicit trade and smuggling of goods both through the back-door bayous surrounding the city and under the noses of officials looking the other way.

Bienville's resignation and move to Paris in 1743 ushered in the last twenty years of French colonial rule, a period of continued political stability and economic stagnation. Indigo provided the main export commodity, but generally prices remained low. The crown's monopoly on goods including tobacco only fed resentment among merchants and encouraged illicit trading. In this post-founder period, a new hierarchy emerged as the planters of the lower river exercised political and sometimes economic and social control through their positions and influence on the ruling Superior Council.[69]

The two appointed governors following Bienville are both generally overlooked in the city's history. French Canadian Pierre de Rigaud de Vaudreuil served from 1743 to 1753 and then returned to Quebec to serve as the last French colonial governor of New France. Lawrence Powell characterizes Vaudreuil's support among New Orleans elites as reflecting the unity between the French nobility and the Canadian-descended gentry in the colony. The Canadian's successor, Breton military officer Louis Billouart, Chevalier de Kerlérec, governed until 1763. His ineffective administration was beset by infighting over money with the colonial *ordonnateur* (comptroller) Vincent de Rochemore, a native of Languedoc, who oversaw colonial commerce, finances, and policing. The latter had allied with French nobleman Jean-Baptiste d'Estrehan and Creole Antoine Philippe de Marigny, both of whom were part of the local planter aristocracy. Through their political connections the men had the governor recalled to France, where he was briefly imprisoned and exiled from Paris before his death in 1770.[70]

Kerlérec was succeeded by two lesser-known interim leaders who served as director general, a position that combined the governor and *ordonnateur* roles. The Gascony-born Jean-Jacques Blaise d'Abbadie began service in 1763 and then died in office from yellow fever two years later, becoming the only French governor to be buried in St. Louis Church. His successor, the French military commander and administrator Charles Philippe Aubry, prepared the colony for the transition to Spanish rule and then served briefly as acting governor following the Creole Revolt of 1768.

During the period following the Seven Years War, Aubry successfully encouraged French Canadian exiles from the Acadia region led by Joseph "Beausoleil" Broussard to settle in the region west of Baton Rouge, where they established the early Cajun community at Bayou Teche. New Orleans residents today generally are unaware of the three governors' minor political legacies. However, their names are memorialized in the Faubourg Marigny–Seventh Ward streets Kerlerec, d'Abadie, and Aubry.[71]

From 1762 to 1766, the colony remained in political limbo. La Louisiane, like many other American colonies, was swept up in the extraordinary international impact of the Seven Years War fought between Great Britain and France from 1756 to 1763. The global war was the culmination of almost six hundred years of conflict between the two European empires. The postwar Treaty of Paris between Great Britain, France, and Spain in 1763 stipulated that France cede the eastern portion of La Louisiane to Britain and that France recognize British sovereignty in Canada, the former French colony of La Nouvelle France.

However, one year before the Treaty of Paris, France secretly initiated the Treaty of Fontainebleau, in which the French crown relinquished La Louisiane to Spain, ruled by King Louis XV's Bourbon cousin, Carlos III. This treaty ensured that the vast colony stretching from the Mississippi River to the Rocky Mountains would remain out of the hands of Britain. Although Spain nominally owned Luisiana beginning in 1762, the first governor Antonio de Ulloa did not assume administrative control until 1766.

As a fitting conclusion to Louisiana's French colonial era, Bienville passed away in 1767 at the ripe old age of eighty-seven in Paris. Although he was born in Montreal, the Canadian spent his last years in the sophisticated French capital, where he rented an apartment at 17 Rue Vivienne in the Second Arrondissement not far from the Palais-Royal. Bienville's decision to retire to Paris, and not to spend his remaining years in the small settlement he founded, speaks volumes. His father had remained in Montreal, the city that he cofounded. But for Bienville, New Orleans and Montreal were no match for Paris. Given the small size and isolation of La Nouvelle Orléans, who would blame such an ambitious man who had probably experienced his fair share of rough living and hard times in the frontier port?

By the 1760s, La Nouvelle Orléans had matured into a stable French colonial village, which remained well within the initial rectangular grid laid out in 1721 by Pauger. Royal cartographer Jacques-Nicolas Bellin's map (*Plan de La Nouvelle Orléans*) from the latter part of the French period reveals the pastoral nature of the settlement and the presence of large garden plots throughout (fig. 5). The plan, which details the placement of individual buildings, conveys how the outer blocks of the grid remained uninhabited and that even the interior blocks were sparsely settled. Based on Bellin's specific location of houses, the residential character represented a mix of buildings. Some buildings on Chartres were recessed from the street with larger garden lots, whereas smaller homes on Royal and Bourbon fronted directly onto the street, a characteristic more in line with the historic neighborhood today.[72]

During the fifty-year period of French rule, the community had surmounted the first environmental challenges of establishing a permanent settlement on the vulnerable site of Bulbancha. French engineers had responded by constructing drainage canals and small riverfront levees to protect the settlement from inundation, feats still essential to the habitation of the city. One must wonder at the fortitude of the original generations of

FIG. 5. This map shows the orderly symmetrical grid plan of Adrien de Pauger that is still in place today, as well as the smaller size (11 × 4 blocks) of the original settlement during the French period. Jacques Bellin, *Plan de La Nouvelle Orléans*, 1764, Historic New Orleans Collection, 1989.15.

settlers who persisted in the flood-prone, subtropical mosquito-ridden locale, and even more those persons who came in bondage but survived in the harsh environment and adverse social conditions.

By the 1760s, the village had the footings of what would become a larger town in the succeeding Spanish era and then one of America's largest cities in the nineteenth century. The settlement underwent a process of creolization in which Indigenous, African, and European residents forged new cultures through foodways, music, languages, and religion. The French Catholic Church, as the official state church, established a social imprint that still resonates in Carnival celebrations, the importance of the Lenten season, and the paradoxical concurrence of virtue and self-indulgence for which the city is renowned.

As La Nouvelle Orléans exited the French colonial period, one sees an ethnically diverse port village that straddled a crossroads of North American and Caribbean-Atlantic worlds. In essence, La Nouvelle Orléans existed as a cross-bred mélange of New France and Saint-Domingue. The French colonial capital differed from its Caribbean or African colonial sisters by its North American orientation and survival that largely depended on both Indigenous and African peoples. Whereas most of France's Caribbean colonies were largely African and French, the lower Mississippi Valley still existed at the intersection of the dominant Choctaw, Wolof, and Atlantic French cultures, all of which left a strong legacy in the foundation of the city.

3

Nueva Orleans

A Criollo *Caribbean Port, 1766–1803*

WHEN SPAIN TOOK administrative control of Louisiana in 1766, New Orleans was a small Caribbean-Mississippian port town. The Catholic Church maintained a strong presence, and the small settlement housed an Afro-Creole population that increased prolifically during the Spanish era when slavery expanded. As the colonial capital, renamed Nueva Orleans, entered a new phase of evolution, the social and cultural elements that distinguished the growing community's reputation and exceptionalism in North America became more defined under Spanish control, which ended in 1803.

Near the end of Nueva Orleans's Spanish era, English traveler and astronomer Francis Baily in 1797 observed an incident that epitomized the social and religious life of the town. The Englishman recalled in his journals that "scarcely had the priest pronounced the benediction, ere the violin or the fife struck up at the door, and the lower classes of people indulged themselves of all gaiety and mirth of juvenile diversions." As soon as the church service ended, the city's inhabitants began their musical street festivities—a phenomenon that continues today. Baily continued, "Singing, dancing, and all kinds of sports were seen in every street. . . . The negroes [*sic*] . . . are suffered to refrain from work on this day. Here arrayed in their best apparel, . . . they would meet together on the green, and spend the day in mirth and festivity."[1]

Baily's observations provide a vivid snapshot of New Orleans life at that time, describing both Catholic rituals and a vibrant Afro-Creole street culture that became defining characteristics of the city. During the Spanish colonial period, the church, through local pastor Pere Antoine (Antonio de Sedella), influenced local politics, society, and culture in the colonial city.

Although Pere Antoine, a Spanish Capuchin priest, was officially appointed as the Supreme Officer of the Holy Inquisition, he did not enforce its strict campaign against less-than-pious behavior. His tolerance allowed the very New Orleanian predilection and reputation for permissiveness to continue.

At the same time, the musical procession through the streets came to define New Orleans within the United States and the broader Atlantic world, and within the context of other Spanish colonies in the Caribbean and Eastern Latin America with similar demographics. By the 1790s, a large and growing enslaved Black and free persons of color population comprised around 50 percent of the town's inhabitants.

Nueva Orleans's population growth in the Spanish colonial era transformed the settlement from a village to a small city. When Spain inherited Louisiana from France in 1762, New Orleans's population was just over 2,500 persons; when the Spanish colonial era ended with the Louisiana Purchase in 1803, the city had grown to a respectable population of just over 8,000. The land area of Nueva Orleans increased as well, as seen clearly when comparing Thomas Jefferys's 1769 map of the town with Carlos Trudeau's plan thirty years later (see fig. 2). Spain's successful efforts to recruit settlers and the expansion of the slave trade were important factors in both this physical and demographic growth.[2]

A Northern Caribbean Community

In 1769, Louisiana's Spanish governor Alejandro O'Reilly ordered the execution of six French Creoles in New Orleans convicted of treason against the Spanish crown. The year before, these rebels, who had served on or had connections to the French Superior Council, had led a local insurrection against Spanish rule in Louisiana. Their brief rule began with the ouster of the first Spanish governor, Antonio de Ulloa, who had arrived two years earlier. Ulloa was a respected scientist but was not politically savvy. The leaders of the Louisiana Revolt of 1768 objected to Ulloa's new restrictive trade policies and wanted to maintain their Creole political authority.

The rebellion initially succeeded, and the rebels took control of the town for nine months—until O'Reilly, the new governor, arrived from Havana with twenty ships and more than three thousand troops to authoritatively reestablish Spanish rule in Louisiana. His sentencing of the six conspirators to death earned him the nickname "Bloody" O'Reilly, and the incident continues to fascinate students of New Orleans history.[3]

But O'Reilly's legacy as a governor is more complex than his nickname suggests. His rule was shaped by the strong political, social, and cultural connections that Louisiana maintained with Cuba and Latin America during this period. As O'Reilly applied Spanish policies of colonial control, Nueva Orleans essentially emerged as an extension of colonial Cuba in its political administration, law, and the influence of the Catholic Church. One could argue that the strong political, religious, economic, and cultural connections with Cuba defined New Orleans as a distinct Caribbean Latin community within North America.

Born in County Meath, Ireland, O'Reilly left his homeland in his youth as part of the "Wild Geese" generation—those who left Ireland to become mercenaries in foreign armies—and began serving in the Spanish military in the 1750s. After the Treaty of Paris ended the Seven Years War in 1763, King Carlos III promoted O'Reilly to the post of commander in Cuba. In this position the Irishman implemented numerous military reforms in both Cuba and Puerto Rico, while establishing close social ties and family connections to Spanish Creole elites in Havana through his marriage to Doña Rosa de Las Casas. After the French Creole insurrection in Louisiana during 1768, Spanish King Carlos III removed Ulloa and appointed O'Reilly governor of the new Spanish colony because of the Irishman's administrative experience and military leadership. Hence, when O'Reilly arrived in New Orleans in July 1769 with the backing of the king, he wielded considerable authority in reestablishing Spanish rule and punishing the rebels for treason.

At that time, Louisiana existed as a dependency of the Spanish Cuban political and military administration. As Louisiana governor, O'Reilly implemented reforms stemming directly from the Cuban system of law, known as Recopilación des las Indias. He replaced the colonial French Superior Council (Conseil Supérieur) in New Orleans with the Spanish Cabildo town council found throughout Latin America. Overturning the very restrictive French mercantilism, he implemented "free trade" solely within the Spanish Empire, a policy his successor as governor, Luis de Unzaga, ignored. O'Reilly's ban on gambling and restrictions on taverns were similarly overturned when he departed for Cuba in 1769.[4]

O'Reilly's changes to the French Code Noir brought about some of the most lasting legacies of his short administration. Known as the Code O'Reilly, the new Spanish Cuban slavery regulations lasted well beyond his departure from New Orleans. O'Reilly outlawed the enslavement of Indigenous peoples, an outgrowth of Andalusian priest Bartolomé de Las Casas's campaign to protect native peoples in the Americas. This ban led to a greater dependence on African labor in Spanish America. In Louisiana, after enactment of this law, most enslaved Indigenous peoples in Louisiana received a new racial designation—as mixed-race Black people in the census—so their chattel status could be maintained.[5]

The most significant Spanish reforms to the Code Noir related to the process of emancipation. Whereas the French Code Noir (Article L) required the Superior Council to approve the freeing of an enslaved person, the new Spanish Cuban law simply required the slave owner's legal statement, thereby eliminating both bureaucratic and political constraints on manumission. Most importantly, O'Reilly instituted the law of *coartación,* in which enslaved persons could establish a contract with their owner to purchase their own freedom. Enslaved individuals could also own property, negating Code Noir Article XXII.

Together with the new law enabling property ownership, and thereby the accumulation of capital, *coartación* made it possible for more than 1,500 persons in New Orleans and over 3,000 within the colony to gain their freedom. Of the emancipations in New Orleans, 452 occurred through self-purchase, and free persons purchased the freedom of an additional 445 persons. As a result, the number of free persons of color surged during the Spanish colonial period from 19 in 1763 to over 1,300 by 1803. The establishment of this larger community of *pardo libre* (free brown) and *moreno libre* (free dark) persons, as designated by the Spanish census, underscored New Orleans's social and legal connections to Spain's Caribbean and Latin colonies and distinguished the town within mainland North America.[6]

O'Reilly's introduction of Cuban (Spanish Indies) laws in the colonial appendage of Louisiana left a lasting impact. These policies provided Nueva Orleans a vital shipping link to Cuba; the New Orleans–Caribbean connection grew stronger in 1776 when Governor Bernardo de Gálvez gained a concession from King Carlos III for New Orleans to trade openly with Cuba, the Yucatán, and the French West Indies. New Orleans therefore maintained and even increased its maritime trade relationship with Mexico

(New Spain) and French Saint-Domingue. At the same time the smuggling that emerged in the restrictive French mercantilist era continued unabated, providing a more tacit trade connection with the islands to the south.

By 1781, however, King Carlos III separated the colonies of Louisiana and Florida from Cuba as a reward to Governor Gálvez for his military conquest of East and West Florida during the American Revolution. Spain supported the American republican rebels, because the War of Independence destabilized the British Empire to Spain's advantage. Initially, Gálvez provided financial aid to the rebels through the Irish New Orleanian financier Oliver Pollock, who had established friendly relations with fellow Irishman and later governor Alejandro O'Reilly while stationed in Havana during the 1760s. Then, the Andalusian governor Gálvez waged a successful military campaign against Britain from 1777 to 1781 that secured Spanish control of Florida.

In his Florida campaign, Gálvez commanded a diverse militia comprising Spanish career soldiers, French Creoles, free men of color, and Choctaw warriors. Gálvez's troops captured Baton Rouge, Mobile, and Pensacola from Great Britain, which had controlled Western Florida: at that time, Florida extended from the panhandle to Baton Rouge on the Mississippi River. Gálvez's military legacy and support for the American cause during the revolt against Britain was honored in 1976 with a statue at the foot of Canal Street adjacent to Spanish Plaza (it was removed for renovations in 2018). He is also memorialized in the cross-town thoroughfare that bears his name—pronounced locally as "GAL-vuz" with the accent on the first syllable.[7]

Gálvez, who served as governor from 1777 to 1786, maintained the city's connections to both France and Spanish Latin America. Before serving in Florida, he fought with the Spanish military in New Spain (Mexico) in the war against Apache bands of the northern provinces in the 1760s. Returning to Spain, Gálvez then served with a Spanish regiment in Pau, a city in Basque country where he learned French, a language that served him well when Carlos III appointed him governor of Louisiana. Marrying Marie Felicité de Saint-Maxent d'Estrehan ingratiated him to the elite French Creole plantation society of New Orleans. When Gálvez ended his term as governor in Louisiana in 1786, Carlos III appointed him to succeed his father as viceroy of New Spain; he died in Mexico City later that year.

Both O'Reilly's and Gálvez's policies and careers reflected the strong political, economic, and social connections linking New Orleans to both Cuba and Mexico, as well as the French Caribbean. Carlos III's reign occurred at the height of the Spanish Empire in the Americas during the 1770s and 1780s, when the Catholic Bourbon crown controlled almost the entirety of South America, much of the Caribbean, Mexico (which included California, New Mexico, and Texas), Florida, and the Louisiana Territory. He died in 1788 and was succeeded by his son Carlos IV, who oversaw the Spanish loss of Louisiana to Napoleon Bonaparte in 1800.

Incendios Católicos

When Spain assumed the title of the Louisiana Territory from France following the Treaty of Fontainebleau in 1762, King Carlos III made the tacit decision not to enforce the strict Catholic doctrine and policies of the Spanish Inquisition in the former French colony. Spain hoped to attract settlers and to succeed where France had failed, and the Spanish crown wisely understood that enforcement of the Inquisition would deter immigrants from settling in Louisiana. In part because of this contradiction of Catholic convictions and crown policy, the former maintained a contentious relationship with the colonial officials over concerns that the local church failed to counter the less-than pious behavior of the city's residents.

Around 1780, Spanish Capuchin friar Pere Antoine arrived in New Orleans to serve nominally as the Supreme Officer of the Holy Inquisition of Louisiana. The Capuchin Order had replaced the Jesuits in the colony, after the latter were evicted from the Americas and western Europe in the 1760s over political and religious differences with the Catholic Church. Historians debate the extent of Pere Antoine's enforcement efforts of the Inquisition in New Orleans. In the end, New Orleans's French Creole residents had a reputation for not abiding by strict Catholic doctrine, and Pere Antoine was well loved by his parishioners.[8]

The Spanish priest's longevity as pastor at St. Louis Church (later Cathedral) speaks to his support from local parishioners. Remarkably, he served in that position for more than fifty years until his death in 1829. After being ordained as a priest in the early 1770s, Antoine was assigned by the church to be both pastor at St. Louis Church and the leading church authority for the colony of Louisiana.[9]

In 1790 the friar's failure to enforce strict church doctrine and his alleged scandalous conduct led the Auxiliary Bishop Cyrillo of Barcelona to call for the expulsion of Pere Antoine from the colony. Esteban Miró, who was then governor, attempted to force Pere Antoine to leave, and a brief conflict ensued between the two men. Initially the friar challenged the expulsion order by invoking the powers of his position as Supreme Officer of the Inquisition to override Miró's authority; he raised the possibility of enforcing the Inquisition in New Orleans and thereby scaring away immigrants to the colony.

The conflict between Miró, Bishop Cyrillo, and Pere Antoine revealed the larger concern over the lack of strict enforcement of church policy in New Orleans's permissive culture. Pere Antoine likely had to balance the pressures of his office with the realities of the behavior of his lax Creole congregants. This balancing act is reflected in the folklore surrounding the pastor. On the one hand, he maintained a reputation, but perhaps only among Protestant American immigrants, as a strict enforcer of the Inquisition. Yet, the friar was also viewed as a populist who expressed concerns over the treatment of prisoners and the enslaved and opposed capital punishment. Rumors also held that Pere Antoine was a Free Mason and lived with a common-law wife and their son. But in the end, the pastor's support and love from his parish at St. Louis Cathedral spoke volumes.[10]

Bishop Cyrillo did not appreciate the social customs and behavior of many New Orleans residents, and like Pere Antoine, the bishop had to respond to the orders of his superiors. When Cyrillo visited the city in 1786, he denounced the "wicked custom of the negros [*sic*], who at the hour of Vespers, assemble in a green expanse called Place Congo to dance the bamboula and perform—hideous gyrations." Clearly, the bishop had no tolerance for the African Sunday dances at Congo Square, which he viewed as crude and un-Christian. Yet, like Pere Antoine, he also opposed the execution of enslaved people and even protested loudly during the execution of maroon leader Juan San Maló on the Plaza de Armas in 1784.[11]

Spanish authorities' sporadic enforcement of royal laws and church doctrine fit in with the general culture of social tolerance that defined New Orleans. The presence of non-Catholics in the colony reflects this important feature of the colony. For example, the Monsanto family were Sephardic Jews who had deep connections in the international slave trade. Immigrating to Louisiana from Dutch Curaçao in the last years of French colonial rule, the patriarch Isaac Monsanto was permitted to reside in Louisiana, despite Article I in the French Code Noir forbidding Jews in the colony.

Monsanto's close business relationship with French governor Kerlérec, along with New Orleans's general laissez-faire attitude, played an important role in the initial non-enforcement of Article I. Governor O'Reilly expelled the slave trader from the colony briefly in 1769 for illegal trading. Yet, O'Reilly's successor, Spanish governor Luis de Unzaga, himself of Sephardic Jewish origins, gave Monsanto a visa allowing the family to return and resume their trade in New Orleans.

Under Spanish rule, the extended Monsanto family lived as socially prominent merchants and ingratiated themselves within New Orleans's elite business circles. Following Isaac's death in 1774, the brothers continued their prosperous trade, and Spanish governor Manuel Gayoso de Lemos even appointed Benjamin Monsanto to a prominent position overseeing the inventories and appraisals of plantation estates. And as a reflection of Pere Antoine's tolerance, he consecrated the marriage of Benjamin's sister Angelica to Scottish immigrant George Urquhart at St. Louis Cathedral.

The social and financial success achieved by the multilingual and very cosmopolitan Monsanto family is a clear example of the lack of enforcement of both legal and religious doctrine in the Spanish colonial era. Their becoming one of the most prominent merchant families represented the founding of the New Orleans Jewish community, giving the city the oldest established Jewish presence in the American South.[12]

Despite Pere Antoine's permissiveness, he did enforce Catholic doctrine during the Good Friday Fire of 1788 that destroyed most of the upper Vieux Carré. The fire started on March 21 at the home of treasurer Don Vicente Jose Nuñez (617 Chartres), one block from the church. The inferno began when candles in Nuñez's private altar lit either the drapes or the ceiling on fire. The flames spread quickly through the French Quarter with the help of gusty southerly winds and the prevalence of structures with exposed cypress shingles and timbers.[13]

Pere Antoine chose at this point to enforce church doctrine, which prohibited the ringing of bells on Good Friday. Without the church bells, no alarm sounded, and the fire raged unabated throughout the residential quarter. In the friar's defense, a fast-moving fire on a windy day in a town filled with wooden structures would be difficult to combat just with buckets of water. And he reported that he did order men, perhaps enslaved workers, to moisten the roofs of the Capuchin monastery buildings. Moreover, Pere Antoine is given credit for prioritizing the preservation of parish records, many of which he saved and can be found today in the New Orleans Archdiocese Archives.[14]

All told, more than 850 buildings were destroyed in the 1788 fire, which ravaged the residential area between Dauphine and Chartres, and Conti to St. Philip Streets. The conflagration destroyed the St. Louis Church, the Cabildo, the *corps de garde* (military barracks), armory, and the jail on the Plaza de Armas. Remarkably, the fire spared the large West Indies–style Government House (destroyed by fire in 1828), the royal tobacco warehouse and powder magazine (on present-day Canal St.), and the old Ursuline Convent in the lower part of the city. The fire also damaged Madame John's Legacy, at the time the residence of the Beluche family. The home was reconstructed in the original style and therefore exemplifies French colonial (West Indies) residential design, even though the structure was rebuilt during the Spanish period.[15]

The 1788 Fire greatly devastated the colonial city, and the rebuilding process represents one of the great examples of the city's resilience in its three hundred-plus years of history. Governor Miró housed the homeless in tents and provided food aid to the destitute. He also relaxed trade restrictions to allow aid from American ports and was sufficiently in the Spanish crown's good graces to receive financial aid.[16]

The fire required the rebuilding of the original town, today's French Quarter. New buildings were constructed in a style reflecting Spanish architectural design—incorporating private interior courtyards, tile roofs, exterior wrought-iron balconies and galleries (verandas), and facades abutting the sidewalk. The use of patio courtyards, tile roofs, and balconies reflected the strong Moorish Arab influence on the architecture of southern Spain. And even though the Vieux Carré is named the French Quarter today, the neighborhood's buildings dating to the rebuilding in the 1790s characterize an Andalusian village.

But in fact, these courtyards, balconies, and tile roofs are present throughout much of the Mediterranean world, including southern France and Italy. The use of *colombage* (bricks between posts) was common to many parts of northern Europe and to pre-Spanish New Orleans. Additionally, the use of stucco to protect the exterior bricks and posts appears to be evident as early as the rebuilding of the old Ursuline Convent in 1753. Today, this exterior coating and iron balconies seem reminiscent of a quaint

European style and certainly distinguish New Orleans from the English-colonial brick Georgian architecture of the Atlantic Coast, as exemplified in old Williamsburg, Virginia, and Boston's Beacon Hill.

The oldest clay bricks in the Vieux Carré are known for being very soft and susceptible to erosion, if not protected from the elements. Some of these "soft reds" were likely mined from river clay and fired in the city. Harder bricks originated from kilns on the north shore of Lake Pontchartrain, where Choctaw inhabitants had pointed out clay deposits to the early French settlers. By the Spanish period, the Creole Cousin family had the largest land grant encompassing Bayous Liberty and Lacombe.

The Cousin family shipped kiln-fired bricks across the lake to New Orleans on a fleet of barges manned by their enslaved workers. The barges carried the bricks directly to the Vieux Carré via Bayou St. John and the newly constructed (1794) Carondelet Canal, which connected the headwaters of the bayou with the back-of-town along the route of the present-day Lafitte Greenway. Today the older and softer bricks can be identified by their orange color and soft texture; they continue to present a challenge to the preservation of the oldest historic structures.

The use of wrought- and cast-iron balconies also distinguishes New Orleans architecturally within the United States. In the Vieux Carré nearly all the galleries and balconies were made of cast iron during the early American period, when new technology enabled the more affordable manufacture and reproduction of cast-iron gallery posts and elaborate patterns. Creating wrought iron during the Spanish period required a much more labor-intensive creative process by a master blacksmith, which explains why it was used much less commonly used than cast iron. Some of the most beautiful wrought-iron examples are the balconies at the Vincent Rillieux residence (341 Royal), the Bosque House (617 Chartres), and the Correjoles House (715 Gov. Nicholls), as well as the decorative entry gates to St. Louis Cemetery #1.

The ornate balconies of the Cabildo on Jackson Square are the most significant representation of the Spanish wrought-iron style in the city. Designed by Canary Island (Isleño) immigrant artisan Marcelino Hernandez, the balconies incorporate the graceful motifs of a crown and rose. The symbols likely represented the Spanish crown and the church, respectively, because the rosary is a common Catholic design motif. Their survival into the U.S. period after 1803 is quite remarkable, considering that these two institutions were contrary to the very American ideas of republican democracy and freedom of religion.

Notary Don Andrés Almonester y Rojas, perhaps the wealthiest Spanish resident in the city, financed the rebuilding of the Casa Capitular (Cabildo), which was completed in 1795. He hired a French architect and surveyor and a Spanish military officer, Gilberto Guillemard, to design the building, which remains one of the grandest from the Spanish era in the Vieux Carré. Like earlier French engineers Pauger and Broutin, the French-born architect Guillemard trained at the Académie royale d'architecture (Royal Academy of Architecture).

While in the service of Spain, Guillemard was stationed in Havana, where he gained a familiarity with Spanish and Mediterranean design. In redesigning the new Cabildo, he drew on the surviving arched walls from the *corps de garde* along St. Peter Street to extend a prominent *portales* arcade across the front at ground level, creating a distinctly Mediterranean or Latin American architectural design motif.[17]

Originally, the Guillemard-designed building contained two levels with a shallow-sloped roof, and the second-floor façade featured a large, arcaded gallery with a fine view of the Plaza de Armas and the Mississippi River. The pediment contained the sculpted seal of Spanish Louisiana, later removed by American officials and replaced with an American military motif designed by Italian artisan Pietro Cardelli. On the second level, the interior grand Sala Capitular (Capital Room), with its elaborately carved fireplace mantle, hosted official meetings of the Cabildo (town council) or Catholic superiors.[18]

Guillemard also designed the new St. Louis parish building, which the Catholic Church upgraded to a cathedral on its completion in 1794. The tall, two-level church was both larger and grander than the original one designed in 1720 by Adrien Pauger. As depicted in the detailed inset illustration of city surveyor Jacques Tanesse's 1817 map, the Spanish-era two-story church façade featured three arched entrances flanked on the ends by tall domed bell towers, with a smaller spire in the center (fig. 6). The design is very similar to that of the cathedral in Cádiz, Spain, which maintained a strong trade relationship with Latin America and New Orleans. The building is also similar in appearance to the cathedrals in Santiago de Cuba and

Havana, where Guillemard studied. In the early American period, esteemed English architect Benjamin Latrobe designed a tall center tower with a bell, which was completed in 1819.

The French architect designed the Presbytère, completed in 1815, in the same design as the Cabildo. The three buildings were renovated to their present three levels in the years before 1850. Guillemard's overall symmetrical and well-balanced architectural ensemble is a distinctive landmark distinguishing New Orleans architecturally from other American cities.[19]

Within the Vieux Carré, several residential properties built after the Good Friday Fire represent Spanish styles of design for both modest and grand homes. Among the smaller residences, the two houses at 840 Governor Nicholls and 709 Dumaine have a Spanish flat roof reminiscent of those in Latin America. The latter house has a decorative Roman tile parapet on the facade and is thought to be designed by Barthélémey Lafon, the noted French planner and architect who laid out Faubourg Marigny and the Lower Garden District.

FIG. 6. This map inset shows the barren Plaza de Armas featuring the impressive new Spanish-style Casa Capitular (Cabildo), St. Louis Cathedral, and the Capuchin Presbytère designed by Gilberto Guillemard after the Good Friday Fire of 1788. Inset from J. L. Roqueta de Wosieri's map of New Orleans, 1803, Historic New Orleans Collection, 1958.41 i–v.

Lafon is also thought to have designed the impressive Spanish-style Bosque residence to replace Don Nuñez's home that burned at 617 Chartres. The home dating from 1799 features a balcony decorated with an elaborate monogrammed wrought-iron *B* (for Bosque), a porte cochère (coach entrance), and a rear covered balcony overlooking a bricked patio courtyard, all indicative of a well-to-do residence in this era.[20]

The Jean François Merieult House at 533 Royal is now a property of the Historic New Orleans Collection and exemplifies one of the grander Spanish homes. Dating from 1792, the large two-story brick and tile residence features a broad wrought-iron balcony overlooking the street and a porte cochère leading to very large patio courtyard originally surrounded by a stable, coach house, pantry, two kitchens, and a wood store.[21] Though some of these buildings have undergone minor alterations, they retain their distinct Spanish character overall.

Notary Don Andrés Almonester oversaw the process of rebuilding within the city. In addition to funding the replacement of the Cabildo, St. Louis Church, and the Presbytère, Almonester also provided financial support for the construction of a boys' public school, a new charity hospital (present-day North Rampart at Toulouse Streets), and a chapel for the Ursuline nuns. For his philanthropy and service, King Carlos IV awarded the Andalusian nobleman a knighthood in the Real et Distinguida Orden Espagñola de Carlos III (Royal and Distinguished Order of Charles III). His full-length portrait painted in 1795 by local artist José Salazar hangs in the Old Ursuline Convent today.[22]

Two other legacies of the Good Friday Fire include the coincidental creation of the city's first suburb Santa Maria (in French, Ste. Marie) and the dedication of the St. Louis Cemetery. In response to the fire's devastation, French merchant Bertrand Gravier subdivided his upriver plantation, partly to provide land on which to rebuild. City surveyor Carlos Trudeau designed the plan for the new neighborhood on the site of today's Central Business District (or American Sector) extending from Canal Street upriver to St. Joseph Street and from present-day Tchoupitoulas back to O'Keefe Street.

Importantly, the creation of the Faubourg Ste. Marie, named in honor of Gravier's recently deceased wife Marie, was the first example of a phenomenon in New Orleans's expansion, in which Creole planters subdivided their plantations to create new neighborhoods. This trend greatly accelerated in the early American period from 1803 to the Civil War.[23]

Trudeau centered the neighborhood around a central Plaza Gravier (today's Lafayette Square), which is the second-oldest park in the city. The surveyor named the streets for local landmarks, saints, and Spanish royalty. In reference to the crown, the Camino Real or the Royal Road is today's Tchoupitoulas. Campo (perhaps a reference to the local term for slave quarters) is today's Camp, and Almazen (named for the royal tobacco warehouse) is today's Magazine, renamed in the later American period for the city's powder magazine. The successive saint streets included San Carlos (St. Charles Avenue), San Francisco (Carondelet), and San Felipe (O'Keefe). Present-day Baronne was originally named de la Barona, likely a reference to the succeeding Spanish governor Francisco Luis Héctor, barón de Carondelet.[24]

St. Louis Cemetery #1 (425 Basin St.), the city's oldest active burial ground, also came into existence in 1788. That year, the city and St. Louis Church designated the land for such use just outside the city limits, and the walled site received its first burials in 1789. New Orleans had also maintained several cemeteries within the Vieux Carré during the French era, including one for the military at Royal and Barracks and another for the Ursuline nuns.

The French colonial-era cemetery, known today as St. Peter Street Cemetery, may have existed outside the village boundaries, as shown on some maps of the time indicating that the lakeside boundary was at Dauphine Street. But maps in the Spanish era consistently show that Nueva Orleans's back-of-town boundary expanded to the present-day North Rampart Street. Therefore, likely for hygiene and sanitation reasons, the town officials designated a burial area outside the expanded limits.[25]

Interestingly, the St. Peter Street burials appear to be done through interment, and not with above-ground tombs, as became the custom beginning with St. Louis Cemetery #1. For this reason, the square between St. Peter, Burgundy, Toulouse, and North Rampart Streets is a sensitive burial site containing unmarked graves underneath the existing structures. In 1984, the *Times Picayune* newspaper recorded the uncovering of several remains during a construction project, and archaeologist and historian Shannon Dawdy noted that the Catholic cemetery built in the French colonial period represented an egalitarian burial process in which bodies were interred regardless of ethnicity, class, or status as free or enslaved.[26]

St. Louis #1, as the oldest existing cemetery, exhibits the longest-standing visible graves and tombs in the city. Above-ground burial tombs generate great interest, because they distinguish New Orleans (and south Louisiana) from other U.S. regions and reflect the city's Latin heritage customs. Although much misunderstanding exists around the burial practice, the use of above-ground tombs in New Orleans represents both cultural influences and environmental factors.

In terms of environment, the high water table of the soil makes in-ground burial of a casket problematic. During heavy rains or floods, buried caskets can rise (or float) to the surface—a fact confirmed today in lower Louisiana floods. Even in local cemeteries without the vaulted tombs, such as Lafayette Cemeteries #1 and #2 or Mount Olivet Cemetery, burials are accomplished by creating a raised cement bed and then covering the casket with a layer of heavy gravel or small stones. In above-ground tombs, the law requires a body to be entombed one year and a day before the remains can be replaced by another deceased body. The policy enabled families to use the same tomb (perhaps with two or three levels) to accommodate multiple generations.

Older cemeteries in both Spain and France use vaulted tombs to hold the deceased or small open votive chapels under which the bodies of the family are interred. In these cemeteries, well-to-do families would construct a tomb or chapel to illustrate their wealth and status, in effect building a stately and beautifully designed "home" for the deceased. The families of those interred at St. Louis Cemetery adopted this same cultural practice when creating above-ground vaulted tombs. Therefore, if one views these cemeteries as cities of the dead, the most beautiful and elaborate "homes" are those of the wealthiest.

St. Louis #1 (and many other local cemeteries) also use mausoleum wall vaults (colloquially referred to as "oven vaults") for interment. This practice is commonly used in older Spanish and southern French cemeteries, as well as throughout Latin America. These stacked simple mausoleum vaults are not as elaborate as the standalone family tombs described earlier; such vaults usually contain those persons who could not afford an elaborate family tomb or were destitute. In reference to the "city of the dead" analogy, the mausoleum vaults would represent apartment buildings surrounding the neighborhood of elaborate houses lining the wide central passages (boulevards) and narrower paths (side streets).

In St. Louis #1, the grandest tombs are those of prominent Creole families, but the Catholic Church buried persons in the same cemetery regardless of ethnicity or status. Among the most well-known historic figures interred in this cemetery are Étienne de Boré, the planter and sugar industry pioneer; Bernard de Marigny, the planter and founder of the Marigny neighborhood; and Homer Plessy, the nationally known civil rights activist and descendant of free persons of color. Voodoo priestess Marie Laveau is purported to be interred in the family vault of her husband, Christophe Glapion. For years Laveau's tomb attracted visitors who left votive offerings. And although the cemetery originally was for Catholics only, the church designated a rear section for the interment of Protestants where the burial sites are not vaulted.

In the annals of the city's history, the Good Friday Fire is often mentioned together with the Great Fire of New Orleans that occurred on December 8, 1794. Together both fires and the subsequent rebuilding shaped the charming appearance of the present-day Vieux Carré. This second conflagration destroyed more than 210 buildings in the upper section of the old town between Bourbon and Decatur Streets. The flames spared several important buildings, including the Government House, the Royal Hospital, and the old Ursuline Convent. The St. Louis Church also survived: its consecration as a cathedral only two weeks later symbolized the new status that New Orleans gained as a Catholic diocese.[27]

Just as Spanish Louisiana began as a political appendage of Cuba in the 1760s, the local Catholic Church continued to exist under the archdiocese of Santiago de Cuba into the early 1790s. At that time, King Carlos IV requested that Pope Pius XI separate New Orleans from Cuba because of his concern about the "deplorable state of religion and discipline" in the colony. In 1793, Bishop Cyrillo was sent back to Cuba, and Pere Antoine returned to Nueva Orleans. More importantly, the pope created a new archdiocese encompassing Louisiana and East and West Florida, underscoring the administrative separation of Louisiana and Florida from Cuba accomplished under Governor Gálvez.[28]

The first bishop, Luis Ignatius Peñalver y Cárdenas, arrived in New Orleans in 1795 from his hometown of Havana to take charge. He remained for eight years before his transfer to Guatemala. Like Bishop Cyrillo of Barcelona, the new bishop was shocked and disappointed by the state of New

Orleans inhabitants' morals and behavior. In his 1799 report, Peñalver y Cárdenas complained of the irreligious behavior and public sin in the city—especially the concubinage between white planters and enslaved Black women—and he stressed the need for greater discipline among New Orleans and Louisiana residents.[29]

Throughout the Spanish colonial period, the church as the official state religious institution continued to have a very large influence on the city's politics, society, and culture. But even as New Orleans remained a distinctly Catholic town, Spanish policy permitted the existence of non-Catholic residents, including Jewish families, some Anglo-Protestant immigrants, African Muslims, and even Afro-Creole voodoo practitioners. These people generally worshiped privately, but some ceremonies were in plain sight, as was the case with Sunday Calinda dances at Congo Square. Hence, the city existed as a contradiction of piety and desire, awkwardly balancing church doctrine with the reality of a very diverse population in terms of religion, class, and ethnic identity.

Relevant Historic Sites

Jackson Square: The site of the Spanish Plaza de Armas features the Cabildo (701 Chartres St.) and the Presbytère (731 Chartres St.). Both buildings were designed by Gilberto Guillemard and constructed after the Good Friday Fire. The Cabildo's balconies on the Chartres Street façade are some of the finest wrought-iron work from the Spanish era in the city, designed by noted Isleño blacksmith Marcelino Hernandez.

Vincent Rillieux Residence, 341 Royal St.: Spanish colonial residence from the 1790s, with decorative balconies exemplifying the artistic use for residential wrought iron.

Merieult Residence, 533 Royal St.: Completed in 1792, the home of prosperous merchant Jean François Merieult is now the property of the Historic New Orleans Collection. The complex is an example of a very large Spanish colonial residence with a patio courtyard and outbuildings.

Bosque Residence, 617 Chartres St.: The site of Don Vicente Nuñez's residence where the Good Friday Fire of 1788 began, this home dating to 1795 is named for Spanish official Don Bartólome Bosque. The house design with porte cochère, patio, and balconies reflects classic Spanish-

Moorish architecture that replaced the original French colonial buildings after the fire. Before 1785, the site housed the residence of Bernardo de Gálvez while he served as governor.

St. Louis Cemetery #1, 425 Basin St.: New Orleans's oldest existing cemetery designated in 1788. The walled "city of the dead" includes elaborate tombs of Creole families, some of which are decorated with graceful Spanish-era wrought-iron crosses.

Congo Square, 701 N. Rampart St.: This corner section of Armstrong Park is the site where African and African-Creole dances were permitted from the Spanish colonial era until the 1840s. Drum circles and ancestor tributes still occur at the large live oak tree in the center.

Spanish Customs House, 1300 Moss St.: The home on Bayou St. John is one of the oldest buildings in the city outside the French Quarter. Dating to 1788, the steep pitched roof, raised construction, and large galleries overlooking the bayou reflect a West Indies style of architecture appropriate for the New Orleans climate.

Pitot House, 1440 Moss St.: Dating to 1799, this home was built by Don Bartólome Bosque (the original owner of the residence at 617 Chartres St.) as a rural retreat on the bayou. Architecturally, the home is a rural two-story variation of Madame John's Legacy. The large galleries and steep-pitched roof are indicative of the West Indies colonial design of New Orleans and surrounding areas.

Acadians, Isleños, and Andalusians

As noted at the beginning of this chapter, Spanish New Orleans experienced a growth in population that surpassed that of the French colonial period. Spain successfully attracted settlers to Louisiana in part because of the crown's policy of not enforcing the Inquisition. Additionally, Governor Alejandro O'Reilly issued liberal land grants to help populate the surrounding hinterlands and bolster the military defense of the colony. Even though many Spanish- and English-speaking settlers came voluntarily, Spain's expansion of the slave trade at that time also increased the African population to support an agro-export economy. As Spanish Louisiana witnessed a population increase, so did New Orleans's population grow to more than eight thousand people, reflecting the effects of Spanish policies.

In Louisiana, Spain's liberal immigration policy aimed to create a substantial population buffer between the British American colonies east of the Mississippi Valley and the Spanish colony of New Spain (Mexico). Before the American Revolution, which concluded in 1783, Madrid believed that Great Britain's presence in North America posed a threat to the crown's lucrative silver mines of Zacatecas in the mountains north of Mexico City. Whether this concern was rational or not, Carlos III feared that Britain might attempt to invade Mexico from the north and seize the mines, thereby depriving the crown of a major revenue source. Thus, a large population strategically placed in Louisiana could theoretically defend Spanish interests in northern Mexico.

Most of the voluntary immigrants to Spanish Louisiana came from three sources: French Acadian refugees from the Seven Years War in Canada, emigrants from the Spanish Canary Islands off the west coast of Africa, and Spaniards from the southern province of Andalusia. In addition, the surge in the slave trade brought to the colony an enslaved population, largely from Central Africa. All four groups contributed to the development of a diverse and distinct Atlantic Creole culture that underscored New Orleans's distinction within the United States and tied the city to the larger sphere of the Atlantic Basin.

Acadian immigrants (Les Acadiens), whose descendants became known as Cajuns, did not initially foresee Louisiana as their destination when they fled the Acadia region of eastern Canada, which today comprises Prince Edward Island, New Brunswick, and Nova Scotia. When the British conquered this region in 1755 during the Seven Years War, the Protestant empire forced thousands of French-speaking Catholic settlers to leave the coastal province in an exodus known as "le Grand Dérangement." The families dispersed across the Atlantic Basin, from western France to Saint-Domingue in the Caribbean and the Anglo-American Atlantic Coast.

These families had descended from rural Pays-de-Loire and Aquitanian immigrants who had populated the Acadia region when France founded the colony of La Nouvelle France in the seventeenth century. Culturally, these Acadians were similar to many of the settlers who had initially come to French Louisiana, sharing western French origins. By the 1750s, when they emigrated after the British conquest, these families might be described as Canadian Creole because of their French American identity, their familiarity with Indigenous cultures and languages, and their adaptation to the foodways of New France.

By the mid-1760s, the Spanish government in Louisiana, first under Governor Ulloa and then under O'Reilly, offered the refugees land grants to help them populate the rural areas around New Orleans and to provide defense of the colony from a possible British invasion. Overall, about 1,500 Acadian families immigrated to Louisiana from the 1760s to the 1790s. The first waves of settlers established themselves upriver from New Orleans near the community of St. Gabriel. A second wave settled in the region along Bayou Teche to the west of the Atchafalaya Basin, where they became small farmers and cattle ranchers on the open prairies that stretched toward Spanish Texas. Some families also resided along Bayou Lafourche west of New Orleans, where they eventually became fishers and ranchers in the upland bayou ridges around Houma and Thibodaux.

Although most Acadian families did not settle in New Orleans proper during the Spanish era, their presence in Louisiana did have an impact on the city. Their post–World War II settlement in the New Orleans suburban areas continues to resonate in the city's culture. Because many families were destitute when they arrived in Louisiana in the late 1760s, feeding them strained local food supplies, requiring Governor O'Reilly to bend the rules that prohibited Spanish trade with Britain. The governor dispatched his Irish Cuban acquaintance Oliver Pollock to procure food stuffs from the Anglo-American colonies on the Atlantic Coast.[30]

These Acadians (the term phonetically evolved into "Cajuns") adapted to their new environment and developed a distinct culture that is essentially the rural equivalent of urban New Orleans's Creole culture. The French Canadians borrowed their hunting and fishing techniques and foodways from their Indigenous neighbors, enslaved and free people of color, and the Spanish and German immigrants who also moved to these rural areas. Their cuisine, which became popular internationally in the 1980s, reflects the blended influences of all these groups. Whereas Cajun food is known for its spicy heat and flavors, like in New Orleans, this attribute likely came from African cooks or their Afro-Creole neighbors.

Today, many Acadian family names such as Bergeron, Boudreaux, Foret, Guidry, Melancon, Pitre, Robichaux, Trahan, and Thibodaux have endured, and their descendants can trace their lineage back to the initial exodus in the Spanish colonial period. But even though residents of the swamps, marshes, and prairies of the areas surrounding New Orleans are often called Cajuns, their lineage is a diverse mix of Acadian French, non-Acadian French, Spanish, German, Irish, English, Native American, West African, and West Indian.

Even though many tourists come to New Orleans expecting to see Cajun culture, the city today is largely urban Creole. However, many residents who descended from Acadians live in the suburbs (especially Jefferson Parish). After World War II and before Hurricane Katrina, some Cajun families did settle in upper Mid-City between S. Galvez and S. Broad streets, where neighborhood bars like the Cajun Pub and the Frenchman Inn catered to French-speaking residents. During the 1960s and 1970s many other Cajuns found job opportunities and settled in the modern-day Jefferson Parish suburbs of Lafitte, lower Marrero, Gretna, and Westwego, as well as Metairie and Kenner. Musician Bruce Daigrepont claims that in the 1960s parishioners at St. Edward the Confessor Church in Metairie popularized the culinary *boucherie* tradition of *cochon de lait* (roast suckling pig), as celebrated at their annual fair in October. Although some authentic Cajun restaurants exist in the New Orleans area, most Cajuns, like New Orleans Creoles, would likely tell a visitor that the best food can be found at their paw-paw and me-maw's home.[31]

The immigration of people from the Canary Islands to Louisiana during the late eighteenth century reflects Spain's larger colonial effort to relocate the islands' inhabitants (referred to as Los Isleños) to the Americas. The tropical archipelago, located off the coast of Morocco, became the first colony of the Spanish Empire (the crown of Castille) founded in the fifteenth century. By the late 1700s, economic woes brought on by the struggling sugar industry, a broad enclosure movement by wealthy noble landowners, and drought led to the displacement of hundreds of farming and shepherding families. In response to this push off the islands, Spain enabled their pull to the Americas by offering land grants in Louisiana, Texas, Cuba, and Mexico.[32]

And so Governor Gálvez gave land to the Isleños, with the understanding that the settlers would provide defense of the colony, if needed. Between 1777 and 1783, about 2,100 immigrants from the Canaries settled in three strategic locations for defense across the lower Mississippi Valley. The Spanish government placed some families along the headwaters of Bayou Lafourche on the west bank of the Mississippi River near present-day Donaldsonville and others across the river at the head of Bayou Manchac, near present-day Galvez in Ascension Parish. Spanish authorities intended these two locations to provide defense against a possible invasion from the Gulf of Mexico up either bayou. Closer to New Orleans, Spanish officials settled Isleños on the bayou ridges in present-day St. Bernard Parish to defend the colony against a potential invasion via the lower river and surrounding wetlands. At that time, the area was known as Terre aux Boeufs (land of the beef cows), and Spanish officials dubbed the settlements La Conceptiòn and Nueva Gàlvez.[33]

In these lands along the river delta, the new immigrants settled in the marshes and small bayous adjacent to the wealthy Creole plantations along the elevated Mississippi River ridge. The émigrés lived and survived as small farmers, hunters, fishers, and fur trappers, maintaining a distinct culture defined by traditions such as the *decima* (a ten-line song form), carved wooden duck decoys, distinct Creole Spanish foodways (*caldo de pescado* and *ropa vieja*), and a unique Isleño dialect.

Over time, the people of the community were referred to as the "Spanish Cajuns." Today, many rural and suburban St. Bernard Parish Isleños are identified by family names such as Nuñez, Fernandez, and Perez. Since the twentieth century these families have mixed with other French Creole, Irish, and Italian immigrants in St. Bernard. At the same time, they have reconnected with the culture bearers of their homeland in the Canary Islands and host an annual heritage festival at the Los Isleños Museum and Cultural Center (1357 Bayou Road) in the village of Saint Bernard.[34]

In New Orleans proper, most Spanish government officials and immigrants originated from the southern Iberian region of Andalusia; more specifically, the Mediterranean coastal province of Malaga. Andalusia maintains the strongest Islamic, North African, and Roma cultures in Spain because of its proximity to Morocco directly across the Straits of Gibraltar, and its history as the longest-existing Moorish-occupied region (711–1492). Appropriately, in the colonial period, this most exotic region of Spain and the birthplace of flamenco music and dance was also the geographic source of Spanish immigration to New Orleans, which holds a similar outsized reputation in the United States as the colorful birthplace of jazz.

The Andalusian influence in New Orleans is most evident in the colonial officials who spanned the Spanish social class system from the *campesino* to *nobleza.* Among the former, the very popular priest Antonio de Sedella (Pere Antoine), who was born Francisco Ildefonso Moreno, grew up in the small rural village of Sedella outside Malaga. From his humble origins, he attended school and was ordained at the nearby Capuchin Monastery in Granada. He was then assigned to be pastor at St. Louis Church in Nueva Orleans where he remained almost his entire life. His formal full-length portrait by Edmund Brewster portrays him in a simple brown cassock with a wooden *chapelet* (rosary beads) around his waist.

In contrast to Pere Antoine, the wealthy notary Don Andrés Almonester y Rojas descended from a noble family of *hidalgos* and grew up in the city of Mairena del Alcor in the province of Seville. Appointed royal notary in New Orleans, he married Marie-Louise Denys de la Ronde, who was from an elite Creole planter family. In his full-length formal portrait from the 1790s, the nobleman is depicted wearing his distinguished medals; within the inset crest, artist José Salazar listed Almonester's philanthropic accolades and formal titles, including caballero de la Orden de Carlos III (Knight of the Order of Carlos III).

The earliest Spanish Louisiana leadership was peppered with Andalusians, specifically those from the province of Malaga. The first appointed governor, Antonio de Ulloa (1766–1769), grew up in the Malagan capital city of Seville. Governor Luis de Unzaga (1769–1777), who succeeded O'Reilly, descended from a noble family of Sephardic Jewish and Basque origins in the coastal city of Malaga. The military hero Governor Bernardo de Gálvez (1777–1783) grew up in a *familia de la nobleza* in the town of Macharaviaya outside Malaga. In the last twenty years of the colony, however, the appointed governors represented more geographic diversity: Esteban Miró was from Catalonia, Hector Luis Carondelet from Flemish France, and Sebastian Casa Calvo from a noble family in Artemis, Cuba.

In truth, the similarities between New Orleans and Andalusia in terms of their relative exoticism was not reflected in the Spanish leaders' comportment. The Andalusians were conservative Catholics, and they did not celebrate the marginalized Moorish or Roma cultures historically associated with the region. Nevertheless, Andalusian history is characterized by the complex coexistence of African Arab, Jewish, and Christian Iberian settlements and the subsequent interactions of their cultures, religions, language, foodways, and architecture.

Although Andalusian immigrants to New Orleans may have exhibited an outward appearance of Catholic respectability, certainly the Andalusian culture of religious and cultural tolerance resonated with the generally permissive nature of New Orleans society historically and even today. Although debates exist over the extent of religious and cultural tolerance in both Andalusia and New Orleans, the general trends of cultural adaptation and absorption characterize both distinct cultures.[35]

The Moorish (North African and Arabic) Spanish legacy may have had its most visible impact on New Orleans architecture. The prevalence of courtyard patios with fountains, wide galleries to protect against the sun and rain, and decorative balconies is a direct link to North Africa, the Mediterranean, and Andalusia. The expansion of the African slave trade in the Spanish period also introduced a new generation of Africans who continued to shape the city's society and distinct musical, culinary, and religious cultures.

Bamboula

Just as Spanish Louisiana began as an appendage of Cuban political administration, law, and the church, colonial officials in the 1760s modeled their plans for Louisiana's development on the growing agro-export economy of Cuba. As the officials sought to create an economy based on the shipping of tobacco and indigo, they expanded the African slave trade in Louisiana. The population of enslaved people in lower Louisiana more than quintupled from 4,598 in 1763 to 24,264 people by 1800. In New Orleans, the population of enslaved persons more than tripled from 859 persons in 1763 to 2,773 by 1803. And in that last year of Spanish New Orleans, the overall population of 4,108 persons of color (enslaved and free) surpassed the number of 3,948 white inhabitants, reflecting a demographic majority that continued into the first three decades of the American period.[36]

The French slave trade had slowed to a trickle from the early 1730s on, and by the end of the French colonial period only a small influx of persons directly from Africa had arrived in the colony. With the Spanish revival of the African trade in the 1760s and 1770s, most of the enslaved people originated from the Congo and Angola in Central Africa. Indeed, historian Ned Sublette refers to the Spanish colonial era as "the Kongo Period."[37] His characterization raises the question: What aspects of New Orleans's Afro-Creole culture might be considered Congolese?

The numerous Bantu dialects of Central Africa, part of the larger Bantu-language family of Central and West Africa, have had an influence on New Orleans foodways and music. Words such as *gumbo, jambalaya,* and *bamboula* (the last describing a drum, dance, and rhythm) all contain the common Bantu letter combinations of *m* and *b* (mb). Many common musical and dance terms in Latin America include the Bantu sounds of "mb" and "ng." Consider the names for several popular Latin American music and dance styles: mambo (Dominican), samba (Brazilian), cumbia (Colombian), and tango (Argentinian), as well as conga (large drum) and bongo (smaller drum).

The Bantu-French noun *gombe/gombo* (okra) evolved into the Louisiana term *gumbo.* In French African markets today, *gombe/gombo* is still used to designate *okra,* a word used in English but of Igbo (Bight of Benin) origin.[38] Hence, the iconic south Louisiana and New Orleans dish of gumbo likely began as a thick stew named for the green African vegetable. And although jambalaya is closely associated with Senegambian *riz jolof* or *thieboudienne,* as discussed in chapter 2, the Louisiana names for both jambalaya and gumbo probably developed in the kitchens of Bantu-speaking cooks in New Orleans and surrounding areas.[39]

Catholicism had influenced the syncretic religions of Central Africa since the Portuguese traders and missionaries arrived in the 1500s. Ned Sublette points out that Kongo people "had a centuries-old tradition of employing the imageries and structures of Catholicism to express traditional African practice." Therefore, many forced immigrants from Central Africa arrived with their own Afro-Catholic beliefs, influencing the syncretic Catholic Afro-Creole belief systems developing in New Orleans and its environs.[40]

In terms of music and dance, the phenomenon of the Sunday calinda continued to grow and develop. During the latter eighteenth century, the term "Place Congo" began to apply to the locations of the African dances and markets. Eventually, the green commons (Place Publique) behind the Vieux Carré developed into the site associated with the Sunday dances. Known today as Congo Square (701 North Rampart), its name is often associated with the Central African people and culture that became prominent in colonial Spanish New Orleans. In fact, however, the name originated from the Congo Circus that existed at that site during the 1810s.[41]

The term *bamboula* is applied to the specific rhythm, dance, and associated large drum used at Place Congo. The repeated bamboula rhythm cell (the repeated pattern: BOM ba dom dom) is known in the Kikongo language as *mbila a makinu* (the call to dance) and is the basis for multiple Afro-Latin music genres throughout the Atlantic Creole world. Many variations of the rhythm are also performed in dances throughout West and Central Africa. In Cuba the rhythm that became known as the *habanera* is evident in the nineteenth-century *contradanza* genre. In Argentina, the rhythmic cell became the basis for the *tango* music genre and dance.[42]

The term *bamboula* is likely a Kikongo-language reference to playing music and dancing in remembrance of a place of African origin. Although this term applied historically to dances at Place Congo in New Orleans, West Indian scholar Dr. Chenzira Davis-Kahina has documented the bamboula as a symbolic dance ritual of resistance, done by female dancers wearing white dresses, throughout the African diaspora of the Caribbean, eastern Latin America, and New Orleans. Today, the dance is strongly identified with the American Virgin Islands and is also practiced by some culture bearers in New Orleans.[43]

The Sunday dances and their so-called "hideous gyrations" offended the conservative auxiliary bishop Cyrillo Sieni (Cyril of Barcelona) on his visit to New Orleans in 1786. In his complaint that was recounted earlier, Cyrillo reported how Africans in New Orleanians danced the bamboula at Place Congo during the hours of vespers. Subsequently, Spanish governor Esteban Miró, himself a conservative Catalonian Catholic, issued a decree to delay the dances—"*los tangos, o bailes de negros*" (the tangos, or Black dances)—until after vespers.

More importantly, African dancing and drumming on Sundays in colonial New Orleans distinguished the city culturally from the more racially restrictive Anglo-American Atlantic Coast, where officials prohibited African dances and music in public. At the same time, the permitted existence of African dance and music in New Orleans provides yet another strong cultural connection to the larger Afro-Caribbean-Latin American world.[44]

After increasing the importation of slaves to Louisiana in the first twenty years of Spanish rule, by the 1780s, officials reacted in alarm at the existence of maroon communities in the surrounding swamps and marshes, which raised planters' fears of a potential slave uprising. Although small maroon settlements of self-emancipated Africans and Afro-Creoles had existed unmolested in the past, in 1784 Governor Miró felt compelled to crack down on several communities in the lower river region of present-day St. Bernard Parish. A Spanish military contingent including enslaved and free persons of color eventually arrested the maroon leader Juan San Maló. To ease white fears and send a message to would-be maroons, San Maló and several captured maroons were executed on the Plaza de Armas that year.[45]

The policing actions in the mid-1780s, as well as the Spanish restrictions on the Sunday dances and even on the perceived rights of people of color, reflected white inhabitants' concerns as the population of 2,600 persons of color grew to constitute 50 percent of the population. During this period, both Governors Miró and his successor Hector Luis Carondelet passed new regulations stemming the importation of enslaved people from Africa. During the 1790s the new rules then applied to Saint-Domingue (Haiti), where the largest rebellion of enslaved persons in history unfolded.[46]

As white fears of racial equality grew with the increase in the population of free persons of color, Governor Miró passed a law in 1785 enacting a dress code for free women of color. This law required the *femmes de couleur libres* to wear a head covering to distinguish their status and ethnic identity. Referred to by some modern historians as the "Spanish War on Black hair," the law led to the wearing of the tignon, a head wrap or decorative cloth that women of color employed fashionably to counter its intended racial degradation. In fact, tignons or head scarves of various names existed throughout Africa and the larger Afro-Latin-Caribbean diaspora to signify status or origin. Ironically, Napoleon's wife Josephine Bonaparte, a native of Martinique, spread the popularity of the tignon as a fashionable headwear in the 1790s. And in New Orleans, the style gradually appealed to white women, who proudly wore the tignon, as evident in formal portraits from the early nineteenth century.

Foodways: African Cooks in the Kitchen

Whereas accounts of the early French period emphasize European and African adaptations of maize corn to their diets, fewer examples exist of this phenomenon in the Spanish period. Evidence does exist, however, of the influence of African cooking on local cuisine during this period, perhaps reflecting the prevalence of enslaved Africans in the Spanish and Creole kitchens of New Orleans.

As mentioned in the previous section, the word *gumbo* has its roots in the Bantu dialect term for *okra*. The earliest known reference to the dish comes from a passage in a document from 1764, as Louisiana transitioned from a French to a Spanish colony. In this French Superior Council transcription of a legal interview in New Orleans regarding the theft of a pig, the interrogator asks an enslaved women Louisa (Conga) if she had "*donné (lui-Louis) un gombeau avec Cezar et un autre negresse*" (given [him, Louis] a *gombeau* with Cezar and another Black woman).[47] One might wonder whether the passage refers to a dish of okra or a stew. But the fact that the passage mentions *un gombeau* (a gumbo) raises the possibility that the interrogator is referring to a specific dish commonly known among both formally educated white Creoles and enslaved Afro-Creoles in New Orleans.

In 1803 during the last month of Spanish administration in New Orleans, the newly arrived French colonial prefect Pierre Clément de Laussat described a sumptuous meal served to celebrate the transition of Louisiana from Spain to France. In his recounting of this elaborately prepared dinner, Laussat wrote, "As a local touch, twenty-four gumbos were served, six or eight of which were sea turtle." Laussat makes a more explicit reference to gumbo as a soup or stew, noting that one of the dishes was a turtle (soup) gumbo. However, one may still wonder about the colors of the roux and the specific ingredients.[48]

The cuisines of the Bantu regions of Africa, stretching from the Congo and Angola northward to the Bight of Benin and Sierra Leone, have much in common with the foodways of New Orleans and south Louisiana. As discussed in chapter 2, okra, black-eyed-peas, stewed greens, sweet potatoes, and rice are all common in this region. Moreover, in coastal regions of West Africa can be found numerous dishes containing fresh fish and shrimp, whereas cooks in inland regions often use chicken as a meat, which is also true in south Louisiana.

The national dish of the Congo and Angola is often considered *poulet à la moambé* (stewed chicken with greens) and is usually served with rice and red peppers. Another very common dish in the region is *saka madesu* (sautéed greens, beans, and rice), which is also served with *piri piri* (red hot pepper). In the Bantu regions, a flavorful red bean soup or stew served with rice is also common, leading one to surmise that the New Orleans dish possibly has its origins in this culinary tradition as well.

But what might be the Spanish or Andalusian culinary legacy in New Orleans? Certainly, one can point to the presence of Creole meat pies as a variant of Spanish *empañadas.* The local chili-gravy-covered hot tamale may be considered an adaptation of Indigenous Spanish American culinary traditions. Some culinary historians might also include jambalaya as a variation of Spanish paella, as explored in chapter 2. Appropriately, the upriver Spanish settlements in Ascension Parish are known for jambalaya (without tomatoes or tomato sauce), and the parish seat of Gonzales hosts an annual cook-off festival for the celebrated rice dish.

The New Orleans king cake, baked to celebrate Epiphany and eaten throughout the Carnival season, finds its closest predecessor in southern France and throughout Spain. Its distinct ring shape and the addition of sugary toppings are closely related to the Spanish *rosca de rey* (king's thread) as well as the French Mediterranean *gâteau de rois* (king's cake) and *couronne des roi* (kings' crown). These three distinct king cakes differ from the northern French Epiphany cake, *galette de rois* (king cake), which is more of a flat, rounded phyllo-dough pastry filled with almond paste (*frangipane*).

The mirliton (*Sechium edule*) grown and used in New Orleans cuisine may also be considered a cultural legacy of the city's historic relationship with Spanish Latin America and the Caribbean from this time period. Indigenous to Mexico (where it is known as *chayote,* a word of nahuatl origin), the squash-like vine fruit is found throughout the extended Spanish and French Creole world from the Canary Islands to La Réunion and Mauritius, where the fruit comprises an important Creole cuisine known as "le chouchou." In New Orleans, the mirliton is used in a number of traditional Creole dishes (stuffed mirliton, dressing, and casserole), and functions similarly to the bell pepper as discussed below.[49]

Stuffed peppers are one of the most recognizable New Orleans foods associated with the culinary traditions of Spain (*pimientos rellenos*) and Mediterranean France (*poivrons farcis*). Baked peppers stuffed with minced meat and vegetables are also common throughout the Mediterranean, Eastern and northern Europe, and as well as northern and southern Africa.

Even though the historical or geographic source of the dish in New Orleans is open to conjecture, stuffed peppers are featured here to symbolize a classic local Creole dish that represents Spanish, Mediterranean French, and African culinary traditions.

*Stuffed Peppers (*Pimientos Rellenos*)*

In New Orleans, stuffed bell peppers use a variety of different fillings. Ask a local for their recipe, and as in many local food traditions, each cook will prefer their own seasonings and ingredients—especially the choice of fillings such as shrimp, pork sausage, ground beef, cornbread, or rice. During the Lenten season, one may find seafood-based filling, whereas at other times of year, pork sausage or minced meat may be common. The mixing of rice into the filling historically provided households a means of stretching the meal to feed more people. The addition of tomatoes and spicy peppers in the filling may be more of an urban New Orleans Creole ingredient. Additionally, the use of bell peppers differentiates the New Orleans style from the long green poblano peppers used in the Mexican-inspired *chile rellenos* of neighboring Texas.

Serves 6

Holy Trinity + Garlic
- **1 cup diced onions**
- **1 cup diced celery**
- **1 cup diced bell pepper**
- **2–4 tablespoons minced garlic (depending on your taste)**

6 bell peppers seeded and with tops cut off
¼ cup cooking oil (or butter)
4 cups cooked long-grain rice
3 cups medium shrimp peeled and deveined
2 cups tomato sauce (optional)
2 cups chicken stock
2 tablespoons chopped fresh thyme
⅛ to ¼ cup fresh (cayenne or bird's eye) peppers (depending on taste)
2 tablespoons salt
1 cup chopped parsley

1. Parboil topped and seeded bell peppers in water for 5 minutes to soften. Set aside and cool.

2. Sauté onions, celery, bell pepper, and garlic in the cooking oil (or butter) until onions are clear and vegetables are soft.

3. Add the chicken stock (and optional tomato sauce), salt and red pepper, and simmer on low for 5–10 minutes to reach a sauce consistency.

4. Stir in the rice gently to avoid clumping, and simmer with the shrimp for 5 minutes. Stuff the seeded peppers fully, filling to a rounded top.

5. Place in a casserole dish insuring that the peppers are firmly standing. Preheat oven to 375° and bake for 25 minutes.

6. When done, remove and sprinkle parsley on top.

NOTE: Although New Orleans stuffed peppers are generally served with the tops removed and placed upright, another option is to cut the peppers in half lengthwise and stuff the pepper halves, laying them on their side in the dish.

Sophisticated Creole Town

The Spanish colonial era ended on paper when Napoleon secretly acquired Louisiana for France in the Treaty of San Ildefonso in 1800. The Corsican French leader dreamed of retaking the former island colony of Saint-Domingue (Haiti), and he envisioned the fertile North American colony as a breadbasket to feed the island's population. Spanish king Carlos IV traded the massive Louisiana Territory in exchange for Napoleon giving the Bourbon Duchy of Parma in Italy to the Spanish crown. Although the final treaty was officially signed in 1801, Spain did not relinquish control of Louisiana until 1803, when the French colonial prefect Pierre Clément de Laussat arrived in New Orleans to assume his duties.

Over the forty-year period in which New Orleans served as the capital of Spanish Louisiana, the burgeoning town had matured and expanded into a town of more than eight thousand residents, who were almost evenly divided between whites and persons of color. But given the town's relatively small size compared to its sister city Havana (more than sixty thousand inhabitants at the time), New Orleans could boast a sophisticated arts community of both artisans and artists, as well as a theater for opera by the 1790s.

In 1796, Andrés Gretry's opera *Sylvain* was presented with a French libretto by Jean-François Marmontel. The production premiered at the Theatre de la Rue St. Pierre, ushering in an era in which New Orleans emerged as one of the opera capitals of North America. That decade, free person of color furniture artisan Celestin Glapion, the future brother-in-law of voodoo queen Marie Laveau, became respected for his large armoires featuring symmetrical black-walnut grain doors and perched on graceful cabriolet legs. These pieces displayed a French-inspired Creole furniture design that distinguished New Orleans within Anglo America.

In the visual arts, Mexican-born painter José Francisco Salazar y Mendoza emerged as the premier portrait painter of the city, elevating the small port city's artistic sophistication. Salazar displayed a keen eye for exquisite detail, capturing the distinctive facial characteristics of the leading figures and their families in Spanish New Orleans. The artist emigrated from Mérida, Yucatán, with his family in 1782 and painted a considerable portion of the city's elite at a time when portraits symbolized one's social status.

Scholars believe that Salazar's daughter Francisca may have painted some portraits attributed to her father, making her paintings even more remarkable for being painted by a female artist. Salazar's portrait of the Dr. Joseph Montegut family, in the Louisiana State Museum collection, is perhaps the most impressive in size and detail (fig. 7). The Historic New Orleans Collection also has several fine portraits, including that of Angelica Monsanto, free woman of color Marianne Celeste Dragon, and Clara de la Motte, in which the artist used a glaze to depict the shimmer of her elaborate dress.[50]

Nueva Orleans displayed an impressive architectural elegance for a town of its size. The symmetry of the Plaza de Armas remains a distinctive feature today. The St. Louis Cathedral anchored the plaza between the arcaded two-story Cabildo on its left and the future Capuchin presbytère on the right. In the front of town, newly constructed grand Spanish-style homes with large courtyards distinguished the Gulf–Caribbean port's sturdy brick and stucco forms and decorative wrought-iron balconies, in contrast to the homes on the federalist Anglo-American Atlantic coast. The adjacent new Faubourg Santa Maria signaled the expansion of the growing town and its future extension into surrounding Creole plantations subdivided into residential enclaves.

The three-tiered social hierarchy of free whites, a growing French Catholic *gens de couleur libres* community, and an enslaved African and Afro-Creole urban population distinguished New Orleans as a Caribbean town as well. The Catholic majority also connected the town to the neighboring

FIG. 7. Mexican artist José Salazar's finely detailed portrait of the Creole Montegut family presents the small port town's visual arts and musical sophistication at the end of the Spanish colonial period. *The Family of Dr. Joseph Montegut,* by José Francisco Xavier Salazar y Mendoza, 1790s, Louisiana State Museum, 04944-04945.

French and Spanish colonies to the south and differentiated New Orleans from the Protestant Atlantic coast cities of the newly established United States. By the time of the Louisiana Purchase in 1803, the Latin Creole port was an important crossroads where the Mississippi River intersected with the Atlantic world and one in which the United States would come to place its enduring stamp of Anglo culture, the English language, Protestantism, capitalism, and republican democracy.

4

American Boomtown

A Creole City in the United States, 1803–1860

In 1803, artist J. L. Boqueta de Woiseri painted a colorful watercolor tableau of the waterfront of the town recently acquired by the United States (fig. 8). From the vantage point of the Marigny plantation's West Indies-style second-floor gallery, Woiseri portrayed the riverfront filled with ocean-going vessels, several of which fly the U.S. colors. In the old colonial Vieux Carré, one can identify the two Spanish bell towers of St. Louis Cathedral, the old Ursuline Convent, and the palisaded Fort St. Charles over which flies the fifteen-star U.S. flag, all in front of a looming cypress swamp.

The artist also included residents going about their business in the town. On the river road headed downriver, one sees several men, including one on horseback and another carrying a long rifle walking with his hunting dog. Adjacent to the man with the rifle and dog are two women of color walking together, one of whom totes goods on her head in the tradition of African women. In the front pasture of Bernard de Marigny's property, a Black man herds two cattle on foot, holding a stick in the fashion of African livestock herders.

Across the top of the painting is a banner proclaiming "Under My Wings Every Thing Prospers." The artist clearly portrays the newly American New Orleans as a port city that would flourish under a non-mercantilist, non-colonial, capitalist economic system. His depiction of the small size of the town would soon be outdated, because within twenty years the city's population quadrupled to more than forty thousand inhabitants and new neighborhoods developed along the river and into the back-of-town swamps. But the diverse population and the significant presence of African or Afro-Creole persons would continue, helping define New Orleans's notoriety

FIG. 8. This detailed depiction of the Vieux Carré in 1803 conveys the cultural diversity of the burgeoning town, and the banner title correctly predicts the explosive growth of the city in the early American period. Boqueta de Woiseri, *A View of New Orleans Taken from the Plantation of Marigny, November 1803,* University of Wisconsin, Milwaukee Libraries, agdm 1582.

within the United States and the city's strong cultural ties to the Creole Atlantic world.

Woiseri's artistic prediction of future prosperity captures well the history of New Orleans in this early American period from the Louisiana Purchase to the Civil War. During this time, New Orleans emerged as a boomtown with one of the fastest-growing economies and populations in the United States. By 1840, with a population of 83,977, New Orleans was the third-biggest city in the nation after New York and Baltimore. In the years leading up to the Civil War, the Creole American municipality grew into one of the busiest ports and immigrant destinations internationally behind London and New York.

The port city stood securely as the national commercial center for cotton and sugar exports and the trade of enslaved persons, and was also the largest city and the financial capital of the American South. During the early 1860s, the American Civil War and emancipation of enslaved persons altered immeasurably the city's social sphere, politics, and economics. By 1877 when racially conservative Democrats regained political dominance, New Orleans stood on the verge of a new era of industrial development and immigration.

Cultural Collisions

On December 20, 1803, the United States gained official control of the Louisiana Territory. That day French colonial prefect Laussat handed over the symbolic keys of New Orleans tied in tricolor ribbons to newly appointed governor William C. C. Claiborne and General James Wilkinson. The ceremony took place in the grand Sala Capitular in the Cabildo and then moved to the large gallery overlooking the Place d'Armes, where the men witnessed the lowering of the tricolor French Republic flag and the raising of the American Stars and Stripes.

The United States acquired Louisiana through a series of complicated diplomatic events occurring in the very first years of the nineteenth century. Napoleon Bonaparte, the French First Consul, had reacquired Louisiana from Spain through the secret Treaty of San Ildefonso in 1800, with the intention of using the vast territory to supply food for his planned reconquest of Saint-Domingue from Haitian rebels. Around the same time, the new U.S. president Thomas Jefferson faced a critical political crisis when Spanish administrators in Nueva Orleans closed the port to western American farmers from the Ohio Valley, who had depended on the Mississippi River entrepôt to export their grain and whiskey.

The angry Americans threatened revolt, forcing the president to take action. Jefferson sent emissaries James Monroe and Robert Livingston to Paris to negotiate for the purchase of the Isle of Orleans from France. By April 1803 when the Americans arrived in France, Napoleon had abandoned his goal of retaking Haiti and no longer needed Louisiana. He therefore offered to sell the entire 530-million-acre territory to the United States for $15 million. With no time to consult Jefferson, Livingston and Monroe agreed to the deal and signed an agreement with France. The news of the treaty arrived on July 4, and it was ratified by the U.S. Congress in October. By December, American authorities had arrived in New Orleans to enact the official transfer at the Cabildo.

Although the handover of Louisiana from France to the United States went smoothly that day, formal balls commemorating the changing of the guard peeled back cultural tensions between the Americans and the French that lurked under the surface. At two balls attended by officials from both nations, altercations erupted between the French and Americans over the dance repertoire. To maintain the peace, French and English quadrilles were supposed to be played, one after the other. But when the repertoire strayed from the intended order, according to Laussat, "bedlam ensued," and American interpreter Daniel Clark spread a rumor that "until two or three Frenchmen have been hanged, we will not rule over this country." Known as the "Battle of the Dance Floor," this cultural disagreement was a harbinger of the Franco-Anglo culture clash in American New Orleans that would persist throughout the nineteenth century.[1]

The French and English had maintained contempt and sometimes open animosity toward one another for more than eight hundred years. This difficult relationship manifested in New Orleans between the native Creoles and the Anglo-Americans in culture, religion, language, economics, and politics.[2] Although France played an integral role in the successful American Revolution against Britain in the late 1700s, in New Orleans the French still found the Americans to be aggressive in their behavior.

Prefect Laussat, after getting to know the Americans moving in after the Louisiana Purchase, considered them to be annoyingly confident about the expansion of the nation. He admitted, "The acquisition of Louisiana has increased their ambition"; the Americans wagered that the United States would have "an open port on the Pacific Ocean within five years." And among those "swarming in from the northern states" they turned over in their minds "a little plan of speculation."[3]

On the American side, the newly appointed Orleans territorial governor William C. C. Claiborne professed equal disdain toward Louisiana Creoles, whom he saw as corrupt and ignorant. And despite Creole republican support for the French Revolution during the Spanish era, Claiborne considered the locals incapable of understanding the American republican democratic system. As he confided to President Thomas Jefferson in 1804, "The fact is, that the people of Louisiana, are not prepared for a Representative Government, and the experiment would be hazardous." However, Claiborne did credit the Creoles of New Orleans with "being tolerably well informed."[4] When the Orleans Territorial Assembly drafted voting rights in 1804, the law initially stipulated that, to be eligible to vote, one must have three years of U.S. citizenship and own two hundred acres of land, thereby excluding any Creole resident of Louisiana. To assuage the furious wealthy Creoles, the assembly then revised the criteria to three months of U.S. citizenship and holdings of fifty acres.[5]

New Orleans French and Creole elites led by wealthy planters Jean Noël Destrehan, Pierre Sauvé, Pierre Derbigny, and others protested the U.S. territorial form of government as not representing the public's interests. In their formal statement to Congress in 1805, the group objected to "the oppressive and degrading form of territorial government." They claimed that Claiborne deprived the Creoles of their "right of election" and that the governor had represented them as "too ignorant to exercise it with wisdom, and too turbulent to enjoy it with safety." Emphasizing the communication gap, the group complained of the "American officials who neither associate with us nor speak our language."[6]

Although the Virginia-born Claiborne only spoke English when he arrived in Louisiana, he eventually adapted to Creole ways in New Orleans. Following the path of many Spanish governors and officials, he ingratiated himself with local elites by marrying a Louisianan, Marie Clarisse Duralde of the Attakapas region. After she died from yellow fever in 1809, the governor married sixteen-year-old Susana "Suzette" Bosque, daughter of French Creole Feliciana Fanguy (Felicité Fangui) and the former colonial treasurer, Don Bartólome Bosque, one of the Spanish officials who remained in New Orleans after the Louisiana Purchase. Over the years, Claiborne appears to have gained political savvy and Creole support, so that once Louisiana achieved statehood in 1812, he won the first gubernatorial election against Creole planter Jacques Villeré.

President Thomas Jefferson also found himself having to ingratiate himself to Creole society during the territorial period. In the lawsuit of *Gravier v. the City of New Orleans,* Jefferson was asked to weigh in on the legal use of the batture, the section of land along the riverfront that became exposed when river levels lowered in the summer and autumn months. The case involved the Creole presumption of public use over the exposed riverfront. Former New York mayor and recent American arrival Edward Livingston was sold a deed to the land on the exposed batture in front of Faubourg Ste. Marie by Jean Gravier (Bertrand's brother). Livingston sought to use the land as his private property, thereby violating Creole norms. The batture controversy represented a conflict between French Creole civil law (Code

Civil) and Anglo-American common law in the new territory. The very complicated case eventually went to the federal courts in 1808, at which point President Jefferson sided with the Creoles in enforcing the civil law, a calculated decision that likely reflected his desire to gain the support of Louisiana's native residents.[7]

Even though the case dragged on to 1813, the conflict led to the resolution of how to balance the two legal systems. By 1808, the Territorial Assembly had codified the bilingual Code Civil based largely on the French Code Civil but with some English common law components. This unique blending distinguishes Louisiana's legal system within the United States today. Although the Louisiana legal system is sometimes referred to as the "Napoleonic Code," the term is a misnomer: the Code Civil had its roots in the laws of the Roman Empire and was in force in France before Napoleon. Although many differences exist between the French Code Civil and Anglo-American common law, the principal ones stem from the Code Civil's reliance on judges to interpret established codes. In contrast, common law emphasizes the importance of juries in determining legal outcomes.[8]

Jefferson, who was the architect of the U.S. Constitution's First Amendment enshrining the freedom of worship, also found himself having to reassure anxious Catholics in Louisiana. In response to a letter from Sister Therese de St. Xavier of the Ursuline order questioning their status under the new republic, Jefferson assured her that their property would be held "sacred and inviolate" based on the Constitution. Furthermore, Jefferson complimented the Ursuline nuns, writing that despite "whatever diversity of shade may appear in the religious opinions of our fellow citizens," the sisters' charitable healthcare and educational contributions "cannot fail to ensure it the patronage of government."[9]

The religious schism that developed at St. Louis Cathedral in 1805 also illustrated the antipathy that Creoles held toward Americans. When the territory was acquired by the United States, the Catholic Church placed the archdiocese of Louisiana under the authority of Bishop John Carroll and Vicar Patrick Walsh in Baltimore. As part of this tumultuous transition, Walsh dismissed Pere Antoine, who in response appealed to his parishioners to retain him as pastor. The majority of parish members voted to retain him at St. Louis Cathedral, where the Capuchin pastor remained until his death in 1829. Not until 1814 did Pere Antoine reconcile with the church and newly appointed apostolic administrator Louis G. V. DuBourg, ending the schism. Most importantly, the vote of the Creole parishioners to reject the American vicar Walsh and retain the Spaniard pastor represented an ironic American-style exercise of democracy in the top-down Catholic Church.[10]

At the same time as Anglo-Americans were increasing their numbers and influence in Creole New Orleans, in 1809 a sudden influx of ten thousand Saint-Domingue refugees infused a strong dose of Caribbean Catholic culture into the American Creole city. A large group of refugees had fled Saint-Domingue during the Haitian Rebellion in the early 1790s and had settled in the eastern Oriente Province of Spanish Cuba, where they were evicted in 1809 as part of the political fallout between Spain and France over the Napoleonic Wars. Most of these Saint-Domingue exiles then sought refuge in New Orleans, where their presence had a considerable political, economic, and cultural impact.[11]

This group of immigrants was almost evenly divided into thirds: free whites, the enslaved, and free persons of color. Generally French Creoles welcomed the free whites and organized aid and support to house and feed the new arrivals. In contrast, Americans such as James Brown and the Irishman Daniel Clark insinuated a connection between the Saint-Domingue Creoles and Napoleon, the Haitian Revolution, and recent activities of privateers such as Jean Lafitte. Despite the U.S. Slave Trade Act of 1807, which prohibited the importation of slaves, the free white immigrants, many of whom owned slaves, received special permission to bring their human property into the territory. Yet, the conservative territorial government only reluctantly allowed entry of the three thousand people of color, most of whom were women, because the government considered free men of color the gravest threat to society and the institution of slavery in Louisiana.

Most of the newcomers settled in New Orleans, where they made their significant mark on the city. French Creole Gilbert Joseph Pilié, who had immigrated in 1805, eventually became a well-known engineer, city surveyor, and architect. He is credited with designing the main house at the famed Oak Alley (Roman) Plantation near Vacherie. And even though Claiborne resisted the immigration of free men of color, some, like Captain Joseph Savary, arrived as veterans of the French resistance in the Haitian Revolution and then successfully defended New Orleans in the Battle of New Orleans.[12]

In addition, many free men of color became respected in the artisan building trades as carpenters, masons, and plasterers, thereby contributing to the distinct architectural heritage of the city. Although folklorist John Michael Vlach argues that the iconic shotgun house of New Orleans is of African and Saint-Domingue origins, the cultural anthropologist Jay Edwards points out correctly that shotgun houses in New Orleans were built after the American Civil War, well after the arrival of the first Saint-Domingue refugees. Instead, the Creole cottage of New Orleans was the most common architectural style of modest homes in the first half of the 1800s, and clearly had its origins in Saint-Domingue.[13]

Likely, these Creole of color tradesmen simply imported the Creole cottage style from the island. This design is most common in the New Orleans neighborhoods developed between 1805 and 1860, such as the Tremé, the Marigny, the Bywater, the Lower Garden District, and the streets of Uptown and Carrollton close to the river. The style is identified by its double-pitched roof slanting parallel with the street and its four openings on the front—usually two entrances on either side and two central windows—with a small stoop leading to the doors.

The traditional Creole cottage lacks hallways in the interior. The structure is two rooms wide and two rooms deep, and it is built around one or two central chimneys that provide heat to all the rooms. The interior chimney is considered typical of French-inspired design, in contrast to the exterior Anglo-American chimneys constructed on the exterior ends of a building. Later American variations of the cottage integrated a central hallway and entrance, incorporating the Greek Revival symmetry common to the early American period from the 1820s to the 1840s.

Numerous fine examples of these cottages can be found in the Vieux Carré and adjacent neighborhoods. Across the street from Madame John's Legacy, at 613–615 Dumaine, are two Creole cottages built in the 1820s that exemplify the distinct style in federal brick form. In Tremé, many classic Creole cottages are centered on one chimney and feature the addition of dormer windows on the second level. Some fine examples can be found in the downriver side of the 900 block of Gov. Nicholls (the original Bayou Road), on the uptown corner of Barracks and Henriette Delille, and the Terrance Cousin twin brick cottages (ca. 1828) where Barracks ends at Marais St.[14]

Louisiana (the Orleans Territory) became a state in 1812 after meeting the minimum population requirement of 60,000 inhabitants for statehood. Reflecting the Americans' presumption of Creole ignorance, the new bilingual state assembly meeting at the Government House in New Orleans enacted a constitution that required property ownership as a qualification for voting, thereby ensuring that only the wealthiest exercised the franchise. Hence, many of the elite Creole planters who owned plantations but lived at their luxurious homes in New Orleans controlled the political machinery of the city. New Orleans, as the original colonial and territorial capital, would remain the center of state government until 1852 when the capital moved to the more centrally located upriver town of Baton Rouge.

Can Frenchmen and Americans Be Slaves?

The year of statehood also marked the beginning of a war between the United States and Great Britain that had a profound impact on New Orleans. The War of 1812, sometimes referred to as the Second American War of Independence, would shift the theater of battle from the Atlantic coast to the lower Mississippi River as Britain attempted to carry out a plan to seize New Orleans and thereby gain control of the Mississippi River Valley and the interior of the United States. During December 1814, British troops under the command of Major General Sir Edward Pakenham moored in the shallow brackish lakes east of New Orleans and disembarked to prepare for a land-based assault of the city. The forces camped for several miserable weeks in the wet and cold winter weather on the plains of Chalmette downriver from the city in preparation for what they thought would be an easy victory.

The Battle of New Orleans pitted American forces under Major General Andrew Jackson against the well-seasoned British Imperial forces under Pakenham, which included the respected Scottish Sutherland Highlanders, the West India Regiment of Free Men of Color, and warriors from the Creek nation. The British troops were hemmed in by the river on the left and the cypress swamp on the right; the soldiers had only a narrow sliver of the natural Mississippi River ridge on which to march toward the city. Even though the Americans were outnumbered, Jackson had prepared several lines of defense along the river ridge and used enslaved workers to construct a mud berm along the old Rodrigue Canal that protected the defending American forces.

On January 8, 1815, Pakenham finally ordered the assault on the city. As the British forces marched upriver in formation, the troops were completely exposed on the open field, where they were quickly decimated by American artillery and rifle shot. Despite the experience and discipline of the British troops, their attack plan disintegrated into chaos. In large part because of the protective berm, the Americans suffered only seventy-one casualties, whereas the unprotected British lost more than two thousand men, including Pakenham.

The Battle of New Orleans served as a unifying event for the residents of New Orleans and surrounding areas. When Jackson arrived in New Orleans with the Seventh Regiment of the U.S. Army, he relied on every available man to fight in the coming battle and called on local women to provide vital support in gathering supplies and then taking care of the wounded—despite some Americans' doubts that local Creoles would defend the city against the British. Jackson understood the importance of overcoming the American-Creole divide in the cause. He therefore asked them, "Can Frenchmen and Americans be slaves to the British?"

The American forces under Jackson reflected the diversity of New Orleans and the region. His soldiers included American regulars, white Creoles, free men of color, Choctaw warriors who were historic enemies of the pro-British Creek nation, the Isleños of St. Bernard Parish, American "dirty shirt" volunteers from upriver, and Baratarian privateers (pirates) under Jean Lafitte.

Integrating these diverse groups into a fighting force presented a challenge to the Americans. Jackson abhorred the idea of serving with the Baratarians, whom he referred to as "hellish *banditti*." At that time and until the American Civil War in 1862, African Americans could serve only as musicians in the army. Governor Claiborne made an exception to allow Black Creole soldiers to serve in combat, given the emergency. In New Orleans, conservative whites feared that free men of color, if armed, might foment a slave uprising. This unfounded concern existed despite the fact many Creoles of color were either veterans of the French Army who fought the rebels in Haiti or had served faithfully in the Spanish colonial militia before the Louisiana Purchase in 1803.[15]

Despite Jackson's animosity toward them, the Baratarians provided the U.S. forces with essential artillery power, given their expertise in using weapons in a maritime context. Their leader Jean Lafitte, who did not actually exercise command at the battle, continues to be a person of legend and mystery. Likely of French origins—Lafitte is a family name in the Bordeaux region—he claimed to be a privateer, that is, someone with a government commission to capture enemy ships. Lafitte possessed a letter of marque from the newly independent Republic of Cartagena allowing his men to seize the ships of Cartagena's enemies in the Gulf of Mexico and the Caribbean.

After confiscating those ships' contents, Lafitte used Grand Isle and Barataria Bay south of New Orleans as a base for selling the goods on the black market. But he ran afoul of U.S. authorities for violating customs laws in the years leading up to the war. In recruiting the Baratarians to provide much-needed artillery in the city's defense, the Americans made a deal with Lafitte to issue him a pardon for his support, on the condition that he leave the state after the fighting ended.

Indeed, Lafitte moved west to Lago Carlos (Lake Charles) and then to Texas, where he established a new headquarters on Galveston Island, after the end of the War of 1812. But his lieutenant, Frenchman Dominique You, continued to live and work in New Orleans until his death in 1830 and is buried in St. Louis Cemetery #2. Another Baratarian, Renato Beluche, grew up at "Casa Beluche" (present-day Madame John's Legacy). After the Battle of New Orleans, Beluche served as the commander of Simón Bolívar's navy in the War of Independence for Venezuela, where the Baratarian is buried. Historian Jane Lucas de Grummond and local Venezuelan historian Thais Solano raise this question: Is Beluche a pirate or a patriot or both?[16]

The dedicated service in the Battle of New Orleans of the white and Black Creoles, Isleños, and Baratarians proved their worth and patriotism to the dubious Americans. Their success provided a moment of celebratory unity and led to a U.S. victory in the War of 1812. Although the Treaty of Ghent between Britain and United States had been signed in December 1814 before the Battle of New Orleans was waged, the American victory ensured that Britain would not have an opportunity to renegotiate its terms in their favor.

Significantly, the battlefield heroics of Andrew Jackson propelled him to national fame, which he then leveraged in his successful runs for president in 1828 and 1832. Although his current reputation is largely colored by the Indian Removal Act of 1832 and the subsequent tragic Trail of Tears, Jackson, in fact, gave a moving funeral eulogy in 1824 for the Choctaw chief Pushmataha, who had earned Jackson's friendship and respect in mobilizing his people to fight for the United States in the Battle of New Orleans.[17]

Uptown, Downtown, and Neutral Ground

Despite the Creole support for the U.S. cause in 1815, the American–Creole rivalry continued to be felt in the culture, geography, economics, and politics of New Orleans. Geographically, the city became divided between the upriver American Sector and the downriver Creole districts. Canal Street became the geographic dividing line between Uptown (upriver from Canal Street) and Downtown (downriver from Canal Street).

A colloquial local term for the median found in wide streets was born around this time: only in New Orleans is a median called a "neutral ground." The reference was first applied to the immense median—actually, a large, grassy area—on Canal Street. In the early American period, the large expanse of grass ran down the center of the 170-foot-wide street, providing a neutral space where Creoles and Americans could, theoretically and metaphorically, exist without conflict in the divided city. A "neutral ground" is now used to designate any median in the city's multiple avenues and takes on special significance during Carnival season. Then, locals use it to designate the side of the street on which they watch parades: the sidewalk or the neutral ground.[18]

Competition between the two sectors was even reflected in entertainment, amenities, and tourism. As the largest and most important financial center in the American South, New Orleans catered to the needs of wealthy businessmen and travelers at two of the most luxurious hotels in the United States. In 1837, the opulent neoclassic Hotel St. Charles debuted in the American Sector to provide fine accommodations for wealthy English-speaking travelers; the site also served as an exchange for the trade of enslaved persons.

The next year, southern French immigrant Pierre Soulé, through his Improvement Company and Bank, constructed the grand St. Louis Hotel and Exchange, which catered to well-to-do Creole businessmen and European tourists in the Vieux Carré. Designed by esteemed French architect Jacques Nicolas Bussière de Pouilly, the landmark building echoed the design of the elegant edifices lining the rue de Rivoli in Paris. The structure served not only as a hotel but also as a bank and an exchange for the slave trade. The domed top floor replaced the smaller New Exchange Coffee House (or La Bourse de Hewlett) as a center of Creole business transactions at the corner of Chartres and St. Louis Streets.[19]

William Henry Brooke's historic illustration from 1842 depicts an estate sale of an enslaved family with two children standing and sitting on the auction block in the St. Louis's domed rotunda.[20] Today, the letters "change" from the original "Exchange" sign in the 500 block of Chartres Street are preserved on the original arches and incorporated into the current hotel that replaced the St. Louis in the 1960s. The letters are one of the few remaining physical remnants of the wretched trade in the city.

Ironically, the city's most important financial institutions opened in the Vieux Carré and not in the American Sector. La Banque de la Louisiane first opened at 417 Royal Street in 1805, a building that later became the home of chess master Paul Morphy and is now the location of Brennan's Restaurant. The Louisiana State Bank conducted business in an elegant Italianate building at 401 Royal designed by the renowned English architect Benjamin Latrobe in 1818. Ten years later, the competing Bank of Louisiana, designed by noted Irish-born architect James Gallier Sr., opened at 334 Royal in a Greek Revival building on the opposite corner.

Although the banking industry gradually migrated to the American Sector in the pre–Civil War period, the federal government placed two important financial institutions in the Creole district, reflecting the prominence that New Orleans held as the economic center of the South. The imposing Greek Revival building of the U.S. Mint at 400 Esplanade Avenue was completed in 1838 on the former site of Fort St. Charles. And in 1845, the federal Treasury Department constructed the U.S. Customs House, where incoming goods were officially declared. The Customs House is a grand Egyptian–Greek Revival building on the upriver edge of the Vieux Carré, close to the riverfront at 423 Canal Street.

Around this time, New Orleans emerged as the opera center of North America, with the location of separate performance venues exhibiting the American–Creole divide as well. The French Quarter hosted several theaters featuring French- and Italian-language performances. As mentioned in the previous chapter, the city's first opera *Sylvain* debuted in the Spanish period at the Théâtre de la Rue Saint Pierre (800 block of St. Peter), which was succeeded in 1808 by the Théâtre de Rue St. Philippe. In 1819 the Théâtre d'Orleans opened at the corner of Orleans and Bourbon. The site existed as the city's grandest French-language theater, regularly attracting troupes for extended residencies in the city. Creoles of color attended the Théâtre de la Renaissance, which hosted the Negro Philharmonic Orchestra, attesting to the sophistication of the Afro-Creole community.

Across Canal Street, British-born promoter James Caldwell opened the first English-language playhouse, the Camp Street Theater, in 1824 and then constructed the very opulent St. Charles Theater to provide entertainment for Americans. Finally, in 1859 the French Opera House, designed by New Orleans architect James Gallier Jr., opened on Bourbon at Toulouse Streets as one of the most luxurious theaters in North America, which free Black and white people, as well as the enslaved, attended at a time when opera was considered popular music.[21]

The vast majority of New Orleans's appointed and elected mayors before the Civil War were French Creole or natives of France. The latter included James Pitot (1804–1805), Nicolas Girod (1812–1815), and Count Louis Philippe de Roffignac, who served from 1820 to 1828. In the mid-1830s, the English-speaking political establishment, chafing at this Francophone dominance, got the city council to issue the Charter of 1836 to separate the American Sector from those neighborhoods below Canal Street. This new geopolitical arrangement gave Anglo-Americans more political control over "le faubourg Américain." The city created three municipalities. The First and Third Districts included the Creole and immigrant neighborhoods from the French Quarter downriver to the Bywater. The Second District included the largely American residential area upriver from Canal to Felicity Street. The districts are clearly marked on B. M. Norman's Plan (Map) of New Orleans from 1849.[22]

This three-municipality system operated similarly to the political administration of arrondissements (neighborhood districts) in Paris. Each municipality had its own council and public services, and the mayor and city council administered all of New Orleans as well. Although this arrangement was intended to reduce political conflict and rivalries, the lack of clarity in powers between the municipalities and the city, as well as the overall inefficiency of the separation, led to its demise in 1852, when the city once again united under a single council and mayor.[23] That same year, the city created the ward system that still exists and is often used to identify one's cultural orientation in New Orleans.[24]

The building of the New Basin Canal provides another example of American–Creole separation and control. In 1838 American businessmen, through the New Orleans Canal and Banking Company, financed and constructed the waterway that enabled them to ship goods from Lake Pontchartrain directly to uptown New Orleans and avoid the Creole districts. The new route completely bypassed the 1790s-era Carondelet Canal, which connected Bayou St. John to the rear of the Vieux Carré adjacent to St. Louis Cemetery #1. The New Basin Canal ran along the routes of present-day West End Boulevard and the Pontchartrain Expressway (Interstate 10), terminating near the current Union Passenger Terminal.

This massive construction process relied on the labor of low-wage Irish immigrants, who are memorialized with the Celtic cross monument in the neutral ground of West End Boulevard. Older historical accounts allege that more than ten thousand workers died from cholera and yellow fever. But Irish sympathizers exaggerated the number of deaths in an era when Americans looked down on the impoverished Catholic newcomers. More likely, around five hundred Irish workers died. Still, contractors found it easier and cheaper to work an Irishman to death, rather than sacrificing the more expensive enslaved labor.[25]

This new "American" canal was an expression of New Orleans's economic importance nationally and the arrival of the transportation revolution of the 1830s and 1840s. During these decades canals were dug and railroads constructed across the country to enable the more efficient shipping of commodities. As early as 1831, the Pontchartrain Railroad realized the long-held dream of shipping goods from Lake Pontchartrain to the river on the five-mile route of current-day Elysian Fields Avenue. The line, later known as "Smokey Mary," was one of the first public railroads in the nation. During the ragtime and jazz era of the 1910s and 1920s, it took passengers out to Milneburg on the lakefront to cool off and socialize during the hot months. And in 1845, the Destrehan Canal (present-day Harvey Canal) on the West Bank was completed using enslaved workers: it connected the Mississippi River to Bayou Barataria and the sugar plantations to the west.

The administrative reuniting of the city in 1852 occurred in the decade leading up to the American Civil War, when conservative Creoles and white Americans both appeared to agree on the economic importance of maintaining the institution of slavery. By the time Louisiana seceded from the Union in 1861, conservative Creoles fully supported the Confederacy's cause of maintaining states' rights in the face of federal talk of abolishing slavery. The 1860s was also the last decade in which the state legislature maintained a bilingual policy. The dominance of the English language by the 1870s reflected the gradual decline of Creole political and cultural differences with the Americans.

Unfree and Free

"All the time the trade was going on, Eliza was crying aloud and wringing her hands. She besought the man not to buy [her son Randall], unless he also bought herself and Emily." This scene is how Solomon Northup, who had been kidnapped into slavery as a free man in New York, described a New Orleans slave market in the 1840s. When a slave buyer separated a young boy from his mother and sister because he claimed he did not have enough money to buy all three, Eliza burst into a "paroxysm of grief, weeping plaintively." She promised "how very faithful and obedient she would be; how hard she would labor day and night, to the last moment of her life, if he would only buy them all together." Still the man only purchased Randall: "Eliza ran to him; embraced him passionately; kissed him again and again; told him to remember her—all the while her tears were falling in the boy's face like rain."[26]

Northup's description of this sale at Theophilus Freeman's slave market reveals the brutality of the slave trade, which was centered in New Orleans after the Louisiana Purchase. The separation of families, along with the physical and emotional ruthlessness of the slave market in New Orleans, unveils a part of the city's history that is difficult for modern-day tourists and residents to accept and understand.

Recently, the city has begun to acknowledge this uncomfortable history through commemorative markers, such as the one at the corner of Chartres and Esplanade Avenue where Freeman's slave market stood. Increasingly, historic home museums in the Vieux Carré such as the 1850 House in the Pontalba Apartments, the Beauregard-Keyes House, and the Hermann-Grima and Gallier Houses interpret the history of urban slavery in their tours and programs.

In 1806, the Assembly of the newly established Orleans Territory issued a revised American Black Code (Code Noir) that removed many of the rights provided under the Spanish Code O'Reilly. The enslaved were still given Sunday as a day off, which was crucial to the continuation of Congo Square in New Orleans. The law also forbade the separation of young children from their families, but this regulation was obviously not enforced, as Northup observed in New Orleans. Most significantly, the process of emancipation became much more restricted. Slave owners could not free anyone under thirty years old, a bond was required, and any newly emancipated person had to leave the Orleans Territory.[27]

New Orleans became the largest slave trade center in the United States due to the convergence of technological, economic, and political factors. By reducing the time and effort to separate cotton boll fibers from the seeds, Eli Whitney's invention of the cotton gin enabled greater profits for the cotton trade. At the same time, the development of steam-powered cotton mills in Great Britain provided a very profitable market, and New Orleans shipped the bulk of America's raw cotton in bales to Manchester and other mill towns in Lancashire, England, and western Scotland.

The timing of the Louisiana Purchase in 1803 coincided with the immense profitability of cotton, which led to the massive development and expansion of plantations in the lower Mississippi Valley. As the economic capital and largest city in the American South, New Orleans became the center of cotton and sugar exports, as well as the trading of enslaved individuals. Indigo and tobacco had been the most important export commodities in the Spanish colonial era, but cotton and sugar quickly emerged as the dominant export crops in the American period.

As did cotton, sugar became profitable due to agro-technological developments. Up until the 1790s, Louisiana planters were unable to grow and refine sugar successfully, despite the prominent model of France's most lucrative colony, Saint-Domingue. Étienne de Boré, the Illinois-born Creole whose plantation is now the site of Audubon Park, pioneered the successful growing and refining of sugarcane in the late eighteenth century. De Boré imported new improved varieties from Tahiti and partnered with Antoine Morin, a refiner. By 1803, the Creole planter's success led to a huge expansion of sugarcane production, and the entire river region below Baton Rouge emerged as the wealthy "Sugar Coast." And as with cotton, the development of the labor-intensive sugar industry led to an expanded market for enslaved labor.[28]

The passage of the Slave Trade Act of 1807 in the U.S. Congress provided the final element in New Orleans's emergence as a national slave trade center. As mentioned, the bill (known officially as the Act for the Abolition of the Slave Trade) outlawed U.S. participation in the international slave trade and prohibited the importation of enslaved people from outside the United States after 1808.

The new law, however, did not eliminate slavery but instead led to the expansion of a very profitable domestic slave trade, through which enslaved workers could be traded, bought, and sold within the United States. So when the Louisiana Purchase and the subsequent agro-technological developments occurred around the same time as the act's passage, New Orleans became the hub of slave sales for the expanding export economy in the region. Despite the law, smuggling and illegal slave trading continued until the Civil War.[29]

In the fifty-seven years between the Louisiana Purchase and the Civil War, the enslaved population of Louisiana grew to more than 300,000 persons. Although some of this population growth can be attributed to natural reproduction, most of the surge occurred through the domestic slave trade. By this time, the center of the American plantation economy in the Virginia Tidewater region had become less productive, which led to a huge shift of enslaved workers from the Upper South to the booming lower Mississippi Valley.

Enslaved people were transported overland through walking caravans and also by boats along the coasts, as recounted by Northup. The growth of the English-speaking Protestant African American population added more diversity to the Black population of New Orleans, and also generally mirrored the cultural and linguistic divide between American and Creole cultures in the city.

In New Orleans, the number of enslaved people increased from 2,773 in 1803 to its peak of 18,208 persons in 1840, making it the largest urban slave population in the nation. Although slavery in the antebellum American South is often typified by laboring on a cotton plantation, enslaved workers in the urban environment of New Orleans worked a variety of occupations. Women often served as domestics: they cooked, cleaned house, did laundry, shopped at the market, and cared for children. Men often worked as stevedores, sailors, common laborers, artisans, and domestics—serving as valets and liverymen, cooks, and caregivers, as exemplified by Harriet Beecher Stowe's elderly and kind fictional character Uncle Tom, who lived in New Orleans before being sold to work and die on a cotton plantation in central Louisiana.

Enslaved men also worked in skilled trades, such as blacksmithing, carpentry, plaster, and masonry, and as dockworkers, warehousemen, or general laborers—for which they were sometimes rented out by their owners to earn extra money.[30] In this regard, Felix Achille Beaupoil de Saint-Aulaire's watercolor of a street scene in Faubourg Ste. Marie from 1821 shows two white men supervising three Black men digging a ditch, along with a Black woman wearing a slave collar featuring three spikes with small bells (fig. 9). Such devices were usually required for enslaved workers who attempted self-emancipation but also reflected the dehumanizing treatment of enslaved people like livestock.

In 1811 the New Orleans area experienced the largest attempted slave rebellion in U.S. history. The Deslondes Revolt occurred upriver from the city when Charles Deslondes, an enslaved overseer for the Andry Plantation, fomented a plan to march on New Orleans with an armed militia and seize the city arsenal to implement a Haiti-sized rebellion. The revolt erupted on January 8 outside present-day LaPlace, and the rebel force of about two hundred persons reached as far as present-day Kenner, just upriver from New Orleans, on January 10. There a white militia from New Orleans drove the rebels to retreat, and a militia from the German Coast upriver clashed with the band near present-day Norco. In the end, quick tribunals were conducted, including one at the Jean Noël Destréhan Plantation, where the judges sentenced the rebels to death.

In a show of barbarian brutality, the planter class decapitated those convicted, placing their severed heads on spikes at the Place d'Armes and along the River Road. This punishment was intended to serve as a dire warning

FIG. 9. This painting of a street scene in the Faubourg Ste. Marie illustrates the public existence of slavery as two white men in the American Sector supervise a group of enslaved persons, including a woman wearing a metal slave collar with bells. Felix Achille Beaupoil de Saint-Aulaire, *Vue d'une Rue du Faubourg Ste. Marie,* 1821, Historic New Orleans Collection, 1937.2.3.

to any person considering such rebellious conduct. The Deslondes Revolt realized the greatest fears of the slaveholding class, confirming to many conservative whites the influence of the successful rebellion in Haiti.

Alongside their fears of a slave rebellion, white elites resented the existence of the large class of free persons of color, whom they saw as setting a poor example of racial caste deference. The slave owners also assumed that free Blacks would contribute to future rebellions, simply based on their racial identity. For this reason, Governor Claiborne reluctantly armed those free men of color fighting in the Battle of New Orleans, which occurred only four years after the Deslondes Rebellion.[31]

But in fact, most free persons of color simply sought social stability and economic advancement. The free person of color population peaked at around 10,000 persons, comprising about one-tenth of the city's population of 102,193, in 1840.[32] As the largest community of free Black people in the American South, their existence reinforced New Orleans's status as a unique community within the United States.

Yet, the American planter class enacted laws that attempted to restrict their lives as free people. Although they had many of the same legal rights as free whites, Creoles of color were not allowed to serve on juries, were required to carry identification papers, and had to show whites deference and respect. During the last two decades before the American Civil War, the number of Creoles of color in New Orleans decreased because many left the state seeking a life of freedom outside the restrictive Louisiana racial caste system. This exodus reflected the harsh racial tensions that existed in the state before the Civil War. Many families moved to France, Mexico, Cuba, Haiti, Canada, and the northern states.[33]

For example, members of the Tio family, who were descendants of Spanish immigrants and the wealthy Creole-Irish Macarty family, relocated to northern Mexico in the 1850s. There they founded the community of Eureka, where their descendants still live. Some members of the family finally returned in the 1870s, with descendants Lorenzo and Louis Tio becoming instrumental in the development of New Orleans ragtime and jazz during the 1910s and 1920s.[34]

Composer Edmond Dédé represented the prolific community of musically educated Creoles of color, which contributed to making New Orleans an exceptional city for music within the United States. Born in 1827, Dédé emerged as a violin prodigy while studying with the respected conductor Ludovico Gabici, director of the St. Charles Theater Orchestra. Dédé left New Orleans to work in Mexico in the late 1840s and spent the remainder of his life in Bordeaux, France, where he lived as a respected conductor and married a Frenchwoman, Sophie Leflet. Dédé made one trip back to New Orleans in 1893, when he attended concerts in his honor, hosted by the members of the Comité des Citoyens, an organization formed to advocate for Afro-Creole civil rights.[35]

Norbert Rillieux is perhaps the best known of the Creole of color expats from this period. He was born the son of a wealthy French merchant, Vincent Rillieux (341 Royal), and Constance Vivant, a free woman of color in 1806. Rillieux was also the cousin of French painter Edgar Degas. The young Creole studied at the Ecole Centrale in Paris in the 1820s and returned to Louisiana as a respected engineer. In the 1830s he helped revolutionize the sugar industry by inventing a more efficient patented refining method. But the free man of color faced degrading racism in New Orleans, and the state legislature refused to adopt his innovative drainage plan for New Orleans because of his racial identity. In the 1850s, Rillieux relocated permanently to Paris, where he worked at the Bibliothèque Nationale and lived with his wife Emily Cuckow until his death in 1894. Rillieux is buried in the famous Père Lachaise cemetery in Paris.

Although New Orleans witnessed the departure of several thousand free persons of color in these twenty years, the majority chose to stay despite or perhaps because of the hardships and racial tensions. Several prominent persons stand out for their commitment to fight restrictive racial policies and for their efforts to improve conditions for their fellow Afro-Creoles.

The Venerable Sister Henriette Delille grew up in a privileged family of French, Spanish, and Afro-Creole origins but dedicated her life to caring for the underserved Black residents in New Orleans, both enslaved and free. A devout Catholic and healer, Delille founded a Catholic order in 1836 to provide aid to the enslaved and elderly, which received official recognition from the Holy See in 1842. Named the Sisters of the Holy Family, the order in the 1850s established a school for girls of color (both free and enslaved) at a time when Louisiana law prohibited the formal education of enslaved persons. In 1989, efforts began to nominate Delille for canonization. Today she is recognized by the dedication of a chapel in her honor at St. Louis Cathedral, and St. Augustine Church in the Tremé honors her with a prayer for racial healing and tolerance.[36]

Military veteran Jordan Noble began his life as a slave in Georgia but earned praise for his service as a brave young drummer conveying battle commands at the Battle of New Orleans. At a time when the U.S. military allowed African Americans to serve only in noncombat roles, Noble continued in this musical military capacity throughout his life, eventually earning his freedom in the 1830s. He served with U.S. forces in the Seminole Wars of the 1830s and the Mexican War of 1848. During the Civil War he helped organize the first African American regiment in the Union Army, known as the 1st Louisiana Native Guards. And during the Reconstruction era, Noble emerged as one of the leading African American politicians, pressing for political and equal rights in the city. After his death in 1890, Noble was buried at Saint Louis #2.[37]

Marie Laveau is now one of the most famous figures in the city's history and is known popularly as the "Voodoo Queen." Laveau worked as a hairdresser and lived as a devout Catholic, healer, and practitioner of Louisiana's unique Afro-Creole religion. She benefited from the popular embrace of religious belief during the nineteenth century among all classes and ethnic identities. Laveau gained a large number of followers, given the insecurity that many residents felt in the face of yellow fever and cholera epidemics that raged through the city. Her standing as a socially powerful woman from the 1830s until her death in 1881, at a time when women and persons of color were politically marginalized, is unparalleled in the city's history. As a free woman of color who practiced her art in the decades before the Civil War, she sought to make a positive difference in society through healing and offering blessings to her followers.[38]

Tourism lore often focuses on the social relations between free women of color and wealthy white men during this period. According to the legend of the "quadroon balls," these women attended special dances to which only Creole of color women and wealthy white men were invited. At these balls, the women allegedly attempted to enter into relationships with the men to serve as their mistresses in return for the men providing for them.

Such an alleged contractual relationship, known as *plaçage,* emerged from popular fiction and legends in the late nineteenth and twentieth centuries to be accepted as fact. A former ballroom on Orleans Street in the French Quarter is often purported to be the site of the legendary quadroon balls, so named for the Spanish designation of a woman with one-quarter African ancestry.

Certainly, many well-known examples of relations between wealthy white men and women of color existed at this time—including the aforementioned French merchant Vincent Rillieux and Constance Vivant, the engineer Barthélémey Lafon and Modeste Foucher, and the businessman Edward Gottschalk and Judith Françoise Rubio. Some of these relationships existed because state law prohibited interracial marriages.

Indeed, quadroon balls did exist in the 1790s, imported from Saint-Domingue by immigrant Auguste Tessier. But historian Emily Clark describes how the dances soon devolved into cheap tourist attractions, differing greatly from the Creole high-society affairs of legend. Clark also argues that no documentary evidence of *plaçage* contracts exists. Instead, Catholic parish records indicate that the vast majority of free persons of color married other free persons of color, underscoring the importance these families placed on traditional institutions and maintaining relations within their community. Therefore, a self-respecting free woman of color would not be likely to attend a cheap dance looking for a white husband.[39]

The quadroon ball and *plaçage* legends depict free women of color as passive and sexualized, thereby diminishing these women's real-life accomplishments as proud, pious, and enterprising entrepreneurs. In fact, real estate records show that free women of color owned properties throughout the Vieux Carré, the Tremé, and the Marigny. For example, the house at 2020 Burgundy was the home of Constance Rixner Bouligny. The residence is now owned by architectural historian and preservationist Eugene Cizek, who has documented the rich history of these women in the downtown faubourgs. Likewise, many free men of color made their living as artisans in the building trades. The contractor-carpenter Jean-Louis Dolliole built his own cottage in 1820 at 1436 Pauger, one of the finest examples of craftsmanship built by this Creole community of skilled artisans.[40]

In the context of increased American racial restrictions during the period of early statehood, the continued existence of Sunday dances at Congo Square appears quite remarkable. Their persistence also reflects New Orleans's permissive attitudes. Numerous accounts of travelers detail the activities at these Calinda dances, showcasing New Orleans's distinctive Afro-Caribbean culture until the decline of Congo Square as a dance site in the 1840s.

For example, in 1808 German tourist Christian Schultz observed "in the rear of town" some "twenty different groups of [African] dancers" performing their "worship after the manner of their country." Schultz described the playing of their "national music" on three or four long bamboula drums "two to eight feet in length" while the principal dancers dressed in "wild and savage fashions." According to Schultz, the dances continued until sunset when one or two city patrols showed their cutlasses "and the crowds immediately dispersed."[41]

Architect Benjamin Latrobe wrote the most detailed description of Congo Square, which he encountered by chance in 1819. Latrobe moved to New Orleans to create a private freshwater system financed by subscriptions. In his journal the architect illustrated and described the playing of a long, deep bamboula drum, along with a long-necked string instrument with a gourd for resonance, a reference to an early banjo-type instrument in New Orleans.

As Ned Sublette points out, the combined performance of the large drums of coastal forest regions of western Africa with the banjo-like string instruments of the inland savanna regions illustrates the process of Afro-creolization of two musical cultures. Importantly, Latrobe concluded his observations by stating, as did Schultz, that "there was not the least disorder among the crowd, nor do I learn, on inquiry, that these weekly meeting of Negros have ever produced any mischief."[42]

The decline of Congo Square as a Sunday public dance space in the 1840s occurred at a time when both the population of enslaved and *gens de couleur libres* began to decrease in the city. More than five thousand Creoles of color in New Orleans chose to seek new lives outside Louisiana, and the number of enslaved workers declined from more than 18,000 in 1840 to just over 14,000 by 1860 in part because of the surge in western European immigration and the rise in low-wage white labor. In 1840, New Orleans became the third-largest city in the United States, and the white population became a majority of residents for the first time since the 1780s.

Creole Plantations to Faubourgs

In 1829 the legendary Spanish Capuchin pastor of St. Louis Cathedral, Pere Antoine, passed away after serving the parish for more than fifty years. His funeral at the cathedral may have been the largest one in New Orleans history, attracting both American Protestant admirers and Catholic parishioners. Only one year before, a mortuary chapel for St. Louis Cemetery had opened at the back of the Vieux Carré (411 N. Rampart St.). In 1833, the Catholic Church consecrated the first parish outside the Vieux Carré.

These years marked a new era in Catholic worship in New Orleans, as St. Louis Cathedral ceased to exist as the only Catholic church in New Orleans. The establishment of St. Patrick's Church on Lafayette Square (Place Gravier) in Faubourg Ste. Marie reflected the phenomenal growth that the city experienced in this early American period. Appropriately, the new church opened in the expanding American Sector, and its worship services reflected the predominant English language of the neighborhood.

Although priests conducted Catholic masses only in Latin at that time, the Creole parishioners of St. Louis Cathedral spoke French, and the mostly Irish congregation at the new St. Patrick's was more likely to speak English.

The trend in establishing new parishes catering to the mother tongues of immigrant communities continued unabated in the city during these years. The growth of Catholic parishes in the city mirrored the arrival of newcomers from France, Germany, and Ireland.

New Orleans underwent a profound population increase in these years, surging from the small Spanish colonial port of just over 8,000 persons in 1803 to the large American immigration hub of more than 170,000 inhabitants by 1860. The city witnessed the arrival not only of Americans from the Atlantic states but also of waves of western Europeans seeking new opportunities and escaping political turmoil and persecution in their homelands. The physical growth of New Orleans is easily measured in the development of new faubourgs and the extension of the city's limits upriver.

Only two years after the Louisiana Purchase, Bernard de Marigny (Bernard Xavier Philippe de Marigny de Mandeville) subdivided his downriver plantation adjacent to the Vieux Carré. The galleries on his large West Indies–style plantation home had provided the vantage point of Woiseri's 1803 painting of the town under the banner "Underneath My Wings Everything Prospers," described at the beginning of this chapter (see fig. 8).

The Marigny family was one of the wealthiest Creole planter families in the Orleans Territory and had descended from French nobility. Bernard's maternal grandfather, Jean-Baptiste d'Estrehan, served as royal treasurer of the colony, and his paternal family were Canadian Creoles of noble Norman origin. In 1798 the family hosted Louis Philippe duc d'Orleans, the future neoliberal "king" of France (1830–1848), at their suburban plantation home. On the death of his father in 1800, Bernard inherited the family holdings, which included the Marigny Plantation downriver from New Orleans and the former Acolapissa lands on the north shore of Lake Pontchartrain, which he developed as the town of Mandeville in 1834.

By 1805 Bernard was land rich and cash poor due to gambling debts and a lavish lifestyle. He clearly saw an opportunity to earn a profit by developing his plantation into the second faubourg in the city after Ste. Marie. Marigny therefore hired French engineer Nicolás de Finiels and the city's top planner and architect Barthélémey Lafon to design a new neighborhood defined by the Vieux Carré on the upriver side and extending downriver to the present-day Franklin Street.[43]

Marigny had apparently directed Lafon to give the new streets rather whimsical romantic French names, some of which changed in 1850 when the city made the streets uniform with the Vieux Carré. For example, Craps, named after Marigny's favorite dice game, became sanitized to Burgundy. Other street-name changes included Les Bons Enfants (good children) to St. Claude, L'Amour (love) to N. Rampart, Grands Hommes (great men) to Dauphine, Casa Calvo (the Spanish governor) to Royal, Bagatelle (pinball) to Pauger, L'Histoire (history) to Kerlerec, and Poetes (poets) to St. Roch.

Some other streets retained their original names but were translated into English. Rue des François, named for the Creole rebels executed at Fort San Carlos in 1769, became Frenchmen Street. Les Champs Elysées (likely named after the fashionable Parisian avenue) became Elysian Fields, which centered on the original axis of the Marigny (Dubreuil) Canal running from the river to the back-of-town swamp. In homage to the city's new American political heritage, Lafon named the faubourg's central green space "Place Washington" (Washington Square).[44]

One important aspect of the Faubourg Marigny's development was its tree-lined avenues, inspired by the classic French landscape design of an allée—a straight line of parallel trees leading to the entrance of a large chateau. The city plan from 1809 shows the original fortified ramparts of the city dividing the Faubourg from the original settlement. But by 1817, Jacques Tanesse's official city map clearly shows a more coherent street plan joining the Vieux Carré and Faubourg Marigny by a wide avenue lined with trees, as well as an allée along present-day North Rampart Street (fig. 10). By 1822 city surveyor Joseph Pilié extended the street to Bayou St. John and named it Esplanade Avenue. One cannot be certain what species of trees the city planted to form this urban allée (perhaps the American sycamore, *Platanus occidentalis*), but the design became the defining landscape template for New Orleans's principal avenues. Today, immense planted live oaks (*Quercus virginiana*) have grown to form gracefully arching arbors providing essential shade and grand elegance to the city's urban landscape.

One year after Marigny established his faubourg, several upriver Creole plantations were subdivided to create the neighborhood now known as the Lower Garden District. Marguerite Duplantier first subdivided her long-lot plantation just upriver from Faubourg Ste. Marie and hired Lafon to draw up a plan. Thomas Saulet and Jean-Baptiste de Marigny (Bernard's brother) followed suit by subdividing their adjacent plantations. Then the Ursuline nuns and former Spanish officer Don Jacinto Panis sold off their long lots. Initially each separate plantation became a faubourg: Duplantier, Saulet,

FIG. 10. French artist de Saint-Aulaire documents the social and economic diversity that characterized the Creole Marigny neighborhood in this crossroads encounter of an Indigenous family and an Afro-Creole father and son scurrying out of the way of a well-to-do white couple riding in a cabriolet. Felix Achille Beaupoil de Saint-Aulaire, *Vue d'une Rue du Faubourg Marigny,* 1821, Historic New Orleans Collection, 1937.2.2.

La Course et Annunciation, Nuns, and Panis. But Lafon created a master plan consolidating all five, which covers the area from St. Joseph Street to Felicity Street today.[45]

Lafon's plan drew on Greek mythology in naming and designing the streets lined with drainage canals, embracing an engineering concept the city has used throughout its development. The theme reflected the early nineteenth-century American obsession with classical Greek architecture, republican politics, and culture. Most of the names of the routes parallel with the river have since been altered. Lafon had designed a large, landscaped circle named Place Tivoli (Harmony Circle), where San Carlos (St. Charles Avenue) merged with Lafon's Nyades, named for the mythical Greek water nymphs. But the city eventually extended the grand St. Charles Avenue farther uptown, thereby eliminating the mythological reference.

On the lakeside of Nyades, Lafon named streets for the Greek and Roman mythological figures of Apollo (Carondelet), Bacchus (Baronne), Hercules (South Rampart), and Dryades, the Greek oak tree nymphs. On the river side he planned Coliseum, named for an arena that never materialized, and Prytania for a proposed French school (Prytanée). Lafon's design maintained the urban planning scheme of centering neighborhoods on a public square to provide a communal green space. And so he created two large public squares: Place de l'Annunciation (now Annunciation Square) and the former Dryades market square.

For the streets cutting toward the river—all of which have retained their names—Lafon chose the nine Greek Muses, the goddesses of the arts and science: Calliope (epics), Clio (history), Erato (lyrics), Thalia (comedy), Melpomene (tragedy), Terpsichore (dance), Euterpe (music), Polymnia (hymns), and Urania (astronomy). Over time, the pronunciations have adapted from the original Greek to the strong New Orleans dialect: "CALeeope," "MELpameen," "TERP sickore," "c 1ten" (for Clio)," and "eRATo." As mentioned, this unified plan eventually became known as the Lower Garden District, in reference to the "upper" Garden District that developed in the 1840s between present-day Jackson and Louisiana Avenues and within the former upriver town of Lafayette.

Lafon left an enduring imprint on the development of New Orleans through his building designs, urban planning, and engineering schemes. Originally from Villepinte, Languedoc (Occitanie), in the southwestern Mediterranean region of France, Lafon's earlier architectural style incorporated Iberian and Mediterranean influences of his native region. He is credited with designing the notable Spanish-style homes of Vincent Rillieux (341 Royal), Don Vicente Nuñez (617 Chartres), and Joaquin de Latorre (707 Dumaine), and as stated, he created the street plans for Faubourg Marigny and the Lower Garden District.

Lafon's fascinating personal life reflects New Orleans's French-Latin-American connections during his time. He had five children with his lifelong companion Modeste Foucher, but Louisiana law forbade them to marry because of her status as a free woman of color. In a clandestine arrangement, Pere Antoine baptized their children as white, of unknown origin, as a way to enable their social mobility during a time of racial caste restrictions. Their grandson Thomy Lafon (b. 1810) emerged as one of the great philanthropists for Afro-Creole education in New Orleans during the nineteenth century.

In the 1810s, Barthélémey Lafon worked closely with privateers Jean and Pierre Lafitte in their maritime smuggling and piracy operations; this arrangement ended with their arrest by U.S. customs agents in 1814. Leading up to the Battle of New Orleans, Lafon served with his French colleague Arsène Lacarrière Latour as leading cartographers in the defense of the city. Lafon then briefly moved to Galveston with the exiled Baratarians, where he not only supported Mexican independence from Spain but also served as a double agent for Spain and the United States. Dying in 1820 as an outcast pauper, Lafon was interred at St. Louis Cemetery #1.[46]

French immigrant Claude Tremé developed the city's third faubourg in 1810, likely to satisfy the great need for housing created by the Saint-Domingue exodus to New Orleans. He started as a milliner in Burgundy, and after moving to New Orleans in 1783 he married Julie Moreau (Moro) of the very wealthy French Creole Morand family. In 1798 he acquired title to the Morand Plantation, which city surveyor Jacques Tanesse subdivided into the Faubourg Tremé behind the Vieux Carré and downriver from the Carondelet Canal.

The area encompassed the original Chemin du Bayou (Bayou Road) ridge, which had been developed into small lots with residences and gardens in the French period. But Claude Tremé added a grid, naming the interior streets St. Claude (patron saint of sculptors) and Tremé, as an homage to himself. Appropriately, the plan also included Marais Street, the French term for swamp or marsh, reflecting the neighborhood's location on the edge of wetlands. The other streets running across North Rampart extended from those already existing in the Vieux Carré. And as with the other faubourgs, the plan incorporated a green square (Place Publique) on North Rampart at St. Peters, which was later known as Place Congo (Congo Square).

The Faubourg Tremé (pronounced Trem-AY or colloquially TREM-ee) is significant as one of the oldest African American neighborhoods in the United States. In the Spanish period, free Afro-Creoles owned the majority of land along Bayou Road, and as the Creole of color population boomed with the Saint-Domingue immigration, many of the new arrivals purchased lots in the new development. The oldest Creole cottages in the neighborhood exist in the 1400 block of Governor Nicholls (formerly Bayou Road). Although Afro-Creoles were the predominant residents, the neighborhood was ethnically mixed. Into the twentieth century the neighborhood maintained a decidedly French-speaking Catholic Creole culture.[47]

Encompassing the Crescent

The city continued to grow in leaps and bounds until the Civil War. The expansion up and down the natural ridge of the river is evident when comparing Jacques Tanesse's 1817 map of New Orleans to Nathaniel Banks's map from 1863. The construction of the New Orleans & Carrollton Railroad (today's St. Charles streetcar line) in 1835 fueled the rapid and speculative subdivisions of more plantations between the Lower Garden District and the town of Carrollton. The city annexed the upriver towns of Lafayette in 1852, Jefferson City in 1870, and Carrollton in 1874, thereby moving the Orleans–Jefferson Parish line from Felicity Street to its current location above Carrollton. In 1870, the city also annexed the West Bank community of Algiers.

Upriver, the city of Lafayette had developed as a diverse town in the 1830s within the newly created Jefferson Parish, carved from Orleans Parish in 1825. The new town included working-class and middle-class homes along the river and the back side of St. Charles Avenue, as well as large garden lots for wealthy Americans between Magazine and the New Orleans & Carrollton Railroad. The eventual name "Garden District" conveyed the distinct character of the wealthy section: its large homes surrounded by lush gardens contrasted sharply with the Spanish architecture of the Vieux Carré. The neighborhood's oldest home is the West Indies–style plantation home known as Toby's Corner (2340 Prytania). Built in 1838, the galleried raised home is atypical; most of the later residences were built in the style of the Greek Revival, sidehall American townhome, and the elaborate Italianate styles appearing from the 1840s to the 1860s.

In the character of Uptown, Garden District homeowners were predominantly English-speaking, wealthy American merchants, with the well-known exception of Michael Musson, a wealthy Creole cotton broker who built his large sidehall American townhome at the corner of Third and Coliseum (1331 Third St.) in 1853. The very elegant, raised center-hall Claiborne-Marigny Creole cottage (2524 St. Charles Avenue) built in 1857 is an example of a Garden District home owned by a prominent blended Creole American family. The original owners were Sophronia Claiborne, daughter of Louisiana's first governor William Claiborne, and her husband Philippe Marigny, son of famed developer and planter Bernard de Marigny.

In the adjacent Irish Channel and back-of-town sections of the city of Lafayette, the neighborhoods of smaller Creole cottages and shotgun-style homes were home to many Irish, German, French immigrants, Afro-Creoles, and African Americans after the Civil War. The names on the family and institutional tombs in Lafayette Cemeteries #1 (1416 Washington Ave.) and #2 (2110 Washington Ave.) clearly reflect the diverse origins of the city's residents in the nineteenth century.[48]

The growth of Jefferson City and Carrollton in the 1830s and 1840s followed the general pattern established for present-day Uptown. The wide avenues featured large homes of well-to-do residents. On the side streets along the river and the back-of-town sections stretching to Claiborne Avenue existed smaller middle-class cottages and shotguns. These working-class communities were patchworks of ethnic and racial diversity. Even the neighborhood that became known as the Irish Channel housed a mélange of western European immigrants, free African Americans, and Afro-Creole residents.

The rapid expansion of the Catholic Church after 1830 mirrored New Orleans's growth and the presence of both European immigrant and Afro-Creole communities. Following the 1833 consecration of St. Patrick's on Lafayette Square, in 1838 the Catholic Church established the new Parish of St. Vincent de Paul (3051 Dauphine) for French-speaking residents of the downtown Third Municipality (present-day Marigny and Bywater).

St. Augustine Church (1210 Gov. Nicholls) in the Tremé opened in 1842 as another French-language church in response to the requests of Creoles of color in that community. The Ursuline nuns donated the land, and Jacques Nicolas Bussière de Pouilly designed the building, which features a tall distinctive steeple that serves as a local landmark. The parish, like the surrounding neighborhood, has maintained a congregation comprising largely of persons of color. As such, St. Augustine is one of the oldest historic African American Catholic parishes in the United States.

The later establishment of new churches in the downtown districts came in response to the settlement of non-Creole Catholic immigrants there. Even though the lower river neighborhoods are often characterized as Creole, in fact they displayed a polyglot of languages and western European cultures. Holy Trinity Redemptorist Church (725 St. Ferdinand), consecrated in 1848, served German-speaking families escaping the political instabilities of Prussia in the mid-nineteenth century. The Third District displayed such a German character that locals called it "Little Saxony," despite the prevalence of immigrants from Catholic Bavaria.

The establishment of the massive Sts. Peter and Paul Church (2317 Burgundy) in 1860 served the English-speaking Irish families fleeing the traumatic potato famine of the 1840s and 1850s. At that time, the poorest Irish immigrants faced severe discrimination, and most men could only find low-wage and dangerous jobs, such as digging the New Basin Canal. The women were hired as domestic servants, contributing to the decline in the number of enslaved domestic workers in the city. For example, the residents of the townhome that is the present-day 1850 House Museum on Jackson Square initially used a small staff of enslaved workers but hired Irish immigrants to do the majority of work by the late 1850s. The city's white population jumped from more than 20,000 in 1830 to 144,601 in 1860, while the enslaved population stayed at just over 14,400 persons during this same period.

Even as most Irish immigrants struggled to earn a living, the example of Margaret Haughery illustrates both the suffering and eventually acceptance of many. Arriving in New Orleans from Baltimore as an impoverished, newly married orphan in 1835, the enterprising young Irish woman rose to become one of the most prominent and wealthiest female business owners in the city, based on the success of her bread bakery in the Faubourg Ste. Marie. She gained tremendous public respect and support when she nursed the sick regardless of their race or class and fed the hungry during the Civil War. Using profits from her business, Haughery donated funds to establish four Catholic orphanages meeting the needs of those left destitute by yellow fever epidemics. On her death in 1882, working people from across the city donated small amounts to fund a statue to her, which was dedicated in 1884 (Margaret Place) in the Lower Garden District. The monument exists as one of the first statues dedicated to a woman in the United States.

Just as the Third District is characterized as Creole, the areas of the Lower Garden District and Irish Channel (then located within the city of Lafayette) are often branded as solely American. In fact, all these neighborhoods were home to the same variety of immigrant groups. The 1850s establishment of Notre Dame de Bon Secours Church (demolished at 900 Jackson Ave. in 1925) reflected the presence of French-language residents of this uptown district. In addition, the parish of St. Alphonsus Church (2030 Constance) was built in 1855 for the considerable English-speaking Irish population of Lafayette (present-day uptown New Orleans).

A few years later, St. Mary's Assumption (923 Josephine) Redemptorist Catholic Church opened directly across the street from St. Alphonsus to serve the growing German-speaking population of the surrounding neighborhoods. The church's elaborate and massive gilded altar and German-language–inscribed stained-glass windows reflect the Bavarian roots of the congregation, and local legend maintains that dedicated parishioners carried the bricks by hand to the site for construction. Today, the parish (rededicated as St. Alphonsus) is home to the shrine and relics of Blessed Father Francis Xavier Seelos, the Bavarian missionary who succumbed to yellow fever in 1867 while attending to those who contracted the mosquito-borne illness.

And around the corner, the former Gates of Prayer (703 Jackson Ave.) became the largest synagogue in the metro area at the time of its founding in 1850 and completion in 1865. The building's size and prominence reflected the large numbers of German Ashkenazi and Portuguese Sephardic immigrants in New Orleans, giving the city the largest and most well-established Jewish population in the antebellum South. And as the neighborhood changed, the congregation moved farther uptown in the 1910s, and eventually to Metairie in the 1970s.

Among this immigrant group, Judah P. Touro, of Portuguese Sephardic origins, arrived in New Orleans in 1801 and later served with the local forces at the Battle of New Orleans. As a successful merchant he became one of the city's wealthiest businessmen and a generous philanthropist, establishing Touro Infirmary, a Jewish hospital. The Reform Touro Synagogue, founded in Uptown during the 1880s as a merger of two German and Portuguese temples, is named in his honor.

The increased number of Protestant churches in New Orleans in the early American period reflected the growth of the Anglo-American and African American populations who arrived from the Atlantic Coast and Upper South. Shortly after the Louisiana Purchase, Virginian William Kenner established the first Protestant church in New Orleans, which evolved into Christ Church Episcopal. When this church opened, the Catholic Church no longer had a monopoly on public religious observance, as it had under both France and Spain.

With the religious revival movement known as the Second Great Awakening, Baptist and Methodist churches gradually spread in New Orleans. Presbyterian houses of worship also became established, with First Presbyterian on Lafayette Square being the largest. By the late 1850s, Pastor Benjamin Palmer of First Presbyterian had emerged as an outspoken defender of slavery. On the verge of the Civil War in 1860, Palmer delivered a famous sermon raising the defense of slavery to a Christian duty, which served as a rallying cry for secessionists across the South.

Among English-speaking African Americans, the establishment of the African Methodist Episcopal (AME) Church enabled institutional independence from the larger Protestant white-led churches. The AME Church had been founded in 1816 by Black Methodists in Philadelphia, and remarkably two churches opened in New Orleans in the racially tense decades leading up to the Civil War. In 1844, St. James AME (222 N. Roman) became the first AME church in the South, and by 1850 St. Peter's AME (1201 Cadiz) became the second, at first sharing space with the white Methodist Church in Jefferson City.

These New Orleans congregations were largely made up of English-speaking free persons of color, but enslaved worshipers attended clandestinely. Thus, the existence of these churches represented a form of passive resistance against slave laws and white control generally. After emancipation in the early 1860s, establishing separate and independent African American churches became an important expression of freedom for many.

Foodways: The Birth of Gourmet Tourism

Creole cuisine, for which New Orleans is known internationally, came to fruition in this early American period. The menus of restaurants established in the nineteenth century still reflect French-inspired cooking traditions using locally sourced seasonal seafoods, sausages, and produce of the lower Mississippi Valley and Gulf Coast. These classic old-school establishments also mirror the experiences of their French and German immigrant founders. The restaurants started as small operations but then developed into Creole fine-dining establishments emblematic of New Orleans's Old World charm, as it has been promoted since the nineteenth century.

Antoine's is the oldest existing restaurant in the city and bills itself as the oldest family-run restaurant in the nation. The establishment's evolution mirrors that of the city's nineteenth-century culinary evolution. The founder, Antoine Alciatore, emigrated at eighteen years old from Marseille to New Orleans. His French first name and his Italian surname reflect the rich Mediterranean cultural layers of his native home in France, and one that fit in with New Orleans as well. Alciatore opened a pension boarding house and restaurant on St. Louis Street in the Vieux Carré, which moved to its current location in 1868. In 1874, Alciatore returned to Marseille, wishing to die and be buried in his hometown.

Alciatore's Alsatian-born widow, Julie Freys Alciatore, and their son Jules continued to run the restaurant as its reputation grew. In the 1870s, Madame Alciatore sent Jules to gain culinary experience at fine restaurants in Marseille, Strasbourg, and Paris. Thus, the restaurant's diverse culinary influences extend from its Mediterranean roots to the fine-dining establishments of Paris and the German-French province of Alsace, all with an emphasis on sourcing local ingredients. Jules's signature dish, Oysters Rockefeller, represents the consummation of these sophisticated European sensibilities and local Creole ingredients.[49]

Tujague's is the second-oldest restaurant in the city, and its history also reflects the immigrant experience and growing culinary sophistication of nineteenth-century New Orleans. The founder, Elizabeth Kettering, emigrated from Bavaria to New Orleans in 1853; ten years, later, she opened a restaurant at 811 Decatur across from the French Market. Eventually naming her restaurant Bégué's Exchange (using her married name), she became well known for serving a "second breakfast" (Bavarian *zweites früstük*) to hungry butchers and workers who worked the early shifts on the riverfront. Tourists soon discovered her restaurant, and Bégué became the first "celebrity chef" in New Orleans's culinary history. Her late breakfast of omelets, various meats and poultry, breads and cheese, and strong coffee is now considered the origin of "brunch," although the tradition has roots in Bavaria and eastern Europe.[50] Bégué's life reflects both the immigrant experience in New Orleans and the subsequent rise of the city as a gourmet tourist destination.

The former location of Maylié and Esparbé's Table d'Hote (1000 block of Poydras Street) is still identified by the classic blue and white New Orleans letter tiles embedded in the sidewalk. The restaurant was established by two Frenchmen, Bernard Maylié and Hypolite Esparbé, who immigrated to New Orleans in the 1860s. They first opened a coffee stall at the Poydras Market serving the working men of the neighborhood and then a *table d'hote* restaurant, where patrons ate side by side at large tables. The establishment also included a "stag dining room" that featured casks of imported wine, in the tradition of a French wine cave.

The restaurant's chef, Madame Marie Esparbé, who grew up with her sister Anna cooking at their parents' French *auberge* (inn), served a *petit dejeuner* (breakfast) at 11 a.m, just as Madame Bégué did. The menu featured a plethora of French-inspired and Creole dishes with seasonal New Orleans ingredients: crawfish gumbo filé, Creole bouillabaisse, Spanish court-bouillon, Creole rice, collard greens soup, Tante Therese's fried soft-shell crabs, baked mallard ducks, braised quail, and much more. The restaurant closed in 1986, but Madame Esparbé's cooking in the nineteenth century exemplified the city's Creole cuisine with its mouthwatering inclusion of French-Spanish-Italian-West African-Indigenous influences.[51]

Creole Court-Bouillon

Gumbo is perhaps the most iconic dish of New Orleans and of south Louisiana. Gumbo—as both a blend and stew—is often used as an analogy to define the cultural mélange of New Orleans's social milieu. Indeed, its cooking methods and ingredients reflect the numerous cultures that form the region's Creole culture and society. The base of gumbo is a French-inspired roux gravy that is sautéed with onions, bell pepper, and celery—the holy trinity base of many south Louisiana and New Orleans dishes—as well as garlic. Then one adds the stock, spices, and meats or greens depending on the type of gumbo: seafood, chicken, and sausage or Lenten des herbes (gumbo z'herbes) using various greens.

The name *gumbo* and the additions of okra and red pepper are West African contributions. Filé (freshly ground sassafras leaves) is an essential Indigenous ingredient to flavor and thicken the gumbo. The addition of rice on the side could be an influence from West Africa, France, or Spain. Therefore, the evolution of gumbo reflects the creolization of New Orleans cuisine. The emergence of the dish as the ultimate Creole culinary experience also illustrates the emergence of New Orleans's gastronomic distinctiveness in the nineteenth century.

In Creole cuisine, many dishes have French origins and names, but the recipes and ingredients changed during the adaptive, improvised process of creolization. Bouillabaisse and court-bouillon are two of the most obvious examples of this phenomenon. Both Creole dishes are quite different from their original French forms. Bouillabaisse originated as a seafood stew that was slow cooked by fishermen and women on the Mediterranean coast around Marseille: the French word means *bouillir* (to boil) *et abaisser* (and lower). As with gumbo in Louisiana, bouillabaisse in Marseille depends on what seafood is available and on each family's traditional ingredients and methods. And as in New Orleans, bouillabaisse Provençal aficionados would also inform a visitor that their mamie's kitchen is where to find the best bowl.

The French court-bouillon is essentially a fish poached in herbs—hence, the translation *court* (short) *bouillon* (boiled), or "short broth." Like bouillabaisse in Louisiana, the dish now has creolized versions. And like the original Provençal fish stew that uses whatever *fruits de mer* are available, Creole court-bouillon (pronounced coo-bee-yon) is also cooked with the catch of the day or even with leftover fish parts. Louis Armstrong recalled proudly in his autobiography that, as a young man in the early 1900s, his mother sent him to the Poydras Market to buy fifteen cents worth of fish heads to make a "big pot of 'cubie yon' which she served with tomato sauce and fluffy white rice with every grain separate."[52]

In fact, both Creole dishes have many of the same variations. Some use roux bases, whereas others use sautéed vegetables with tomatoes and seasonings as a base. Family and geographic variations therefore make the concise descriptions of the two dishes nearly impossible. If one asks a group of Cajun or Creole cooks today what are the differences between them, their answers and recipes will likely vary greatly.

This period of New Orleans culinary history is characterized by nineteenth-century French immigrants adapting and creolizing their traditions to New Orleans's ingredients and tastes. In contrast to the colonial period during which most French settlers came from the northern French provinces such as Normandy, in the early American period, Louisiana attracted more French émigrés from the Mediterranean coast, who moved with their distinct food traditions such as bouillabaisse. Therefore, the recipe of Creole court-bouillon exemplifies the early American period when this new creolization process occurred and when New Orleans developed a culinary tradition that evolved into gourmet tourism.

Serves 6

Holy Trinity + Garlic
1 cup diced onions
1 cup diced celery
1 cup diced bell pepper
2–4 tablespoons minced garlic (depending on your taste)
½ cup flour
½ cup cooking oil (or butter)
4 large seeded and skinned tomatoes (or 1–2 cans of stewed tomatoes)
¼ cup diced serrano or jalapeño peppers (or less according to heat tolerance)
1 quart fish stock (can be made from leftover fish parts and bones)
1 tablespoon salt
1 tablespoon black pepper
1 tablespoon cayenne pepper
2–3 pounds firm white fish (redfish, red snapper, or whatever is available) cut into small pieces
1 cup red wine
¼ cup finely chopped parsley
1 bunch chopped green onions
1 large serving bowl of cooked rice

1. In a cast-iron pot (preferably), make a roux with the oil and flour over medium heat. Constantly stirring the roux for 20–30 minutes should be an enjoyable, almost meditative experience as the roux becomes a dark-brown color.
2. Add onions, celery, bell pepper, and garlic and cook 10 minutes until soft.
3. Add tomatoes and one cup of fish stock, wine, and seasonings; cook on medium-low heat for 30 minutes until the sauce is formed.
4. Add the remaining fish stock and cook for another 30 minutes on low or until the sauce is thick. Add the fish and cover the chunks without stirring and let cook for 15–20 minutes until the fish is flaky.
5. When done, serve on a plate (or in a shallow, wide bowl) garnished with chopped green onions and parsley and with cooked rice on the side.

NOTE: A variation of this dish follows the same recipe but substitutes uncooked fish chunks with fried fish filets that are placed in the sauce and cooked for only 10 minutes.

Paris on the Gulf of Mexico

On February 9, 1856, a ceremony at the former Place d'Armes dedicated the statue of President Andrew Jackson. Downtown Creoles had organized the unveiling to honor the hero of the Battle of New Orleans. Jackson as a

Democrat also represented the party that appealed to recent European immigrants like those in New Orleans, as well as small farmers and supporters of slavery. The Clark Mills–designed statue, the first in the city, depicted the Tennessean dressed in military uniform, mounted on his rearing horse Duke, and waving his cockaded hat in victory on January 8, 1815.

Five years earlier, the city had renamed the historic Place d'Armes as Jackson Square after the president. The new name also reflected the physical transformation of the square in the late 1840s. During this decade, the city added third-floor mansard roofs and cupolas to both the Presbytère and the Cabildo. The latter had ceased serving as the city hall in 1848 with the dedication of the new Greek Revival Gallier Hall in the American Sector on Lafayette Square. At the same time, the archdiocese renovated St. Louis Cathedral to be the same three-story height as the adjacent buildings. The new cathedral, designed by Jacques Nicolas Bussière de Pouilly, included a grander center bell tower with a clock and topped with a cross and was flanked by two smaller copper-shingled towers to replace the old Spanish bell towers from the 1790s.

Most significantly, in 1850 Micaela Almonester de Pontalba built two large and very fashionable row houses, now known as "the Pontalbas," along the upper and lower sections of the square, which she had inherited from her father. The daughter of Spanish notary and philanthropist Don Andrés Almonester y Rojas and wealthy Creole Marie-Louise Denys de la Ronde, she had received a great sum of money on their deaths. The baroness had lived in Paris, and successfully achieved a divorce after her husband, the New Orleans–born Baron de Pontalba, attempted to murder her in 1834. During the 1848 republican revolution in France, Micaela returned to New Orleans where she created the building complex that hears her name today.[53]

The Baroness de Pontalba's inspiration for the elegant new three-story federalist brick townhomes with large cast-iron galleries was Paris's oldest public square, the stately Place de Vosges. On her return to New Orleans, she envisioned and then implemented a plan to renovate the barren Place d'Armes into a beautifully landscaped park complemented by modern townhomes. Pontalba hired city surveyor Louis Pilié to create a formal French-style garden with graceful walkways in the square. The son of esteemed surveyor-architect and Saint-Domingue immigrant Gilbert Joseph Pilié, Louis designed the sturdy cast-iron fence topped with *fleur de lys* and Egyptian palmette figures that surrounds the square, as well as the impressive double iron gates at the entrance to the Cabildo.

In the three decades leading up to the Civil War, the construction of new three- and four-story brick row houses throughout the Vieux Carré transformed the neighborhood's appearance from a Spanish town into a more modern American-style city. The Pedesclaux-Lemonnier "skyscraper" house built in 1811 is considered to be one of the first examples of the multistory phenomenon at 640 Royal Street in the Vieux Carré. But the newer American architecture is most evident along upper Decatur and Canal Streets, where the first floors were designated for commercial use and the upper floors for residences or offices. In this period, the style also extended into the burgeoning American business district across Canal Street.

For her new townhomes on the Place d'Armes, the baroness commissioned esteemed Irish New Orleanian architects James Gallier Sr. and Henry Howard, who designed perhaps the most elegant example of the brick rowhouse style in the city. Whereas the Place de Vosges is bordered by arcaded walkways similar to those near the Cabildo and Presbytère, the baroness's new townhomes incorporated fashionable and modern cast-iron posts that supported wide galleries decorated with a delicately laced cast-iron design bearing her initials "AP" (Almonester Pontalba) in the center crest. The Pontalba Buildings' second-floor verandas have some of the finest ornamental cast-iron work in the city that is known for its beauty and complexity.[54]

The new industrial-age technology of the mid-nineteenth century enabled the mass production of cast iron. In contrast to Spanish-era wrought iron that used individual iron pieces created by an artisan to form a simple, graceful design, the new cast-iron technology enabled the less-expensive reproduction of a more delicate design through the creation of one cast that could then be repeated endlessly. As a result, cast-iron posts and balcony decorations were used throughout the French Quarter, the Garden District, older commercial districts on lower Magazine Street, and downtown neighborhoods as well.

Some of the finer residential examples of lacy cast-iron galleries are found at the Miltenberger House (900 Royal), the LaBranche House (710 Royal), and the Robinson House (1415 Third). The decorative style defines New Orleans's architecture within the United States. The use of cast-iron supports for wide galleries hanging over the sidewalk also reflects the unique New Orleans design that placed a gallery on the front of a building. Reminiscent of the West Indies style, these wide, covered walkways provided both residents and street pedestrians protection from New Orleans's strong sun and rain showers.

Pontalba's design for Jackson Square yielded a lush park in 1851 that represents New Orleans's European and Latin American character. Adrien de Pauger's original Place d'Armes in 1721 centered the Vieux Carré similar to many public plazas in Latin America. Pontalba's and Pilié's nineteenth-century French-inspired landscaping and buildings, combined with the Spanish-era Cabildo and Presbytère that symmetrically flank the tall bell towers of St. Louis Cathedral, contribute to the Old World charm of the square. Although visitors are likely unaware that the Place de Vosges inspired this plan, the historic charm of the square is unequaled by any other American city. The park's graceful elegance is Baroness de Pontalba's gift to the Creole-American city.

As an American who lived much of her life in Paris, Pontalba also represents the strong connection between New Orleans and France during this period when thousands of French immigrants settled in the city. Their numbers dwarfed those recruited by the French crown to the colonial river village in the early eighteenth century. The Catholic cultural infusion brought by new immigrants from Saint-Domingue, Ireland, Bavaria, and western and southern France—along with new western European Jewish immigrants—continued to distinguish New Orleans within the American South and the nation at large as a distinctly Catholic city, but with layers of Protestantism, Judaism, and Afro-Creole religious beliefs.

The emergence of several prominent portrait artists in this period also was facilitated by the strong connections that New Orleans's Creole society maintained with France, as well as by the artistic sophistication that marked the city during this period. Jean-Joseph Vaudechamp had trained at the esteemed L'Ecole nationale supérieureur des beaux-arts de Paris, and beginning in 1831 he spent seven profitable winters painting portraits of notable Creole elites in the French neoclassical style at his studio in the Vieux Carré.

Lured by Vaudechamp's success, French artist Jacques Amans followed in the 1840s and became the most sought-after portrait artist not only of well-to-do Creoles such as Baroness de Pontalba but also of others includ-

FIG. 11. Classically trained French artist Jacques Amans's mesmerizing portrait of a woman of color wearing a red tignon reflects New Orleans's elevated artistic status in the years before the Civil War, as well as the city's distinct Creole American culture. Jacques Amans, *Portrait of Creole Woman in Red Headdress,* ca. 1840, Historic New Orleans Collection, 2010.0306.

ing Margaret Haughery and President Andrew Jackson. One of Amans's most distinctly New Orleanian portraits is of a young female Creole of color wearing a red tignon (fig. 11). Another one is of the Frey children and their family servant Bélizaire; this latter painting is appreciated as a rare portrait of an enslaved person from the period. Artists Adolph Rinck, originally from Metz, France, and Franz (François) Fleischbein from Bavaria represent German-speaking artists who also found success in New Orleans from the 1830s to the 1850s. The combined works of these five artists document Creole society in New Orleans before the Civil War.

New Orleans also continued to maintain strong ties to Latin America and the Caribbean. In 1849, the Appleton Map of North America clearly showed New Orleans's principal maritime trade connections to Veracruz, Mexico and Havana: these shipping routes formed a well-trafficked triangle of trade across the Gulf of Mexico. During the Mexican-American War of 1848 and 1849, New Orleans was the principal port of military embarkation and shipping.

The first commercial red pepper vinegar sauce appeared in the city shortly after the war, when Battle of New Orleans veteran Maunsel White marketed a red pepper sauce in the 1850s. In the 1870s, the McIlhenny family created Tabasco sauce, named after the Mexican state and pepper. During the late 1800s, the oak barrel–aged McIlhenny sauce made in Iberia Parish west of New Orleans became internationally famous and helped make the region synonymous with spicy cuisine. Even though Tabasco is famous internationally, many natives prefer the locally made Crystal Hot Sauce, which was first produced in the 1920s.[55]

New Orleans also served as the place of asylum for liberal Mexican and Cuban political exiles. During the 1850s, future Mexican president Benito Juárez found refuge in New Orleans where he wrote the "Plan de Ayutla," an important declaration of Mexican republican values. During this exile from 1853 to 1855, Juárez worked as a cigar roller for a free woman of color in the Tremé and befriended liberal Cuban author and exile Pedro Santacilia, then living in the city. Juárez again sought refuge in New Orleans during 1858 before returning to Mexico, eventually evicting French forces under Emperor Maximilian de Habsburgo-Lorena and overseeing the ascendance of liberal republican democracy. In 1965, Juárez was honored for his New Orleans connections with a prominent statue on Basin and Conti, located near the neighborhood where he resided.[56]

Composer Louis Moreau Gottschalk embodies the deep cultural connections that New Orleans maintained with both France and the Afro-Caribbean-Latin world. Born in 1829 to an Ashkenazi German Jewish London-born father Edward Gottschalk and a Saint-Domingue-born French Creole mother Aimée Marie Bruslé, the young boy studied piano and was soon recognized as a child prodigy in the musically rich Creole-American city. At age thirteen, Gottschalk moved to France to study at the Paris Conservatory but was denied admittance because of his American nationality. Despite this rejection, his public performances earned the respect and support of esteemed composers Franz Liszt and Frédéric Chopin. In this period of Romantic-era "local color" music and literature, Gottschalk composed "Bamboula: Danse des Nègres" (Dance of the Blacks) in 1849, which drew on the bamboula rhythm and Afro-Caribbean-Creole melodies of his youth.

This composition is credited with being the first classical music piece to integrate African rhythms into a formal western composition. The piece also presented New Orleans's Afro-Creole musical culture to the world. For the rest of his career, Gottschalk traveled throughout the Caribbean and Latin America, drawing on the region's musical traditions for his inspiration in such compositions as "Souvenir de la Havane" and "Souvenir de Puerto Rico." In the era of larger-than-life performers on the big stage, Gottschalk became an international star and the first major music icon of the city—preceding figures such as Louis Armstrong, Fats Domino, and Lil Wayne. Gottschalk's integration of French and Afro-Caribbean music represents an important intersection of these two cultural threads in New Orleans writ large on the international stage. No other city in the United States could have produced such a complex and popular musical artist. As such, Gottschalk represents most clearly New Orleans's exceptionalism at the time.[57]

Gottschalk's death from yellow fever in Brazil in 1869 also made clear that the deadly disease posed a threat to many cities in the Americas, particularly swampy New Orleans. The worst yellow fever epidemic, which swept the city in the summer of 1853, killed nearly eight thousand New Orleanians, close to 10 percent of the city's population. Although the source of the disease (*Aedes aegypti* mosquito) was then unknown, the city's resilience in the face of these epidemics reflected a communal endurance after devastating fires, fierce hurricanes, wars, and river floods. Indeed, only four years before the great epidemic of 1853, a levee break upriver (in present-day River Ridge)—known as Sauvé's Crevasse—flooded East Jefferson Parish and New Orleans, producing a level of destruction similar to that of Hurricane Katrina flooding in 2005.

By 1860 the city's striking expansion during the early American period overshadowed these environmental, sanitary, and health challenges. During the fifty-seven-year period from the Louisiana Purchase to the Civil War, the urban footprint had grown to encompass the entire natural sediment ridge upriver to Carrollton and downriver to St. Bernard Parish, and across the river to Algiers and the new West Bank towns of McDonoghville, Gretna, and Mechanickham. New canals for drainage and shipping were dug, and two railroad lines (NOO&GWRR and the NOJ&GNRR) connected the city to surrounding regions to the north and west. Although the city no longer served as the state capital of Louisiana, New Orleans remained the economic center of the American South and one of the nation's busiest ports.

In the past, the antebellum era has been characterized as the "golden age" of New Orleans in terms of its wealth and economic growth. But the enslaved workers and immigrants who lived in and around the city did not share in that prosperity. In the early 1860s, the enslaved welcomed the emancipation and freedom that marked the decisive end of the pre–Civil War period. The survival of Afro-Creole and African American people throughout the brutal era speaks to the endurance of the city's residents. This resilience can be attributed both to a strong spirituality and an appreciation for the distinct cultural traditions and celebrations that ease the pain of trauma. At the same time, the residents' commitment to the location—a sliver of land surrounded by water and threatened by the environment—reflects the power of place and a long history.

Relevant Historic Sites

Creole Cottages, 1100 block of Governor Nicholls: The location of free persons of color residences on Bayou Road dating to the 1790s and early 1800s.

Chalmette National Battlefield & Cemetery, 8606 W. Saint Bernard Hwy., Chalmette: The site of the Battle of New Orleans includes a museum and visitors' center operated by the National Park Service

Dolliole House, 1440 Pauger: Designed and built by free man of color Jean-Louis Dolliole in 1819, the home exemplifies the craftsmanship of Creole of color architects and tradesmen in the nineteenth century.

St. Louis Cemetery #2, 200–400 blocks of N. Claiborne Ave.: Established in 1823, the cemetery contains the tombs of Jordan Noble, Henriette Delille, Dominique You, Pierre Soulé, and many other notable residents.

Le Musée de FPC (Free Person of Color Museum), 2336 Esplanade Ave.: The museum interprets the history of the free persons of color community in New Orleans.

Whitney Plantation Museum, 5099 LA-18, Edgard, Louisiana: The former Haydel Plantation interprets the history of slavery through historic buildings and memorials.

Pontalba Buildings, 500 blocks of St. Peter and St. Anne on Jackson Square: The luxury apartments built by Micaela de Pontalba around 1850. The 1850 House Museum (523 St. Anne) recreates and interprets a luxury townhome from the period.

Gallier House, 1132 Royal: The personal residence of James Gallier Jr. that he designed with cast-iron galleries, a porte cochère, indoor plumbing, and slave/servant quarters.

5

The Simmering Gumbo Pot

Civil War to the Ragtime Era, 1860–1910

LAFCADIO HEARN, the Irish American journalist, observed in post–Civil War New Orleans: "It is a little curious how the creole element preserves its ancient customs and manners in the very heart of the changes that are going on about it." Hearn described the downtown district of New Orleans in the late 1870s this way: "The old French town is asleep; the streets are deserted; and the shadow of the pedestrian makes a moving black speck against the moonlight on the pavement only at long intervals." Hearn continued, "Creoledom wakes up as slowly and cautiously as possible; and has not fairly begun to enter upon the business of the day until the sun has warmed the streets."

Contrasting the city's two cultures, Hearn wrote, "The comparatively new generation of American citizens, when brought into contact with this older population, is utterly unable to understand the difference of character, and shuns as much as possible the transaction of business with it—which contents the Creole perfectly well." Hearn concluded that Creoles "seem to tolerate those who understand them, and to abominate those who do not, and propose to live in the good old way as long as possible."[1]

Hearn lived and worked as a journalist in New Orleans from 1877 to 1887, where he chronicled the city's Creole culture and characters, which fascinated him. Historian Fred Starr has argued that Hearn's writing popularized the image of New Orleans as a place of mystery and exoticism, thereby cementing the notion of New Orleans exceptionalism in the American mind. During these ten years, Hearn collected and published Creole proverbs and recipes, becoming the first unofficial folklorist of the city's Afro-Creole culture. His characterization of the cultural dichotomy of the city after the Civil War provides a portrait of New Orleans's French and African characteristics in language, religion, cuisine, and temperament that distinguished the city well into the American Gilded Age.[2]

The Civil War and Reconstruction brought profound social, political, and economic transformations to the city. The gradual process of emancipation altered the labor and racial caste system that had characterized prewar New Orleans. The emergence of modern industry after the war brought a new era of modern cotton mills, national railroads, and international shipping to the riverfront. The French Creole wealth that characterized the city in the early American period dissipated with the economic disruptions of the war. But at the same time, the city's Creole culture continued to exist in the shadows of the modernizing American city.

In the thirty years after the Civil War, new American boomtowns such as Chicago, Cleveland, St. Louis, and San Francisco all exceeded New Orleans in population. But as the economic and shipping capital of the American South, the port city experienced a profound influx of immigrants from the Mediterranean Basin, eastern Europe, and southeast Asia—thereby adding new layers of Catholic and non-Catholic cultures to the existing base of America's gumbo pot.

Laboratory of Reconstruction

Generally, the Civil War and postwar Reconstruction periods are not celebrated in New Orleans history. Residents are often uncomfortable with the extreme political and racial divisions in the city then, as well as the trauma of death, violence, military occupation, and economic decline. On the one hand, white conservatives lamented the loss of the Confederate cause—that of preserving slavery and their wealth during the war. Afro-Creoles and African Americans, still largely divided by language and culture, bitterly regretted the opportunities for racial, social, and political advancement that disappeared at the end of Reconstruction in 1877, despite the overall positive impact of emancipation. The racial violence that marked the period is perhaps the most uncomfortable subject for all and one that the city's tourism industry often overlooks.

New Orleans's location as the economic heart of the American South certainly led to the city and state's official support for secession from the Union in 1861. But in fact, the city was hardly unified behind this separatist cause. Secession was largely supported by white Anglo-Americans and some white Creoles and Frenchmen, such as Pierre Soulé, who identified with the conservative racial ideals of the Confederacy. Yet, many shipping merchants and Creole sugar planters such as André Roman preferred to avoid fully seceding from the United States and had identified with the Republican Party's predecessor, the Whig Party.

The antebellum Whig Party, which morphed into the new Republican Party of Abraham Lincoln during the 1850s, supported state investment in the development of infrastructure (railroads and canals), centralized banking, and tariffs on sugar imports but refrained from taking a definitive stance on the system of slave labor.[3] In contrast, the more dominant southern Democratic Party was singularly focused on preserving slavery. The Democratic Party also found support from recent urban immigrants in New Orleans, who identified with its platforms supporting small artisans and anti-temperance. Creoles of color in the city, who could not vote, associated the Democratic Party with the cause of white supremacy and therefore nominally supported the Union cause and the Republican Party.[4]

After the war began in April 1861, the city spent a year under Confederate control, during which separatist rebels took over all federal military facilities such as Jackson Barracks and government offices such as the Customs House and the U.S. Mint, which then printed Confederate money. Early in the war, the Union implemented a naval blockade of the South, known as the Anaconda Plan, that essentially brought New Orleans's exports to a standstill. Any commerce associated with maritime trade immediately felt the pinch, and the city suffered from food shortages throughout the war. The inability to ship goods from the port had a profound impact on cotton exports, which provided the city's bread and butter. Because New Orleans was the main source of raw cotton to Britain's mills, the blockade led to industrial layoffs in the Lancashire region on the west coast of England around Liverpool and Manchester. This dire period is known in the United Kingdom as the "cotton famine," illustrating the international economic impact of the blockade.

One year into the war, the Union Navy's Gulf Squadron under Admiral David Farragut successfully ran the gauntlet of Confederate defenses downriver and captured the city. Farragut had spent his youth in New Orleans and had served as a teenage officer in the U.S. Navy during the War of 1812. With the arrival of some fourteen thousand Union troops in early May 1862, Confederate commander Mansfield Lovell withdrew his troops to the north shore of Lake Pontchartrain. Farragut threatened to lay siege to the city if the Confederates did not surrender; Mayor John T. Monroe refused to do so and was imprisoned. However, the Union did not follow through on its threat to use force, which ensured preservation of the Vieux Carré's historic architecture and character.[5]

The Union occupation began immediately in May 1862, and the city soon became a laboratory for Reconstruction. New Orleans became the first major southern city to experience property seizures by the Union, the gradual emancipation of enslaved persons, the eventual enfranchisement of men of color, and the implementation of formal racial integration. These profound social and political changes provide another example of New Orleans's unique position in the South. In this period, the federal government enforced liberal Republican policies in the South's largest city, which served as a harbinger of conflicts and resolutions, tensions and accomplishments that the nation as a whole experienced during Reconstruction and into the twentieth century.

In the first seven months of the occupation, General Benjamin Butler's enforcement of the federal Confiscation Acts against wealthy Confederates in New Orleans spawned immense resentment and animosity against the Union and Butler personally. The acts allowed the federal military to seize the property of those who refused to take an oath of loyalty to the United States. Union forces confiscated personal property for auction, as well as enslaved persons, who were officially designated as contraband. The corrupt and self-serving Butler acquired the name "Spoons Butler" for his seizure of silverware from New Orleans's elite families. His issuance of General Order No. 28, which labeled as a prostitute any woman who disrespected a Union officer, earned him even more vitriol and outrage from the city's anti-Yankee residents.

Butler's unpopularity led to his removal in December 1862, because the Republican administration hoped to win the hearts and minds of the city's resentful inhabitants. The wartime diary of teenager Clara Solomon reflects the experiences of those whose hearts softened during the occupation. Solomon, who grew up in a well-to-do Sephardic Jewish home, expressed complex views that mirrored many Jewish southerners' support of the white supremacist Confederate cause.

Initially, the teen was repulsed by the sight of "Yankee" soldiers and was afraid of the newly emancipated African Americans. But over time, she had favorable encounters with Union soldiers and came to appreciate their humanity. As she observed, children taunted the soldiers on Hercules Street in her Lower Garden District neighborhood by waving the rebel "Bonnie Blue" flag, and yet the soldiers seemed to "appreciate them" regardless. The impressionable teenager admitted, "I hear that their deportment has always been most gentlemanly, and I also heard that there were many handsome ones."[6]

With the Union occupation, self-emancipated persons from the plantations along the river sought refuge in New Orleans and the surrounding area. These newly freed persons flocked to Union military camps such as Camp Parapet in East Jefferson Parish, where the women served as washerwomen and nurses and the men as cooks, carpenters, and orderlies. Labeled as contraband, however, their official emancipated status remained in limbo.

Butler needed more troops to police the city, but the loyal volunteers of Irish and German immigrants made up only three regiments. Therefore, with the approval of the War Department, Butler created the 1st Louisiana Native Guards, the first regiment of African Americans in U.S. history. Jordan Noble, the well-respected musician and army veteran, recruited and organized the regiment, after initially forming regiments of free men of color under the Confederacy to avoid any threatened persecution for lack of fealty. In the enlistment process, recruiters did not ask whether the men were free or enslaved but equipped them with weapons confiscated from local rebel families.[7]

The Army used the Louisiana Native Guards only for guard, picket, and engineering duties during the fall of 1862. In the spring of 1863, the African American soldiers finally engaged in combat. One of the fiercest encounters occurred at the siege of Port Hudson north of Baton Rouge, part of the Union Army's campaign to control the Mississippi River and divide the Confederacy. On May 27, Captain André Cailloux and sixteen-year-old Lieutenant John Crowder died in the assault. Crowder and his mother, a free woman of color and seamstress, had moved in 1849 from Louisville to New Orleans, where she became active in the AME Church and educated her son. Despite his youth, Crowder's intelligence and ability enabled him to earn the rank of second lieutenant before he died in the assault.

Cailloux was born enslaved to the Duvernay family in Plaquemines Parish but was granted his freedom in 1846. He married a free woman of color, Félicie Coulon, and raised a family of four while working as a cigar maker and entrepreneur. A supporter of education and the local Institute Catholique for Afro-Creole children, Cailloux emerged as a leader in the community of free persons of color during the tense 1850s. His combat death at Port Hudson earned him the status of martyr locally and became a rallying cause for more recruitment of African American soldiers. On his widow's request, the French-born abolitionist priest Claude Paschal Maistre officiated his funeral at St. Louis Cemetery #2. The nationally syndicated *Harper's Weekly* published an illustration of the funeral procession, in which mourners lined the streets of the Tremé. This image provides the earliest depiction of a New Orleans funeral march led by a brass band.[8]

As part of the reconstruction of the South, in 1864 Louisiana was readmitted to the Union and held a gubernatorial election. Local Democrat Michael Hahn, a moderate loyal Unionist, won the election on the Republican ticket, at a time when Democrats' refusal to take oaths of loyalty caused their party to dwindle into oblivion. *Leslie's Illustrated* published an illustration of Hahn's well-attended inauguration at Lafayette Square, in which Patrick Gilmore, the composer of "When Johnny Comes Marching Home," led a massive brass band "monster concert" in an obvious attempt to appeal to the music-loving masses of the city.

Hahn had immigrated to New Orleans in the 1840s as a youth from the German Palatinate via New York. He rose in local Democratic circles when the party was reaching out to recent European immigrants in American cities. Hahn's victory made him the first German-born and ethnic Jewish governor in U.S. history. From 1864 to 1865, Hahn resided at the temporary Governor's Mansion in the Garden District, the home at 1448 Fourth Street known today as Colonel Short's Villa.[9]

Soon after the war's end, Afro-Creoles and African Americans in New Orleans made efforts to realize their goal of equal rights and political participation in a campaign that was part of the city's long history of civil rights activism. In the spring of 1867 Black men and boys protested the continued existence of segregated streetcars; mule-drawn cars for African American riders were then designated by the symbol of a star. The activists staged Rosa Parks–style sit-ins in the cars, and up to five hundred persons gathered for a peaceful protest at Congo Square. Given the potential for racial violence across the city, mayor Edward Heath implemented a policy of desegregation that lasted until 1902, when state law reinstituted legal segregation on public transport.[10]

Although New Orleans did not experience any street combat during the war years, much violence broke out on the city streets in the era of Reconstruction. During the military occupation that lasted until 1877, Union troops served as an arm of the Republican Party, enforcing martial law against the former Confederate Democrats. Those Democrats opposed federal efforts to implement a liberal agenda of racial equality and voting rights for African American males, based on the passage of the Fourteenth and Fifteenth Amendments to the U.S. Constitution.

The Mechanics Institute Riot of 1866, which spawned the city-wide event known as the New Orleans Massacre, exists as one of the most notorious and deadly racial conflicts in the nation during Reconstruction. In this incident, armed African American activists marched to the Mechanics Institute, at the site of present-day 130 Roosevelt Way, to draw up articles for the new Republican-backed state constitution that was intended to guarantee equal rights for all citizens. There, they encountered a white mob and militia of former Confederates, and the two groups engaged in combat; the white militia stormed the Mechanics Institute and attacked African Americans in the street.

The riot ended with 36 deaths and 114 wounded; nearly all the victims were freedmen. The violence made the headlines of national news journals; the cover of *Harper's Weekly* depicted a former rebel shooting point-blank at Reverend H. Horton, who is holding an American flag alongside a white flag of surrender (fig. 12). The riot reflected the profound racial and political tensions that existed not only in Louisiana but across the American South. The wanton violence of the white mob caused outrage among liberal Americans. In response, Radical Republicans in Congress imposed a strict form of Reconstruction on the former Confederacy, dividing the region into five military districts.[11]

Numerous armed conflicts erupted between the white militias and the Republican-backed Metropolitan Police during the Reconstruction years,

FIG. 12. This illustration of the New Orleans Riot of 1866 clearly conveys the brutality of political and racial violence that characterized the Reconstruction era in the city, as well as the national importance of New Orleans in shaping congressional policy at the time. Cover illustration from *Harper's Weekly*, August 25, 1866, Louisiana State Museum, 1984, 001.2.30.

as the Republican Party maintained political control of New Orleans with the support of newly enfranchised African American men. In 1869, however, it encountered resistance in conservative Jefferson City (present-day Faubourg Bouligny), just upriver from New Orleans. When the Metropolitan Police marched on the town to take over the police station, a pitched battle erupted with the white militia defenders, which resulted in a military occupation of the town. And in what could be viewed as a hostile takeover, Republican New Orleans annexed Democratic Jefferson City in 1870, and then Carrollton in 1874, thereby extending the city boundaries all the way to the current Orleans–Jefferson Parish line.

That same year, the Battle of Liberty Place erupted in what became the final pitched battle between the two forces. In this conflict, the Metropolitan Police sought to intercept a shipment of arms to the White League militia on the riverfront at the foot of Canal Street. Five thousand armed White League members faced off against the 3,600 Republican-backed troops on Canal Street. Overpowering the police and state militia, the White League laid siege to the city before federal troops arrived and retook control. Although the siege only lasted for a short time, the victory portended the collapse of Republican Reconstruction in New Orleans and the return of conservative white Democrats to power.[12]

By 1877, the national political crisis caused by the undecided 1876 presidential election resulted in the Hayes Compromise, in which Democrats acknowledged the victory of Republican candidate Rutherford Hayes as president in exchange for removing the last remaining federal troops from the occupied South. The departure of the troops led to the creation of a one-party system of conservative Democratic rule in New Orleans and across the South that lasted until the post–World War II years. Although some Republican parishes continued to exist into the 1880s, by the late 1890s Louisiana was solidly under control of the Democratic Party, which then passed laws enforcing racial segregation.

In this period of war and reconstruction, New Orleans experienced profound demographic and social changes. In the 1860s, the white population had declined by about 5,000 people due to combat losses in the war, and the city gained about 25,000 African Americans—most of whom were freed persons who sought new opportunities in the city. With emancipation, many white Creole families' wealth disappeared with the loss of their chattel property. Numerous Creole planters based in New Orleans were forced to sell their plantations to upstart American investors. With this decline in French Creole wealth, the formerly prestigious Vieux Carré lost its allure, and luxurious townhomes gradually transformed into immigrant tenements.

New Cotton

In the fall of 1872, French painter Edgar Degas visited the cotton factor offices of his extensive Creole family in New Orleans. During the cotton harvest season in the lower Mississippi River Valley, the city's docks filled with paddlewheel boats loaded with large bales of the white fiber from plantations upriver. The wharves of the cotton district in front of the American Sector teemed with African American roustabouts stacking and moving the bales for shipment to spinning mills in both the American Northeast and the west coast of Britain. Degas, who was later known for his impressionist paintings depicting Parisian scenes of French ballerinas, absinthe drinkers, and horse races, captured the activities in the New Orleans offices where his cousins judged the quality of cotton samples and recorded shipments while his uncle casually read the newspaper.

The busy scene belied the insecurity of Degas' uncle Michael Musson's business in postwar New Orleans; in fact, that business went bankrupt within a year of Degas' visit. The disruption of war had brought economic hardship, from which recovery proved elusive, and like many formerly well-to-do Creoles, Musson lost his fortune. During Reconstruction, he was forced to sell his beautiful Garden District sidehall townhome and rent a house on Esplanade Avenue in the downtown Creole neighborhood on the edge of the Tremé and Bayou Road. Although the young painter intended to portray a bustling American business for a European audience, his painting documented the fragility of the postwar cotton industry as the city struggled to regain its prewar economic status.[13]

In 1884 city boosters hosted a world's fair, billed as the Industrial and Cotton Centennial Exposition, to promote New Orleans as the economic hub of the post-Reconstruction "New South." The Expo nominally commemorated the hundredth anniversary of the cotton industry in Louisiana, dating to the Spanish era when the fiber first made its appearance in the colony. Ironically, the fair was held at the former site of the de Boré Plantation, where sugar was first granulated in the late 1790s and which was later developed in the 1890s as Audubon Park stretching from the river to stately St. Charles Avenue.[14] The famous illustration, "The City of New Orleans and the Mississippi River," promoted the fair from the bird's-eye perspective of the West Bank looking north over Uptown toward Lake Pontchartrain. The colorful print, updated from an 1850 illustration, depicts the uptown riverfront bustling with paddlewheel steamboats and three-masted ocean-going ships lining the wharves of the city. The Creole districts of the downtown neighborhoods remain in the background, as if they were but an inconsequential afterthought.[15]

Indeed, the city's economy and transportation system had become more diverse, industrial, and modern—moving beyond its antebellum reliance on the cotton and slave trades and river traffic. One year after the end of Reconstruction, the opening of the Eads Jetties at the mouth of the Mississippi proved an engineering feat that enabled maritime ships to enter the river without fear of being stranded on sandbars. By the late 1870s, New Orleans had once again become an important port center for grain shipments from the upper Mississippi Valley. At the same time, the city provided land grants to railroads, realizing that economic success required a modern commercial transportation network that could compete successfully with other Mississippi Valley and Great Lakes hubs such as St. Louis and Chicago. By the time of the World's Cotton Expo, a network of new rail lines crisscrossed the city and riverfront, connecting New Orleans to the Atlantic coast, up the Mississippi Valley, and westward to Texas.[16]

The cotton economy also modernized by becoming more industrial and streamlined. Before the war, New Orleans exported the majority of its raw cotton to the mills of Britain and New England. But the city now housed two of the largest urban cotton mills in the nation. The massive Lane Cotton Mills at Napoleon Avenue and the river opened in 1864, and the Maginnis Cotton Mills began operation in 1882 on the edge of the cotton district in the American Sector with some twelve thousand textile looms. A year after the New York Cotton Exchange opened in 1870, the New Orleans Cotton Exchange debuted in 1871 at 231 Carondelet, near Cotton Factor's Row (800–822 Perdido) where Michael Musson had his offices. The exchange streamlined operations for international brokers, and the development of futures trading in the market made New Orleans competitive with New York and Liverpool in the post-Reconstruction era.

Although old-line Creole families struggled in the postwar period, a wave of Americans and older Anglo-American families profited from the new economic model of "free" labor, railroads, and commodities exchanges. Politician and planter Duncan Kenner remained one of the wealthiest and most powerful figures after the war by embracing wage labor after emancipation, working with Republicans, and supporting African American suffrage as a pragmatic way to end Union occupation.

In the 1830s, Kenner had married Anne Bringier, a daughter of one of the wealthiest Creole families before the war that had gone bankrupt during Reconstruction. Kenner's accumulated capital enabled him to acquire his in-laws' vast property portfolio on the Sugar Coast, while keeping his offices at 257 Carondelet in New Orleans. Embracing the new economic model of cotton, Kenner founded the Louisiana Sugar Planters' Association in 1876 to serve as a lobbying arm for the two hundred wealthiest planters in the lower Mississippi Valley. The opening of the New Orleans Sugar Exchange in 1884 on Front and Bienville Streets in the Sugar District symbolized the economic sophistication of that industry as well.[17]

Kenner's embrace of the "New South" political order reflected the new economic structure that produced extreme wealth for those at the top of the pyramid in New Orleans. Along upper St. Charles Avenue and the Audubon Park district, large homes displayed the opulence that accompanied the new cotton economy. For example, William Smith, the president of the New Orleans Cotton Exchange at the turn of the century, built his impressive home on the large live-oak-shaded lot at 4534 St. Charles. Two blocks farther uptown, "Cotton King" William Perry Brown built his stately Romanesque Revival mansion at 4717 St. Charles Avenue. Brown had become one of the wealthiest men in the city based on his manipulation of cotton futures in 1903, when he and local cotton broker Franklin Brevard Hayne cornered the global market through the New Orleans Cotton Exchange.

In this era of modernization and industrialization, the city's infrastructure struggled to keep pace with residential and industrial development. Thomas Hardee's 1878 map of New Orleans illustrates how the city had settled all the available lands along the natural river ridge and along the Bayou Sauvage (Gentilly) Ridge (fig. 13). The map shows the area of Mid-City and all the lakefront and New Orleans East as undeveloped cypress swamp. But the plan also details the city's efforts to engineer a modern drainage system for the low-lying areas that filled with rainwater after heavy showers and storms. In two locations Hardee includes depictions of "draining machines," steam-powered paddlewheels that pushed water from Mid-City and the outer Seventh Ward through the Orleans and London Avenue "outfall"

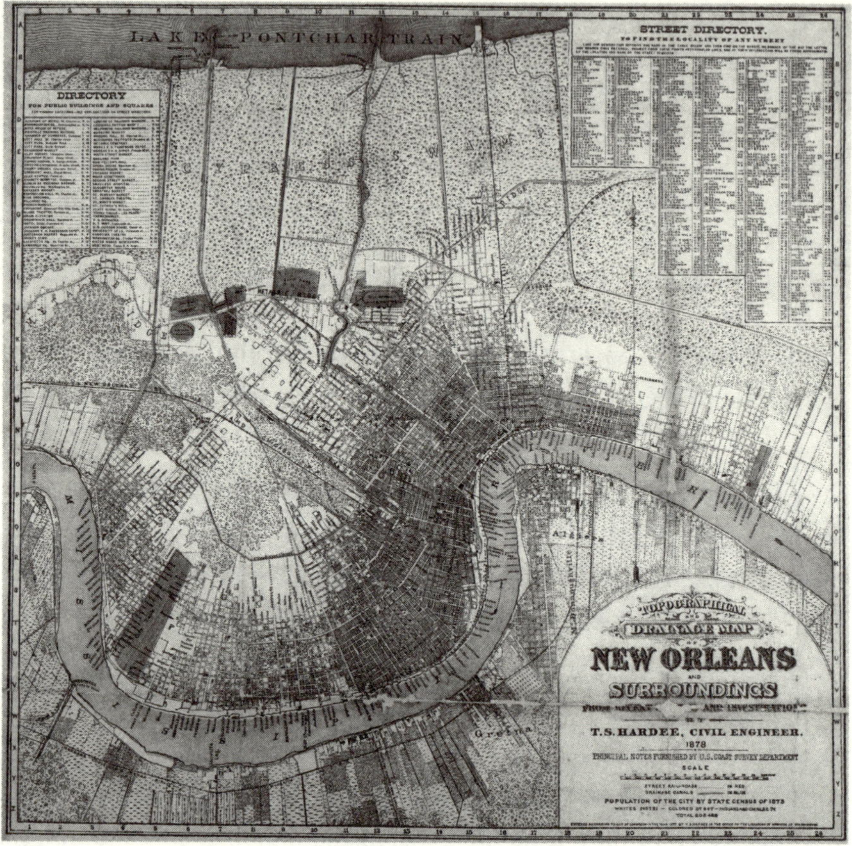

FIG. 13. This map illustrates how the city of New Orleans expanded to occupy all the naturally elevated sections along the river and bayou ridges by the late nineteenth century, while also portraying the uninhabited low-lying wetland areas of present-day Mid-City, Old Metairie, the Lakefront, New Orleans East, and the Lower Ninth Ward. T. S. Hardee, *Topographical Drainage Map of New Orleans and Surroundings,* 1878, Louisiana State Museum, 09379A.02.

canals to the lake. Because this draining method remained ineffective, however, these lowest-lying wetland areas remained undeveloped until the turn of the century.[18]

In the 1890s, New Orleans took important strides in water management with the appointment of a Drainage Advisory Board, which then created the Sewerage and Water Board. The new agency established a modern sewerage and drainage system and infrastructure for a modern water-purification system. But although wealthier neighborhoods along the tree-lined avenues received the amenities of modern plumbing and covered drainage canals, the poorer working-class communities struggled with unpaved streets, open ditches, and outhouses into the post–World War II era.[19]

Similarly, the arrival of electric power came in fits and starts to the commercial districts and eventually to wealthier neighborhoods in the 1880s and 1890s. The Southwestern Brush Electric Light and Power Company was chartered in 1883 as the first major provider of electricity in the city, which initially was used mostly for street lighting. Five years later, the Edison Electric Illuminating Company provided services for incandescent lighting and power. By 1900, more than two hundred companies operated in a confusing and inefficient marketplace.

Following this same chaotic model, the streetcar system in New Orleans was operated by six competing companies that went from using mule or steam power to electric propulsion in the 1890s. The St. Charles Street line, the oldest continually operating streetcar line in the city dating to 1836, became the first line to go electric in 1893, and others followed suit. By 1905, the six lines consolidated under the New Orleans Railway and Light company.

Passenger railroad service also existed in a marketplace of numerous competing interests. As the city became a railroad hub in the years after Reconstruction, three major stations connected passengers to regions across the nation. Union Station, built in the modern hip-roofed "Chicago School" style, opened in 1892 (1100 S. Rampart) to serve the Illinois Central Line to Chicago, as well as Southern Pacific's Sunset Limited to Los Angeles, which required passage across the Mississippi by railroad ferry. At the foot of Canal Street, where a modern shopping center is now located, the Louisville and Nashville built a station in 1902 that connected the city to Mobile and then much of the Great Lakes region. And in 1908, the Southern Railway opened its grand terminal at Basin and Canal (1125 Canal St.) that provided service to most major southern cities and as far north as Washington, DC. For many tourists coming from the Northeast, the famous Crescent line brought them to the heart of New Orleans; it terminated at the edge of the infamous Storyville red-light district, with its mansion brothels fronting the tracks on Basin Street.

The emergence of New Orleans's industrial economy in the Gilded Age coincided with the consolidation of conservative Democratic Party power and the rise of legal segregation. Although the city's power brokers often looked to the past for racial caste and labor models, the economy and the process of industrialization ushered in a very modern era based on new technologies. As mentioned, New Orleans's most important power brokers were American businessmen, and much of the city's residents in the downtown Creole districts, the working-class riverfront, and back-of-town neighborhoods uptown did not share in the wealth generated during this era. In these diverse neighborhoods that were patchworks of new immigrants, old immigrants, Creoles, and African Americans, the residents worked their day jobs and raised families in an era when labor unrest and racial animosity marked the reality of rough lives for many.

Relevant Historic Sites

St. Louis Cemetery #2 (section 1), 200 N. Claiborne Ave.: The burial site of numerous historically important African Americans from the Civil War, Reconstruction, and post-Reconstruction eras, including Henriette Delille, André Cailloux, Jordan Noble, Oscar Dunn, and Rodolphe Desdunes.

Chalmette National Cemetery, 8606 W. St. Bernard Hwy, Chalmette: Burial site of African American Union veterans from the Civil War era.

Spanish Fort (remains), 6400 Beauregard Ave.: The site of a Civil War fort and a lakefront resort in the post-Reconstruction era.

Factors Row, 800–822 Perdido: The central location of cotton merchants in the nineteenth century designed by Lewis Reynolds.

New Orleans Cotton Exchange Building, 231 Carondelet: Site of the original Cotton Exchange established in 1871. The current building was completed in 1921.

Plessy v. Ferguson Historical Marker, Press at Royal St.: Marker at the site of Homer Plessy's arrest in 1892.

Beauregard-Keyes House, 1113 Chartres St.: Greek Revival residence and historic house museum of the Giacona family, ca. 1900.

Notre Histoire

On June 7, 1892, Homer Plessy boarded an East Louisiana Railroad passenger car at the Press Street station in the lower Faubourg Marigny near the river. As a Creole of color, Plessy's presence in the whites-only car flouted the new state law requiring white and African American passengers to ride in separate cars. Plessy's light complexion enabled him to purchase his ticket without any objection. But when seated in the car, the porter J. J. Dowling acknowledged Plessy's racial status and asked him to move to the car reserved for "colored" passengers. Plessy's refusal to move caused Dowling to call on the station detective C. C. Cain to arrest him for violating state law.

Plessy's act of civil disobedience had been carefully planned by a local civil rights organization, Le Comité de Citoyens (Citizens Committee), to test the new segregation law and thereby challenge the legality of racial segregation on public transport. The Citizens Committee included members of New Orleans's Creole of color community, many of whom were active in pushing for equal rights during Reconstruction and who then battled against conservative whites' efforts to establish legal racial segregation after Reconstruction. The Separate Car Act passed in 1890 was only one of the many segregation laws enacted in the years after Reconstruction ended.[20]

Following the withdrawal of Republican-backed Union troops from New Orleans in 1877, the Democratic Party gradually assumed political control of local and state governments, undoing the racial equality efforts supported by the Republican Party. The socially liberal wing, known as the Radical Republicans, grew out of the abolitionist movement and sought equal rights for all U.S. citizens in the Reconstruction era. This liberal agenda came to fruition during the 1860s and 1870s in the context of a global emancipation movement and the rise of political republican democracy throughout Europe, Latin America, and the Caribbean.

Plessy had spent his youth in Reconstruction-era New Orleans experiencing a temporarily transformed society in which public transportation and schools were racially integrated, African American men exercised the right to vote, and interracial marriages were no longer prohibited. His family, like many other politically active Creoles of color, had arrived in New Orleans during the 1790s as free people of color fleeing the Haitian Revolution. Growing up in this community, Plessy earned his living in the shoemaking trade and lived in the Tremé with his wife, Louise Bordenave Plessy, whom he had wed at the St. Augustine Church in 1889. When Democrats outlawed racially integrated schools in 1879 and then defunded public education in the 1880s, Plessy became politically engaged in the issue of school reform.[21]

Creoles of color and African American activists in New Orleans organized to fight against the post-Reconstruction conservative reforms and the reversal of civil rights gains. In the Creole community, activists such as poet and historian Rodolphe Desdunes, attorney Louis A. Martinet, journalist Paul Trévigne, philanthropist Thomy Lafon, and Dr. Charles Louis Roudanez promoted the cause of civil rights through the media and through educational, political, and legal means.

In 1864, Roudanez founded *La Tribune de la Nouvelle Orléans*, the first daily African American newspaper in the United States. Paul Trévigne, who was the nephew of Catholic philanthropist Sister Henriette Delille, served as editor of *La Tribune*, which promoted political rights and racial equality for African Americans across the South until it ceased publication in 1870. During this time, Afro-Creole activists found common ground in supporting the Couvent School, the former Institute Catholique dedicated to educating orphans of color in the Creole district. They also organized politically under the Young Men's Progressive Association in the 1870s and then L'Union Louisianais in the 1880s.[22]

In committing the act of civil disobedience, Plessy emerged as a principal figure in the debate over civil rights not only in Louisiana but also across the United States. In Le Comité des Citoyens' fight against the Separate Car Act of 1890, their lawyer Albion Tourgée represented Plessy in the Orleans Parish Court, where presiding judge John H. Ferguson failed to dismiss the charges. Le Comité then sued Ferguson in a new case, *Plessy v. Ferguson*, in which the conservative Louisiana Supreme Court at the Cabildo unanimously ruled in favor of Judge Ferguson's dismissal. The activist organization appealed the case to the U.S. Supreme Court. In a landmark ruling, the highest court ruled 7–1 that Plessy's arrest did not violate the Fourteenth Amendment of the Constitution, thereby sanctioning racial segregation in the United States.

The ruling is often interpreted as "separate but equal," in terms of the law requiring segregated but equal public facilities including schools, transportation, and accommodations. The case gained national significance for enabling a legal pathway for white conservative state legislatures to enact segregation laws across the nation: it thereby ushered in the age of formal racial segregation, known euphemistically as "Jim Crow." Thereafter, segregation remained legal in the United States until 1954, when the Supreme Court overruled the Plessy decision in *Brown v. the Board of Education.*

The erosion of African American rights in the 1880s and 1890s occurred at a time when Creole culture became increasingly marginalized in New Orleans. Conservative white French Creoles, as exemplified by Louisiana historian Charles Gayarré, dreaded the idea of racial equality. They began to claim the term "Creole" as one designated for whites only, while identifying Afro-Creoles as mulatto.

Thus, white Creoles' cultural claim on the term coincided with the segregation of New Orleans society and the general designation of any Afro-Creole person as "Negro" in terms of civil and voting rights and social caste.[23] The new claim by whites resulted in the confusing and ever-shifting definition of the term *Creole,* which originated in the sixteenth century as a Spanish-Portuguese term (*Criollo/Crioulo*) designating any person born in the Americas regardless of ethnic identity.

Afro-Creole activists including Rodolphe Desdunes continued to push back against what they saw as whites' ridiculous claim of ownership of the term *Creole.* In 1895 he completed his book *Nos Hommes et Notre Histoire* (published in 1911), which chronicled the historic contributions of Afro-Creole New Orleanians in the arts, the military, sciences, literature, and education. Desdunes's book followed in the wake of Armand Lanusse's book *Les Cenelles,* published in 1845, heralded as the first African American poetry anthology produced in the United States. As the founder of the Institute Catholique Creole in 1848, Lanusse served as an important inspiration for postwar activists. Regarding Afro-Creole costuming traditions of New Orleans from this era, the oldest formally organized Black Masking Indian group, the Creole Wild West, claimed to have chosen its name after viewing Buffalo Bill's Wild West show in New Orleans in the 1880s.[24]

In the late nineteenth and early twentieth centuries, the French-speaking Afro-Creole community and English-speaking African American community remained culturally divided in their social activities, churches, and schools. But several African American activists did fight to maintain civil rights after the war and into the post-Reconstruction era. Military veterans Jordan

Noble and James Ingraham became politically active in local and state government. Noble, who had helped recruit soldiers for the Louisiana Native Guards, became president of the Convention of Colored Men of Louisiana, which held its convention in New Orleans in 1865. Ingraham, who succeeded André Cailloux as the captain of E Company in the Native Guards, was elected state senator from Orleans Parish. Ingraham also cofounded the Central Congregational United Church in Christ, which provided a meeting place for African American politicians in the Reconstruction era.

The biracial Louisiana Unification Movement was founded during Reconstruction by moderate white and Black leaders to find a path to political unity and racial advancement in the city. Emerging from the Reform Party in 1872, the organization included both Democrats and Republicans who abhorred the violence and corruption endemic to the times. Creole activist and *Le Tribune* owner Charles Louis Roudanez lent his support to the cause, while Jewish businessman Isaac Marks served as chairman. Former Confederate general and St. Bernard sugar planter P. G. T. Beauregard served as president of the group's committee of resolutions, which issued a remarkable statement calling for full social and political equality for the state's residents. Although Beauregard had ordered the first Confederate shot fired in the Civil War, his political activism after the war endorsed civil and voting rights for African Americans.[25]

Despite the efforts of the Reform Party and Unification Movement, the return of conservative Democrats to power after 1877 eroded Reconstruction-era strides toward racial equality and voting rights. The state legislature passed laws that segregated schools in the late 1870s and public transport in 1890. In 1898, the overtly white-supremacist state constitution required poll taxes to be paid annually, decreasing state voter rolls from nearly 204,000 in 1896 to 76,870 in 1900. Drafted largely by conservative businessmen and planters, the constitution represented the culmination of post-Reconstruction era racial conservatism and resulted in significant political disfranchisement for both Black and white voters that remained until the Huey Long era in the 1930s.

In the 1880s, the city also began to create monuments to Confederate heroes. A large column supporting a statue of Robert E. Lee was erected in 1884 at the former Tivoli Circle on St. Charles Avenue. Seven years later, the city placed a monument on Canal Street honoring the White League's casualties in the Battle of Liberty Place. In 1910 the city named the new wide avenue in Mid-City for Jefferson Davis and placed a statue of its namesake in its neutral ground. These monuments were intended to nominally commemorate the sentimental Confederate "Lost Cause" of the Civil War. In reality, however, these memorials celebrated the defeated rebels' complete political control and their cause of white supremacy in New Orleans and across the South.

A King Like Me

In 1898, the *Blue Book* guide to the brothels of New Orleans advertised the luxurious Mahogany Hall at 235 Basin Street. Considered to be the most opulent of New Orleans's brothels, the mansion boasted marble floors and stained-glass windows, as well as five parlors and fifteen *en suite* bedrooms catering to wealthy white men. Many of the men were tourists—sex tourists in the notoriously decadent and exotic New Orleans. In the era of formal racial segregation, the allure of illicit interracial sex appealed to rich businessmen and professionals, who sought the exoticism synonymous with the southern city of sin. The brothels also promoted the services of New Orleans's finest women; like the nearby mansion of "Countess" Willie Piazza at 317 Basin Street, Mahogany Hall highlighted liaisons with octoroons, a colonial-era term used to designate a person of one-eighth African ancestry. The juxtaposition of segregation and sexual power in Storyville reflected Jim Crow's contradiction of separate but equal.

Lulu White, the owner of Mahogany Hall, and Willie Piazza promoted their status as New Orleans octoroons largely as a marketing gimmick, since they grew up in rural Alabama and Mississippi, respectively. White was one of the wealthiest independent businesswomen in New Orleans, and her status as a woman of color operating the fanciest mansion of prostitution in the city underscored the contradictions inherent within the formal system of segregation at the time. Similarly, many of the women who advertised as octoroons in the infamous *Blue Book* were also likely not from the exotic backgrounds they claimed.[26]

The brothels operated in the legally sanctioned red-light district known as Storyville. Named after city alderman Sidney Story, who sought to control and consolidate prostitution in the city, the district existed from 1897 to

1917, when the U.S. military forced its closure as the United States entered World War I. Story's efforts to control prostitution reflected the new impulse for reform that emerged from the debris of the post-Reconstruction era when labor unrest, child welfare, alcoholism, and prostitution were considered major ills of society.

In this era of formal segregation, African American men were permitted to work in the white Storyville but were prohibited from being customers. The African American tenderloin district existed uptown across Canal Street in the mixed African American and Jewish neighborhood along Perdido, Liberty, and South Rampart Streets. Louis Armstrong, who grew up in the neighborhood, remarked, "Life was just about the same [there] as it was in Storyville except that the chippies were cheaper." And as he recalled, "Our hustlers sat on their steps and called to the 'Johns' as they passed by. They had to keep an eye out for the cops all the time, because they were not allowed to call the tricks like the girls in Storyville."[27]

In a landmark civil rights case from early 1917 before Storyville was shut down, Willie Piazza filed suit against the city of New Orleans, contesting a new city law that prohibited African American women from working in "White Storyville." The new rule would have required Piazza to relocate her brothel to "Black Storyville." In her lawsuit, Piazza was joined by Lulu White and twenty other women of color who sought to protect their investments and resented the possibility of a forced relocation to the less prestigious back-of-town area above Canal Street. After the city denied her suit, Piazza appealed her case to the Louisiana Supreme Court. In an irony befitting the racial contradictions of Jim Crow, the very conservative higher court ruled in Piazza's favor, thereby allowing those successful African American women to continue operating in the segregated white Storyville.[28]

The fascination with the exotic, as exemplified by the marketing of octoroons in Storyville, was also reflected in the themes of Carnival and the appreciation for Latin American music in this era. The first formal Carnival organization, that of the Mistick Krewe of Comus, was founded in 1857, inspired by the older Cowbellians New Year's Eve parade in Mobile, Alabama. Comus presented the first parade to use mule-drawn floats on a formally sanctioned route. The Krewe of Momus followed in 1871, and the following year the new Krewe of Rex presented the "King of Carnival," enabling its elite white members to mimic European royalty for a day.

The birth of the formal Carnival parade reflected elite New Orleanians' desire to bring order to the Catholic holiday, which had been celebrated historically in the city as a day of unorganized costuming and chaotic frivolity. Popular costume designs in the Reconstruction era satirized Charles Darwin and northern "carpetbaggers," whereas the costume and ball themes of the later nineteenth century idealized the exoticism of East Asia and Indigenous Latin America.

In this era of white global imperialism and racial segregation, New Orleans well-to-do white men often embraced ancient and romanticized themes. On the invitations to their krewe's exclusive balls, one sees colorful illustrations depicting ancient European royalty; Greek, Roman, and Egyptian mythology; tropical and desert scenes; exotic wild animals; and idealized and sexualized women in a fantasy world for New Orleans's wealthiest residents.

In 1909, the Zulu Social Aid and Pleasure Club organized the first African American parade with decorated floats and an African-inspired theme. Originally calling themselves the Tramps, the parade's founders were inspired by the vaudeville production, "There Never Was and Will Be a King like Me." The club subsequently adopted the costume of a Zulu warrior wearing black face paint, a curly-haired wig, and a grass skirt.

The Zulu king is often characterized as a satire of Rex's King of Carnival. Where Rex acted like a benevolent ruler, majestically waving his jeweled scepter to the crowds along the route, King Zulu wore a crown made out of a lard can and held a banana-stalk scepter while engaging the crowd in banter and self-deprecating humor. Louis Armstrong, who watched the first Zulu parades as a youth in his neighborhood, recalled, "The members march to the good jumping music of the brass bands, while the king on his throne scrapes and bows to the cheering crowds."[29]

In the Jim Crow era, the very existence of the Zulu parade made an important statement about the public presence of African Americans in New Orleans. Although the Zulu procession was not officially sanctioned by the city, the club proclaimed its right to stage a spectacle on the backstreets of "Black Storyville," the Tremé, and the Lower Garden District. The notion of an African American king emphasized the pride that many African American New Orleanians had in the entertaining comedic parade. Furthermore, wearing blackface and curly wigs and straw skirts not only reappropriated the demeaning depiction of Black people from minstrel shows and vaudeville but also provided an inexpensive way to costume. Their signature hand-decorated coconuts presented an affordable means of giving one-of-a-kind "throws" to the adoring spectators.

The popularity of Carnival parades in this era also reflects New Orleans's appreciation and love for a procession of any type, but especially those led by a marching brass band. John Philip Sousa was the country's most popular band leader and composer of this era. His enduring compositions "Washington Post March" and "Stars and Stripes Forever" fostered the marching band phenomenon that swept small towns and larger cities alike during the late nineteenth century.

In New Orleans, the city embraced military brass band performances and parades, as exemplified in the 1863 funeral procession of André Cailloux, and by the "monster concert" performance of Patrick Gilmore at Michael Hahn's inauguration in 1864. Later in the nineteenth century, the city hosted the (mostly) white Fischer's Band and Jack Laine's Reliance Brass Band, as well as Joseph Othello Lainez's Onward Brass Band and Théogène Baquet's Excelsior Band—both made up of formally trained Afro-Creole musicians. Importantly, these marching bands included many younger musicians who became the founding generation of jazz performers.

The popularity of the "Mexican bands" in New Orleans during this period also reflects New Orleans's historic Latin American cultural connections and the city's affinity for melodic music from Spanish-speaking nations to the South. The city's World Cotton Centennial held in 1884 had a Mexican exhibit, which featured the Mexican 8th Cavalry Band orchestra, popularly called "the Mexican band."

Composer Juventino Rosas's famous waltz "Sobre Las Olas" (Over the Waves) made its U.S. debut at the exposition and later became a standard in New Orleans jazz and a popular song to accompany circuses and trapeze acts. Following the expo, many of the band's musicians remained in the city, likely taking advantage of New Orleans's affinity for "Spanish" music. The local music publisher Junius Hart issued a very popular "Mexican Series" of compositions, underscoring the city's unique musical heritage and tastes.[30]

During the 1890s and 1900s, the lakefront resorts at West End and Spanish Fort hosted summer concerts and dances featuring variations of "Mexican bands," as well as an orchestra led by New Orleans–born professor

George Adrian Paoletti. These social events featured a variety of operatic themes and popular dances of the time, such as polkas, schottisches, one-steps and two-steps, waltzes, and dances associated with ragtime music.

Musicians such as George Paoletti were among the cross section of European and Latin American musical immigrants who moved to the largest southern city, drawn by its musical diversity and sophistication. The French Opera House, which opened in 1859 in the Vieux Carré, cemented New Orleans's status as one of the leading opera performance centers of the Western Hemisphere; opera and formal concert music remained popular with all levels of New Orleans society into the early 1900s.

Whereas the lakefront amusement parks catered to white crowds seeking to cool off amidst the shoreline breezes, African Americans in New Orleans visited the Lincoln and Johnson Parks on Carrollton Avenue: they featured hot-air balloon rides, a skating rink, and sporting, musical, and dancing entertainment. Some of the early ragtime–jazz artists, including Buddy Bolden, performed at the parks in the formative years of the distinct New Orleans jazz style.

At the turn of the century, the city began to produce and publish the newer styles of music. Ragtime, which had begun as a syncopated piano-based music form in the Mississippi Valley, gradually was adapted to performance by brass bands and dance bands pioneered by a younger generation in New Orleans. The first-ever published blues song, "I Got the Blues," was composed by New Orleanian Italian immigrant Anthony Maggio in 1910 and deftly combined a blues chords formation with a ragtime song structure. Maggio's composition based on African American song forms reflects the social intersections that defined the era of both racial segregation and Sicilian immigration.

Eleven Sicilians

George Paoletti was perhaps the best-known New Orleanian of Italian descent in the post-Reconstruction age. His musician father Joseph and his mother, Tasilda Tena, had emigrated from Italy to New Orleans before the Civil War, at a time when most European immigrants arrived from Ireland, Germany, and France. After Reconstruction, New Orleans witnessed a second wave of immigrants, who differed from the antebellum wave in having origins in eastern Europe, the Mediterranean Basin, and southeast Asia. But like those in the previous wave, many of these newer immigrants continued to reinforce the city's Catholic religious orientation and culture. From the 1870s to the years before World War I, families migrated from Sicily, Albania, Croatia, (Maronite) Lebanon, the Philippines, and the Guangdong (Canton) Province of southwestern China. Ashkenazi Jews also came to New Orleans, escaping persecution and the feudal economies of eastern Europe and Russia.

After the Civil War, sugar plantations along the lower river sought new sources of workers. The managers recruited workers from both Italy and China, believing that these immigrants would be easier to control and perhaps less demanding than freed persons, many of whom sought to move to New Orleans or to earn their living as independent farmers.

The Millaudon Plantation, for example, on the West Bank directly across from uptown New Orleans, recruited Cantonese laborers from Cuba and California to work the sugarcane fields in 1870 (fig. 14). One of the largest plantations in the state before the Civil War, Millaudon had been recently acquired by northern investors. Other plantations along the river and west to the Atchafalaya Basin also recruited a Chinese workforce in an age when cheap Chinese laborers were exploited "coolies." By 1871, the Boston-based newspaper *Every Saturday* reported that most Chinese workers were already dissatisfied with the poor pay and working conditions on the plantations.

Refusing to negotiate with their employers, the Cantonese workers simply left the plantations to find work building levees or as cigar rollers, a skill many had picked up in Cuba. Chinese merchants who catered to the new immigrants soon arrived in New Orleans; there they opened restaurants and laundry services, a trade acquired in the mining and railroad camps of the American West. So many Cantonese immigrants arrived that one newspaper proclaimed them a "Chinese Invasion." Despite the transient nature of the workforce, many of the new immigrants settled in New Orleans, where a small Chinatown developed in the area of South Rampart and Common Streets, on the edge of Louis Armstrong's back-of-town neighborhood.[31]

Filipino and Chinese fishermen also settled in the marshes and bays south of New Orleans in this period. The first Filipino fishers arrived before the Civil War; many were former sailors attracted to the subtropical wetland environment that was similar to their former homes in the Philippines.

FIG. 14. This illustration of Chinese workers at the Millaudon sugarcane plantation (present-day Marrero) depicts how northern investors recruited new laborers to replace emancipated African American workers during Reconstruction. Alfred Waud, "Chinese Cheap Labor in Louisiana—Chinamen at Work on the Millaudon Sugar Plantation," Historic New Orleans Collection, 1974.25.26.259.

They lived as subsistence fishermen. In the days before motorized trawlers, catching shrimp was labor intensive. On the coastal marshes, the Filipinos, as did the French before them, laid out their catch in nets in their rowboats and hauled them to shore; there, men pulled the heavy nets onto dry ground where the shrimp and fish were harvested.

Today, one often finds small packets of dried shrimp at grocery store checkout counters across New Orleans and southeast Louisiana. According to historian Winston Ho, this product can be traced to the process of shrimp dehydration developed by Chinese fishers in the late nineteenth century. The fresh shrimp were laid out on a large flat deck and left to dry in the hot sun. When the shrimp were fully dry, men danced on them to crack and remove the outer shells before packaging. Dehydration today is accomplished through mechanized shrimp dryers.[32]

Nineteenth-century illustrations of Filipino and Chinese settlements south of New Orleans depict villages built on tall wooden pilings that raised the buildings well above the tide level. In 1883 writer Lafcadio Hearn visited the Filipino village of San Maló on the east shore of Lake Borgne in St. Bernard Parish, where Juan San Maló's maroon community resided in the Spanish era. The five illustrations published in *Harper's Weekly* to accompany Hearn's article show modest wooden homes built on stilts and incorporating the large galleries and hipped roofs of the West Indies Creole style.

The origins of this Filipino fishing community are not well documented, but one legend holds that survivors of a Spanish galleon wreck established this settlement. After San Maló was destroyed in a hurricane in 1915, Manila Village in lower Barataria Bay became the most well-known Filipino wetland settlement in the twentieth century; it was photographed extensively in the 1930s.[33]

The construction technique of using raised pilings was common in much of Southeast Asian coastal architecture, where elevated homes are built well above normal tide levels. The raised-floor design is also found in the historic Creole coastal communities of West Africa and in eastern Latin America and the Caribbean during the colonial era. Coastal fishing camps in the marshes of south Louisiana continue to be built on stilts, which raises the question of the origins of this architectural style in the region.

The inspiration for this building technique in the region is still debated. Although *lacustres* (raised homes on pilings) existed along lakes in the Préalpes of eastern France and Switzerland, no such tradition exists in Atlantic French architecture. In the Les Landes (moors) region of Gascony in southwest France, the boggy ground required shepherds to walk on stilts across the marshes. Yet, even in this wet environment, Gascon residents constructed their wooden cabins on natural ridges using stone blocks, and not on stilts, to raise them above the wet ground.[34]

The method of raising buildings found in Les Landes was used by the early French settlers and Creoles when they built cabins and cottages in the rural areas of south Louisiana (and colonial French New Orleans). But at least from the nineteenth century on, the resident Cajun and Indigenous inhabitants of the coastal marshes realized the advantage of pilings and adopted that elevated design.

With the collapse of the Habsburg Empire at the turn of the century,

Croatian men immigrated to New Orleans, where they also became integral to the fishing culture of the region. They settled in the lower river communities of Buras, Empire, Olga, and Port Sulphur in Plaquemines Parish. French oyster fishers had certainly harvested oysters commercially on the Louisiana coast in the nineteenth century. Yet, the new Croatian immigrants had generations of experience cultivating oysters and are credited with developing the modern commercial industry among the marshes south of New Orleans. In the era before modern pumps and dredges, both Croatian men and women seeded the oyster beds with shovels and then harvested them by hand with tongs.

Some Croatians also settled in New Orleans, where they later opened wholesale and retail seafood shops, as well as restaurants. Coming from a country where the Catholic Church was very strong, the immigrants brought their deep faith with them to historically Catholic New Orleans. And because Carnival was celebrated in their native lands, the local observance of the season was comforting, along with Saint Anthony's Day in July. The Croatians also continued to revere the saints and celebrate the holidays associated with their villages in the home country. Thus, they added a new layer of Catholic culture to New Orleans's unique mix of traditions.[35]

As a wave of eastern Mediterranean peoples from the Ottoman Empire sought new lives in the Americas, Maronite Lebanese and Orthodox Greek immigrants were attracted to New Orleans, one of the United States' major ports of entry. The Maronite rite is one of many liturgical traditions within the Catholic Church. Once in New Orleans, these Lebanese migrants occasionally attended services led by traveling Maronite priests. However, in most cases, they were simply absorbed into existing Catholic parishes throughout the city and surrounding region. Many of the new immigrants became traveling merchants and eventually opened retail stores, in which women played an important role in the sale of merchandise.

As Arabic and French speakers, the Maronites kept a low profile in New Orleans. But many family names such as Moises, Reggie, Khoury, and Mahfouz are still found in New Orleans and the surrounding region today. Were these Arabic speakers accepted and their rights as Americans respected in segregated New Orleans?

As with other new immigrants, the Maronites' ability to register to vote and assimilate likely depended on their educational level, ability to speak

English, social networks, and even their physical characteristics. An interesting example of social segregation is the "Arabian" section of the historically African American cemetery of Mount Olivet in Gentilly, which was established around the time of World War I. Although many Maronites found acceptance in white Catholic parishes, the process of assimilation—or not—for Middle Eastern immigrants in the era of racial segregation remains largely unexplored.[36]

Greek Orthodox immigrants, along with other Eastern Orthodox Christians from Turkey, Syria, and the Balkans, also settled in New Orleans and surrounding areas during this post-Reconstruction era. Greeks had in fact been living in New Orleans as early as the Spanish period, when Athens-born Michel Dragon (Draco) served as an officer in the Spanish military. He also maintained a relationship with free woman of color Marie Françoise Chauvin Beaulieu de Montplaisir, whom he initially could not marry because of the "O'Reilly Code." Esteemed Mexican artist José Salazar painted the portraits of both Michel Dragon and his daughter Marianne Celeste Dragon, who is depicted wearing a beautiful blue dress and holding a bouquet of delicate white and pink flowers. Marianne, who was baptized as white, married Greek-born Andre Dimitry, thereby establishing the first Greek community in the city.

The Orthodox community established the Holy Trinity Greek Orthodox Church in 1864, the first Orthodox Christian church in the Americas. Parishioners first held services at the Bayou Road home of Chios native Nicholas Benachi. Then, in 1867 Holy Trinity's church building opened at 1222 North Dorgenois in the Tremé, around the corner from the Degas-Musson home on Esplanade Avenue. At that time, the small community of Orthodox Christians in the city lived along Bayou Road and Esplanade Avenue, as the Tremé evolved into a mixed neighborhood of Creoles of color and more recent Italian and Eastern Orthodox immigrants.[37]

During Reconstruction, the city witnessed a massive influx of new Italian immigrants, the majority of whom came from the southern island of Sicily. Like the earliest Chinese settlers, the Sicilians arrived through sugar planter recruitment schemes to replace African American workers. Also like the Chinese, the Sicilian immigrants found the conditions intolerable and soon quit for higher-paying jobs. Many families began operating truck farms in Jefferson and the River Parishes, forming a distribution network to supply produce to the French Market in New Orleans. Those in Tangipahoa Parish developed strawberry farms: by the early twentieth century that area had emerged as an important center of strawberry cultivation in the American Southeast.

Many of the new Sicilians also settled in the Vieux Carré, marking a transformation of the city's oldest neighborhood. The prestigious community had been home to wealthy Creoles in the pre–Civil War era, but the postwar period was characterized by the subdividing of older homes into inexpensive tenement apartments. The neighborhood gradually became known as "Little Sicily" or "Little Palermo," reflecting the origins of the new residents. As one of the least expensive areas in New Orleans at that time, many African Americans moving to the city from surrounding rural parishes also settled in the Vieux Carré, which led to the development of close ties between Sicilians and Black New Orleanians in this period.

The Sicilian immigrants added their cultural imprint onto the lower French Quarter, which developed into a distinct neighborhood. Those immigrants from the dry, rocky, and hilly environs of Palermo, where the sea is a deep blue, had to adjust to the humid climate, muddy bayous, and lush vegetation of south Louisiana. But at least those who lived in the Vieux Carré likely felt at home with the Mediterranean-style architecture, which featured iron balconies and galleries and cool courtyards that remained cut off from the noisy and bustling streets.

At the turn of the century, Italian produce sellers operated the stalls at the old French Market and ran corner-store markets in neighborhoods throughout the historic districts. Their growing dominance of the produce trades reflected the networks that Sicilians had maintained with their home country, as well as the truck farms their families operated in the surrounding parishes. Numerous Sicilian-owned macaroni factories also operated in the neighborhood. At 617 Ursuline Street one can still see the original entrance tiles of the first café of Angelo Brocato, known for its home-made cannoli, the crunchy cream-filled Sicilian pastry. Around the corner at 1116 Chartres Street is St. Mary's Chapel attached to the Old Ursuline Convent. There Sicilians attended mass, although the stations of the cross remained in the original French language of the previous Creole residents.[38]

The raised Greek Revival house at 1113 Chartres across the street from St. Mary's, known today as the Beauregard-Keyes House, was the residence of the Giacona family. Patriarch Pietro Giacona owned a successful business selling wine out of the family house. One night in 1908, four men from the

Black Hand racketeering gang, a new criminal element that arrived with the southern Italian immigrant wave, confronted Giacona at his home: the incident ended in bloodshed with three of the men dead. Even though locals praised Giacona and his son for defending themselves against the gang, the father and son were nevertheless indicted for murder. In the court, a jury found the two men not guilty, and they continued to live at their home until the 1920s.[39]

The early Sicilian history in New Orleans is one of families, like all immigrants, seeking a chance to establish a new life or to return home with enough money to build a better life in their homeland. However, local media and legends often sensationalized the role of organized crime in the history of Sicilians. Both Creoles and Americans may have held their own cultural biases against the new immigrants from all backgrounds, and by the 1890s social tensions rose to a fevered pitch.

The murder of New Orleans police chief David Hennessy in 1890 culminated in a well-publicized trial that led to a New Orleans social and political calamity. Although New Orleanians distrusted and looked down on Irish immigrants before the Civil War, Chief Hennessy was upheld as a revered and trusted law enforcement official for battling Sicilian vice in the city. Hennessy's assassination by an unknown assailant came as shocking news and unleashed an unprecedented vitriol against recent Italian immigrants.

Following the sensationalized trial in 1891, in which the jury acquitted the eleven men charged, an outraged mob formed at the Henry Clay statue on Canal Street at St. Charles Avenue and then marched on the Orleans Parish Prison in the Tremé. The mostly white crowd stormed the prison, seizing the eleven Sicilians and dragging them from their cells. In their frenzied quest for vigilante justice, the mob lynched two of the men and executed the others in the prison. This incident is indicative of the social tensions that plagued New Orleans in the late nineteenth and early twentieth centuries as segregation and white supremacy became legalized. Yet the murder of the eleven Sicilian men represents the uncommon occurrence of mob justice against Europeans during this period of social unrest.

Mob rule also reigned nine years later in the incident known as the Robert Charles Riot of July 1900. A wave of racial violence swept through the city in the hot summer days after African American militant Robert Charles killed a policeman during a confrontation near a Garden District home and then shot and killed two more policemen when they came to serve a warrant for his arrest at his residence on Fourth Street. As the news spread, white mobs formed and began attacking, beating, and killing random innocent African Americans across the city, while Charles fled to a building in the 1200 block of Saratoga Street. After police discovered his hideout, they set fire to the building, and Charles died while attempting to escape. The mob mutilated Charles's body and then continued their rampage, burning the Thomy Lafon School and a second Black school.[40]

Although the city generally maintained a reputation for social tolerance and Old World charm, in the Gilded Age of the late nineteenth century, New Orleans's social tensions reflected the grim reality of a society in which incidents like the murder of Chief Hennessy and Robert Charles's killing of several police lit the fuse on a powder keg of ethnic and racial friction. On a day-to-day basis, the residents of New Orleans worked and lived together humanely and cooperatively. But in response to actions that challenged the notion of white supremacy and law and order, white mobs unleashed their unbridled fury and violence.

Yet, in this same period before World War I, many African Americans and Italians in New Orleans worked and lived together and bonded over their shared plight of social marginalization. The Tremé developed into a Black and Sicilian community like the adjacent French Quarter. Some of the earliest Sicilian American jazz musicians such as Sharkey Bonano, Tony Parenti, and Louis Prima became enamored with the hot style of Black New Orleans music. While growing up in the Tremé, Prima followed the second-line parades and idolized and copied the style of Louis Armstrong. Conversely, African American costumers in the Mardi Gras Indian tradition began to conclude their masking season on the evening of March 19, St. Joseph's Day, which honors the patron saint of Sicily who provided nourishment to those in need. Even today, Italian homes and bars and Catholic parishes host a St. Joseph's altar during the day, and African American Indian maskers parade on the backstreets of the older neighborhoods in the evening.

Foodways: The Creolization of Mediterranean Food Traditions

The term "Italian Creole" is used to describe the adaptation of Italian culinary traditions to local south Louisiana ingredients and tastes. The creation of New Orleans–specific dishes rooted in Sicilian food customs represents the city's food culture evolution beyond its foundation of French-Senegalese-Spanish-Congolese creolized food traditions that marked the first two hundred years of New Orleans's foodways.

One might focus on the muffuletta sandwich or stuffed eggplant or stuffed artichokes to represent Italian Creole foodways in New Orleans. The history of the muffuletta is recounted in the next chapter. A hearty sandwich developed in the "Little Palermo" section of the French Quarter during the early twentieth century, the muffuletta remains a distinctive Sicilian-inspired food from New Orleans.

Stuffed artichokes and stuffed eggplant are also staples of Sicilian Creole foodways. The former is made by stuffing a mixture of breadcrumbs, southern Italian cheese, herbs, and garlic into the spaces between the leaves of a whole boiled artichoke and then baking the prepared dish until the stuffing mixture is golden brown. Because the artichoke is indigenous to the Mediterranean Basin and serves as the base of many foods from the region, stuffed artichokes reflect the process of creolization in which the southern Italian foodway became identified with New Orleans cuisine.

Stuffed eggplant, which is found through the Mediterranean from North Africa to southern Italy and Greece, is another dish that has become identified with the New Orleans Creole tradition. One can find these dishes on the menus of New Orleans's old-school Sicilian Creole restaurants such as Liuzza's, Pascal's Manale, and Mandina's, along with classic Italian Creole items such as oyster and artichoke soup, cream of artichoke and shrimp soup, or pasta with eggplant and shrimp sauce covered in fried eggplant medallions. These foods are essentially Italian Creole in their blending of traditional Sicilian ingredients and recipes with locally sourced seafood.[41] Many of these dishes evolved during the twentieth century when Sicilian Creole restaurants became integrated into the local food landscape and culture.

Croatian restaurants also emerged as an essential aspect of the local culinary identity. Most residents of New Orleans are less familiar with Croatian culinary traditions, but oysters are central to the heritage of coastal Croatia, and mollusks from the fishing region of Ston, near Dubrovnik, are now internationally known for their taste and quality. *Gregada,* a simple fish (and potato) soup associated with the historic port town of Hvar, is considered a staple of the region's seafood culinary traditions dating back to Greek settlement two thousand years ago. The Croatian fish stew *brodet* could be considered a variation of Marseillaise bouillabaisse or Louisiana Creole court-bouillon.

Drago's, a restaurant founded by the Cvitanovich family in the 1960s, is a great example of Croatian Creole cuisine. Their signature dish of char-broiled or grilled oysters has since been adapted by restaurants across the city and suburbs and has become increasingly appreciated well beyond south Louisiana.

Grilled oysters represent the classic creolization of Mediterranean food traditions. The oyster industry based largely in Plaquemines Parish is dominated by Croatian Creoles. Tommy Cvitanovich grew up working in his family's restaurant; he created the recipe for grilled oysters by adding what he views as the ingredients of classic Italian garlic bread—butter, garlic, and Parmesan cheese—to oysters grilled over an open flame cooked in their own salty brine. Although Tommy sees the ingredients as Italian, the dish is quite similar to *gratiné de coquillage,* the traditional dish of broiled shellfish (covered in a mixture of butter, garlic, herbs, and breadcrumbs and/or cheese) found on the Mediterranean coast of southern France.

Grilled Oysters (Oysters Gratinée)

Although the dish of grilled oysters is in many ways a modern feature of New Orleans culinary traditions, its evolution and recipe are quintessentially Mediterranean Creole. The recipe created by Tommy Cvitanovich builds on the French culinary tradition of *gratinée* or *au gratin,* where the main ingredients are baked or broiled, with a covering of breadcrumbs or cheese creating a golden crust that locks in the flavors. This dish is representative of this period of New Orleans history in its blending of French, Italian, and Croatian inspirations with locally sourced seafood.

Serves 6

24 fresh shucked oysters—loosened in their half-shells
¾ cup melted butter
3 tablespoons finely chopped garlic
1 teaspoon cayenne powder
1 teaspoon oregano
⅛ cup pastis (anise-flavored spirit)
¼ cup breadcrumbs
¼ cup grated Parmesan and Romano cheese
2 tablespoons chopped parsley

1. In a small bowl combine the breadcrumbs and cheese.

2. Melt the butter in a small saucepan, and add the garlic, pepper, oregano, and pastis—stirring for a minute or two until mixed thoroughly.

3. Lay out the oysters on the half-shell, placing shell-side down on a fire grill over medium heat. Ensure that the brine is retained in the shells.

4. Spoon the butter sauce over each oyster and then spoon the breadcrumbs, cheese, and parsley mixture to cover each oyster.

5. Grill for approximately 5 minutes or until the oysters become plump and the cheese is slightly golden.

6. Serve on a platter, being careful to avoid spilling the brine-butter sauce out of the shells. Garnish the oysters by sprinkling the chopped parsley over them.

The Fading Creole Past

In the decades after the Civil War, New Orleans's distinct Creole culture receded further into the shadows of the city's daily existence. Many who identified as Creole became bilingual, especially in commerce, and the once-fashionable Vieux Carré became a neighborhood of Sicilian immigrants and African Americans from the hinterlands seeking new opportunities. Yet, the cultural divide between Uptown and Downtown in terms of culture, language, and religion remained strong among both Black and white residents. The novelty of Creole Catholic culture continued to remain a defining trait of New Orleans's exceptionalism in the United States. And city tourism promoters continued to use the city's unique Creole charm to attract visitors in the age of railroads and streetcars.

The 1904 streetcar and railway map, published by the New Orleans Railway Company, highlighted tourist sites of interest to traveling white businessmen and perhaps their families. The guide listed business districts, monuments, parks, theaters, hotels, and recreational sites such as the West End Resort on the Lakefront that were all accessible by streetcar. The map also included, in a narrative inset, a suggested streetcar ride "That Every Tourist Should Take" along the Canal and Esplanade Belt Line through the "old section" of the city "known as the French portion" that "contains many quaint and aristocratic mansions of French and Spanish origin."

Continuing from Canal Street to Rampart Street, the guide noted Congo Square (ironically renamed for Confederate General P.G.T. Beauregard in 1897) as "the place where the Congo and other negroes held the weird dances and in Spanish days where bull and bear fights took place." The narrative then brought attention to the rear of the square, noting the location of "the scene of the Mafia Lynching." And, as the streetcar then turned on to Esplanade Avenue, tourists could view the "aristocratic streets and avenues of the later Creole Days."[42]

By the first years of the twentieth century, New Orleans's Creole history and culture appeared to be a phenomenon of the past, as were African dances. The site of the recent horrific Sicilian lynching (only thirteen years earlier) was viewed almost with a passing fancy. But at the same time, the inclusion and acknowledgment of these sites on the map also reveal how the exotic facets of Creole and African cultures, along with mob violence, could be promoted as a tourist draw, distinguishing the city in an age of growing tourism within the United States.

In this post–Civil War period, Lafcadio Hearn emerged as one of the first writers to document the city's distinct Creole life. While working as a journalist covering New Orleans for the national magazines *Harper's* and *Scribner's,* he grew fascinated by the people and culture of the downtown Creole district. Hearn also published two books, *Gombo Zhèbes: Little Dictionary of Creole Proverbs* (1885) and *La Cuisine Creole* (1885), a collection of recipes. Both works reflect Hearn's seminal role as an early folklorist of the city's distinct culture. Seeking new exotic adventures, Hearn moved to Martinique in 1887 and then to Matsue, Japan, where he settled permanently, documenting the rapidly disappearing folktales of his adopted land.[43]

The local-color literary genre, which highlighted distinct regional cultures, dialects, environments, and customs, was popular during the late nineteenth century. While living in New Orleans, Hearn collaborated with local-color author George Washington Cable in documenting old Creole songs, proverbs, and folktales. Together they developed the subgenre of English-language literature that aimed to capture Creole life and culture in the city.

The native-born Cable became a journalist and writer in the 1870s after serving in the Confederate Army during the Civil War. His most famous works *Old Creole Days* (1879) and *The Grandissimes* (1880) addressed the complex racial relations in New Orleans's French Creole and Creoles of color society. During the post-Reconstruction era, open hostility toward his liberal and controversial views on race in the 1880s led Cable and his family to leave the city permanently and relocate to Massachusetts. In this era of racial segregation, Cable's exposure of the paradoxes of race relations, historic miscegenation, and white supremacy in New Orleans led to his self-imposed exile.

Writer Kate Chopin also became captivated by the Creole culture of New Orleans and rural Louisiana. Like Cable, she published several short stories and novels that explored race relations and miscegenation. Although her mother descended from Creole Louisiana roots, Chopin was born in St. Louis where she was raised in a devout Catholic family. Chopin married and moved to New Orleans as an adult and spent time in the rural Cane River country near Natchitoches. Although she first gained praise for her writing on Creole people and culture, her novel *The Awakening* (1899) presents the story of a woman disillusioned with her life as a well-to-do housewife in New Orleans. *The Awakening* is now heralded as one of the first feminist works by a southern writer. Like Hearn and Cable, Chopin also left New Orleans, moving to St. Louis in the 1880s after the death of her husband.

As recounted earlier in this chapter, activist and writer Rodolphe Desdunes published *Nos Hommes et Notre Histoire* (1911) to combat attempts by white conservatives such as writer Charles Gayarré to discredit the history of mixed-race Creoles. The book chronicles the rich accomplishments of New Orleans's Creoles of color in the arts and letters, music, education, and the military during the nineteenth century; as such, the work is an important contribution to documenting New Orleans's cultural distinction.[44]

Like Cable, Desdunes permanently relocated from New Orleans, seeking an escape from the city's environment of racial hostility. Desdunes joined his son Dan, a classically trained musician, who had settled in Omaha in 1904 after visiting the city while on a theatrical tour of the Midwest. The elder activist's life mirrored the dramatic social changes that New Orleans underwent after the Civil War.

Born a free man of color before the Civil War, Desdunes lived as a young adult through the years of racial progress and integration during Reconstruction, serving in the Metropolitan Police at the Battle of Liberty Place. By the 1890s, Desdunes had experienced bitter losses and disillusionment in the fight against racial segregation as a member of the Comité des Citoyens, which had provided legal support for the *Plessy v. Ferguson* case. Years after the brutality of the Robert Charles Riot of 1900, the proud Creole left the city of his family to seek a life outside the segregated South.[45]

Thus, the four greatest documentarians of Creole culture in the late nineteenth century—Hearn, Cable, Chopin, and Desdunes—all left the city from which they drew inspiration. And for Cable and Desdunes their departure was spurred by their indignation at the city's social conditions. New Orleans's racial tensions during this period became too much for these literary artists to bear. And yet, the city continued to grow in population. The metropolitan footprint expanded to completely fill the high ground along the river, while moving farther along the Esplanade Ridge connecting to Bayou St. John and encroaching more into the low-lying, working-class back-of-town.

As Creole culture and the associated dialect declined in New Orleans, American culture and the English language gained salience. Families who resided in the downtown Creole district still maintained their French Catholic pride and traditions, but the children of the post–Civil War generations spoke English as their first language and gravitated to the emerging American music and entertainment trends of ragtime and vaudeville. Likewise, the children of immigrants from the Mediterranean, eastern Europe, and Asia also adapted to their new American home, often while living and working alongside newly arrived African American rural migrants seeking opportunities in the South's largest city. From this wave of new arrivals, New Orleans emerged on the international stage as the homeland of America's greatest musical export.

6

The Birthplace of Jazz

Modern American New Orleans, 1910–1950

IN THE DECADES leading up to World War II, New Orleans still reigned as the "Queen of the South." The region's largest city, New Orleans strove to be as modern as the nation's biggest cities with its newly built skyscrapers, paved highways, port facilities, electric power grid, and efficient water systems. But the queen also maintained a foot in the past, with its dependence on cotton exports, a Carnival season that celebrated make-believe royalty, and the city's distinct Creole culture, still evident within the pockets of French-language neighborhoods and institutions. As city boosters trumpeted in 1915, New Orleans married "the romance of the old" with "the progress of the new."[1]

The cultural divide between English speakers and French Creole-patois speakers largely faded, even though the vast wave of immigration between the Civil War and World War I made social relations more complex. Not all English speakers were Protestant, and not all Catholics were Creoles. Although Canal Street still represented a geographic and cultural divide, New Orleans remained largely a city of very diverse neighborhoods, in which new immigrants, African Americans, white Americans, and Creoles often lived side by side or block by block.

Louis Armstrong spent his formative youth in the Third Ward area known as back-of-town, located along Perdido and South Rampart Streets today. The famous entertainer later described the nuances of race relations among his ethnically mixed community on the uptown side of Canal Street: "The neighborhood consisted of Negroes, Jewish people, and lots of Chinese." He admitted how "the Jewish people in those early days were having problems of their own—along with the hard times of other white folks nationalities who felt they were better than the Jewish Race." Armstrong, who worked for the Karnofsky family as a young man, claimed his Jewish neighbors and employers "had a better break than the Negroes. Because they were white people. That's what was so puzzling to me."[2]

Armstrong experienced the complex nuances of race relations while working on the junk and coal wagon of the recently immigrated Russian Jewish family. He admired their hard work ethic, ability to earn and save, their kindness and support, and generosity. The Karnofsky family often invited the young Louis into their home, where they fed him dinner and where he first heard the sad melodies of traditional Jewish lullabies that sounded reminiscent of the blues. Most importantly, the family loaned Louis the money to buy his first cornet from a pawn shop. As Armstrong recalled, "After blowing it a while, I realized I could play 'Home Sweet Home'—then here come the Blues. From then on, I was a mess and Tootin' Away."[3]

Armstrong's experiences with the Karnofsky family provides one snapshot of interracial relations during this time of segregation. His recognition that, as Jews, they had also experienced hardship and prejudice enabled him to feel a kinship with them. At the same time, he understood the advantages of their white status, which eventually enabled them to move into a nicer neighborhood. Armstrong's recollections are important because they also provide insight into the social context during the emergence of New Orleans jazz, a powerful musical symbol of the city's cultural polyglot blend in the 1910s.

Although jazz is often viewed as an African American musical style, many early jazz musicians in New Orleans came from immigrant Italian and Jewish communities that were largely marginalized within New Orleans society. As first-generation Americans, the sons of these immigrants were "white" but often experienced social discrimination similar to that affecting African Americans in New Orleans. Given their marginalized social status, many members of this first generation related to the African American experience and became attracted to the ragtime–jazz music of Black musicians. Jewish musicians such as Monty Korn, Charlie Fishbein, and Meyer Weinberg might have found themselves playing in the same ragtime–jazz bands with Sicilian Americans Tony Almerico, Frank Federico, and Louis Prima.[4]

Indeed, the social integration that occurred in New Orleans's "patchwork" neighborhoods, where African Americans and white immigrants lived and worked side by side, helped facilitate the spread and appeal of ragtime–jazz music. Just as educated Creole of color families felt the weight of segregation in the early 1900s, many of the downtown Creole children of this World War I generation, including Jelly Roll Morton, Sidney Bechet, and Freddie Keppard, gravitated to the celebratory dance music of uptown African Americans in the city.

During this era New Orleans produced a new style of music that took the world by storm. Racial segregation, the social marginalization of immigrants, and the influx of rural African Americans from plantation districts along the Mississippi River all played vital roles in the development of the new musical phenomenon. In the age of the phonograph, the new technology enabled the rapid spread of the raucous style that appealed to a new generation coming of age during World War I.

Farewell to Storyville

World War I is tied to the closing of Storyville, when the War Department and the U.S. Navy issued a rule forbidding zones of prostitution to be near military facilities. Yet, the red-light district had been in decline for years before that, hastened by Charles "Gyp the Blood" Harrison's point-blank shooting and murder of Billy Phillips at the Tuxedo Dance Hall in 1913. By legalizing and regulating prostitution, Storyville reflected the Progressive-era penchant for reform, but the experiment never succeeded completely. Prostitution continued to exist in surrounding neighborhoods, including Louis Armstrong's, and spilled over into the back of the Vieux Carré as well.

With the closing of the district in 1917, the vice trade generally migrated to the area of the French Quarter that became known as the "Tango Belt," named for the Argentinian dance that swept the world in a craze in 1913. During Prohibition, a number of notorious clubs including the Pup, the Dog House, the Cadillac Club, the Orchard, and the Fern Dance Hall were located in the Tango Belt, where they served alcohol illicitly (fig. 15). During the 1920s, the rum-running trade became lucrative, given the proximity to smuggling routes along the bayous and marshes surrounding New Orleans. With the end of Prohibition in 1933, entertainment migrated to nearby Bourbon Street, which emerged as the new center of bars, dance clubs, and live music.[5]

FIG. 15. This photograph of elaborately dressed sex workers and a male pianist conveys the luxury and elegance of the more extravagant mansion brothels such as Hilma Burt's along Basin Street in Storyville. These brothels sometimes featured musical entertainment from the city's emerging ragtime–jazz artists. *Hilma Burt's Mirror Ballroom in Storyville,* Louisiana State Museum, Jazz Collection, 1978.118(B).00883.

Storyville's history is often romanticized in the history of New Orleans jazz. Early historians sought to sell the sex appeal of jazz's development by associating the music with the notorious red-light district. According to these early histories such as *Jazzmen* (1939), the closing of the district in November 1917 led to the exodus of all the jazz musicians in New Orleans to Chicago, New York, and California. But the fact is that local musicians were leaving the city to seek new opportunities since well before World War I.[6]

This exodus of musicians from New Orleans to larger economic markets in the 1910s was a response to the few opportunities available to young men in New Orleans. The relocation of bands like the Original Creole Orchestra to California and the Original Dixieland Jazz Band to Chicago and then New York can be viewed as the musicians' effort to find musical fame, a sense of adventure, but mostly better economic conditions.

For African American musicians, the move also reflected a desire to escape segregation. For example, Joe Oliver, who was Louis Armstrong's mentor, had arrived in New Orleans in the 1900s. Oliver grew up in the Mississippi River plantation hamlet of Aben not far from Baton Rouge, and like many rural African Americans in this period, he sought new opportunities in the big city. But by 1918, despite his success as "king" of the cornet in New Orleans, the constant harassment of police at his gigs led him to depart for Chicago, where he eventually gained national fame. His protégé Louis Armstrong followed suit in 1921.

The United States' entry into World War I provided some new opportunities for federal defense work and jobs at related infrastructure projects. The Algiers Naval Base provided work repairing small ships serving in the Gulf of Mexico and Caribbean zones. Because New Orleans remained an important railroad and maritime hub, the military constructed the New Orleans Military Ocean Terminal, often referred to as the "Port of Embarkation." Eighteen-year-old Louis Armstrong remembered working on that project, likely as a common laborer. He wrote in his autobiography, "You can imagine how tough things were when many well-known musicians had to work on that job." Yet Armstrong admitted, "I was rather proud of that big yellow button I wore for identification when I went in and out of the yard."[7]

The large military port facility is located at the intersection of the Mississippi River and the Inner Harbor Navigation Canal. The waterway, more commonly known as the Industrial Canal, was first excavated during the war years and opened in 1923. Realizing the long-time dreams of the city's shipping interests, the canal connected Lake Pontchartrain to the river through a lock. Because the draft had siphoned off so many young Americans into the military, the U.S. government recruited workers from Puerto Rico, who provided much of the labor. Again, Armstrong noted the paradoxes of race relations with these immigrants, whom he described as having "scarcely any clothes, and some of them were barefooted like the boys in my neighborhood." But as he observed, "they had the nerve to look down on us because we were colored. . . . We ignored that and managed to get along with them fairly well."[8]

In New Orleans and across the American South, racial labor policies during World War I dictated that African American men had to "work or fight." The Selective Service rule meant that able-bodied males had to be either employed in essential defense industries or enlist in the military. So, when Armstrong no longer worked on the Port of Embarkation construction project, he found employment at the C. A. Andrews Coal Company, where he drove a coal cart pulled by a mule named "Lady" and shoveled coal for fifteen cents a load. "I loved it," he recalled, and "felt like a real man when I shoveled a ton of coal into my wagon." The artist later wrote the song "Coal Cart Blues," in which he proclaimed in the chorus, "I got the Coal Cart Blues / I'm really so confused / I'm about to lose my mind / Worry, worry all the time / These blues will make you cry / Feel like you just want to scream."

Not surprisingly, the moment that Armstrong found out that the armistice was declared, he abandoned Lady in the street in front of Fabacher's Restaurant on St. Charles Avenue: "I immediately dropped the shovel, slowly put on my jacket, looked at Lady and said, 'So long, my dear. I don't think I'll ever see you again.' . . . I cut out leaving the mule cart, load of coal, and everything connected with it; I haven't seen them since." Although Armstrong always prided himself on having a strict work ethic and respect for his employers, bucking the forced "work or fight" order must have felt liberating.[9]

Armstrong actually did register for the draft, listing his occupation as musician and his boss as New Orleans club owner Peter Lala.[10] Likely he thought that he might be recruited into a military band, where he could gain more formal musical education and also avoid combat or the common labor "engineering" duties given to most African Americans at the time. But he likely did not qualify for military service because of his young age, and so he worked the jobs mentioned earlier. However, other New Orleanian musicians including Jack Laine and Manuel Perez trained at military camps in central Louisiana or surrounding states. Some like Jim Robinson saw service in France, where he began by digging ditches but found a more enjoyable occupation (and tips) playing trombone in a small traveling military band.

Women's experiences in New Orleans during World War I depended on their social status and race. The shortage of men because of the draft opened a large number of employment opportunities to women: they drove wagons and trucks, worked in the service industries, and provided healthcare. These new experiences contributed to the generational shift in social mores from the more conservative Victorian older generation to the more socially liberated youth of the Jazz Age. In New Orleans, as in most American cities, women's dress lengths shortened from the ankles to the knees, high Victorian collars and long sleeves gave way to more bare skin on the arms and shoulders, and the long hair in a bun was replaced by the short bob. Scandalously, respectable women also dared to smoke and drink alcohol in public.

In the rest of the country, the 1920s are considered the Jazz Age because of the unconventional social behaviors associated with the new music style. But the Jazz Age came early to New Orleans. During the 1910s, the music described as "hot" by the early musicians was embraced by all levels of society from the dance halls of back-of-town and the Creole Tremé to the white-owned lakefront camps at Milneburg, the fraternities at Tulane University, and the high-society Southern Yacht Club and recently established New Orleans Country Club.

Therefore, even as New Orleans may not have been a very modern city in the 1910s compared to New York or Chicago, the new generation of music lovers certainly reflected national trends. Perhaps New Orleanians' love of music, dancing, socializing, and imbibing provided a natural environment for the raucous and rough music style to germinate. Thus, New Orleans's lifestyle and wide-open social mores yielded the special celebratory culture that gave birth to the Jazz Age.

Tropical Cruises

New Orleans took steps toward modernization in the early twentieth century. Given the continued importance of the river for trade and the city's location as an entrepôt for the Mississippi Valley, the Port Commission streamlined the complex and congested railroad traffic on the river by creating the city-run New Orleans Public Belt Railroad. Along the waterfront, it constructed modern wharf sheds to protect goods being loaded and off-loaded. By the 1910s, the riverfront was dedicated solely to commerce, remaining largely cut off from citizens and tourists until the opening of the "Moonwalk" in front of Jackson Square in 1976.[11]

In the modernized maritime port, cotton dominated the riverfront trade, with compresses and gins strung up and down the river from the Warehouse District to Uptown. In 1915, the state-run Port of New Orleans created the sixty-two-acre Cotton Warehouse and Terminal along the river, where a three-story 100-ton compress compacted cotton for shipment overseas. The white staple remained vital to the port in the first decades of the twentieth century, until the 1930s when the spread of the boll weevil and plummeting prices signaled the end of cotton's dominance in the city.[12]

The sugar trade still centered on the wharfs in front of the upper French Quarter, where the Sugar Exchange Building served as an international market exchange for sugar planters until its closure in 1963. During the 1910s and 1920s, two of the largest sugar refineries were constructed along the Mississippi. Upriver in Reserve, the sugar company founded by Jewish French immigrant and planter-industrialist Leon "Sugar King" Godchaux built a massive and very modern complex that functioned into the 1980s: it was admired for its use of the modern rail system to transport cane to the refinery. Downriver in St. Bernard Parish, American Sugar built a second refinery, which was completed in 1927 and was known as the Domino Sugar Refinery. Together the two complexes formed the two largest sugar refineries in the world, signaling an important step toward industrialization of the riverfront.

In the early part of the twentieth century, the tropical commodities of coffee and bananas attained greater importance, signaling a diversification of the continuing trade with Latin American and Caribbean nations that had existed since the earliest days of the city. As the largest and most modern southern port, New Orleans naturally emerged as the logical destination for the sale and distribution of these two important tropical products.

By the 1920s, the city housed dozens of import companies that sold green coffee beans to roasters globally during a time when the industry was largely decentralized and communications with Latin America were unreliable. Ships offloaded the green beans at the Poydras Street Wharf, and then the beans were moved to the Kentucky coffee warehouse at 111 Lafayette Street. A row of coffee import offices and roasting facilities lined nearby Magazine Street, where up until the 2000s, the scent of warm coffee roasting pervaded this section of the Warehouse District now characterized by upscale restaurants and museums.

Among the top brokers was Jacob Aron, who founded J. Aron and Company. The young man, who had learned the business from his uncle, a meatpacking agent in Chicago, owned and marketed several major brands. Their French Market Coffee, which is still found on market shelves, continues to feature chicory. This very dark and rich coffee blends ground beans with the roasted roots of the chicory plant: it was shaped by the tastes of French immigrants in the nineteenth century, yielding a coffee culture that, outside France, one only finds in New Orleans. Even though the West Coast has more recently made a claim to dark-roast coffee, New Orleans has always maintained a taste for the strongest brews based on its French heritage.

In the first decades of the twentieth century, New Orleans also emerged as the international center of the banana trade. The Vaccaro brothers—Joseph, Luca, and Felix—established Standard Fruit after taking over their father Stefano's produce business when the elder retired and moved back to Sicily in 1893. The Arbrëschë (Albanian Sicilian) family had emigrated from the village of Contessa Entellina outside Palermo after the Second War of Italian Independence in the late 1850s. The brothers expanded vertically by purchasing land in Honduras for orange groves. In that Central American country, they received land grants from President Miguel Dávila in exchange for developing a modern infrastructure of railways, highways within the nation, and deepwater wharfs at La Ceiba on the north coast. They then turned to growing bananas while pioneering the use of refrigerated ships to transport the fruit to New Orleans.

Standard Fruit's biggest competitor was Cuyamel Fruit, owned by Sam Zemurray. Growing up on a wheat farm in Moldova, the young Samuel immigrated with his family first to New York and then to Selma, Alabama, during the 1890s; the family settled there and opened a dry-goods store. As a young man Zemurray built a business by buying overripe bananas from the docks of Mobile and then reselling them for a small profit farther inland. At the turn of the century, Zemurray began buying land in Honduras to cultivate bananas. In the fields of Honduras, Zemurray gained a reputation for doing hard labor and pioneering efficient growing techniques. Like the Vaccaro brothers, he developed roads, bridges, and railroads for harvesting and shipping the bananas. In 1905, Zemurray moved the headquarters of his business to New Orleans, where he invested in a fleet of ships.

The competition between Zemurray and the Vaccaro brothers came to a head in 1911, when the former hired mercenaries from New Orleans to stage a coup in Honduras. In the subversive military operation, Zemurray's mercenaries overthrew President Dávila, who had worked closely with the Vaccaros, and replaced him with President Manuel Bonilla, who favored Zemurray's company. From these actions emerged the euphemistic term

"Banana Republic," referring to a "democratic" Latin American nation that was subject to outside political and economic control of its monoculture agricultural commodity market, usually by the United States, at the expense of its citizens.[13]

By the 1920s, Zemurray's United Fruit, headquartered with a new office building at 321 St. Charles Avenue, was the largest fruit company in the world. The Vaccaro brothers' Standard Fruit and Steamship Co. stood as the second-largest company at 222 Carondelet Street. Zemurray, known as "Sam the Banana Man," was a quiet philanthropist who generously funded Tulane University and infrastructure projects in Central America. Joseph Vaccaro, who was known as the "Ice King" because he owned the majority of ice refrigerators in the city, funded hospitals in Honduras.

Both companies owned fleets of ships that not only moved goods but also offered "gay and carefree" tropical tourist cruises. United Fruit's Great White Fleet and the Vaccaros' Standard Fruit Steamship Company maintained New Orleans's historic connections with Cuba, Honduras, Jamaica, Haiti, Nicaragua, Panama, and Colombia from the 1920s through the 1960s. Standard's development of the port town of La Ceiba also provided one of the main connections for Hondurans who immigrated to New Orleans beginning in the 1960s. In this major migration wave, many of the earliest immigrants had connections to Standard Fruit, and their presence in New Orleans distinguished the town's Latin American culture with Honduran "Catracho" food and *musica tropicale.*

The coffee and banana trades had reverberations in New Orleans beyond shipping and immigration during the 1910s and 1920s. In an era when yellow fever and other tropical diseases threatened the lives of those in New Orleans and Latin America, Zemurray funded the establishment of the Tulane School of Public Health and Tropical Medicine in 1912 as the first such institution in the United States. In part, Zemurray's motive was economic: to protect his workforce. But healthcare professionals in the Progressive era hailed the public health effort as vitally important to combating deadly tropical diseases.

In addition, several well-known New Orleans culinary innovations are related to the tropical imports. In the 1880s Jules Alciatore of Antoine's Restaurant created the hot cocktail called Café Brûlot Diabolique—a concoction of dark coffee with sugar, spices, and flaming cognac. In 1951, Brennan's chef Paul Blangé and Ella Brennan invented the popular dessert Bananas Foster, which similarly uses bananas with sugar, spices, and flaming rum for a dramatic fiery effect at the tableside.

The banana trade also supplied steady work for men on the riverfront. United Fruit operated the Thalia Street Wharf, where offloading the fruit, known as "banana budding," provided daily jobs for those in need (fig. 16). Workers carried fifty-pound bunches of green bananas from the ship's hold to the wharf shed. During World War I, when musical performances were prohibited, Louis Armstrong had to take "odd jobs of all kinds." In addition to his construction and coal cart jobs, he worked as a banana budder on "the levee." He recalled, "Sometimes we worked those big ships all day, and sometimes all night. When we finished up, we would light out for Savocas' honky-tonk to line up on the sidewalk to get our pay." Although many of his coworkers gambled away their earnings in nearby honky-tonks, he said, "I

FIG. 16. "Banana budders" hustle to unload a train car full of the ripening tropical fruit in the 1920s when New Orleans continued to maintain strong cultural and economic ties to the Caribbean and Latin America. *Unloading Bananas, New Orleans 1920s,* Arnold Genthe Collection, Library of Congress, LC-G391-1423 [P&P].

couldn't afford to do that because I was the sole support" of his mother and two siblings.[14]

New Orleans's coffee and banana trade maintained the strong cultural connections with the Caribbean and Latin American nations that dated back to the earliest days of the city. The influences of the region to the south, however, were strongest in the musical culture of the city, as evident in the nineteenth century with composer Louis Moreau Gottschalk and the Mexican bands of the 1880s and 1890s. Latin music would later shape the development of jazz, as the *habanera* rhythm associated with Cuban *danzón* of the nineteenth century and the *tango* of the 1910s became vital aspects of early jazz. This distinctive musical phenomenon that directed an international spotlight onto the city's rich musical heritage and lifestyle reflected the blending of the Afro-Creole, European, and Latin-Caribbean cultures of New Orleans, as incubated in the years around World War I.

Jass It Up

On the night of December 4, 1919, New Orleans's famed French Opera House caught fire. By the next morning the smoldering shell of the structure at the corner of Toulouse and Bourbon Streets in the French Quarter revealed all that remained of the grand theater, deemed the most opulent in North America at its debut in 1859. The timing of the building's demise coincided with the fading of opera as the most popular form of music in the western world for people of all social classes and educational levels. The fire also corresponded with the rise of ragtime–jazz that appealed to the generation of youth coming of age in the post-Victorian era.

Two years earlier, on February 26, 1917, the Original Dixieland Jazz Band from New Orleans recorded "Livery Stable Blues," the first song released in the new genre called jazz. Although the band members were exposed to opera in their youth, the composition represented everything that opera was not. The song combined a modern foxtrot dance rhythm with a syncopated bass drum. Its title revealed the influence of the novel African American blues form, and the words "livery stable" referred to the instrumentalists' imitation of uncouth barnyard sounds. In the song's signature break, Larry Shields's clarinet mimicked the rooster crow, the cornet of Nick LaRocca bugled a horse's neigh, and Eddie Edwards's trombone brayed like a donkey. The vocalized barnyard sounds were rough enough to offend the ears of Victorian parents everywhere and, in doing so, delighted the youthful generation that sought to proclaim their modern mores.

To add to the sensationalist nature of the raucous new sound, the term "jazz" was a vernacular sexual term, and not one the earliest musicians would use publicly. The first generation of jazz musicians in New Orleans referred to themselves as ragtime musicians. Only when the music migrated to Chicago around 1916 did audiences coin the term "jass" to describe the catchy new sound from New Orleans. Within the year, ragtime musicians playing foxtrot dance music quickly adopted the inappropriate slang term to market the music style and their bands.

New Orleans jazz's blend of diverse musical elements reflected the cross-pollination of Afro-Creole, American, and European cultures that characterized New Orleans in the early twentieth century. At its foundation, New Orleans ragtime–jazz was dance music. The rhythmic core of the foxtrot was one of the new "animal" dances that developed out of ragtime and vaudeville theater during the 1910s. Dances such as the bunny hop, the grizzly bear, the turkey trot, and the foxtrot were especially popular among the new urban generation that came of age during the World War I era throughout the United States, Europe, and Latin America.

As mentioned earlier, the music had strong American ragtime roots. The "ragging" style evolved as an African American musical form in the lower Mississippi Valley between St. Louis and New Orleans during the 1890s and 1900s. Its syncopated melodies were characterized by "ragged" off-beat rhythms and by a three- or four-part song structure (AA, BB, C, A), both of which were incorporated into New Orleans jazz. The animal dances and ragtime elements thus reflect New Orleans's identity in the early twentieth century as a truly American city.

The premier New Orleans jazz style also reflected New Orleans's rich African American musical traditions stemming from the blues and from gospel music in Protestant and Evangelical churches. Buddy Bolden, whom many credit with being the first "king" of the cornet and the first "hot" musician of the early 1900s, is also acknowledged for integrating the heavy rhythms of the Black Baptist Church into the music, giving it the booty-shaking lilt that added to the music's appeal. Importantly, the spiritual "When the Saints Go Marching In" is perhaps the most well-known New Orleans jazz song internationally.

As "Livery Stable Blues" indicates, many of the earliest jazz instrumental songs in New Orleans were based on the blues, the African American song form and sound that emerged in the lower Mississippi Valley at the turn of the century. New Orleans's location as the largest southern city and the trade center of the valley ensured that the city absorbed the newer music styles as they developed. Appropriately, the first published song with a blues title, "I Got the Blues," was composed in 1908 by Antonio "Anthony" Maggio, an Italian immigrant in New Orleans. Underscoring the crossover between music styles during this era, the blues composition was actually promoted as a ragtime two-step, incorporating both the standard blues chord structure (I-IV-I V-IV-I) and the three-part ragtime song structure.

In addition, the melodic instrumentation—using cornet, clarinet, and trombone in three distinct conversational voices—reflected the European orchestral roots of many of the early jazz musicians. Although the ragtime-jazz style was generally improvisational, and therefore not composed in the formal western tradition, the interplay of the violin or cornet lead melody, the clarinet *obligato* second voice, and the trombone's lower bass notes reflected the melodies and countermelodies one heard in European symphonies. Conversational melodies also could be found in formal orchestras and Sousa-era brass bands, which comprised a large part of the New Orleans musical soundscape in the early twentieth century.

Afro-Creoles such as Ferdinand "Jelly Roll" Morton, Sidney Bechet, Alphonse Picou, and other downtown musicians incorporated their formal musical education and exposure to classical music into the new style as well. Morton, one of the first great jazz pianists and composers, claimed that he was inspired to take up the piano as a youth after attending a formal musical performance at the French Opera House. Despite growing up in conservative Creole families, musicians like Morton and Bechet became attracted to the ragtime and blues of uptown African Americans, integrating classical elements into their rich flourishes and arrangements.[15]

New Orleans's historic Latin-Afro-Caribbean influences also became an integral aspect of the music's style. Jelly Roll Morton famously described the *habanera* Latin American bass rhythm in early jazz as the "Spanish Tinge" that distinguished and defined New Orleans jazz. He claimed, "If you can't manage to get tinges of Spanish in your tunes, you will never be able to get the right seasoning, I call it, for jazz." Indeed, the incorporation of the syncopated dance rhythms of the Cuban *danzón* and popular Argentinian tango into Morton's piano compositions expressed the enduring cultural and musical connections between the port city and Latin America.[16]

Ragtime-jazz melded all these cultural elements of the city's heritage into a new style that quickly found an audience throughout the nation and the western world—in part because the phonograph enabled the music to spread quickly and easily. During the 1910s, the technology became affordable for most households and gradually replaced published sheet music in middle-class households with pianos. Louis Armstrong, as a teen, was proud to have purchased the white Original Dixieland Jazz Band's "Tiger Rag," along with 78 rpm phonograph records by popular singers such as Canadian radio star Henry Burr and Irish tenor John McCormack, as well as Italian opera greats Amelita Galli-Curci, Luisa Tetrazzini, and Enrico Caruso, who is credited with being the highest-selling recording artist of the era.[17]

Even as the music blended styles from multiple genres within New Orleans, the reality of neighborhood, class, and racial identity shaped the artists' experiences. Uptown African Americans such as Armstrong and drummer Warren "Baby" Dodds commented on the differences between themselves and the Creole of color musicians they encountered. Dodds recalled that in his youth the downtown Creoles "had French and Spanish style blended together" while "we had one style: that's Negro." He added, "If someone moved in who did talk [Creole], your mother kept you away from those people."[18]

Louis Armstrong distinguished himself musically during his teen years by teaching formally trained Creole of color musicians to "swing." He greatly admired the formally trained band leader John Robichaux, who led the orchestra at the Lyric Theater, where all the top African American touring shows performed in the Tango Belt. When Robichaux hired Armstrong and trombonist Edward "Kid" Ory to play in their brass band for a funeral, the older musicians played the dirges respectfully in the procession to the cemetery. But after the burial, when New Orleans tradition calls for an upbeat joyous dance parade, Armstrong claimed that "those old fossils just couldn't cut it" and that he and Ory "came in with flying colors." He proudly bragged, "After that incident, those stuck-up guys wouldn't let us alone. They patted us on the back and wouldn't let us alone."[19]

The exploding popularity of jazz in New Orleans created a dance craze and a wide-open market for those bands that remained in the city after the closure of Storyville in 1917; they found steady work in New Orleans and surrounding regions in the boom times of the Jazz Age. Oscar "Papa" Celestin, who had migrated from the sugar plantation region of Assumption Parish in the 1910s, led the Tuxedo Orchestra, one of the top dance bands. The flush market enabled his trombonist William "Bebe" Ridgley from suburban Jefferson Parish (Shrewsbury) to form his own dance band. Sam Morgan, who had moved to New Orleans with his brothers Andrew and Isaiah from nearby rural Plaquemines Parish, led a popular dance band that played a weekly circuit of halls and clubs between New Orleans and Pensacola, Florida, during the period.[20]

And with the generational shift and changing mores of the post–World War I era, women became a fixture of the dance band stage. The tradition in which females provided entertainment in middle-class Victorian homes by performing popular songs of the day on piano led to band leaders recruiting the young ladies for their musical ability and sexual appeal in the 1920s. Jeanette Salvant became the featured pianist for Celestin's Tuxedo Orchestra, and when Bebe Ridgley split from Celestin, the trombonist recruited the young Emma Barrett to perform with his orchestra. During the decade, the three Goodson sisters—Sadie, Wilhelmina (Billie), and Ida—moved from Pensacola to New Orleans, where they all found work in local dance bands. All these women played important roles in a largely male-dominated profession, and they continued to be respected performers well into the 1980s and 1990s.[21]

The 1920s also witnessed the rising popularity of female singers nationally, and New Orleans's own Boswell Sisters found great fame and popularity as part of this trend. The vocal trio, comprising Helvetia "Vet," Martha, and lead singer Connie, had grown up in a well-to-do uptown family and received classical music training. But like most of their generation, they fell in love with the blues and jazz. The sisters gained national recognition while performing in a live radio broadcast at the Orpheum Theater. By the early 1930s, "The Bozzies" had become the most popular jazz vocal group nationally, influencing the next generation of female vocalists such as the Andrews Sisters and Ella Fitzgerald. They seamlessly transitioned from the older vaudeville style into modern swing music by the mid-1930s, after which the sisters retired to raise their families.

But given the rapidly changing evolution of popular music, the instrumental New Orleans ragtime-jazz style became dated and was considered somewhat old-fashioned by the late 1920s. Ironically, Louis Armstrong helped encourage this change by popularizing songs with catchy vocals, scatting made-up lyrics, and playing well-structured and virtuoso extended solos on his trumpet. By the 1930s, Armstrong had made his way to Hollywood and billed himself nationally as the "King of Jazz." The internationally famous artist inspired Tremé native and Sicilian Orleanian Louis Prima, who mimicked Armstrong's singing and trumpet styles effectively, and became part of the next generation of popular New Orleans jazz artists in the post–World War II era.[22]

Many of the original jazz greats, however, failed to adapt as New Orleans–style jazz faded from popularity during the 1930s. The Original Dixieland Jazz Band, Jelly Roll Morton, and Armstrong's mentors Joe "King" Oliver and Edward "Kid" Ory retired and lived in obscurity and in poverty. During the Great Depression, New Orleans ragtime–jazz became superseded by the new sounds of Kansas City swing and the big bands of New York.

Yet, the emergence of jazz in New Orleans provides a mirror into the city's early twentieth-century cultural attributes: neighborhoods in which white immigrants and African Americans lived side by side, a historic Afro-Creole presence, Latin American roots, and a celebratory lifestyle that fed the development of dance-based music. Although many recent rural migrants found greater opportunity in New Orleans, an equal number of locally born Orleanians sought new adventures and bigger music markets in cities across the nation. During the World War I era, a new generation of liberated women found a public role and acceptance in an age of more openly expressed sexuality.

Relevant Historic Sites

400 block of S. Rampart St.: The remnants of Buddy Bolden's Eagle Band performed at the Eagle Saloon (401) in the 1900s. The Iroquois Theater (413) was an African American vaudeville theater, where Louis Armstrong saw shows and performed as a youth. Armstrong's employers lived at the Karnofsky home (427). The building collapsed during Hurricane Ida in 2021.

Buddy Bolden Residence, 2309 First St.: The home of the first ragtime–jazz legend, Charles "Buddy" Bolden.

Joe "King" Oliver Residence, 2712 Dryades St.: Home of the jazz cornetist and band leader who mentored Louis Armstrong.

Edward "Kid" Ory Residence, 2135 Jackson Ave.: Home of the jazz trombonist and band leader whose Sunshine Orchestra was the first African American jazz band to make a recording.

Nick LaRocca Residence, 2218 Constance St.: Home of the jazz cornetist who co-led the Original Dixieland Jazz Band, the first white jazz band to make a recording.

Boswell Sisters Residence, 3937 Camp Street: The childhood home of the famed jazz vocal trio.

John Robichaux Residence, 4727 Camp. St.: Home of the Afro-Creole band leader who directed the Lyric Theater Orchestra in the 1910s and hired Louis Armstrong and Kid Ory to perform in his brass band.

Progress of the New

As jazz music presented a new soundtrack to a younger generation during the first decades of the twentieth century, New Orleans evolved into a modern American city. Whereas the post-Reconstruction period witnessed the explosion of railroads, the coming of electricity, and a new sewerage and drainage system, the early twentieth century welcomed the new automobile culture, the construction of steel-framed office buildings, and an improved mastering of the historic wetlands on which the city developed. With the new engineering feats, New Orleans expanded into the marshy edges of the city with modern white-only suburban developments.

The Central Business District (CBD) began to take on its role as the hub of large modern office buildings during this period. Completed in 1911, the eleven-story Whitney Bank building at 228 St. Charles Avenue ruled the skyline as the tallest building in the city, that is, until the completion of the Hibernia Bank Building at 810 Gravier Street ten years later. The latter building at twenty-three stories is topped with a distinctive neoclassical cupola and was the tallest building until the 1960s. One block down at 200 Carondelet Street, the National American Bank building represented the most modernist of the three buildings when completed in 1929. Designed by local architect Moise Goldstein, the Art Deco gold finial and the Hibernia cupola stand out as distinctive early twentieth-century twin landmarks, especially from the perspective of Bourbon Street looking uptown from the historic Vieux Carré.

Within the CBD, an inconspicuous monument at the corner of Common Street and St. Charles Avenue marks the southern terminus of the Jefferson Highway connecting Winnipeg to New Orleans. Erected by the Daughters of the American Revolution in 1917, the bronze plaque acknowledged the completion of the modern paved highway that crossed the lands of the original Louisiana Territory. A project initiated by the New Orleans Chamber of Commerce in 1915, the highway reflected the arrival of the automobile tourism age. As cars began to replace train travel, the new age of modern highways connected New Orleans to the rest of the continent.[23]

The Federal Highway Act of 1921 created the first modern U.S. highway system forty years before the interstate system of the post–World War II era. Despite the original plans for a direct route to Winnipeg, the new east–west Jefferson Highway in New Orleans became integrated into U.S. 90. This modern federally built axis crossed the southern portion of the nation, paralleling the old Southern Pacific railway line. Coming from the west, Jefferson Highway hugged the natural ridge along the Mississippi River through Jefferson Parish from Kenner to the Orleans Parish line. Passing through New Orleans, the highway became Claiborne Avenue in Uptown and then Broad Street in Mid-City. The road extended along Gentilly Boulevard, hugging the old Bayou Sauvage ridge in the downtown section and then continued east on Chef Menteur (Old Gentilly) Highway toward the Rigolets and the Mississippi Gulf Coast.

Although Chamber of Commerce officials planned in 1915 for the original "Jefferson Highway" to connect New Orleans to Canada, federal highway planners reconfigured the nation's central north–south axis as U.S. Routes 61 and 51, which connected New Orleans to Chicago and the Great Lakes along the Illinois Central railway route. Beginning as Common Street and then Tulane Avenue, the road eventually became known as Airline Highway during the 1930s, as it extended in a straight line through rural East Jefferson Parish toward Baton Rouge and the Mississippi Delta.

And in the 1920s, the new U.S. 11 provided a highway connection from New Orleans to New York State. A privately built bridge was the first automobile crossing of Lake Pontchartrain past the marshes along Bayou Sauvage in Michoud. Completed in 1928, the toll bridge at the time was the longest concrete bridge in the world. Sold to the state in 1938, the operational bridge has withstood the most destructive hurricane tidal surges since its opening.

As New Orleans continued to grow in population, the city expanded from the natural ridge of the river toward the marshy shores of Lake Pontchartrain. During the 1910s and 1920s, the new automobile era of American suburbanization gave rise to new neighborhoods: Lakeview, Broadmoor, Gentilly Terrace along the old Bayou Sauvage Ridge, and Old Metairie along the winding Metairie Bayou Ridge in Jefferson Parish. Born in the age of segregation, these modern developments enforced white-only covenants. They therefore represented a departure from the classic New Orleans model of "patchwork," racially and ethnically mixed residential areas. Moreover, the new suburbs represented the first daring efforts to build in the wetland swamps that existed outside the natural river and bayou ridges and thus were below sea level.

The invention of the Wood screw pump in 1913 radically opened up new possibilities of "reclaiming" the lowlands of Mid-City and the Lakefront in Orleans Parish. Historically, the areas were left undeveloped because of their proneness to flooding during the heavy subtropical showers that flooded the streets and the hurricane tidal surges from Lake Pontchartrain. Tulane engineering graduate A. Baldwin Wood addressed the chronic drainage issue by pioneering a motorized high-volume horizontal pumping system that enabled large debris such as trees and branches to pass through without clogging, using hydrodynamic energy to lift and expel water at astonishing rates. And although Wood receives credit for improving the city's drainage, the invention of the Wood screw pump occurred within a bureaucratic system authorized to build essential infrastructure.

The Sewerage and Water Board of New Orleans installed Wood screw pumps at the lowest parts of the city. The new diesel-engine–powered machines replaced the old steam-powered paddles that attempted to push floodwaters toward the lake. The initial design from the 1890s drained storm water eastward via the Florida Avenue Canal toward Bayou Bienvenue behind the Lower Ninth Ward, but the system proved problematic. In the 1920s engineers redirected the water outfall toward Lake Pontchartrain. One can still view these operating pump houses along Broad Street where the various outfall canals begin. Even today, these pumps, which are more than a century old, are essential to the drainage of the city's streets. When they break down, they cause localized street flooding to the dismay of today's residents.[24]

As developers dared to build on the marshy lowlands, foresighted housing contractors used architectural designs that allowed for the possibility of heavy rains and floods. Throughout these new residential areas, houses incorporated the concept of the New Orleans basement, where the ground level would be used for storage (and sometimes as a residence), and the main floor of the home is elevated above the sea-level flood line. To provide extra height and security for the residents, some developers also constructed terraced berms as a foundation for the home. Today, one can see this style of home throughout Gentilly, Broadmoor, parts of Mid-City, and in the older parts of Lakeview north of the ancient Metairie Bayou Ridge.

Architecturally, the new Arts and Crafts style replaced the older Victorian styles that characterized homes from the late nineteenth century. Gentilly Terrace became the quintessential California bungalow-style enclave. Yet, principal characteristics of the Arts and Crafts bungalow appeared throughout the city in both new square cottages and the more traditional rectangular shotgun-style houses. The bungalow style was based on house designs from southeast Asia, and the umbrella-style southern Asian roof design provided a perfect match for the torrential rains of south Louisiana.

The shotgun house had come of age in the late nineteenth century, replacing the Creole cottage as the most common home design for middle-class and working people after the Civil War. The bracketed Italianate shotguns, the most common style during that era, incorporated rooflines that ended flush with the side of the home: they required gutters to ensure that rainwater did not pour down the sides of the homes and threaten the integrity of the structure. In contrast, the new Arts and Crafts style extended rafter tails to support the roofline one and a half feet beyond the sides of the home, thereby keeping the runoff from heavy rains well away from the wooden frame and siding.

Nevertheless, the city's lowlands remained vulnerable to flooding caused by both rain runoff and tidal surges from Lake Pontchartrain. In this age before named storms, the Great Hurricane of 1915 left a legacy of destruction. Louis Armstrong, who made his way home that day on the streets by foot, later remembered that the storm was "one of the worst New Orleans ever had" and that "houses were blown down."[25] Indeed, the storm irreparably damaged the Old St. Louis Hotel in the French Quarter, caused the collapse of the Horticultural Hall from the World's Cotton Expo of 1884 in Audubon Park, and severely damaged the Henry Howard-designed First Presbyterian Church originally built in 1857 on Lafayette Square.

The 1915 storm also unleashed a destructive tidal surge from Lake Pontchartrain into New Orleans's low-lying lakefront. But because the marshy areas of cut-over cypress swamp had no residential developments yet, the lack of levee protection from lake flooding failed to emerge as an important infrastructure issue. However, once white residents who had a political voice settled in the new developments in Lakeview and Gentilly, the issue of lakefront flood protection became a priority.

Beginning in 1928, the Orleans Levee Board constructed a concrete seawall that dramatically transformed the lakefront. Extending the old lakeshore a half-mile northward, the board built a stepped concrete seawall and raised the newly reclaimed area by ten feet above the surrounding marshes. In the process, the Levee Board dismantled all the recreational camps extending into the lake at Milneburg, from which jazz incubated in the 1910s. From West End to the Industrial Canal, the area changed from a swampy shoreline to one that prevented tides from surging inland.

As the city continued to fill in the lands between the river and the lake during this period, the Mississippi River once again forced the city to address the threat of the annual spring inundation. The Great Mississippi Flood of 1927 threatened the region's economic stability and investments, as the waterway appeared to be bursting at its seams.

The modern river levee system was created by the federal Mississippi River Commission (MRC) and was managed by the U.S. Army Corps of Engineers. Beginning in the 1880s, the MRC established a "Levees Only" policy giving the federal government the authority to create a contiguous levee system, thereby completely severing the river from the historic bayou distributaries (Manchac, Lafourche, Barataria, and others) that deposited freshwater every spring in the surrounding wetlands. But the severity of the 1927 flood created great anxiety for city boosters, who feared a levee break that would inundate the entire city.

To relieve the water pressure on the river levees in 1927, city leaders chose to dynamite the levee downriver from New Orleans at Caernarvon in

St. Bernard Parish. The subsequent breach flooded the entire parish, displacing trappers, fishers, and small farmers, many of whom were descended from the original Isleño settlers. This intentional flooding led to bitterness and resentment among many St. Bernard natives, who saw their well-being as sacrificed for the greater good of New Orleans. Engineers acknowledged the vulnerability of a rigid "Levees Only" policy, which had no system for relieving the water pressure on existing levees from exceptional river flood levels such as occurred in 1927.

Thereafter, the MRC and Army Corps of Engineers created the Bonnet Carré Spillway system in St. Charles Parish to allow a controlled release of floodwaters from the river to flow into Lake Pontchartrain. Authorities used the flood gates successfully for the first time in 1937 and have implemented the system numerous times whenever spring snowmelt waters reach the tops of the federal river levees.[26]

Theoretically, this system ensures that New Orleans will never face inundation from a levee break. But in practice, the "Levees Only" policy on the Mississippi River has had deleterious effects on protection from river floods. The engineering feat designed to alleviate river flooding has led to subsequent land subsidence and loss along the coast, and thereby greater vulnerability to hurricane tidal surges.

As scientists and engineers discovered in the mid-twentieth century, the lack of the annual snowmelt water in the spring degraded the ecosystems of freshwater swamps and brackish water marshes surrounding New Orleans. The lack of freshwater has led to salt-water intrusion through transportation canals in the coastal marshes. And the increased land subsidence combined with the death of freshwater cypress swamps eliminates natural buffers that protected the city from exposure to hurricane winds and tides from the Gulf. Peoples of Indigenous, Acadian, Isleño, and Afro-Creole descent living in the coastal wetlands are losing their homes and cultural homelands. Hence, the loss of land and culture from the "Levees Only" policy is now a crisis for the entire New Orleans metro area, and its effects continue like a slow bleed.

The construction of the modern spillway system coincided with the election of Huey P. Long as Louisiana governor in 1928. Long presented himself as a modernist, and his development of massive construction projects during the Great Depression reflected a new forward-looking optimism.

Under his administration, in 1935 the state completed the first bridge across the lower Mississippi River in suburban Jefferson Parish. For the first time, the Huey P. Long Bridge enabled automobiles on U.S. Highway 90 to cross the river; the Southern Pacific Railroad no longer had to transfer cars to a railway ferry at Elmwood.

Governor Long, a populist dictatorial political figure, helped transform the state by modernizing its highways, healthcare institutions, and educational systems. He hoped to use federal public works funds to carry Louisiana into the twentieth century. However, in New Orleans, a political stalemate existed between Long and the Old Regular Democrats, under the leadership of New Orleans mayor T. Semmes Walmsley. At the same time, the Roosevelt administration was reluctant to provide Works Progress Administration (WPA) funds to Louisiana for fear of the money being misappropriated.

Nevertheless, Long was able to implement some of his vision. The Lakefront Airport is perhaps Long's greatest legacy in New Orleans; its terminal on the lakefront embodied the modern era of travel and its sophistication. Long commissioned the New Orleans firm of Weiss, Dreyfous, and Seiferth to design the Art Deco terminal. The elegant structure featured eight aviation-themed murals by Spanish artist Xavier Gonzales; in front was placed the New Orleanian Mexican artist Enrique Alférez's Fountain of the Four Winds. Today the renovated airport is considered a prime example of Art Nouveau design.

Although Long grew up in rural north Louisiana, he focused much of his political energies on New Orleans. In the city he bought a mansion in the exclusive gated Audubon Place adjacent to Tulane University, but he lived mostly at his twelfth-floor suite at the Roosevelt Hotel, where manager and part-owner Seymour Weiss remained a confidant. In 1935, Long recruited the hotel's orchestra director Castro Carazo to co-write a song for his populist-themed "Share the Wealth" campaign for the presidency. The chorus of the song titled "Every Man a King!" is, "You can be a millionaire / But there's something belonging to others / There's enough for all people to share."

As the political strongman of Louisiana, Long modernized the state, but his iron-fisted political style created enemies as he made the move from governor to U.S. senator in 1932. When he set his sights on the presidency in the 1936 election, he became an even greater threat to President Roosevelt. The senator was assassinated in September 1935 before he could begin his presidential campaign.

After that, the federal government allocated Works Progress Administration (WPA) funds for infrastructure projects in the city. At the same time, the Old Regular Democrats in the impoverished city made a deal with Long's successor, Governor Richard Leche. The new governor agreed to provide state support and restore the city's financial independence on the condition that the Old Regulars endorse Robert Maestri, a Long supporter and New Orleans native, for mayor.[27]

Maestri, who was one of the wealthiest men in the city, served as mayor for ten years after Long's death, during which time he successfully oversaw the modernization of the city's finances and the drainage system, as well as the completion of new public housing. Segregated developments for white residents included St. Thomas in Uptown and the Iberville and Florida projects below Canal Street. New developments were built for African Americans at Magnolia and Calliope in Uptown and Lafitte and St. Bernard in Downtown.

These new housing developments incorporated local Creole architectural elements such as cast-iron galleries and courtyards into attractive three-story brick units. The process of "slum clearance" led to the demolition of the old Storyville district in 1939 to create the new all-white Iberville housing project. Before the demolition, the first jazz historians romanticized the neighborhood's faded past while salvaging souvenirs from Lulu White's infamous Mahogany Hall brothel on Basin Street.

With WPA funds, the city renovated Audubon Zoo, first built in 1914 on the former site of the Cotton Centennial Exposition in Audubon Park. The WPA also funded the extension and expansion of City Park all the way to the new lakefront. Today, the park is filled with Art Deco reliefs and monuments by artist Enrique Alférez; he also created the gates of the City Park Stadium (now Tad Gormley) built in the late 1930s. At the end of the park near the lakefront, the U.S. Department of Agriculture built a modern research facility to study the possible industrial uses of southern agricultural products, the sector of the southern economy whose value plummeted during the Great Depression.

The 1939 opening of the new "Big Charity" Hospital became Robert

Maestri's (and hence Huey Long's posthumous) crowning legacy in New Orleans. The institution had its roots in the French colonial period, when French shipbuilder Jean Louis had included in his will money for the establishment of a facility to care for the poorest in 1836; it continued to exist as the second-oldest public hospital in the nation. Managed by the Daughters of Charity since the early American period, the hospital providing free care for the poorest citizens had functioned in a two-story building at 1500 Tulane Ave. (Common St.) since 1832. By the early twentieth century, the original building was well past its prime. As a populist governor, Huey Long created a state healthcare system and had wanted to construct a new facility as its flagship.

After Long's death, the federal authorities contracted Weiss, Dreyfous, and Seiferth to design the massive twenty-story Art Deco healthcare facility. Enrique Alférez's artistic aluminum grill, titled "Louisiana at Work and Play," greeted guests above the front entrance. The second-largest hospital in the nation at the time, Charity served a large proportion of the city's population: its quality natal care led many to proudly proclaim, "I am a Charity baby."

By 1939 New Orleans emerged from the depths of the Great Depression and entered a new period of economic prosperity. As the United States began to mobilize to support the Allied cause with the outbreak of World War II, the city became an important hub for defense industries, a center for military training, and a regional port of embarkation. The newly reclaimed lands along the open lakefront were transformed from open marshes and pastures into Lagarde Army Hospital (at West End), a Naval Air Base (at Milneburg), and the Consolidated-Vultee aircraft plant making PBY Catalina scout planes to the east.

Under Roosevelt's orders, the War Department decentralized defense manufacturing from the concentrated industrial corridor of the northeast Atlantic Coast to the rest of the nation. New Orleans stood to gain from the president's efforts to bring manufacturing to the impoverished American South. The city, along with other coastal communities, emerged as a shipbuilding center.

This employment boom attracted impoverished rural job seekers from the southern hinterland who relished the idea of earning the unprecedented high wages of the new manufacturing jobs. In some cases, federal defense jobs paid in one hour what most rural southerners had made in one day in agricultural work. For example, Delta Shipbuilding Company of Cleveland constructed Liberty Ships on the Industrial Canal, hiring more than ten thousand workers at wages that began at more than one dollar per hour.

Industrialist Andrew Jackson Higgins exemplified the promise of the new industries that war mobilization brought to the city. Beginning as a manufacturer of small flat-bottomed boats that could navigate shallow bayous in the 1930s, his firm Higgins Industries quickly grew from one plant on St. Charles Avenue to four plants around the city: they built PT boats and landing craft (LCVP) that became essential in the Allied landings in the Pacific Islands and on D-Day in Normandy. Additionally, Higgins acquired a large plywood plant in the marshes of New Orleans East that had the potential to be a major industrial site. Although the 1947 hurricane dashed Higgins's expansion plans, in the 1960s the site eventually developed into the Michoud Assembly Facility, which built rockets for NASA.[28]

During the war, the influx of migrant workers from inland regions gave the city a more southern and American character. Jazz journalists noted that one was more likely to hear "hillbilly" music than jazz on Bourbon Street. In fact, many of the local jazz musicians relocated to central Louisiana, where the prevalence of military camps provided many opportunities to perform. The military bases on the lakefront also brought in Americans from around the nation, further diluting the Creole character of the city.

At the same time, military and employment experiences exposed provincial Orleanians to the wider world. For African American veterans especially, fighting for democracy and against fascism inspired a postwar commitment to civil rights activism. Thus, the war not only had an overall beneficial effect on the New Orleans economy but also ushered in a new political era in which the unjust system of segregation became untenable.

Foodways: Creolizing Cuisine in the Jazz Age

Throughout the automobile age, New Orleans continued to grow as a tourist destination that played on the city's Creole past. In the 1920s, the oldest restaurants in the city such as Antoine's defined New Orleans's unique Creole culinary heritage. Two newer restaurants, Galatoire's and Arnaud's, founded in the early 1900s, also bolstered the French-inspired dining experience associated with the Old World charms of the Vieux Carré.

Jean Galatoire and his wife Gabrielle Marchal had immigrated to the United States in the 1880s from the western Atlantic-Pyrenees mountain village of Pardies, France. After landing in Birmingham, Alabama, the Galatoires moved to New Orleans, where they first opened a saloon on Canal Street and then purchased a small restaurant at 209 Bourbon Street in 1905. Fourteen years later, Jean and Gabrielle's three nephews, who had immigrated in the years before World War I, bought the restaurant. Their initial menu was based on the cuisine of the family's region and featured dishes with creamy Bearnaise sauce. Gradually, the kitchen included more classic Creole dishes such as turtle soup, shrimp and okra gumbo, trout Meunière amandine, and oysters en brochette with Meunière sauce that drew from locally available seafood with a classical French influence. The three nephews provided an elegant French dining experience as well.

Arnaud's Restauarant also has its roots in the Atlantic-Pyrenees region of France. The founder, Arnaud Cazenave, had originally moved from the small western Pyrenees village of Bosdarros to study medicine in Mississippi during the late nineteenth century.[29] After running a café at the Absinthe House, Arnaud—an expert in French wines and cuisine—bought a restaurant at 811 Bienville Street in the Vieux Carré. Cazenave first hired Madame Pierre to serve as chef at the establishment that served an elaborate variety of local seafood cooked in classic French sauces; soups; fowl, steaks, and chops; and French salads and imported cheeses. Most importantly, Cazenave tried to convey his French dining philosophy, often foreign to Americans, that the "art of cooking" is the "soul of festivity." He believed that "eating should be a pleasure" and that a well-chosen dinner, prepared and served, "is a joy to all senses, and an impelling incentive to a sound sleep, good health, and a long life."[30] One could say that his philosophy is echoed by New Orleanians to this day.

The esteemed Fabacher's provided a unique German Creole dining experience in New Orleans during this period. Franz Joseph Fabacher, who immigrated to New Orleans in the 1840s, opened the original Fabacher's Restaurant, Oyster House and Hotel at 137 Royal Street with his wife Magdalena in 1880. The restaurant specialized in local seafood dishes including oysters "served up any style," crayfish on ice, redfish court-bouillon, sheepshead au gratin, as well as an assortment of wild game from squirrel to geese. The restaurant also offered various classic Bavarian schnitzels (breaded fried cutlets), imported Munich beers, and the local Jax Bohemian Beer, brewed by owner Anthony Fabacher's brother Lawrence. Jax, brewed at the large complex at 600 Decatur Street in the French Quarter, was one of the most prominent German beers before and after Prohibition.[31]

The "Original Fabacher's" closed in 1915, perhaps because of the prevalent anti-German sentiment preceding the U.S. entry into World War I. Peter, one of Anthony's sons, continued the family tradition by opening Fabacher's Rathskeller on lower St. Charles Avenue, where Louis Armstrong abandoned his coal cart after he heard about the Armistice in November 1918. The Rathskeller served a mid-day lunch and stayed open late as a German-style beer and dance hall, where Max Fink's orchestra performed in the early Jazz Age. This second Fabacher's closed during Prohibition when agents raided the site and arrested Peter in 1921 for selling alcohol.

At the same time that fine Creole dining experiences came of age in this period, the development of the muffuletta and po-boy sandwiches attested to the importance of hearty affordable meals for everyday working people in New Orleans. The muffuletta's roots are found in the Sicilian grocers and bakers of the "Little Palermo" section of the lower French Quarter during the early 1900s. The sandwich is not native to Sicily but uses the Sicilian muffuletta loaf as the base; it likely emerged from the All Saints Day tradition in Palermo, where the bread is seasoned with olive oil, oregano, anchovies, and local cheeses.

The New Orleans variation apparently developed when farmers visited Central Grocery (923 Decatur Street), where they bought the round sesame loaves and ate them with Genoa ham, mortadella, thinly sliced mozzarella or provolone cheese, and olive dressing. During the early 1900s, owner Salvatore Lupo began to offer the combination as a sandwich, which other nearby corner stores and delicatessens soon began to sell as well. By the 1950s, the sandwich was offered on local menus under its current name, representing the classic process of creolization in local foodways. Old-timers claim that the sandwich is better on the second day when the olive oil dressing has been thoroughly absorbed into the bread.[32]

The po-boy or "poor boy" sandwich received its name during the labor unrest of the post–World War I period. In 1929, the owners of Martin Brothers' Coffee Stand, Bennie and Clovis Martin, supported the striking streetcar operators of Division 194. The Martins offered them free hot meals at their store located at North Peters and Ursuline Streets in the French Market—just around the corner from Central Grocery of muffuletta fame. The sandwich was essentially roast beef "debris" (gravy and beef trimmings) served on a French bread loaf sliced lengthwise. Whenever a striking conductor came in to get a sandwich. the brothers would call out, "Here comes another poor boy."

Gradually, the name "poor boy" began to apply to the style of sandwich on long French bread loaves. German and Austrian bakers had dominated the bread trade by the mid-nineteenth century, changing the traditional French baguette (with a thick crust) to a lighter loaf with a thin crispy and flaky crust. Gendusa Bakery, owned by Sicilian immigrant John Gendusa, supplied the Martin Brothers with the "special" poor-boy loaves, baked with a long evenly shaped loaf and not the tapered ends of a baguette: these new loaves made for better sandwiches. He had been inspired by the bread he grew up with in Sicily: the classic "French bread" loaf in New Orleans today represents the process of creolization from French, German, and Italian bakers in the city.[33]

Before the development of the iconic sandwich made with roast beef debris, New Orleanians had been eating similar-style sandwiches called simply a "loaf." Even the upscale Original Fabacher's menu proclaimed that their specialty was "Trout, Chicken, Crab, or Oyster Loaves" before it closed in 1915. Whereas the Martin Brothers used roast beef debris as an affordable way to provide a hearty meal to the striking carmen, the New Orleans loaf sandwich tradition, as exemplified by Fabacher's, often used local fried seafood as the main ingredient, distinguishing it from other loaf sandwich traditions of the Atlantic Coast that used cold cuts or hot beef. The addition of a spicy cocktail sauce to the seafood sandwich also became a unique hallmark of the New Orleans loaf and poor-boy sandwiches of the twentieth century. The local term "dressed" (or "fully dressed") came to designate a sandwich with lettuce, tomatoes, pickles, mayonnaise ("mynez"), and hot sauce.

The experiences that Louis Armstrong had growing up in New Orleans are revealing about the lives of families with little means in the city during the 1910s and 1920s. His recounting of local foodways, in particular, shows how poor and working-class families ate during this period. In his autobiography, *Satchmo: My Life in New Orleans*, the author obsessively discusses food, reflecting the social and cultural importance of meals for the city's residents. In reference to the sandwich discussed earlier, Armstrong recalled with pride his working with the "old hustlers" at the C. A. Andrews Coal Yard during World War I. He wrote, "At lunch time I would sit with them with my ten-cent mug of beer and my poor boy sandwich. Most of the time I would just listen, but when I threw in my two-cents' worth, the idea they would even listen to me just thrilled me all over."[34]

Armstrong also related how his mother, in the tradition of New Orleans families, passed on her culinary knowledge to Louis and his sister Mama Lucy. He bragged, "Mayann taught us how to cook her best dishes. Her jumbalaya [*sic*] was delicious." To the classic New Orleans jambalaya recipe, she added "diced Bologna sausage, shrimp, oysters, hard-shelled crabs mixed with rice and flavored with tomato sauce." He also wrote, "Her creole gumbo was the finest in the world. Her cabbage and rice was marvelous. As for red beans and rice, well, I don't have to say anything about that. It's my birthmark."[35]

Indeed, Armstrong identified so strongly with that simple dish that he often signed his letters, "Red beans and ricely yours." And in *Satchmo,* he makes numerous references to the classic meal. Armstrong proudly proclaimed that when he was very young, his parents trusted him to watch over his younger siblings and to cook a pot of beans while the adults worked outside the home. But he admitted, "Whenever I cooked a big pot of beans and ham hocks they would manage to eat up most of it before I could get to the table."

When he returned home after playing with Fate Marable's Orchestra on the summer riverboat excursions around 1920, his mother Mayann welcomed him with his favorite meal. As he reminisced, "She went to Zatteran's [*sic*] grocery store" where "she bought a pound of red beans, a pound of rice, a big slice of fat back and a big red onion." Back at home "she boiled the jive down to a gravy, and I'll tell you that when we came we could smell her pot almost a block away."[36]

Armstrong also mentioned in his writings how red beans and rice became creolized in his neighborhood, around the intersection of South Rampart and Common Streets: "The Chinese finally moved into a little section of their own and called it *China Town,* with a few little *beat up* restaurants serving *soul* food on the same menu with their Chinese dishes." Armstrong used to hear the locals bragging about the Chinese-made red beans and rice, which he claimed "wasn't bad at all." Even though "colored people cook the best *Red* Beans + Rice," Armstrong admitted that for a "special occasion" his parents treated him and his sister Mama Lucy for a meal in Chinatown: "And we felt we were having something Big. We would also order Fried Rice and *Liver Gravy* with our Red Beans. And *ooh, God*—you would *lick* your *fingers* it would taste so good."[37]

Red Beans and Rice

In honor of Louis Armstrong's association with early twentieth-century New Orleans, red beans and rice is the featured recipe for this chapter. As Armstrong suggests in *Satchmo,* the ingredients were inexpensive and often varied depending on the meat available for seasoning.

The recipe for red beans, like many New Orleans dishes, likely came from many sources and culinary traditions. In the Lauragais region of southwestern France, red beans (*les haricots rouges*) are an important crop and part of local food customs. The hearty bean casserole *cassoulet* from this region is similar to a New Orleans red beans dish in its liberal use of pork sausage and ham for a smoky flavor. In the Congo region of central Africa, *madesu* (red bean stew) is also an essential food tradition and is often served with rice and *piri piri* red peppers. In the Caribbean, the meal *riz collé aux haricots rouge* (sticky rice with red beans) is a staple in Haiti (formerly Saint-Domingue); a variation is also found in the neighboring eastern Cuban Oriente Province, where the stew known as *frijoles colorados* is paired with rice. Indeed, the presence of a beans and rice staple is common throughout much of the Atlantic Creole world.[38]

In New Orleans, many cooks use only the local Camellia brand of beans. For seasoning, locals often prefer pickled tips—essentially the tips of pork ribs that have been pickled. Others swear by smoked D&D sausage. In 2005 when New Orleanians found themselves temporarily settled in other cities following the devastation of Hurricane Katrina, one often heard the lament that none of these local products could be found and they could not wait to return to cook their favorite comfort food with the proper ingredients.

But as Armstrong described, sometimes he and his mother used meats such as pork fatback or ham hocks. In fact, his own archived recipe for red beans calls for the use of both salt pork and ham hocks.[39] Many cooks combine these meats and sausages in the process of cooking the bean dish. Red beans are like gumbo and other local dishes, in that each person may have their own special recipe passed down through their family. Therefore, endless variations of the recipes are used throughout the city. But one of the defining characteristics shared by all the recipes is the creamy consistency of the beans, mixed with the smoky flavor of the meat seasoning.

Serves 6

Holy Trinity + Garlic
3 large chopped onions
4 stalks chopped celery
2 seeded and chopped bell peppers
6 to 12 cloves of chopped garlic (depending on your taste)
1 pound red beans cooked
1 pound white rice cooked with 2 tablespoons of butter
1 pound pickle tips (or substitute seasoned or smoked ham cut into chunks)
1 pound diced or thin-sliced smoked sausage
3 tablespoons vegetable oil (canola or sunflower oil)
4 whole bay leaves
3 sprigs fresh thyme or 1 tablespoon of dried thyme
2 tablespoons chopped parsley
4 tablespoons of Creole seasoning (even mixture of salt, cayenne, black pepper, and garlic powder)

1. Soak the dried beans over night to rehydrate.

2. Rinse the beans, place them into a 6-quart pot, and add 3 quarts of water.

3. Boil and then turn down to a medium-low simmer.

4. Add the seasoning, bay leaves, and half the holy trinity/garlic mixture to the beans—and let them cook for 3 hours.

5. While the beans are simmering, rinse the pickle tips and cook them in a large pot of water for 30 minutes. Repeat the process, which removes the saltiness of the meat. When the tips are tender, drain the water and set aside.

6. In a large pan, heat the cooking oil and sauté the rest of the holy trinity/garlic on medium heat until the onions are clear and soft. Add the tender pickle tips (or ham) and diced smoked sausage, and sauté until the meat is slightly browned.

7. Add the thyme, cooked meat, and remaining holy trinity mixture to the cooked beans, and continue cooking on medium-low heat for 30 minutes. If the beans are not creamy enough, some cooks prefer to mash them (using a spoon)

as they cook to ensure the correct texture. Continue to gently stir to make sure that beans do not stick to the bottom of the pot.

8. To cook the rice, bring to a boil and add the butter. Once boiling, reduce to a very low simmer and only stir at the early boiling point to prevent sticking. When the water is evaporated and the rice is tender, set aside.

9. When the beans are ready, serve in a bowl with a scoop or large spoonful of the cooked white rice on top. Garnish with parsley and your favorite red pepper vinegar sauce.

Romance of the Old

In 1939, New Orleans existed as a locale where boosters and tourists romanticized the Old World ambience of the historic neighborhoods, which provided a welcome contrast to the rapidly modernizing world and homogenized American suburbs. On the threshold of World War II, the city was about to welcome new defense industries while also trying to hold onto its historic role as the "Queen of the South." As other younger cities such as Atlanta, Dallas, and Houston matured into business-friendly southern metropolises, New Orleans hoped to keep pace while sustaining a certain charm distinguished by its Creole past.

In city leaders' push toward modernism, emerging preservationists provided an equal push back for maintaining the historic character of the city, especially the French Quarter. The Hurricane of 1915 severely damaged the old St. Louis Hotel, which was soon demolished. In the preceding decade, the entire adjacent block upriver along Royal and Chartres Streets had been cleared to make way for the new State Courthouse that was completed in 1910. With the fiery destruction of the French Opera House in 1919, the city proposed the demolition of several square blocks in the Vieux Carré to make room for a new municipal auditorium, and thereby replace the Opera House as the site of the elite Mardi Gras ball hosted by the old-line krewes of Rex and Comus.

Although many New Orleanians saw the Vieux Carré merely as an Italian and African American slum, the city's proposal alarmed a small group of influential citizens who feared it would destroy the historical fabric of the French Quarter. Several organizations made up of people in literary, arts, and society circles formed to protect the old neighborhood, and by 1925 Mayor Martin Behrman and the city council had created the Vieux Carré Commission (VCC) to study the preservation of historic buildings of interest in the neighborhood. Finally, in 1936, the state gave the VCC authority to enforce the preservation and regulation of buildings within the historic neighborhood, outside Canal Street. On a national level, New Orleans emerged as one of the earliest U.S. cities to pioneer and prioritize historic architectural preservation.[40]

In this post–World War I period, the French Quarter attracted artists and writers, who were inspired by this American city with European charm. Following in the footsteps of the local-color writers of the late nineteenth century, a new generation of romantics, including artist Alberta Kinsey and writers Lyle Saxon, Sherwood Anderson, and William Faulkner, settled in the bohemian neighborhood. In the rapidly modernizing United States, such artists and literary figures viewed New Orleans, and specifically the Vieux Carré, as the "Paris of the West," where café culture and European sensibilities characterized the lifestyle.[41] Often, outsiders and tourists searched for remnants of a bygone era when visiting New Orleans.

Adherence to a romantic past also attracted the earliest jazz historians to the cradle of the music genre. By the late 1930s, big band swing music from Kansas City and New York were the most modern elements of popular culture, while New Orleans jazz lay forgotten as a souvenir from an older time. Charles Edward Smith, who co-wrote the first history of jazz, *Jazzmen,* visited the city in 1939 and was saddened by what he saw and heard. Describing a down-and-out city where the good times were forgotten, he wrote, "If you ask [a New Orleans musician] what killed the music business in that town, he'll tell you any one of a number of things—the radio, the talking picture, the filling in of the lake front, poverty."[42] This, despite the fact that some esteemed jazz artists, such as Steve Lewis, Fats Pichon, Joe Robichaux, and Tony Almerico, still performed regularly in the city.

At the end of World War II, New Orleans–style jazz experienced a nostalgic resurgence among music lovers who failed to appreciate the modern pop sounds of swing and longed for the 1910s. Writers Rudi Blesh and Harriet Grossman Janis founded Circle Records in New York in 1946 to record New Orleans musicians from the first era of ragtime and jazz. Their 1946 album *Jazz à La Creole* not only embodied a longing for older music but also documented the continued existence of New Orleans Creole culture into the 1940s.

Drummer Warren "Baby" Dodds led the album's "Creole" band, despite his growing up in a strict uptown household during the early 1900s where his mother discouraged any association with French-speaking Creoles. Dodds gained national fame while playing drums in King Oliver's popular Creole Jazz Band with Louis Armstrong in the early 1920s. Realizing that the term "Creole" provided an appealing marketing hook for New Orleans culture in the 1940s, Dodds's Circle Records band included New Orleans musicians Albert Nicholas on clarinet, George "Pops" Foster on bass, and Danny Barker on guitar, as well as two New York musicians, James P. Johnson and Don Ewell, on piano.

The album featured several songs that Albert Nicholas and Danny Barker sang in patois. Both had grown up in downtown Creole households, but in their adult years had worked as jazz artists in New York City. While the producers Blesh and Janis romanticized the "pure" jazz of the recordings, in fact, the musicians themselves lived a very modern existence in New York, not wedded to a romanticized segregated New Orleans of their youth. But the songs "Les Oignons" and "Mo Pas Lemmé Ças" utilized the Creole patois while drawing from contemporary Afro-Caribbean rhythms that had come to New York at the time and had some precedent in New Orleans.

The album's contemporary attributes reflected the combined romanticism and racial reality of modern New Orleans at the time. As outsiders, Blesh from Oklahoma and Janis from New York intended the album for an audience of "traditional" jazz lovers who romanticized the past. But the artists themselves really considered themselves contemporary. All the musicians lived in New York and had essentially left New Orleans permanently after World War I, because of greater opportunities and to escape the oppressive environment of racial segregation.

The exodus of jazz musicians, and their occasional return to New Orleans, reflects the dilemma that many native New Orleanians faced in the years preceding and following World War I. On the one hand, many New Orleanians remained in the city enticed by the comfort of their families, as well as the rich culinary heritage, the unique celebration traditions, and the warm weather. On the other hand, the greater economic opportunities elsewhere and, for African Americans, a life without Jim Crow drew many others away. As long as the antiquated and unjust system of segregation existed, New Orleans would be held back from reaching its potential for business, tourism, and global acceptance in the post–World War II modern world.

7

America's Most Interesting City

Sunbelt and Suburbs, 1950–2000

IN 1949, the "King of Jazz" Louis Armstrong realized a lifelong dream by serving as King Zulu on Carnival Day in New Orleans (fig. 17). He very proudly rode as the monarch of the historic African American parading club that had originated in his back-of-town neighborhood in 1909. Armstrong's reign was the first guest appearance by a celebrity monarch in any Mardi Gras parade. As a sign of his global fame, *Time* magazine featured his image wearing a crown of trumpets, marking the first appearance of an African American on the cover of the respected news magazine.

In the years following World War II, Armstrong emerged as the smiling face of the United States on the international stage. Traveling the world as "Ambassador Satch," the New Orleans native promoted the ideals of American democracy on tours sponsored by the U.S. State Department in Latin America, East Asia, the Middle East, and Africa. In 1957, the movie *Satchmo the Great* documented his cultural visit to the newly independent nation of Ghana, underscoring the importance of American support to developing states. By the late 1950s, Armstrong's ability to transcend barriers was so great that a Mischa Richter *New Yorker* cartoon sardonically questioned whether "Satchmo or [Secretary of State John Foster] Dulles" could resolve "a diplomatic mission of utmost delicacy" for the State Department under President Eisenhower.

At the height of the Cold War, the United States promoted itself as the bastion of democratic values internationally while tolerating racial injustice at home. Privately, Armstrong resented the hypocrisy of the State Department using him to promote American standards while segregation existed in the South, including in his hometown. In many respects, New Orleans's

FIG. 17. Despite deciding to live away from New Orleans for his entire life after 1921, Louis Armstrong visited the city numerous times over the years, including to celebrate his proud reign as King Zulu in 1949. *Louis Armstrong as King Zulu on Mardi Gras Day,* 1949, Louisiana State Museum, Jazz Collection, 1978.118(B), 07032b.

Cold War–era racial conservatism reflected the city's and country's awkward straddling of the past and the modern age.[1]

While Armstrong promoted U.S. ideals abroad, the very conservative 1956 Louisiana legislature banned interracial performances in the state (Act 579) in reaction to the growing civil rights movement. Although Armstrong rarely revealed his political beliefs publicly, by the 1950s he began to take a more open stand against segregation and racial injustice. After World War II he made a point of racially integrating his "All-Stars" band with artists such as Jack Teagarden, Eddie Shu, Marty Napoleon, and Barrett Deems. In 1956, his band included Filipino American drummer Danny Barcelona. As long as the law banning interracial performances remained on the books, Armstrong used the opportunity to boycott appearances in the state—including his hometown. Although the local hero had visited numerous times in the late 1940s and early 1950s, Armstrong did not perform again in New Orleans until 1965 after the passage of the Civil Rights Act.

In a bitter expression of his love-hate relationship with New Orleans at the time, Armstrong proclaimed angrily, "I don't care if I ever see that city again. . . . They treat me better all over the world, than they do in my hometown. Ain't that stupid? Jazz was born there, and I remember when it was no crime for cats of any color to get together and blow." His bitterness and regret reflected the anger many African Americans held toward the city during the civil rights era and beyond.[2]

For the first time, New Orleans no longer held the title of the American South's largest city. Since 1950, Houston at 596,163 people and the nation's fourteenth-largest city had surpassed New Orleans, which had grown to 570,445 people but fell to sixteenth in size. Although Houston had once looked to New Orleans for cultural inspiration and sophistication, the tables had turned in the post–World War II years.

During this period, younger southern cities such as Atlanta, Dallas, Memphis, and Houston grew at a faster pace than the charming southern historic port cities of Charleston, Savannah, Mobile, Galveston, and New Orleans. The modern inland cities seemed to attract new businesses, despite adhering to the system of segregation. As a result, New Orleans made every effort to emulate the model of economic modernity that defined the booming Sunbelt of the post–World War II American South and Southwest.

In 1946, the youthful deLesseps "Chep" Morrison was elected mayor of New Orleans. His victory reflected white voters' support for a forward-looking political environment. Morrison presented himself as a clean-cut and well-spoken veteran who was returning home to reform the city's government, after the city's decade of political rule by the less sophisticated Huey Long supporter, Robert Maestri.

The young reformer gained the support of the city's business community, returning white veterans, and well-educated women, who staged parades in which marchers carried brooms to symbolize Morrison's commitment to sweeping out corruption. The "Broom Brigades" showcased the power of these white female voters in the postwar era. Some women leaders, such as liberal activist Edith Stern, even sought to increase African American voter registration to reflect their idealistic vision of an advanced southern city.[3]

Under Morrison's leadership, New Orleans gained a reputation nationally as an urban model in the American South. As a modernist, Morrison upgraded the Port of New Orleans and city services, created the New Orleans Recreation Department (NORD), constructed highway and street overpasses, expanded public housing, and promoted urban renewal. Under his watch, the city built a new, larger airport, Moisant Field, leasing the site from the town of Kenner and designing a modern terminal that opened in 1959. And despite the decline of passenger railroads, Morrison built a central railroad and bus terminal that replaced the private stations—the L&N, the Southern, and the Southern Pacific—that served rail travelers along the Canal Street corridor.

And as did other modern cities, New Orleans replaced the streetcars with a modern bus system. For historic preservation and tourism reasons, the city kept the old St. Charles line, which continues as the oldest operating streetcar line in the nation. Ironically in these post–World War II years, New Orleans became well known for Tennessee Williams's 1947 play *A Streetcar Named Desire*, titled for the line that ran along Royal Street between the French Quarter and the Upper Ninth Ward, ending at Desire Street. By 1951, the famous movie adaptation of *Streetcar*, starring Marlon Brando and Vivien Leigh, already presented an outdated vision of New Orleans, because the city had replaced the Desire line with buses in 1948.

Morrison sought to build on New Orleans's historic relationship with the tropical nations to the South. Billing the city as the "Gateway to the Americas," he relentlessly courted trade with Latin American nations. The widening and reimagining of Basin Street—the former front entrance to Storyville—presented an opportunity to create an homage to great Latino political figures.

After the city's railroad system was centralized in the new terminal on Loyola Avenue, the old Southern Railway Station at Basin and Canal was demolished. Basin Street was reconfigured into a wide avenue with a neutral ground, on which were placed statues of Venezuelan patriot Simón Bolívar, nineteenth-century Central American leader Francisco Morazán, and Mexican president Benito Juárez, who had worked as a cigar roller in the nearby Faubourg Tremé during the 1850s. The statues remain today as a reminder of the mayor's efforts and the city's historic Latin American connections.

In the mid-1950s Morrison also had built a new modern glass-and-steel city hall on Perdido Street, into which city government moved from the Greek Revival Temple on St. Charles Avenue, which was designed by James Gallier Sr. in 1848. The new city hall was much larger and more functional than the old one, and the contemporary structure symbolized Morrison's embrace of the urban renewal movement. The complex, which opened in 1957, included a large green space across the street named Duncan Plaza and an annex constructed in a similar design to the main building. A very modern main branch of the public library, designed by local firm Curtis and Davis, opened in 1958 at the other end of the plaza.

To build the city hall complex, the city leveled several blocks in the back-of-town area behind the CBD. Homes were demolished, and apartment buildings and stores were torn down and replaced with surface parking lots for the nearby CBD and city government. Many of the original Jewish residents, such as the Karnofskys, had already moved to quieter neighborhoods such as Lakeview, although some still operated their shops and stores along South Rampart.

The neighborhood around Common Street had already lost its Chinese inhabitants, who followed the move of Chinatown to the central French Quarter during the 1930s. In the postwar era, the Chinese community largely moved out to suburban Jefferson Parish, where the popular House of Lee on the new Veterans Highway in Metairie made the Lee family well known. The owner's son Harry Lee later became a larger-than-life political figure who served as parish sheriff from 1979 to 2007. As a law enforcement figure, he sported his iconic cowboy hat and instituted a law-and-order policy that civil rights activists viewed as racist.

The demolition included the 1100–1300 blocks of Perdido Street, where Louis Armstrong lived as a youth at 1233 Perdido. Louis Armstrong did not publicly comment on the loss of his childhood landmarks in the 1950s, but his love–hate relationship with New Orleans continued. In a later private conversation with New Orleans Jazz Club president Helen Arlt, Armstrong expressed regret and sadness at the destruction of his birthplace. Like most of his musical peers, he chose to live outside the segregated South. In the 1940s he and his wife Lucille bought a house in the middle-class African American neighborhood of Corona, Queens, in New York City. Today, his home is a public museum dedicated to interpreting his life and career.[4]

In the meantime, Mayor Morrison remained committed to segregation to preserve his political career. Yet, even as he set his sights on the governorship in the elections of 1956, 1960, and 1964, his urbane sophisticated manners and his cooperation with Black leaders in New Orleans earned him the statewide reputation as "the NAACP candidate." Racial conservatives charged that Morrison was soft on segregation and therefore not aligned with the values of white Democratic voters. In fact, the mayor initiated the massive new Desire public housing development and adjacent George W. Carver High School for African Americans so New Orleans could remain a segregated city.

Likewise, in 1955 Morrison attended the ribbon cutting for the Pontchartrain Park subdivision on the eastern lakefront. Funded by local philanthropists Edith and Edgar Stern and Rosa and Charles Keller, the modern suburb provided ranch-style housing and an eighteen-hole golf course for middle-class African Americans. The following year, the new Southern University New Orleans opened next to Pontchartrain Park, highlighting the city's efforts to maintain racial separatism in higher education.[5]

The contradiction of southern segregation existing in juxtaposition to professed American democratic values created a national political and social crisis that became manifested locally. New Orleans desired modernity but also maintained an antiquated and undemocratic racial caste system. In 1960, the city emerged on the global stage as the battleground for civil rights and racial segregation. That year, New Orleans became the first southern city to integrate its public elementary schools.

The Problem We All Live With

On November 14, 1960, three young girls—Leona Tate, Gail Etienne, and Tessie Prevost—walked through the doorway of the McDonogh #19 School in the Lower Ninth Ward along St. Claude Avenue. That same day another child, Ruby Bridges, entered William Frantz Elementary on North Galvez on the other side of the Industrial Canal in the Upper Ninth Ward. In doing so, these four girls, later known as the "New Orleans Four," became the first African Americans to integrate the segregated New Orleans public school system. Their enrollment became a global focal point for the U.S. civil rights movement.

After desegregation of the Little Rock, Arkansas, public high schools in 1957, the integration of elementary schools in New Orleans became the second globally publicized effort to enforce the end of racial segregation in American public education. In 1954, the U.S. Supreme Court case of *Brown v. Board of Education* ruled that segregated schools were unlawful. In doing so, the court overturned the idea of "separate but equal," the rationale for the New Orleans–based *Plessy v. Ferguson* ruling that legalized segregated train travel in Louisiana in the 1890s.

The "New Orleans Four" are quite remarkable because at only six years old the brave children became civil rights heroes for those who supported the end of segregation. The four girls had been selected to serve this role because of their ability to hold up to the immense pressures of the integration process. Their gender was also a factor in their selection: integrationists who oversaw the challenge viewed young girls as less threatening and more sympathetic than boys.[6]

When they arrived at the schools, the girls faced taunts, racial slurs, and even death threats yelled by white supremacist protesters. Federal marshals accompanied the young students for protection. Four years later, American painter Norman Rockwell depicted this scene in a painting titled *The Problem We All Live With,* which was published in *Look* magazine. In the painting, a lone young girl dressed in white, depicting Ruby Bridges, walks surrounded by federal marshals, passing a wall with a racial epithet painted next to a stain from a rotten tomato.

Rockwell's perspective centers on the child, and the marshals are shown from the shoulders down, thereby bringing the viewer's focus on the experiences of the lone student. Since the 1930s, Rockwell had generally depicted more idyllic scenes with less social commentary in the *Saturday Evening Post,* but his new contract with *Look* enabled him to address more controversial issues. *The Problem* showed how New Orleans's racial troubles mirrored the delicate national transition toward a post-segregation society.

If Mayor Chep Morrison wanted to position New Orleans as a modern Sunbelt metropolis open for international business, the televised footage of angry white crowds protesting school integration certainly did not help the city's image. Yet Morrison felt compelled to support segregation to retain support from his base of conservative white Democrats. The Orleans Parish School Board, like many other southern school districts at the time, foresaw the legal challenges to segregation and in the 1950s had built schools for African Americans that could be seen as equal to white schools. In 1954, the very modern Phillis Wheatley Elementary opened on Dumaine Street in the historic Afro-Creole Tremé neighborhood as an example of the city's efforts to justify "separate but equal."

In the early 1960s, the city experienced a wave of civil rights protests against segregation in public transport, stores, and accommodations. In May 1961, "Freedom Rides" became a form of activism in which interracial groups rode buses from Washington, DC, to southern communities, including New Orleans, to challenge segregated interstate public transportation. The riders sometimes encountered extreme violence from white supremacists along the way. The freedom riders arrived in New Orleans by plane, because the bus company refused to transport them, fearing fire bombings and attacks. The group found housing at Xavier University with the support of the young activist dean Norman Francis and ate a meal at Dooky Chase Restaurant. The young protesters then attended a peaceful rally at New Zion Baptist Church, whose pastor, A. L. Davis, had emerged as one of the most outspoken religious leaders advocating for equal rights in the 1950s and 1960s. The rides would continue throughout 1961, bringing some four hundred activists to New Orleans.

In 1957, the Southern Christian Leadership Conference, a civil rights organization of African American Baptist activists across the South, was founded at New Zion Baptist Church (2319 Third Street). The group elected the youthful Martin Luther King Jr. as its first president and proceeded to stage nonviolent protests against segregation across the South. As a southern city with nearly 235,000 African Americans in 1960, New Orleans represented an important location for manifesting the future of post-segregation America.[7]

Locally, activists in the Consumer League began organizing boycotts and protests of stores in the city's principal shopping district of Canal Street and on Dryades Street, where African Americans comprised more than 90 percent of shoppers but were not hired as clerks or managers. By 1960 the nationally based Congress of Racial Equality (CORE) organized student activists to participate in Canal Street sit-ins and to join the Freedom Ride movement.

A diverse group of young activists committed themselves to the protest movements on Canal Street. College students targeted the Woolworth's on Canal at North Rampart Street and McCrory's Five and Dime at 1005 Canal. The racially integrated group included Xavier student Rudy Lombard, Lanny Goldfinch of Tulane, Dillard's Cecil Carter Jr., and Southern University of New Orleans's Oretha Castle Haley, who also focused on Dryades Street boycotts. Teenager Dodie Smith-Simmons participated in these actions as well, getting arrested for protesting the segregation policies of Loew's Theater on Canal Street.[8]

Although Morrison and his successor Vic Schiro positioned New Orleans as a business-friendly city, they both refrained from creating any policies that would prohibit segregation in private businesses. The Canal Street sit-ins continued through 1964, when the passage of the Civil Rights Act that year brought the federal enforcement of integration to the city. After the bad publicity from attempts to integrate the schools in 1960, the business community urged Schiro to avoid public conflicts that could present New Orleans as having a hostile business climate. Such attitudes were inspired by Houston's and Atlanta's quiet implementation of desegregation, without any publicity or fanfare.

Schiro therefore took some small steps—without media attention—to begin the process of integration within the municipal government. In 1961, New Orleans schools continued to integrate, and in contrast to Morrison's policy, Schiro ordered the city police to keep protesters four blocks away from schools. The following year, the mayor ordered the integration of public parks, but he closed all public swimming pools until 1969.

By August 1963, Schiro had integrated all public facilities, including city hall, without any fanfare or backlash. However, the city hall cafeteria remained segregated because the private vendor under contract refused to allow it to be integrated. In a well-publicized incident—the kind that Schiro had hoped to avoid—activist reverends Avery Alexander and A. L. Davis, among others, staged a nonviolent sit-in at the cafeteria, from which New Orleans police literally dragged Alexander away by his feet and placed him under arrest. Footage of Alexander's head banging against the steps of the building brought more negative publicity to the city, yet the cafeteria did not integrate until 1965.[9]

Higher education in New Orleans had also made nominal efforts to apply the new directives. In 1962, Schiro ordered the desegregation of Delgado Trades School (now Delgado Community College) without any media attention. In 1963, Pearlie Hardin Elloie, Edwin Lombard, and Barbara Marie

Guillory became the first African Americans to attend Tulane University, following its board's 1961 decision to integrate—even though nineteenth-century benefactors Paul Tulane and Josephine Louise Newcomb stipulated that admission should be limited to white students. However, the Ford Foundation had informed Tulane that the university would not receive any future funding if it maintained a discriminatory enrollment policy.[10]

Five years earlier, the brand-new Louisiana State University New Orleans (present-day University of New Orleans [UNO]) enrolled fifty-five African American students. The integration process resulted from a federal lawsuit initiated by civil rights attorneys A. P. Tureaud and Ernest "Dutch" Morial, both raised in the city's historic Afro-Creole Seventh Ward. Morial had been the first African American graduate of the Louisiana State University Hebert School of Law in 1954 and then worked as Tureaud's protégé.

The first class of African American students at LSUNO (UNO) encountered hostility, but by the next year the incoming Black freshmen recalled an atmosphere of indifference. Even so, student activists staged sit-ins at the school cafeteria, privately operated by the Morrisons chain. In the fall of 1960, university president Homer Hitt gave an ultimatum to Morrisons: integrate or lose its contract. The chain chose the latter, and the university contracted with a new integration-friendly service the next school year. Student activists like Raphael Cassimere—who later became a history professor at UNO—then used the momentum of their efforts to stage sit-ins at Woolworth and McCrory's on Canal Street.[11]

Even as activists worked to integrate New Orleans's schools and public accommodations, the city's music culture was characterized by interracial cooperation. During the late 1950s, musical artists like Antoine "Fats" Domino, "Little Richard" Penniman, and Lloyd Price became hugely popular internationally, once again placing New Orleans at the epicenter of the sounds of a new generation. But even though African American rock 'n' roll artists embodied the face of the city to the world, their music was produced through a biracial collaboration mirroring the casual social integration that marked much of New Orleans's residential and work life during the period.

The team of Dave Bartholomew and Cosimo Matassa collaborated on producing and recording the hits that emerged from New Orleans. Matassa had grown up in the "Little Palermo" French Quarter of the mid-twentieth century and had worked in his family's segregated bar at 1001 Dauphine

Street, serving Black and white patrons in different sides of the bar. Matassa easily formed friendly relationships with the African American customers and after World War II worked at his uncle's J & M Music shop at 838–840 North Rampart Street, where he learned the skills of a recording engineer. At J & M, Matassa met and established a working relationship with local big band leader Dave Bartholomew. Together they formed a dynamic partnership.

After World War II, Bartholomew helped create a sound that mixed big band jazz with New Orleans signature Afro-Latin elements. The young trumpeter was born in the river town of Vacherie and moved to the city as a youth in the 1930s; there, he took lessons from Louis Armstrong's first music teacher, Peter Davis. In the postwar era of rhythm and blues (R&B)—the industry's term for African American music—Bartholomew and Matassa began to record and produce emerging artists such as the young Afro-Creole pianist from the Lower Ninth Ward known as "Fats" Domino.[12]

By 1955, the new phenomenon of "youth" music labeled artists like Domino as rock 'n' roll and promoted them to an expanded audience of both Black and white teenagers. Domino scored several international hits with "Ain't That a Shame" (1955), "Blueberry Hill" (1956), and "I'm Walkin'" (1957). During the 1950s, Domino became the second-highest-selling recording artist in the country after Elvis Presley. And although Domino had the opportunity to move anywhere, he chose to build a two-story ranch-style home in his childhood neighborhood, next door to his older shotgun on Caffin Avenue (renamed Fats Domino Avenue in 2021).

J & M produced the sound of "big beat" rock 'n' roll youth culture and recorded musical icons of the era such as pianist-singer Little Richard, whose outrageous style was captured in "Tutti Frutti" (1955) and "Long Tall Sally" (1956). In a more pop vein, J & M recorded singer Lloyd Price and scored a number one hit with "Personality" in 1959. On the heels of this studio's success, local pianist and composer Allen Toussaint produced many popular songs, including Ernie K-Doe's "Mother in Law," which topped at number one, and Lee Dorsey's "Ya Ya" and "Working in a Coal Mine." Producer Wardell Quezergue recorded the female vocal trio, the Dixie Cups, earning another number one hit, "Chapel of Love," in 1964.

As New Orleans was emerging as a center of rock 'n' roll, the traditional "Dixieland" jazz sound also developed as a form of interracial protest. In

1962, young activists Allan and Sandra Jaffe relocated to the French Quarter from Philadelphia. The couple soon began staging integrated jazz concerts at Larry Borenstein's art gallery as a form of dissent. The performances also provided a steady income for the numerous elderly artists such as trombonist Jim Robinson and the piano-playing Goodson Sisters, whose careers stretched back to the dance band craze of the 1920s. Their new venue, Preservation Hall, offered alcohol-free, family-friendly concerts (not dances) in the cozy front room of an old Spanish-style home at 726 St. Peter Street. The reputation of its authenticity spread quickly, and the hall soon became a tourist hotspot off Bourbon Street and one with roots in the civil rights movement.

As New Orleans musical artists became international stars, the great popularity of the rock 'n' roll sound often meant that these former rhythm and blues artists now played to white and integrated audiences. To those conservatives opposed to the civil rights movement, the new sound represented a social transformation and the emergence of a younger generation with its own musical tastes that differed greatly from those of their parents.

Although the music was not overtly political, the new sound and the sexually suggestive nature of the lyrics set the new generation apart. Like jazz, the music's name "rock 'n' roll" emerged as a euphemism for sex, and song titles like Shirley and Lee's "Let the Good Times Roll" from New Orleans underscored the connection. Appropriately, New Orleans had earlier created celebratory dance music without any overt political references but that by its very nature was rebellious and anti-authoritarian. That the biracial team of Matassa and Bartholomew found success in producing the new youth phenomenon underscored the understated nature of New Orleans's role in the social revolution that served as the apolitical soundtrack to the civil rights movement.

The largely biracial nature of rock 'n' roll ended with the British invasion and the rise in popularity of the Beatles during 1964. Ironically, these white English rock artists all listened to and were greatly inspired by African American singers and musicians from New Orleans—often covering their songs or composing new music in the style of their heroes. Indeed, when the Beatles first performed in New Orleans in September 1964, they invited Fats Domino to their green room before going on stage at the City Park Stadium.

That year the passage of the Civil Rights Act outlawed racial discrimination and segregation, profoundly affecting New Orleans society and politics. Yet, just as integration became law, the music industry became largely resegregated, divided between white rock artists and Black soul music performers. The New Orleans sound declined in popularity and with it the fortunes of the many artists who had enjoyed success during the rock 'n' roll and civil rights movement years.

New Orleans gradually emerged from under the shadows of racial segregation and the stigma it held for a city that strove to be modern and business friendly. In this new political and social climate, Mayor Vic Schiro sought to maintain New Orleans's historic position as an economic center of the region and the nation. Yet the social and political consequences of integration became clear as white families began to abandon the city for the surrounding suburbs where they could still enroll their children in white schools and live in all-white neighborhoods.

In 1960 New Orleans reached its peak population of 627,525—reflecting the population density created by large Catholic families living in modest shotgun houses and Creole cottages in integrated neighborhoods. During the 1950s, more than 100,000 New Orleanians had moved to neighboring Jefferson Parish. In the early 1960s, many white families immediately pulled their children out of the Orleans Parish public school system and moved to more racially conservative Jefferson and St. Bernard Parishes. Over the decade, these suburban parishes would gain another 150,000 residents, most of whom departed in white flight.

This exodus had a huge demographic and social impact on the city. Many historic communities such as the Irish Channel and Lower Garden District in Uptown, and the Tremé, the Bywater, and Holy Cross neighborhoods below Canal Street, lost their biracial patchwork character, as white residents fled to Metairie, Gretna, Arabi, and Chalmette. Within ten to twenty years, many of these neighborhoods were largely all-Black communities. In the 1970s, the city became majority African American for the first time since the 1830s.

School integration may have served as a strong push for racially conservative white families, but the modern suburbs also provided a great pull away from New Orleans. The federal GI Bill provided accessible financing for white military veterans seeking affordable modern brick houses with yards, a huge step up for many who grew up in crowded wooden shotgun houses with no yards or indoor plumbing. In 1956, the Causeway connected the New Orleans area to the north shore of St. Tammany Parish. By 1958 the Greater New Orleans Bridge across the Mississippi River provided easy access to the largely rural West Bank where new suburbs like Aurora Gardens and Terrytown quickly developed.[13] Likewise the construction of modern freeways such as the Pontchartrain Expressway and then Interstate 10 provided quick access to suburbs in a postwar world where cheap fuel and automobiles enabled affordable transportation. The 1960 opening of Lakeside Mall with a sea of parking spaces along Veterans Highway and Causeway Boulevard spelled the decline of Canal Street as the main fashionable shopping district.

If It's Good for New Orleans

In May 1965, an anonymous person threw a homemade bomb at the door of Dooky Chase Restaurant, damaging the entrance and bar at 2301 Orleans Avenue (fig. 18). The building only received minor damage, and no patrons were injured. But the destructive intent reflected the social tensions of the civil rights era. The Creole restaurant—owned by Edgar "Dooky" Chase Jr. and his wife Leah—served as a symbol of civil rights activism in New Orleans. During the Morrison mayorship and into the early Schiro period, the restaurant had hosted integrated meetings in its upstairs camelback room in which civil rights and labor relations were discussed and resolved. By 1965, new federal laws had seemingly addressed the issues of integration and voting rights, yet that year marked the emergence of a new community threat.

New Orleans mayor Vic Schiro had made the construction of new freeways an important part of his overall agenda of modernizing the city. Under the Federal Highway Act of 1956, the U.S. Department of Transportation developed a plan to build a new Interstate 10 through the heart of New Orleans. In the engineers' initial designs—largely inspired by the freeway proponent Robert Moses—the new federal highway would encircle the French Quarter via a riverfront viaduct along the Mississippi River, and a second stretch would be built along Claiborne Avenue, the business heart of the historic African American neighborhood of the Tremé.[14]

FIG. 18. In 1941, Edgar "Dooky" and Leah Chase opened their restaurant in the Faubourg Tremé, providing a sophisticated Afro-Creole dining experience and a safe harbor for civil rights activists; it gained international recognition in the years after segregation. Here the Chase family stands outside the restaurant, 1960s, Historic New Orleans Collection, 2017.0034.07.

In the era of segregation, more than one hundred African American businesses on Claiborne, known within the Black community simply as "the avenue," provided essential services, like Charbonnet Funeral Home, and shopping at stores like Circle Grocery. Large live oak trees—the landscape template for the city's large avenues—lined Claiborne between Canal Street and Elysian Fields Avenue. The neutral ground often served as a green park space for neighborhood residents. All that would be destroyed by the planned expressway.

Vic Schiro's motto was "If it's good for New Orleans, I'm for it." But the motto did not sit well with African American residents who realized too late the plans to build the elevated freeway along Claiborne Avenue. During the early 1960s, local activists such as Dodie Smith-Simmons focused their energies on protesting segregation on Canal Street and speeding up integration. They overlooked the long-term impact of freeway construction on the heart of the Tremé.

And so in 1965, the city began to implement the federal plan for Interstate 10: it bulldozed the stately live oak trees, replaced the green neutral ground with pavement, and erected concrete pillars to support the elevated interstate—now referred to as "the bridge." The buyout required the city to purchase 155 properties, a process tinged by racist assumptions that greatly undervalued Black-owned properties. Bitterness still resonates today among the older residents of the community. And the despair over the loss of the Claiborne green space is deepened by the fact that white preservationists successfully thwarted federal plans to construct the other section of the interstate planned for the French Quarter riverfront.[15]

Indeed, New Orleans became the first U.S. city to halt the construction of an urban interstate in the years following the Federal Highway Act of 1956. By the early 1960s, concerned citizens viewed the proposed "Riverfront Expressway" as a dire threat to the integrity and charm of the French Quarter. Where African Americans were focused largely on civil rights issues at the time, local white preservationists led by political activist Martha Gilmore, young lawyers William Borah and Richard Baumbach, and the Vieux Carré Property Owners, Residents & Associates (VCPORA) organized a campaign to stop the expressway.

The preservationists faced a powerful coalition led by Mayor Schiro and the city council, local media, labor and construction interests, and the U.S. Department of Transportation. During the 1960s, many city and suburban residents still considered the aging Vieux Carré a dangerous Italian and African American slum with little historic value. But the preservationists succeeded through well-organized legal representation, a creative propaganda campaign, persistence, and their use of political connections.

On July 1, 1969, Secretary of Transportation John Volpe in the administration of Richard Nixon canceled the project, admitting that the expressway would have "seriously impaired the historic quality of New Orleans's famed French Quarter." Bill Borah claimed that the victory represented a challenge to "the way the power structure worked"—echoing the language of civil rights activists. He added correctly, "We set an example for the rest of the country, but it was not what the business and political elite wanted." For African American residents of the Tremé, the Riverfront Expressway cancellation served as a reminder of their limited political power in the 1960s and left a bitter aftertaste of passive racism.[16]

As mentioned, Schiro's support for the new interstate was part of his overall mission to keep New Orleans competitive with the other Sunbelt cities of Houston, Dallas, and Atlanta. Indeed, in his pitch for "What's Good for New Orleans," Schiro initiated several projects to refashion the city during the era of the Cold War and the demise of segregation. Even though the success of preservationists in canceling the Riverfront Expressway underscored the importance of the historic past in the city's identity, Schiro pushed projects that looked forward—positioning New Orleans as a city with new industries, high-rise office buildings, a professional sports team with a modern stadium, and new tourist experiences beyond the French Quarter.

Schiro's efforts to bring a NASA rocket assembly base to New Orleans was perhaps one of his most ambitious and successful projects. Working with local congressmen Edward Hebert and Hale Boggs, Schiro recruited a committee to pitch the old Higgins Michoud plant in New Orleans East as the location for one of the coveted NASA rocket assembly plants. Appealing to former Nazi rocket scientist Wernher von Braun, who chaired NASA's Apollo program under President Kennedy, Schiro and his team landed an assembly contract in 1961. Constructing Saturn rockets in the U.S. race for the moon, the Michoud plant employed more than five thousand workers contracted by Chrysler and Boeing.

In the era of Sunbelt growth, the renewal of the World War II–era Michoud facility stood as a hopeful symbol of New Orleans's growth potential and ability to attract new industries. The location of the plant along the Intracoastal Canal in the marshes east of the city also spurred the growth of New Orleans East. As the last undeveloped portion of Orleans Parish, the area provided an opportunity for the city and private developers to construct a modern suburb with shopping and other amenities for the families of the NASA employees. Initially, promoters heralded New Orleans East as the "City of the Future," promising a modern residential lifestyle only minutes from the city center on Interstate 10.

Even as the cancellation of the Riverfront Expressway reflected preservationists' appreciation for history, Schiro focused on modernizing Canal Street and the CBD. In 1964, the city converted the Canal streetcar line to buses, leaving the historic St. Charles Avenue line as the only one using the old-fashioned 1920s-era green Perley Thomas streetcars. At the foot of

Canal Street the city built a modernist-style Convention Center designed by local firm Curtis and Davis. The Rivergate Center opened in 1968 across the street from the impressive new thirty-three-story World Trade Center, showcasing New Orleans as the "International City" promoted by Schiro.

The new development transformed lower Canal Street and anchored the lower section of Poydras Street, which Schiro planned to promote as the "Park Avenue of the South." In a radical revision of the thoroughfare in 1965, the mayor ordered the demolition of forty-seven properties on the downriver side to create a new six-lane street that connected the riverfront to Interstate 10. Over the next two decades, major oil companies such as Shell, Amoco, Texaco, and Mobil built large office buildings on Poydras—befitting New Orleans's position as the national center of offshore oil production in the Gulf of Mexico. Schiro's modernist vision led to Poydras Street emerging not as a Park Avenue residential enclave but as a glass-and-steel canyon of energy-related high rises stretching from the Mississippi River to the I-10.

The city's landing of the Saints professional football team realized another of Schiro's plans for New Orleans as a top-tier American city. Since 1961, the mayor and local businessman Dave Dixon had been courting the National Football League (NFL) in hopes of acquiring an expansion team. On November 8, 1966, the NFL awarded New Orleans the league's sixteenth franchise. The team's name reflected the city's Catholic heritage, and the team colors of black and gold symbolized New Orleans's connections to the "black gold" of the oil industry. The Saints made their debut in 1967 and played at Tulane Stadium until 1975, when they moved to the newly completed Superdome. Despite their years of miserable defeats and losing seasons, the Saints built an enthusiastic fan base that supported the team and made football games into another New Orleans–style celebratory social ritual.

But the lingering shadow of segregation almost ruined the city's chances for landing the Saints. In 1965 the American Football League (AFL) agreed to have New Orleans host the AFL All-Star game as a showcase of its hospitality in the post-segregation era. But when African American players came to town, they were refused service by racist taxi drivers, nightclub operators, and restaurant managers in the French Quarter. Before the game, the Black players staged a strike in protest of their ill treatment. The AFL quickly moved the game to Houston, serving as a wake-up call for New Orleans's hospitality industry in the new era of integration. Dave Dixon and city tourism leaders agreed to make a greater effort to accommodate African Americans in the future, and the NFL then awarded New Orleans the franchise.

At the upper end of Poydras, Schiro's vision of a new multipurpose stadium also came to fruition during these years. In 1966 voters approved a bond that initiated financing for a new domed stadium that would outshine Houston's one-year-old Astrodome, the world's first such enclosed structure. Designed by Curtis and Davis in 1967, the state-financed Louisiana Superdome took over the former site of the Illinois Central railroad yard, with construction starting in 1971 and its completion four years later. Next to the railroad yard lay the site of the Girod Street Cemetery deconsecrated in 1957 (present-day Champions Square and Benson Tower), which provided lore of an alleged curse that haunted the New Orleans Saints' performance for decades.

In the early 1960s, the Spring Fiesta, an antebellum-themed showcase of historic homes first organized in 1937, served as the only tourist festival in New Orleans. To increase tourism, Schiro dreamed of creating a jazz festival that would rival the well-regarded Newport Jazz Festival held each summer in Rhode Island. After asking Newport festival producer George Wein to stage a similar event in New Orleans, Schiro invited Wein and his African American wife Joyce to visit the city. Forbidden to stay with his wife at the same hotel because of segregation laws, Wein informed city leaders that a festival would not be possible until segregation ended. With the passage of the Civil Rights Act in 1964, Wein returned to the city, expressing a willingness to help produce a new festival.

In 1970, the city hosted the first New Orleans Jazz and Heritage Festival, eventually known popularly as Jazz Fest. The weekend-long event was held at Beauregard Square (officially renamed Congo Square in 2011) and featured a mix of local cuisine, daily parades by brass bands and Mardi Gras Indians, and, of course, music. Three small stages showcased gospel, blues, and Cajun music. The adjacent Municipal Auditorium hosted formal evening concerts in which big names such as Duke Ellington, Pete Fountain, and Mahalia Jackson performed. At the time, Jackson was the top gospel singer globally, and her headline billing was considered a homecoming of sorts for the woman who grew up in the Greenville (Carrollton) neighborhood and had left New Orleans for Chicago as a youth in the 1910s.

Most importantly, the festival was organized by the nonprofit New Orleans Jazz and Heritage Foundation, which was overseen by a multiracial board. The composition of the new board offered an important accomplishment for New Orleans in presenting a new face of racial inclusion and cooperation in the post-segregation era. In many respects, the board's ethnic makeup realized the dreams of festival producer George Wein and his wife Joyce to see New Orleans embrace a vision of racial cooperation in the modern era.

The festival crowds also reflected this ideal, as the initially small crowds included Black and white, old and young, conventional and hippie. The festival quickly outgrew Congo Square and moved to the New Orleans Fairgrounds in 1972. More importantly, the festival's popularity initiated the explosion of cultural and music festivals that characterize the city today.

With the passage of the Civil Rights Act, Louis Armstrong returned to New Orleans. His grand homecoming in 1965 served as a bright symbol of the new post-segregation era. One year after he earned a number one hit with "Hello Dolly," Armstrong stayed at the new Royal Orleans Hotel in the French Quarter, received the keys to the city, and visited the new Jazz Museum on Dumaine Street with his old music professor Peter Davis. But the homecoming was also bittersweet.

That year, Schiro had approved the demolition of Armstrong's birthplace on Jane Alley to make room for a modern New Orleans Police headquarters on Broad Street. The city also demolished the Colored Waif's Home on City Park Avenue, where Armstrong had received his first formal music lessons as a young teen, again to build an administrative center for the police and fire departments.

And in one of the most controversial and sadly ironic urban renewal projects in this period, Schiro proposed demolishing a large portion of the Tremé, considered the nation's oldest historic African American neighborhood, to create a park honoring Armstrong. Schiro's successor, Mayor Moon Landrieu, inherited the project, which cleared thirty-two acres of historic buildings and displaced more than 1,900 residents, most of whom were African American. Preservationists did manage to save Perseverance Hall, the site of early jazz performances. But the remainder of the site was transformed into green space, concrete-lined lagoons, parking lots, and the Mahalia Jackson Center for the Performing Arts.

Although resisted by local residents, African American activists, and preservationists, Armstrong Park finally opened in 1980. But many residents still see the park as a symbol of the city's blind efforts to erase African American history in the name of revitalization, and Moon Landrieu later expressed regret at the destruction and division caused by the project.

One of the greatest infrastructure legacies of this era emerged as an unintended consequence of Hurricane Betsy, which hit New Orleans on September 9, 1965 (fig. 19). The powerful storm flooded much of the Ninth Ward and suburban St. Bernard Parish, causing hundreds of million dollars of damage and more than seventy deaths. Remarkably, residents had to rebuild their homes without the benefit of federal monies or flood insurance. President Lyndon Johnson arrived immediately at the behest of local congressmen Edward Hebert and Hale Boggs and toured the devastation by plane and on land. Johnson and the congressmen vowed to address the

FIG. 19. In September 1965, an extremely strong tidal surge from Hurricane Betsy flooded large sections of downtown New Orleans and adjacent St. Bernard Parish, requiring the rescue of many residents by boat and leading to a federal policy of levee protection for the entire metro area. *Rescuers and Boats Moored at Judge Seeber Bridge following Hurricane Betsy,* September 1965, Historic New Orleans Collection, 1974.25.11.76.

problems the metro area faced in securing protection from the tidal surge and the high costs of rebuilding and renovating ruined homes.

In response to the coordinated efforts of local Democrats and the politically powerful Johnson, Congress passed the Flood Control Act of 1965. The new law required national flood insurance for homes vulnerable to inundation and set a new standard for federal financial support for homeowners facing the high costs of recovery. At the time, residents in the Lower Ninth Ward were quite self-sufficient and skilled in the building trades. Carpenters, plasterers, plumbers, and roofers all generally cleaned up and rebuilt without federal assistance, often helping one another. In St. Bernard Parish, older locals recalled bitterly the devastating crevasse flood of 1927.

The national government also worked with the U.S. Army Corps of Engineers to build a new fifteen-foot-high levee system for $56 million that would ring the city along the lakefront and the marshes to the east, protecting the city from hurricane tides that could flood the lower-elevation parts of the metro area. The New Orleans lakefront from West End to the Industrial Canal became protected by the new improved levee system, which represented a much more effective barrier than the well-intended sea wall of the late 1920s.

But over time, the flood protection effort, known as the Lake Pontchartrain and Vicinity Hurricane Protection Project (LP&VHPP), provided a false sense of security to many residents. A dangerous combination of underfunding, incompetence, natural soil subsidence, and coastal erosion resulted in a system that was incomplete and under-engineered. And as the residents of Orleans and St. Bernard Parishes discovered with Hurricane Katrina in 2005, such a system required constant professional maintenance and citizen vigilance to safeguard lives and properties.

The simultaneous construction of the shipping canal in St. Bernard Parish known as the Mississippi River-Gulf Outlet (MRGO) in 1965 also provided an unobstructed path for salt water from the Gulf of Mexico to enter and degrade the freshwater ecosystem of the Bayou Bienvenue swamp east of the city. Although intended to facilitate maritime shipping to New Orleans, the canal left area residents more vulnerable to heavy tidal surges and strong winds. By the 2000s, the once-lush freshwater bayou swamp basin had become an open, brackish-water lake. This dramatic metamorphosis of the Bayou Bienvenue Basin served as a tragic symbol of the region's increasing vulnerability to salt-water intrusion and the subsequent loss of important freshwater swamp forests that buffered the metro area from destructive hurricane winds.

Disneyfication

In 1966, Walt Disney, with Mayor Vic Schiro at his side, revealed a new attraction at his signature theme park in Anaheim, California. Promoted as New Orleans Square, the new experience re-created the French Quarter of the 1850s, complete with antebellum buildings fronted by laced iron galleries overlooking winding streets at a bend in the park's River of the Americas, where the Mark Twain paddlewheeler offered rides. Later additions included a Pirates of the Caribbean ride across the river inspired by the legend of Jean Lafitte and a Haunted Mansion playing on the paranormal aesthetic of the city. The park also began hosting "Dixieland and Disneyland" performances, featuring live concerts by New Orleans jazz greats, including Louis Armstrong. Walt Disney personally oversaw the vision of New Orleans Square: his fascination with the French Quarter reflected the charm and appeal of the neighborhood to tourists internationally.

In the grand opening of New Orleans Square, Disney made an off-hand remark to Schiro that the streets of his attraction were cleaner than those of the real French Quarter. Indeed, during the 1960s the French Quarter had a reputation as an historic neighborhood with a certain European charm but also with a seedy side characterized by the burlesque dance clubs and boozy atmosphere of Bourbon Street. Schiro accepted Disney's joke good-naturedly, but the sardonic comment rang true.

Where Mayor Schiro's push in the 1960s helped propel the city into a new era of modern mass tourism, the 1970s and 1980s witnessed the French Quarter transform into a more family-friendly tourist location, along with the city as a whole. New Orleans never did become a Disneyland, but the French Quarter evolved from a residential neighborhood with some visitor attractions to one that sacrificed its authentic residential character for tourist kitsch.

Schiro's successor Moon Landrieu oversaw the changes that characterized the new era of family tourism. As the city moved beyond the antiquated system of segregation, hotel chains such as Marriott, Sheraton, Hilton, and

Holiday Inn invested heavily in creating high-rise tourist accommodations along Canal Street and the adjacent streets. The French Market gradually changed from a collection of family-run produce and seafood stands to a collection of souvenir stalls. Bourbon Street also transformed from a place of jazz clubs and burlesque halls to a pedestrian mall with tourist trinket and t-shirt shops, rock bands, and bars serving large "go cups" filled with beer or sugary boozy drinks.[17]

Under Landrieu's administration, the city also began to envision a renewed connection with the Mississippi River. As other cities worldwide began to deindustrialize their waterfronts, so did New Orleans. In 1976 the city removed the 1900s-era wharf sheds in front of Jackson Square to allow easier tourist access to the Mississippi River. The new levee promenade was named "the Moonwalk" in honor of the mayor. During this period, the streets surrounding Jackson Square were transformed into a pedestrian mall paved with large flagstones, underscoring the historic charm of the park and surrounding buildings.

That same year, the riverfront adjacent to the World Trade Center was redeveloped as Spanish Plaza, reinforcing the city's historic relationship with Spain. During the 1980s, the city continued to reclaim the riverfront in the name of tourism, removing the wharf sheds upriver from the Moonwalk toward the GNO bridge. The new green space became Woldenberg Park and featured the Aquarium of the Americas, which opened in 1990.

Landrieu also oversaw the political transition from the white-dominated New Orleans of the 1960s to the Black-majority city of the mid-1970s. He had raised his family in the racially mixed neighborhood of Broadmoor, and he had always been sympathetic to concerns of civil rights activists. In contrast to Schiro, Landrieu opened city government and services to provide employment opportunities for African Americans, especially in white-collar positions. Many racial conservatives came to resent his liberal values and politics. By the time he completed his second term in 1978, the city's loss of white residents to surrounding suburbs led to a Black political majority.

Landrieu's successor, Ernest "Dutch" Morial, the first African American to serve as mayor, benefited from the new political demographic and was elected with a coalition of African Americans and white liberals. Since the Voting Rights Act of 1965, Black New Orleanians had become increasingly politically active and organized. African American politicians were elected to the city council, school board, the state legislature, and Congress. Civil rights activist Reverend A. L. Davis became the first Black council member in 1970; he was soon followed by James Singleton, Sidney Barthelemy, Lambert Boissiere, Dorothy Mae Taylor, and others.[18]

Yet racial tensions did not abate in New Orleans; occasional incidents highlighted the lingering effects of racism. In 1970, the Black Panthers began providing pest-control services, free breakfasts, and educational programs to the residents of the Desire public housing development in the back of the Upper Ninth Ward. At that time, law enforcement authorities across the United States considered the Panthers a grave threat to the social order. In New Orleans, state and local police brought armored vehicles to confront the Panthers at Desire, resulting in a tense days-long standoff that made national news but ended with no deaths.[19]

Three years later, an ex-Navy enlistee and radical Black activist, Mark Essex, launched a deadly sniper attack on New Orleans citizens from the roof of the Howard Johnson Hotel across from city hall. In a day-long siege that resulted in Essex's death, the sniper shot twenty-one people, including two policemen, of whom nine died. For some, the episode resonated as a second Robert Charles moment.

In these years, African Americans continued to have tense relations with New Orleans police, even as the department increasingly employed a larger number of African American officers. In 1985, Mayor Morial promoted Warren Woodfork as the first Black police superintendent to oversee the troubled department, which faced budget shortfalls, criticism for corruption and abuse, and a wave of crime associated with the surging crack cocaine epidemic.

As the city attempted to move forward in race relations, preservationists gained momentum in protecting the city's rich architectural heritage by revitalizing historic neighborhoods. In 1966, Congress created the National Register of Historic Landmarks to offer protection to historically significant communities. Immediately, the Vieux Carré applied and qualified for the designation. Over the next three decades the city's oldest communities along the natural river ridge, as well as Mid-City and Esplanade Ridge, gained preservationists' protection.

Some of the efforts coincided with the process of gentrification that occurred gradually during the 1970s and 1980s in the Lower Garden District,

Faubourg Marigny, and other neighborhoods that had been neglected since World War II. In the Lower Garden District, a new generation of preservationists invested in refurbishing stately old homes around Coliseum Square and formed the Lower Garden District Association (LGDA). At the time, the neighborhood was partly blighted by the Greater New Orleans Bridge, built in the 1950s when little residential support existed for protecting the historic community.

Eventually, the LGDA successfully lobbied for the removal of the Camp Street westbound on-ramp to the bridge, thereby enhancing the livability of the area. The LGDA also partnered with the newly established Preservation Resource Center (PRC), founded in 1972 to provide institutional support for the architectural protection of endangered historic buildings and to encourage investment in dilapidated structures. That same year, local preservation activists formed Save Our Cemeteries to highlight the threats posed by the neglect of New Orleans's famous "cities of the dead" and their historic tombs. Some critics, however, labeled the efforts of these organizations as white gentrification at the expense of maintaining income diversity in the historic neighborhoods.

The 1984 World Exposition led to one of the largest and most successful efforts to revitalize an overlooked neighborhood: the Warehouse District. By the late 1960s, city business boosters in the Council for a Better Louisiana sought to bring new investments to New Orleans and expand tourism beyond the French Quarter. Through the nonprofit Louisiana World Expo, they landed the "World's Fair" of 1984 and chose the derelict area of warehouses upriver from the Rivergate as its site. Top attractions included a monorail ride and an aerial gondola ride across the Mississippi, as well as exhibits promoting Louisiana, the United States, and numerous countries around the world—all against the backdrop of construction of the second span of the bridge crossing the river, now called the Crescent City Connection.

The Expo, like others of its day, was a financial loss. But momentum from its development led to the complete revitalization of the Warehouse District. The Great Hall exhibit space evolved into the new Morial Convention Center only two decades after the construction of Rivergate, which was demolished to make way for the state's first and only land-based casino. The International Riverfront exhibition hall became repurposed as Riverwalk

Mall. By the 1990s, the Warehouse District had become a neighborhood of top-rated restaurants, tourist hotels, and luxury condominiums.

Stretches of Camp and Magazine Streets developed as the city's Museum District. Preceding the World Exposition, the Contemporary Arts Center opened in 1976, spurring the first efforts at revitalization. By the early 1990s, Julia Street emerged as an important arts district hosting gallery and exhibit openings on the first Saturday of every month. The Ogden Museum of Southern Art debuted in 1999, focusing on local and regional visual arts. Around the corner, the D-Day (now World War II) Museum opened in 2000 to honor New Orleans's connection through Higgins Industries to the Allied D-Day landing at Normandy in June 1944.

In the mid-1980s, New Orleans began to feel the effects of the global downturn in oil prices, often referred to locally as the disastrous "oil bust." The major multinational oil producers that had built the high-rise office buildings along Poydras Street in the late 1970s and early 1980s gradually moved their workforces to Houston. At the same time, New Orleans began to rely more on the hospitality industry to sustain the city's economy. But whereas oil-related jobs provided high incomes for white-collar and offshore workers, local tourism-related jobs often paid meager wages.

New Orleans's sluggish economy failed to attract new transplants seeking a more prosperous economy. Many locals with a college education simply moved to cities like Houston, Atlanta, New York, or Washington, DC, where opportunities were more plentiful. Educated African Americans also moved to cities where they saw a chance for upward mobility. In contrast, New Orleans's lingering "plantation economy" often employed white managers who oversaw a Black workforce, hindering chances for their advancement.

Yet, despite those other cities' reputations for economic vibrancy and opportunity, New Orleans still attracted a wave of foreign immigrants in the 1970s, adding a new layer of religious culture to the Catholic city. At the end of the Vietnam War in 1975, Archbishop Philip Hannan of New Orleans visited Fort Chaffee, Arkansas, where Vietnamese refugees had located temporarily after the fall of South Vietnam. Hannan informed the camp residents, many of whom were Catholic, that New Orleans would welcome them with open arms. The archbishop told them that the region's subtropical climate and marshy surroundings would provide a familiar and comforting environment for many.

Soon, a trickle of South Vietnamese Catholics settled in the Michoud area and the neighborhood of Village de l'Est (Village of the East). The small subdivision, which was first developed in the early 1960s, became known as Little Saigon. Mary Queen of Vietnam Catholic Church opened in 1983 to serve the local population, and the canals were soon lined with gardens providing the food comforts of Vietnam. The surrounding bayous and marshes provided sustenance for the families of fishers, who found the area to be very similar to the coastal environments of South Vietnam. New Orleans's French heritage and historic rice-based culinary culture also represented important touchstones for the older immigrants who had grown up in the French colony of Indochina.

Over the next decades, more Vietnamese families immigrated to New Orleans, including many Buddhists and North Vietnamese. By the 1990s, New Orleans had one of the most diverse Vietnamese communities in the United States, and many of the initial immigrant families had found homes in the West Bank and suburban Jefferson Parish. New Vietnamese Creole seafood shops and restaurants opened across the metro area, and many families formed strong connections with relatives on the Gulf Coast of Texas.

New Orleans's historic banana trade connections with Honduras led to a wave of middle-class migration from the Central American nation beginning in the 1950s. Standard Fruit had developed the city of La Ceiba as a major port with strong connections to New Orleans through the Standard Shipping line. The various political coups, strikes, hurricanes, and floods of the 1950s and 1960s pushed a large number of Hondurans to New Orleans, where they found a familiar climate and Catholic culture.

Many families settled in the Lower Garden District and attended the Spanish-language services at St. Theresa of Avila Catholic Church. In the 1970s, station KGLA on AM radio programmed *musica tropicale* reflecting the Honduran community's musical tastes. In the 1980s, many families began moving to suburban Jefferson Parish, especially the West Bank and Kenner. By this time, Hondurans represented the largest Hispanic group in New Orleans, differentiating the city from Mexican American Houston and Cuban Miami.[20]

Around the same time, New Orleans served as the destination for Middle Eastern immigrants. In the 1960s the first mosques opened in response to the emerging pan-African Islamic movement. Later, in the 1970s, Muslim immigrants came mostly from the West Bank of Palestine and Pakistan. Like other immigrants before them, newly arrived savvy Palestinian entrepreneurs operated small corner stores in older neighborhoods. Eventually, these businesses grew to include gas stations and became popular for their crispy fried chicken. By the 1990s, many Muslim families began settling in the suburbs of Jefferson Parish, especially Harvey and Kenner. The population of Jefferson Parish came to reflect a modern American suburb, in contrast to the gradually gentrifying Black and white New Orleans.

Foodways: Creolization and Cajunization of Culinary Traditions

In the process of creolization, a new wave of restaurants opened after World War II, shaped both by the maturation of older immigrants and the adaptation of new arrivals. The opening of Brennan's Restaurant at 417 Royal Street in 1956 challenged the notion that only French Creole families and chefs could present a fine dining experience in New Orleans. The Brennan family had lived in the Irish Channel and had opened a successful restaurant in the Old Absinthe House on Bourbon Street during World War II. The relocation to Royal Street presented an opportunity to raise the dining experience to a more sophisticated level of service quality and setting. Brennan's elevated the New Orleans culinary reputation nationally beyond the older French Creole restaurants from the turn of the century. Its table service set a new standard for presentation, and the restaurant's success led to the development of restaurants by other branches of the Brennan family's younger generation.

In 1969, culinary pioneer Ella Brennan opened Commander's Palace on Washington Avenue in the uptown Garden District. Providing an elegant atmosphere that resonated with both tradition and modernity, Brennan had an intuitive understanding of management and hired a series of chefs who defined and reinvented New Orleans cuisine during the 1970s and 1980s. In the era before American chefs embraced the idea of local and seasonal foods, Ella Brennan employed chefs Paul Prudhomme, Frank Brigtsen, and Emeril Lagasse, who heightened New Orleans's reputation as a city of international culinary exceptionalism.

Paul Prudhomme left Commander's in 1979 and with his wife Kay opened their own restaurant, K-Paul's, at 416 Chartres Street in the French Quarter. The very unpretentious Prudhomme served meals that drew from his Cajun upbringing and emphasized the use of fresh, seasonal ingredients—thereby reflecting the new phenomenon of farm-to-table cuisine popularized by Alice Waters in California—but adding a Louisiana twist. The couple sourced local ingredients such as pecans, sweet potatoes, and fresh speckled trout or redfish. Crowds began to wait in long lines at K-Paul's, which was soon credited with kicking off the Cajun food craze that took the world by storm in the mid- and late 1980s. Soon every major city opened a Cajun-themed restaurant, and people began to use Cajun and Creole spices to add a kick to their dishes.

The appreciation of New Orleans's culinary traditions then reached new heights. Successive Commander's Palace chefs continued the culinary trend. In 1986, Prudhomme's protégé Frank Brigtsen opened a restaurant with his wife Marna in a narrow shotgun in the Riverbend area, using the same philosophy of local and seasonal ingredients to guide their menu. Brigtsen's successor Emeril Lagasse took over at Commander's in 1982 and departed in 1990 to open his own restaurant, Emeril's, in the Warehouse District. He soon enhanced New Orleans's reputation as a city of cutting-edge culinary development and popularized the new Creole cuisine with television appearances and a modern marketing team.

As the haute cuisine experience in New Orleans furthered the city's reputation internationally, local African American chefs and their restaurants also gained greater exposure and publicity. With the end of segregation, African American establishments welcomed integrated crowds. Beginning in the 1970s several restaurants gained fame for their New Orleans cuisine. Since its opening in the 1930s, Dooky Chase had provided a fine dining experience for African Americans in New Orleans. Owners Edgar "Dooky" and Leah Chase sought to provide an elegant culinary atmosphere during segregation that matched the reputation of New Orleans's finest restaurants. After integration took hold in the 1960s, their location on Orleans Avenue gained international fame for its Creole gumbo, fried chicken, and seafood po-boys.

Dooky Chase presented a white-tablecloth dining experience with food to match, but other, less fancy downtown establishments also gained recognition during the 1960s and 1970s. For years, African American patrons—

especially the members of the Black Musicians Union AFL #496—had appreciated the red beans and rice at Buster Holmes's restaurant at 721 Burgundy in the French Quarter. After segregation ended, celebrities including Woody Allen, Vincent Price, and Louis "Red Beans and Ricely Yours" Armstrong sang Holmes's praises. His red beans and rice were featured at the first New Orleans Jazz Fests along with Vaucresson's Creole sausage as historic dishes representing local culinary traditions.

Eddie's at 2119 Law Street in the outer Seventh Ward emerged as another outstanding representative of Creole cuisine outside the white tourist districts. During the 1970s, the restaurant, owned and operated by Eddie Baquet, became well known for its Creole gumbo. Reviews in the local press warned white guests that the exterior might be discouraging, but the interior offered warmth and its food stood above the rest. In earlier generations, George and Achille Baquet had been formative in the development of ragtime-jazz during the 1910s. By the 1980s, the Baquets had become valued as a local family that represented generations of Creole culture and culinary authenticity. Although the original Eddie's closed in the 1990s, the next generation continued the family enterprise under other names.

Chef Austin Leslie's Chez Helene at 1540 N. Robertson became recognized as a top destination for lovers of authentic (non-touristy) Creole cuisine. The menu offered varied and well-respected local Creole favorites, especially the chef's specialty: crispy, well-seasoned fried chicken. Leslie, always wearing his trademark white ship captain's cap, took over the restaurant from his aunt in 1975. In the late 1980s, the CBS comedy-drama series *Frank's Place* depicted a fictionalized version of Chez Helene, helping further promote the culinary reputation of Leslie and New Orleans during the "Cajun" food craze.

In this era, Vietnamese cuisine represented the new epoch of creolized New Orleans culinary culture. The downtown corner store Manchu became well known in the Seventh Ward and beyond for its party trays of peppery fried chicken wings and drumettes. Vietnamese-owned shops like Broadview Seafood became well liked for their super-spicy boiled seafood—meeting the fiery standards of south Louisiana and New Orleans–area taste buds.

In New Orleans East, the Vietnamese restaurant and bakery Dong Phuong became well known for its stuffed king cakes and flaky mini-French baguettes, known as pistolettes, representing the French (Belgian) boulangerie tradition that Indochina adopted during the colonial era. The small loaves are ideal for the bakery's fresh banh mi sandwiches. When these "Vietnamese po-boys" became more common in the 2000s, restaurants across the metro area sourced pistolettes directly from Dong Phuong.

Grilled Pork Banh Mi

The banh mi represents this culinary era in part because the sandwich is a Gulf Coast Asian variation of the classic po-boy sandwich. The bread, especially that baked at Dong Phuong, has a delicately flaky crust and is soft in the middle, like the classic po-boy bread of the famous older bakeries Leidenheimer's, Alois Binder, and Gendusa's. Banh mi can be eaten with meat and seafood fillings—Viet ham, liver pâté, Chinese sausages or meatballs, toasted shrimp, or fish patties—and there is even a veggie option using a soy-based ham product.

This recipe uses grilled pork, which is used in classic Vietnamese cooking and harkens to the common use of grilled pork in traditional Cajun cooking. And although pistolette bread is easy to find in New Orleans, the small loaf may be less available in other regions or countries: one can always substitute a traditional light and crusty French baguette or any long loaf that can be cut into smaller sections for a sandwich. The spicy green jalapeño slices add a touch more common on the Gulf Coast, where Vietnamese immigrants to Louisiana and Texas use peppers to meet local taste preferences. The peppers, which are even made special to order at the Dong Phuong bakery counter, are optional.

Serves 6

Marinade

2 tablespoons oyster sauce
2 tablespoons fish sauce
2 tablespoons vegetable oil
1 tablespoon rice wine—or dry sherry
1 teaspoon sesame oil
1 tablespoon minced lemon grass
5 cloves of minced garlic
1 tablespoon honey
1 tablespoon molasses

Condiments

½ cup of Bò (Vietnamese mayonnaise)—or homemade French-style mayonnaise
2 peeled cucumbers cut lengthwise into thin slices
1 cup of sliced fresh jalapeños (optional)
1 cup of Asian pickled carrots

1 or 2 bunches of cilantro (depending on taste) removing any tough stems

2 pounds (1 kilo) of pork shoulder cut to ¼ inch thick slices

6 pistolette loaves—or equivalent longer loafs cut to 8 inch lengths

1. Mix the marinade and marinate the pork slices for 4–6 hours or overnight in a cool location.

2. Grill the pork slices on medium heat, ensuring that the exterior is slightly charred but the inside is tender.

3. Slice the pistolettes lengthwise, if possible keeping one side intact.

4. Spread the Bò mayonnaise evenly on both sides of the bread. Layer the pork slices evenly and then distribute the condiments evenly over the pork. Cilantro can be added as a garnish or layered evenly on top of the condiments.

The Big Uneasy

New Orleans's Carnival experience finally entered the post-segregation age in 1969. As a show of interracial cooperation and tolerance, the city brought the Zulu parade into the mainstream on Carnival Day. That year, the historic African American Zulu Parade preceded Rex—King of Carnival and the symbol of New Orleans elite—on the main St. Charles Avenue to Canal Street route. Four years earlier, Rex had invited the heralded St. Augustine High School "Marching 100" band to perform in its parade. The presence of the top-quality historic African American high school band in the old-line parade was a harbinger of a new era of inclusion for the city's globally famous celebration.

In the 1960s, New Orleans began to place all its proverbial eggs in the tourism basket, and Carnival season attracted more tourists than ever. The parade experience became even more spectacular with the new phenomenon of super-krewes. These larger-than-life parades, staged by Endymion (1967), Bacchus (1968), and eventually Orpheus (1994), featured celebrity monarchs and distinctive double-decker two-trailer floats in a fabulous lighted spectacle with thousands of riders heaving a constant shower of beads and other throws to the adoring crowds.

New Orleans continued to brag about its idiosyncratic culture into the 2000s. At the time, a popular t-shirt sold in the tourist districts printed the quote, "America has only three cities: New York, San Francisco, and New Orleans—everywhere else is Cleveland." The quote was attributed to Tennessee Williams, who lived in the French Quarter from the 1940s throughout much of his life into the early 1980s. And although Williams may or may not have made that claim about New Orleans, the statement highlighted the city's self-identified stereotyped exceptionalism as a mixed Latin-Caribbean, Black, bohemian, gay, decadent, and proudly "non-Puritan" community.

Since the 1920s, the artistic literary quarter had existed as a quiet, queer-friendly community, spawning some of the oldest gay bars in the nation.[21] During the 1970s, the lower French Quarter emerged as an unabashedly gay neighborhood, and Tennessee Williams was celebrated as its icon. Just as the Stonewall riots emerged as a liberating moment for New York's gay community, the tragic Up Stairs Lounge fire of 1973 provided a similar seminal event. The hate-based arson at the lounge at 604 Iberville Street resulted in the deaths of thirty-two persons and led to soul searching about New Orleans's reputation for tolerance (or hate) and the safety of gay and transsexual men and women in the city.[22]

During the 1970s, gay bars became more open on the streets of the French Quarter and the Marigny. Although Carnival had historically offered cover for men dressing as women, contemporary Mardi Gras became the day when gay men became celebrated for their outlandish and intricately designed costumes, all judged in the now-famous Bourbon Street Awards for the best drag regalia. At the same time, gay krewes such as Yuga, Amon-Ra, and Petronius, which had held their annual Carnival balls quietly during the 1960s, now celebrated their costumed kings and queens more openly. Every Labor Day weekend, the city hosts the six-day pride event known as Southern Decadence, attracting more than 300,000 LGBTQ tourists from across the South and the nation.

Around the same time, unique African American costuming traditions emerged from the backstreets to be celebrated not only by African Americans but also by a new generation of white youth. Photographers like Jules Cahn and Michael P. Smith began to expose white audiences to New Orleans's Afro-Creole masking tradition known as "Mardi Gras Indians" or Black Masking Indians. Local young African American photographers such as Girard Mouton III, Christopher Porché West, Eric Waters, and Chandra

McCormick also gained new heralded recognition for authentically capturing African American street life and cultural traditions.

The Black Masking Indians' elaborate Afro-Creole costumes and beadwork gained mainstream exposure in daytime parades at the first Jazz Fests at Congo Square. In the early 1970s, the Wild Magnolias from Uptown recorded their traditional repertoire, as well as new compositions like "Smoke My Peace Pipe" and "New Suit" backed by the Gaturs, a local hard funk band led by keyboardist "Wille Tee" Turbinton and his saxophonist brother Earl. Soon thereafter, the Thirteenth Ward's Wild Tchoupitoulas recorded an album that united the Neville Brothers and the Meters. Their repertoire was partly based on traditional Mardi Gras Indians' chants, and their sound promoted New Orleans's Afro-Latin-Caribbean percussive rhythms and grooves to a new global audience.

The New Orleans funk sound became well known, and the influential but initially unheralded pianist Roy "Professor Longhair" Byrd became internationally appreciated for his Latin-inspired funky bass lines and blues riffs. Longhair's yodeling style of singing popularized songs like "Tipitina," which inspired the founding of the famous uptown music club featuring a new generation of New Orleans dance music artists. At around this time the popular singer and pianist Mac "Dr. John" Rebennack presented a psychedelic and funky sound with voodoo spiritual themes. Partnering with New Orleans native, producer Harold Batiste, Rebennack appealed largely to the counterculture but also crossed over to mainstream radio with songs like "Right Place, Wrong Time" in 1973. And in the period of politically aware soul music, songs like Aaron Neville's "Hercules" addressed social problems, reflecting a new willingness to move beyond the more apolitical dance and love themes that had characterized earlier New Orleans music.

New Orleans had changed socially and politically over the three decades from the 1960s to the 1990s. White flight had given way to a city that was more than 60 percent African American, in which many of the poorest residents were left marginalized and underpaid in a low-paying hospitality industry. Despite the promises of integration, many African Americans also headed to areas like New Orleans East, the West Bank, and Jefferson and St. Charles Parishes to escape the crime and crack cocaine epidemics ravaging many of the older neighborhoods and housing developments in the city. In these years, Orleans Parish's public school system was staffed by dedicated educators, but they struggled to educate the city's youth in a system that was more than 90 percent African American. In this educational environment, those parents who could afford to often enrolled their children in private or Catholic parochial schools.

Yet, New Orleans continued to exist as the "City That Care Forgot," where social problems were often buried or ignored by a culture of good times. Even as the city maintained a reputation as a place of sin and debauchery, many locals found solace through spiritual release at their neighborhood churches and the new mega-churches. Others overcame difficult times by cooking and eating familiar foods with their families and friends, consuming alcohol (and drugs), listening to funky music and dancing, and sometimes attending and making elaborate costumes for Carnival. Whereas New York promoted itself as the "Big Apple," New Orleans chose to market itself as "the Big Easy," reflecting the philosophy that life existed with no stress and hardship.

In reality, life was never easy for a considerable portion of the population who struggled with low-wage jobs, decrepit housing, dysfunctional families, drug use, poor education, police brutality, and endemic poverty. Although a political awakening arrived with the civil rights movement, both Black and white residents often found it easier to carry on with front-porch parties, lakefront picnics, crawfish boils, Mardi Gras parades, and second lines. However, even as many locals took their unique lifestyle for granted, an impending environmental and engineering disaster in 2005 brought the city's plight into focus around the globe.[23]

Relevant Historic Sites

J&M Music Shop, 840 North Rampart Street: The original site of the historic J&M recording studio operated by engineer Cosimo Matassa and producer Dave Bartholomew from 1945 to 1956. Historical markers commemorate this location where the two men recorded a number of internationally popular rock 'n' roll records by artists such as Antoine "Fats" Domino, Little Richard, Ray Charles, Roy "Professor Longhair" Byrd, and others.

The TEP (Tate, Etienne, Prevost) Center, 5909 St. Claude Avenue: This museum, located at the site of the former McDonogh 19 Elementary

School, interprets the history of the Lower Ninth Ward neighborhood and New Orleans school desegregation.

Dooky Chase Restaurant, 2301 Orleans Avenue: The historic Creole restaurant established by Edgar "Dooky" and Leah Chase in 1939 was the site of important meetings addressing pressing civil rights issues during the 1950s and 1960s. In 2024, the family created an exhibit and monument to New Orleans's civil rights history in the camelback (second half-story) dining room.

The Moonwalk, on the river in front of Jackson Square and Washington Artillery Park: The promenade opened in 1976 in Mayor Moon Landrieu's effort to reconnect residents and tourists with the Mississippi River. Prior to the construction of the Moonwalk, public access to the historic waterfront had been blocked for a 70-year period as the New Orleans Dock Board built wharf sheds to serve the port.

Up Stairs Lounge Fire Historical Marker, 604 Iberville Street: The historical plaque on the sidewalk memorializes the 1973 arson attack on the Up Stairs Lounge gay bar, which killed 32 persons and remains the deadliest fire in New Orleans history.

Dong Phuong Bakery, 14207 Chef Menteur Highway, New Orleans: This Vietnamese bakery and adjacent restaurant are situated in the historic Little Saigon neighborhood in New Orleans East, where Vietnamese immigrants first settled in the city during the late 1970s. During Carnival season, long lines queue along Chef Menteur to purchase the bakery's popular king cakes.

8

"Ain't Dere No More"

Post-Katrina Resiliency and Tourism, 2005–2025

DURING THE 1970S AND 1980S, New Orleans residents began to openly acknowledge the distinct but fading older working-class "yat" culture of the city. The term stemmed from the common old-school greeting of "Where y'at?" The term "yat" was originally associated with the white working-class culture of the historic neighborhoods. But the recognition and comedic use of the term extended to the broader dialect of New Orleans, which became more pronounced as the city became more mainstream American. In this dialect, sometimes defined by neighborhood or ward, authentic New Orleans speakers tended to speak with a strong accent and to use colloquial terms that confounded and fascinated outsiders. The dialect reflected the linguistic distinction that made (makes) New Orleans stand out within the United States.

Some early "yat" examples include the Meters' 1975 song, "They All Ask'd for You," which celebrates New Orleans dialect, patois, and unique local foods. In the carefree song, drummer Joseph "Zigaboo" Modeliste recites the praises of crawfish étouffée, red beans and rice, and Creole gumbo, while proclaiming numerous times "Eh la bas! (Over there!)" in reference to an older Creole jazz song and expression from World War I. The ensemble then sings-shouts in the rowdy chorus: "They all 'axed' [asked] for you!"

By the late 1970s, local cartoonist Will "Bunny" Matthews created the popular "Vic and Nat'ly" series that satirized an older couple, Vic and Nathalie Broussard, who ran a corner-store po-boy shop and bar in the Ninth Ward and who spoke in a heavy dialect filled with New Orleans vernacular slang.[1] Although Matthews's satire may have offended some people, the characters represented a New Orleans culture that faded with increasing Americanization and the prevalence of mass culture.

Within two decades, the genre of "yat" humor had become synonymous with New Orleans "cultcha." The publication of *The Joy of Y'at Catholicism* (2007) by Earl J. Higgins added to the intended humor, reaching an audience of locals, curious transplants, and tourists who appreciated the remaining distinctiveness of New Orleans's way of life. *The Yat Language of New Orleans* (2007) and *The Yat Dictionary* (2012) added to the self-deprecating assessment of the cultural phenomenon.[2]

The acknowledgment of "yat" colloquialisms offered a way for older New Orleanians to poke fun at themselves. The humor also documented the decline of local institutions such as neighborhood corner stores and provided a distinct lens through which New Orleans interpreted itself. In this self-effacing vein of culture, local music group Benny Grunch & the Bunch released "The Twelve Yats of Christmas" in 1996 as a New Orleans–themed satire of the classic Christmas carol. In the song, the group references crawfish caught in Arabi, K&B drug stores, French bread from McKenzie's Bakery, Dixie Beer, the phrase "ate by ya' mama's," the Lower Ninth Ward, working at the Chalmette refinery, and a dozen Manuel's tamales—all in an exaggerated dialect.

Benny Grunch & the Bunch's follow-up song "Ain't Dere No More" provided a humorous but poignant acknowledgment of the changing landscape in the age of chain stores and modern tourism. Like "The Twelve Yats," the song references vanished iconic local institutions—the department stores on Canal Street, K&B, Schwegmann's Grocery with its bar inside, and McKenzie's Bakery. The song begins with the chant in "yat" dialect: "Where are all da stores? Ain't Dere No Mo!" The chorus, sung to the melody of "Jingle Bells," proclaims, "Just hotels / Just hotels / More are on the way."

At once, the song created a local catchphrase used to acknowledge the disappearance of famed landmarks, and more profoundly, the lyrics recognized the degree to which New Orleans's landscape had changed dramatically since the 1980s. National chains had replaced the ubiquitous local K&B drug stores and Schwegmann's supermarkets, and most of the classic neighborhood corner stores began to disappear. The old department stores on Canal Street, which had been the target of segregation protests in the 1960s, had either closed or moved to the suburban malls during the 1990s. Hotel chains renovated the sites of the departed Maison Blanche, Krauss's, and D. H. Holmes, and the transformation of Canal Street, the once grand shopping street, continued.

During the early 2000s the French Quarter became even more of a tourism hub and less of a residential neighborhood. Many apartments transformed into condos or time-shares, and the Quarter lost much of its community character (and characters). However, many traditions continued. Long Friday lunches at Galatoire's remained a social ritual for well-to-do residents. The city's distinct culture of second-line parades, clubs and lounges, small churches, and distinct dialects survived on the backstreets of many older African American neighborhoods. Although many residents remained complacent about the city's current state and future, the impending hurricane would bring about a renewed appreciation of the city.

Is This America?

On the Saturday night of August 27, 2005, Max Mayfield—head of the National Hurricane Center in Miami—called New Orleans mayor Ray Nagin at his home on Bayou St. John. He informed Nagin that Hurricane Katrina was now headed straight for New Orleans. The Category 5 storm was so powerful—encompassing the entire Gulf of Mexico on satellite imagery—that he urged Nagin to call a mandatory evacuation of the city. No such order had ever been given in the history of New Orleans, and Nagin was reluctant to declare one. But in consultation with Governor Kathleen Blanco, Nagin agreed to issue the unprecedented evacuation call.

Mayfield understood that New Orleans was especially vulnerable to strong winds and a heavy tidal surge from a powerful hurricane. Well before the storm, scientists had issued dire predictions that if the fifteen-foot post-Betsy hurricane levees surrounding the city were to break, a catastrophic tidal surge would inundate the areas of the city below sea level. Half the city—essentially every neighborhood built in the former wetlands and marshes after 1900—could flood catastrophically.

Even with the mandatory evacuation order, a sizable portion of the city's population stayed put for a number of reasons. Many remained because, in their life experience, no such storm was imaginable. These residents had stayed in the past without any problems; they figured that they might be without power for a week but could not imagine the levees breaching. Others stayed because they had no means to leave. Many residents felt obligated to care for elderly family members or pets. Because no public shelters existed, the mayor informed the remaining citizens that the Louisiana Superdome would serve as a "shelter of last resort." Thus, many vulnerable families trekked by foot to the stadium for protection from floodwaters and powerful winds.

As the hurricane made landfall as a Category 3 storm, the 100-mph gusts toppled trees and powerlines, broke windows in high-rise buildings, and damaged roofs across the metro area. Heavy rainfall flooded lower-lying areas of the downtown neighborhoods, leading some residents to seek shelter in two-story structures or attics. The powerful winds ripped a huge hole in the Superdome roof during the night, frightening those sheltering there. And outside the levee system along the lakefront east of the city, a fifteen-foot tidal surge drove residents from their homes and destroyed the Interstate 10 bridge across the eastern portion of Lake Pontchartrain. By the time the winds calmed on Monday August 30, however, the worst of the storm appeared to have passed.

In fact, the extraordinary fifteen-foot tidal surge from the lake had placed such enormous pressure on the levee walls of drainage canals within the city that they caused the barriers to bend or breach entirely. The outfall canals built to drain rainwater from the city instead served as throughways for the rushing water to pour into low-lying neighborhoods. Levee failures occurred at the 17th Street Canal in West End and along the London Avenue Canal in Gentilly. A massive breach in the Industrial Canal flooded the Lower Ninth Ward with such force that the wave of water washed wooden shotgun houses completely off their foundations and tossed cars and trucks haphazardly.

The city's floodwaters covered the areas that were marked as cypress swamp or wetland on the historic 1878 T. S. Hardee Map (see fig. 13). While the historic neighborhoods along the natural river ridge remained high and dry, the lower parts of the city—Mid-City and Broadmoor, the Lakefront and Gentilly, New Orleans East, and the Lower Ninth Ward—all flooded from four to fifteen feet depending on the elevation. Areas of neighboring East Jefferson Parish, which had sent their drainage pump operators to safe locations, flooded when water draining from the natural river ridge in East Jefferson Parish backed up south of Metairie Ridge and along the lakefront levee. And the massive tide surge inundated all of St. Bernard Parish, even the area of the elevated natural ridge along the river.

The international media covered the scenes of devastation, providing a global view of New Orleans dysfunction and poverty. Aerial footage showed mile after mile of flooded neighborhoods, most with African Americans stranded on their rooftops pleading to be rescued. Soon news stories covered chaos at the Superdome and Convention Center where desperate crowds, including tourists, remained in the sweltering heat with little or no food and water. Looting broke out when no help arrived from the federal government in the form of transportation, law enforcement, shelter, or sustenance. Although some images showed the criminal theft of goods, most people who "looted" were searching for something to eat and drink, fresh clothes, and diapers. The scenes continued for five days as local, state, and federal authorities wrangled over political control and blame. With no cellphone or landline service, communication became almost impossible.

The world watched in disbelief as the destruction of one of the most famous American cities revealed a side of the United States that few had seen before: New Orleans appeared like an underdeveloped nation. Finally, after five days of chaos, the U.S. military's Joint Task Force Katrina arrived. Under the command of Lieutenant General Russel Honoré, a Louisiana native, the troops restored order, provided food and water, and offered bus transportation to shelters in neighboring states for the stranded residents. The hospitals were finally evacuated. The National Guard forcibly evacuated the entire city, with the exception of essential healthcare and law enforcement personnel. And the world breathed a sigh of relief, even as New Orleanians cried from sadness, loss, trauma, and despair. No one knew how long the city's recovery would take or even whether New Orleans would recover.

The damage to New Orleans's infrastructure and reputation was unfathomable. The city remained off-limits for residents until mid-October, when authorities finally allowed the return of those residents who lived in the neighborhoods along the natural river ridge uptown that had not flooded. But residents of a large portion of the city could not return to start the recovery and rebuilding of their homes and neighborhoods. Public schools did not reopen until the following school year, so families with no workplaces or schools for their children remained stranded in cities and towns all over the United States—from Baton Rouge to Houston, Seattle, Austin, Denver, Phoenix, Memphis, and New York. Although some New Orleanians found new opportunities and better housing and schooling in their new communities, others experienced intense homesickness and found life difficult without their favorite foods and the New Orleans lifestyle of weekly second-line parades and a culture of street parties.

In this context, the displaced residents, and even the larger world, gained a new appreciation for the city's unique cultural institutions that were gravely imperiled or lost. The first Mardi Gras celebration after the storm provided an emotional lift for those who could attend. The media depicted Black Masking Indians, back home temporarily, parading in costumes past giant piles of storm debris on the sidewalks of their communities. The gradual reopening of familiar restaurants and even grocery stores provided something to celebrate. And with the rebuilding labor force, new restaurants and food trucks appeared, reflecting the arrival of a wave of Latin American workers to the city.

The utter devastation of the Lower Ninth Ward revealed class and racial tensions that had remained largely buried before the storm. Many residents of the historic African American community felt bitter about their displacement. Some claimed that the devastation of the neighborhood was intentional, to provide a way for developers to stage a land grab. Fats Domino's ranch-style home, from which he had to be rescued by boat from the second-floor balcony, continued to stand empty.

As wealthier, white parts of the city such as Lakeview recovered, Black neighborhoods such as the Lower Ninth Ward continued to struggle. New Orleans East, home to many middle-class and wealthy African Americans, some of whom lived in the gated Eastover community before the storm, rebuilt its housing stock but initially failed to attract national restaurant chains and big box stores like Walmart, as well as essential medical services such as Methodist Hospital that had existed before the storm. Finally in 2013 a Walmart opened, while the renovated Methodist opened as New Orleans East Hospital in 2014.

New Orleans's recovery became an international symbol of resilience, despite the slow pace in poorer communities. The city had endured fires, wars, floods, and epidemics, and the fervor for rebuilding was fueled by a renewed pride and a drive to reform the problems that plagued the community before the storm. In the new era, charter schools replaced the parish public school system, giving more independence to individual schools. Laid-off teachers expressed great bitterness with the transformation, and parents found the plethora of new school choices daunting. But overall, educational standards improved under the new system. The city also reformed the tax assessor system. Before the storm seven separate offices assessed the value of each home, and the assessors were subject to influence at the neighborhood level. In the post-storm reform, the system employed only one citywide assessor, who created an objective assessment system that yielded more accurate and equitable property taxes to fund city coffers.

Most importantly, the city reformed the system that oversaw flood protection. In an analysis of the levee engineering failures that led to the massive flooding, forensics engineers discovered that the outfall canal levees were constructed with inferior designs and materials. In many places, metal sheets were driven vertically into the soft soil along the edges of canals with no anchoring to withstand the pressure of extreme water levels. Many of the earthen levees built to protect New Orleans East used inferior peat soil from nearby marshes, and not the heavy clay that could withstand a tidal surge. Overall, records showed that the Army Corps of Engineers inspectors had not provided a professional assessment of the levee infrastructure for years. Critics often argued that, even though Katrina brought a destructive tidal surge, the flooding resulted from levee breaches caused by federal negligence.

As a wave of anger focused on the Army Corps of Engineers, the agency admitted its past wrongdoing. After intense lobbying by advocates of the city and Senator Mary Landrieu, Congress allocated billions of federal dollars to rebuild the flood protection system to withstand a Category 5 storm. The Army Corps put locally born and openly accountable managers in place, making the case that with its local staff, the agency remained committed to construct a system to protect their families, neighbors, businesses, and the larger community.

The Army Corps installed an expanded pumping system and gates that could close the 17th Street and London Avenue canals, Bayou St. John, and the Industrial Canal during severe storms, thereby cutting off potentially damaging tides. In New Orleans East and St. Bernard Parish, federal engineers installed a new 1.8-mile-wide barrier, "the Great Wall of Louisiana," on the MRGO to prevent a tidal surge from the Gulf. And importantly, the Orleans Levee Board, long subject to allegations of corruption, was incorporated into two larger professional-appointed flood control organizations for the east and west banks of the metro area.[3]

These reform efforts were largely initiated by women activists from the wealthier uptown neighborhoods near Tulane University. Citizens for 1 Greater New Orleans and Women of the Storm devoted the time and energy to lobby for the educational, infrastructure, and political reforms that characterized the post-storm years.

During the years after Katrina, African Americans continued to face many challenges in returning and rebuilding their homes and neighborhoods. The state's program to fund recovery efforts, Road Home, was poorly administered. Insurance companies also received a great share of criticism for not honoring claims, especially those from Black residents, who became exhausted and embittered as they fought the bureaucracy and red tape put in the way of homeowners' recovery.

Mayor Ray Nagin voiced the frustration of the African American community in his famous Martin Luther King Day speech in January 2006. All along Nagin had claimed that the slow federal response reflected the Bush administration's indifference toward a Black-majority Democratic city characterized by poverty and an un-American lifestyle. In his speech given four months after the storm, Nagin proclaimed, "It's time for us to rebuild a New Orleans, one that should be a chocolate New Orleans." And in a not so oblique reference to rich white residents, Nagin continued, "I don't care what they are saying uptown or wherever they are. The city will be chocolate at the end of the day."

Although the speech offended and angered white conservatives, many African Americans felt supported and hopeful that the city could rebuild its flooded neighborhoods, schools, and businesses, and also sustain the locale's special Afro-Creole-Caribbean culture, traditions, communities, and foodways. But just as culturally liberal whites and African Americans celebrated the comeback of Black New Orleans, the city also felt the effects of gentrification in the historic neighborhoods.

Five years into the Katrina recovery, the New Orleans metro area faced yet another environmental catastrophe with BP's Deepwater Horizon oil spill. The well explosion in the Gulf of Mexico south of the city killed eleven workers, and the resulting leak caused the largest oil spill in U.S. history. A massive amount of crude oil (estimated to be 210 million gallons) floated into the sensitive marsh environment south and east of New Orleans in Terrebonne, Plaquemines, and St. Bernard Parishes, threatening aquatic wildlife and shutting down fisheries and seafood harvests. The well was finally capped three months later, but the painful experience reflected residents' exasperation at facing another environmental disaster.

Many affected coastal residents showed the resilient spirit that characterized the city's recovery from Katrina. But the spill also reflected the troubled relationship that the region had with an economic sector that provided well-paying jobs but also caused ecological degradation. Many locals blamed the oil industry for dredging canals that laced the fragile marshes to the south, thereby increasing salt-water intrusion and killing off healthy freshwater ecosystems. And because New Orleans no longer served as the center of offshore energy exploration and production by the 2010s, the city shifted its focus to tourism as a major economic engine. But as mentioned, the hospitality industry did not support high-paying jobs.

Bike Lanes and Coffee Shops

On February 7, 2010, New Orleans Saints quarterback Drew Brees hoisted his young son Baylen in the air, as he celebrated the NFL football team's first (and perhaps only) Superbowl victory. Just as people across the nation had watched New Orleans drowning and the roof torn off the Superdome only five years earlier, they now cheered for the Saints, who represented the great underdog city that staged a remarkable comeback as a community. The victory represented a heartfelt triumph for the resilient city, but especially for long-suffering residents and Saints supporters around the world.

Brees moved to New Orleans to play for the Saints in 2006. He and his wife Brittany had been attracted by the opportunity of relocating to the unique city and being part of the rebuilding process after Katrina. In doing so, the Texas native and his wife personified a post-storm wave of newcomers and transplants who wanted to experience the city's special culture and participate in the city's recovery. Brees lived and worked as one of the most high-profile transplants, joined by thousands of young adults from around the nation who also found a new home in a city where housing was more affordable than other culturally rich cities like New York or San Francisco.

The new arrivals' appreciation for New Orleans culture mirrored renewed citywide support for the city's endangered cultural practices and institutions. In 2008, the New Orleans Museum of Art (NOMA) staged an exhibit featuring the elaborate African-inspired beaded suits of Victor Harris, chief of the Mandingo Warriors, Spirit of the Fi Yi Yi Black Masking Indians. The exhibit, which was part of the Prospect 1 art biennial in which works by renowned local, national, and international artists were placed around the city, represented the first time that a formal art museum had recognized and celebrated the complex artful designs of the long-standing Afro-Creole masking tradition. Prospect 1 placed installations in African American neighborhoods that had been overlooked or avoided by many white residents before the storm, but were now embraced and appreciated by art lovers as rich communities intrinsic to New Orleans's deep social and cultural fabric.

In historic downtown neighborhoods, several new museums opened after the storm that showcased African American costume traditions while receiving financial support from national academic institutions. The Donald Harrison Sr. Museum and cultural center in the Upper Ninth Ward promoted educational programs on New Orleans's African music and masking heritage. Ronald Lewis's House of Dance and Feathers in the Lower Ninth featured colorful suits, costumes, and memorabilia associated with several local parading groups. Six years before Katrina, visionary curator Sylvester Francis had opened the Backstreet Cultural Museum as a showcase of New Orleans's African American parading culture. After Katrina, the Tremé institution became recognized for its expansive collection of costumes related to second lines and Indians. But even as these historic cultures came to be openly celebrated by residents and tourists, the process of gentrification presented a threat to maintaining older traditions.

As early as the 1990s, the Tremé emerged as the battleground between parade traditions and gentrification. Many locals proudly thought of the neighborhood as the heart of the city's brass band second-line culture, one in which a loud celebratory funeral parade could roll through the neighborhood in the wee hours of the morning without causing any offense to the neighbors. The community's first non-natives bought into the culture. But then some newer residents objected to the free-form brass band culture and noise. In 2007, police swarmed a late-night gathering of brass band musicians at Tuba Fats Square where the crowd honored the recently deceased tuba player Kerwin James, the brother of Rebirth Brass Band founders Keith and Philip Frazier. Police arrested drummer Derrick Tabb and his brother Glen David Andrews for parading without a permit and disturbing the peace.

The arrest of the musicians sparked an outcry from both locals and transplants across the city, and the issue of recognizing African American street traditions came to the political forefront. Only two months before Katrina, famed Black Masking Indian chief Allison "Tootie" Montana suffered a fatal heart attack after making an emotional plea to the city council about the importance of the masking tradition and chastising the police for harassing Indians on the streets. In the wake of the Tremé arrests in 2007, the city held a formal dialogue between the police and African American musicians and maskers—openly acknowledging the historic and cultural importance of New Orleans backstreet traditions.

After Katrina, the Bywater neighborhood—site of several Prospect 1 installations in 2008—also began to attract non-native artists and culture lovers seeking New Orleans authenticity and affordable housing. Before the storm, outsiders rarely ventured into the neighborhood downriver from the French Quarter, doing so only for work or to imbibe at a few neighborhood bars. But starting in the late 2000s, the neighborhood began attracting attention for its new farm-to-table restaurants, hipster bars, budding art gallery scene, and the construction of the new Crescent Park along the Mississippi River. As with all gentrifying communities, many locals and artists were pushed out by the new wave of home buyers willing to pay five to ten times more than the value of properties in the 1990s. The gentrification process gradually spread across to the St. Claude neighborhood and up St. Bernard Avenue into the Seventh Ward.

In Uptown, gentrification had begun in the Lower Garden District with Preservation Resource Center's "Operation Comeback" of the 1990s—or "Operation White Bread," as a tagger spraypainted on the sign welcoming people to the neighborhood. In the 1990s gang conflicts continued in the area, which was the geographical crossroads between the housing developments of St. Thomas along the riverfront and the Calliope farther back-of-town. Then in the early 2000s the New Orleans Housing Authority demolished the St. Thomas "projects" built in 1939 and began constructing one- or two-family homes to replace them. A new Walmart Supercenter was built next to the site, despite some controversy, and the surrounding Irish Channel neighborhood underwent the process of gentrification.

In the early 2000s, the New Orleans Housing Authority, with the generous support of the U.S. Department of Housing and Urban Development under President George W. Bush, implemented a plan to demolish all the public housing developments built between 1939 and 1965 and to replace them with smaller, less dense singles and duplexes. Desire, the largest complex with some 260 buildings, was torn down in 2003. In 2004, the Fischer Projects in Algiers were imploded. After Katrina, the older developments of Calliope, Melpomene, and Magnolia in Uptown were demolished. In Downtown, the Iberville, Lafitte, and St. Bernard all came under the wrecking ball. Many outraged residents and newcomers questioned how the city and federal government could demolish this public housing, given the dire state of post-Katrina housing options, especially for low-income residents.

In a process that began before Katrina, often those families seeking public housing instead were given Section VIII vouchers—federal government rental subsidies for privately owned rental units. Subsequently, many families moved into apartments in New Orleans East. Although these families simply sought affordable, stable, and safe housing, the once idyllic suburb, originally billed as the "City of the Future" in the 1960s, suffered from the effects of the 1980s oil bust, and many apartment complexes fell into neglect during the 1990s. As a stark symbol of the section's transformation, the Lake Forest Plaza shopping mall, which opened in 1974 with 130 stores and a star-studded publicity blitz, gradually lost tenants during the 1990s. The Katrina floodwaters hastened the nearly empty mall's ultimate demolition in 2007.

Beginning in the late 1990s and early 2000s, New Orleans once again gained international fame for a new style of music: the distinct hip-hop dance style referred to as "bounce." The name denoted the shaking or "twerking" of female dancers' backsides to the music. Before Katrina, the dance and music style appealed mostly to an African American audience. As with most New Orleans music, the genre was meant for dancing, fun, and release. The lyrics did not address political issues, in contrast to more "conscious" rap from the East Coast. Most songs called out specific dances or required call-and-response shout-outs to New Orleans's neighborhoods, wards, and housing projects.

From Uptown, rapper Master P (born Percy Miller) initiated a wave of New Orleans musical popularity in the mid-1990s unmatched since the days of the "big beat" in the early 1960s. By the late 1990s, the Hot Boys, with the production team of Bryan "Birdman" and Ronald "Slim" Williams, recorded hip-hop songs that glorified an outlaw lifestyle while bragging about sexual conquests, material goods, jewelry, and expensive cars. From the Hot Boys, the rapper Juvenile along with DJ Mannie Fresh and Lil Wayne scored a national hit in 1999 with "Back That Thang Up," which has endured as a Gen X dance anthem. The group also popularized the term "bling" in reference to an expensive, fancy, or shiny aesthetic. For the nation at large, their songs promoted the distinct New Orleans bounce style characterized by fast tempos, with drum machine beats, rapid high-hat cymbals, and hand claps.

Although the music was largely a regional phenomenon before Katrina, the post-storm years witnessed explosive mainstream success for rapper Lil Wayne (born Dwayne Michael Carter Jr.) and New Orleans bounce. During the late 2000s, the raw southern "crunk" rap style dominated national radio, and Wayne ("Weezy") became one of the most popular American music artists internationally. His cartoonish voice and creative lyrical references to New Orleans and pop culture provided an appealing combination. He sported long dreadlocks and often showed off a shirtless torso covered with tattoos. One of his first "tats" commemorates the intersection of Apple and Eagle Streets in the Hollygrove neighborhood, where he grew up. After Katrina, "Weezy" relocated to Miami, where he then became a superstar. He often claimed New Orleans as his cultural home, but like Louis Armstrong he preferred to live elsewhere.[4]

With the rising tide of the "Dirty South / crunk" dance genre in the late 2000s, the once obscure bounce music gained international appeal. New Orleans bounce rappers, dominated by Big Freedia, began to spread the gospel of the sound at music festivals, often giving demonstrations of the twerking style and encouraging audiences to join in the fun. The transsexual orientation of many of these artists appealed to the Gen X generation, who identified with the music, much as earlier generations of jazz and rock 'n' roll lovers identified with those styles. With the demolition of public housing in New Orleans after Katrina, the dance and hip-hop music associated with the "projects'" lifestyle suddenly became gentrified along with the neighborhoods.

Thus, the post-Katrina "safety" of the gentrified older neighborhoods signified the new respectability, acceptance, and novelty of the rap and dance style. The mainstream profile of bounce and twerking became evident at a

Guinness Book of World Records event held during the 2014 Central City Festival. In the officially monitored group dance in her home neighborhood, Big Freedia (born Freddie Ross Jr.) joyously led her song “Duffy,” setting the official world record for the largest number of people (406) twerking simultaneously. Gaining international fame, Big Freedia subsequently collaborated with superstar Beyoncé, pop star Kesha, singer-rapper Drake, Lil Wayne, and others. Her reality TV shows have been especially popular with the drag audience; they also reflect the historic culture of African American cross-dressing performances in New Orleans at the historic Dew Drop Inn (2836 LaSalle) during the 1950s and perhaps earlier.

By the late 2010s, the short-term rental phenomenon brought New Orleans tourism to a new level of authentic experiences for nonlocals, but produced headaches for many neighborhoods. Rental accommodation and guide apps for smartphones brought tourists into the backstreets and enabled them to experience authentic local culture. Nonlocals could now easily find second-line parades and discover brass band shows at neighborhood bars like Bullet’s in the Seventh Ward. They could take laid-back bike tours that visited po-boy joints in the Lower Ninth Ward. Even the site of the Katrina breach on Jourdan Avenue in the Lower Ninth became a tourist attraction. Visitors wanted to see firsthand the neighborhood made famous in the post-storm media and the modern shotgun homes that Brad Pitt’s Make It Right Foundation funded for the pre-storm residents who chose to return.

The nature of tourism also changed to reflect the new appreciation for African American culture and history, becoming more sensitive and nuanced in its understanding of New Orleans’s past. Downtown experiences such as the Backstreet Cultural Museum (1531 St. Philip St.), Leona Tate’s Lower Ninth Ward Living Museum (now the TEP Center at 5909 St. Claude Ave.), the Donald Harrison Sr. Museum (1930 Independence St.), and Ronald Lewis’s House of Dance and Feathers (1317 Tupelo St.) enabled more post-storm tourists to learn the fascinating history of these communities and their rich traditions.

A greater sensitivity was applied to the interpretation of once overlooked subjects. Tours offered nuanced explanations of Indigenous Bulbancha, voodoo and spirituality, enslavement and resistance, immigration, violent racist episodes, and civil rights. Bourbon Street restaurants no longer hired Black women in colorful antebellum hoop dresses to promote their menus, and the history of Afro-Creole women no longer focused on their sexuality but on their social and economic accomplishments. And even though tourism also became more theatrical and entertaining with the increased number of night-time ghost and vampire tours, a younger generation of guides also prioritized greater historical accuracy and focused on stories of the city's overlooked "dark history."[5]

But with the new tourist experiences came displacement. The unregulated booking phenomenon encouraged investors to buy houses in transitioning neighborhoods and convert them to short-term rentals. As real estate prices shot up, so did rents and property taxes, forcing many marginal renters and homeowners to find more affordable housing in the suburbs and exurbs. Even as the city made efforts to regulate the practice in the late 2010s and 2020s, rents for half of a shotgun house rose to between $1,500 to $2,000 a month, making it difficult for many residents to remain. Outpriced residents often moved to New Orleans East, Slidell, St. Rose, LaPlace, or Reserve.

Meanwhile, older main thoroughfares like St. Claude Avenue became hipster strips. New music clubs for locals appeared at places other than Frenchmen Street, which had become as popular as Bourbon Street with tourists. St. Claude even gained status as a new Arts District, with openings on the second Saturday of each month at the new galleries that lined the avenue. The old St. Roch Market, which was a walkup seafood and poboy market before Katrina, was reinvented as an upscale food hall, catering to wealthier locals and tourists who could afford the artisan meals and cocktails.

Uptown, the old riverfront industrial street of Tchoupitoulas now housed craft brew pubs, transforming the road into a popular center of nightlife for young adults. The historic African American shopping district of Oretha Castle Haley Boulevard (formerly Dryades St.) was repaved with wide bike lanes and landscaped with a tree-lined neutral ground to match the importance of its new businesses, museums, nonprofits, restaurants, and bars.

The transition of neighborhoods and the city overall was acknowledged in local Mardi Gras Indian rapper Flagboy Giz's song "Gentri Fire in the

City." Sung to the old-time Indian standard "Shallow Water," Giz (born Aaron Hartley) called out the process of older neighborhoods transforming to "where all the Black people gone." In a city where political and social commentary remained uncommon to the musical heritage, Giz sang, "Hurricane Katrina sped up the plan / pushed the Black people out like the Indians." And with a wry wit, Giz added how the "transplants can't pronounce the street names / and there goes the neighborhood when you see the bike lane." In the chorus he rapped in sing-song, "Gentrifying your favorite spot / it's gentrified now it's a coffee shop."[6]

Indeed, in the post-Katrina era of Mayor Mitch Landrieu, son of former mayor Moon Landrieu, many neighborhoods transformed into communities of artisan coffee shops where bike lanes indeed reflected the presence of non-native, post-automobile urban youth. As some neighborhood housing prices surged, older residents who bought their homes for less than $5,000 in the 1960s then sold out for $300,000 and moved to St. Tammany Parish, the suburban West Bank, or the River Parishes.

As controversial as gentrification remains in New Orleans, the process occurs worldwide in historic urban areas subject to mass tourism, digital nomadism, and the retirement of the well-to-do. Across the globe, urban-core neighborhoods in Seville, Cartagena, Paris, Mexico City, Rome, Atlanta, Accra, and London have all been transformed by the short-term rental market and rising housing costs. Although bitter conspiracy theories exist about the displacement of African American residents in New Orleans, the global march of mass tourism and urban hipsterism is not unique to the Crescent City.

At the same time, many of the post-Katrina transplants themselves moved on to other locations with more affordable housing. The COVID pandemic and the slowdown of the tourist economy in New Orleans pushed a new wave of youth to other cities where job opportunities are more readily available. Subsequently, many younger adults with deep family roots in the city feel disinclined to invest their lives and futures in the city. Although the most recent Orleanian ex-pats may miss the laid-back, carefree lifestyle and their close families, the comforts of home are not strong enough to retain them. The increased ease of travel and communication technologies enable people to stay close to their families, making life away from home more bearable in the modern age.

Foodways: Gentrifying Creolized Cuisine

The age of post-Katrina gentrification witnessed the opening of new restaurants—many of which characterized the farm-to-table seasonal menus that were pioneered by Paul Prudhomme and his protégés beginning in the 1970s and 1980s. Small farms such as Covey Rise in Tangipahoa Parish grew to meet the year-round demand for fresh local produce and meats. Because of the high costs of the farm-to-table experience, the restaurants serving the seasonal food were often characterized as expensive and hipster and therefore reflected a facet of gentrification when located in older, transitioning neighborhoods.

In 2014, the "kalegate" controversy reflected the clash of hipster food trends, New Orleans culinary pride, and the limited availability of nutritional foods. Natives and seasoned transplants reacted to a *New York Times* travel piece by Lizzy Goodman that focused on touring New Orleans through the experiences of recent arrivals. In the article, Dutch actress Tara Elders commented, "New Orleans is not cosmopolitan. There's no kale here." Elders's observation may have been either a compliment or a diss to the city, but the ensuing backlash defended the availability of the trendy green at many restaurants and markets. More importantly, the local reaction also highlighted the sensitive subject of affordability and access to healthy food options for many of the city's struggling residents, who lived in "food deserts."

Older African Americans and those Vietnamese with garden plots, many of whom grew up in rural areas, never associated fresh produce with hipsters or expensive restaurants. Well before Katrina, the Lower Ninth Ward was populated largely by Afro-Creole families who had rural roots but chose to live in an area of the city where they could maintain a garden and raise chickens. More urbanized or suburban New Orleanians often looked down on this section of the city as being backward or "country." But the old-timers, who raised their own food, paid no mind. Similarly, in the Michoud and Village de l'Est areas of eastern Orleans Parish, older Vietnamese immigrants grew their own food and bought and sold their fresh produce at the Saturday morning farmers' market in Little Saigon.

Although the merging of Asian and African American food traditions may appear an oddity to many Americans, the creolization of Afro-Asian foodways became an important aspect of New Orleans culinary history and heritage in the twentieth century. As mentioned earlier, Vietnamese immigrants adapted well to the spicy tastes of south Louisiana, as attested by the popularity of Asian seafood and fried chicken stores in African American neighborhoods.

Yakamein is a striking example of the intersection of the two food cultures in New Orleans.[7] The dish is essentially a Creole Asian noodle soup. Before Katrina the comfort food was found mainly at markets in older neighborhoods. Locals sometimes facetiously referred to yakamein as "Ghetto Pho," in reference to the corner stores' locations and the soup's similarity to Vietnamese pho. Yakamein's origins are unclear, but legendary chef Leah Chase thought it originated in New Orleans's Chinatown, near where Louis Armstrong grew up and sometimes ate. Historian Winston Ho found examples of the dish at Chinese restaurants in New Orleans dating to the 1900s. Some locals even argue that returning African American Korean War veterans enabled the increased popularity of the dish in the 1950s.[8]

In the post-Katrina era, yakamein has gone mainstream and global. Like bounce music, the dish emerged from the backstreets to become an icon of the city's culture. The gentrification of yakamein mirrors the global trend where traditional foods of working people are gradually embraced by wealthier people in the context of culinary reinvention. Shrimp and grits is another simple meal that is now found in the nicest restaurants. And although yakamein has not yet been elevated to a five-star level of respect, the dish is emblematic of the renewed appreciation that locals and the world brought to New Orleans cultures overlooked before Katrina. As some locals might say, yakamein got "bougied up."

In post-storm New Orleans, Miss Linda Green emerged as the premier chef of the yakamein to the point that she became known as the "Ya ka Mein Lady." After Katrina, one found Miss Linda serving her dish at second-line parades, street festivals, Jazz Fest, and her hospitality station for police working the uptown Carnival route. Just as she learned to cook the soup watching her matriarch elders, one may find her children and grandchildren assisting her in serving the steaming bowls. Typical of New Orleanians who gain international fame, she remains exceptionally friendly, engaging easily in a conversation and always willing to pose for a photo. Yet, Green remains serious about her craft.

Miss Linda's yakamein is a dark beef broth with a rich spicy flavor, chunks of beef, spaghetti noodles, and garnished with chopped chives and a sliced boiled egg. Like gumbo, the dish is perfect for cooler weather. Historically locals gave it the nickname of "old sober" for its purported qualities of curing a hangover.

Yakamein

Yakamein, as with numerous dishes in the region, has as many recipe variations as the families that cook the dish. This recipe includes some of the essential ingredients—noodles, beef and broth, and a boiled egg. The recipe is never complicated, which makes it a dish that relies on the rich flavor of the broth and beef for intensity.

Serves 6

2 pounds boneless chuck roast
3 tablespoons beef bouillon
3 teaspoons Creole season mix
½ cup Worcestershire sauce
½ cup soy sauce
1 pound spaghetti
6 hard-boiled eggs—peeled and quartered or sliced into fours
2 bunches of green onions chopped into 2 cups
Garnish Options
1 cup chopped hot red peppers
1 cup each of lightly steamed cauliflower, carrots, or broccoli
2 cups boiled shrimp, peeled and deveined

1. Make two quarts of beef bouillon and add the beef roast and Creole seasonings; bring to a simmer and cook on low heat for 1 to 2 hours or until tender.

2. Remove the beef and let cool for 20–30 minutes.

3. Once cool, chop the beef into small pieces. Add the Worcestershire and soy sauces to the broth and adjust to taste. When ready to serve, reheat the broth.

4. Divide the cooked spaghetti evenly among eight medium-sized bowls, evenly adding the pieces of beef, green onions, and egg quarters.

5. Ladle 1–2 cups of hot broth over the base, and add garnishes of shrimp, chopped red peppers, and steamed vegetables as desired. One can also top the steaming bowl with an additional sprinkle of chopped green onions. As with most New Orleans savory dishes, the dish can be served with the option of a red pepper vinegar sauce to provide extra heat and tang.

Still a Creole City?

One might wonder and ask: Is New Orleans still a Creole city? Given the prominence of its French Catholic roots in its foundation and development, as well as the prevalence of the traditions that continued throughout the nineteenth century, what is the legacy of Creolism that survives today? As acknowledged in the introduction, the word has evolved over time to encompass a variety of definitions. Today, Creole in New Orleans identifies a distinct local culture with strong ties to France and the larger Creole world of the Atlantic Basin encompassing the Caribbean, eastern Latin America, and western Africa.[9]

In post-Katrina New Orleans, the gentrification of downtown neighborhoods such as the Tremé and the Seventh Ward led to a greater Americanization of these historic Afro-Creole communities. The transition led some residents and historians to question the continued existence of the historic uptown–downtown cultural division in the city. Certainly, many Creole families from these communities have moved to suburban areas.

But one can still find many residents of these neighborhoods who favor the historic Creole Catholic culture and heritage of Downtown and look down on Uptown as the residence of "waspy" Americans who only venture below Canal Street to have lunch in the French Quarter. Indeed, many older uptown Orleanians may have no reason to venture to the Tremé, the Marigny, or the Bywater and are perfectly content staying in their local area and going to work in the CBD.[10]

In terms of language and identity, New Orleans is largely American. A few physical reminders of the original French and Creole languages remain, however. Some older churches such as St. Louis Cathedral and St. Mary's Catholic Church on Chartres in the French Quarter maintain their stations of the cross in the French language. The wrought-iron entrance gate to the old Etoile Polaire Lodge at 1433 North Rampart Street speaks to the continued existence of French as the language of the downtown Seventh Ward Afro-Creole community into the twentieth century.

Although older generations of Creoles continued to speak French as their first or second language into the post–World War II era, the passing of those generations spelled the decline and almost complete erasure of both the old French and the Afro-Creole dialects in the city. Those New Orleanians who had Cajun or Creole relatives in rural areas may continue to speak the language at home, but on the whole, French patois is very rarely spoken among the residents of the city.

French names remain common among a large portion of the population, often reflecting their French roots. Yet, Americanization, mass media, and pop culture have shaped several generations since World War II, for whom English is the first and often only language, even among those with French last names. But the decline or loss of language is only one factor in the survival of Creole culture and its legacy in shaping modern life in the New Orleans.

In the city today, the term *Creole* is most often applied to foodways, such as Creole gumbo or Creole cuisine. Creole tomatoes are grown in the local soil and thereby signify a *terroir* and environment that yield a distinct local flavor. Additionally, many people commonly refer to the architectural design of the classic Creole cottages found sprinkled throughout much of Downtown and in some uptown neighborhoods along the river.

Many people of Afro-Creole descent still actively identify with the label, while also identifying as African American in the context of modern society and the complex American racial categorization that reflects social developments after Reconstruction and the modern civil rights movement. In their cultural identification, New Orleans Afro-Creoles usually draw not only on their family's Catholic heritage but also on the passing on of Creole food traditions.

Perhaps the strongest Creole legacy in the city is the celebration of Carnival. Even though the tradition has Catholic origins, the modern celebration incorporates everyone from all backgrounds and religions. Therefore, Carnival may be one of the best examples of the way that the process of creolization—embracing and adapting to the unique cultural attributes of the city—is applied today.

Through the process of creolization, the city's immigrants always adapted themselves to their new environment. In the colonial era, Indigenous Americans, Europeans, and Africans formed a new culture reflecting the origins of the three groups. More recent immigrant groups—Vietnamese, Hondurans, Palestinians, and post-Katrina American transplants—have all adapted themselves to the city to various degrees. The terms "Creole Italian" and "Vietnamese Creole" are commonly used to describe foodways.

And although the notion may not often be acknowledged, many of the persons who moved to New Orleans after the storm have also embraced and adapted their lifestyle to the unique rhythms and customs of life in the city. During the 2010s and early 2020s, the city continued to welcome a new wave of West African and Latin American residents—from the Dominican Republic, Senegal, Colombia, Ghana, Venezuela, Cuba, and Central American nations, underscoring the city's historic relationship and cultural connections with these regions in the larger Atlantic Creole world.

New Orleans remains exceptional in the United States for its historic Creole-Caribbean past and identity, but the city has also transformed over the last two centuries into one that is American in its language, economy, political systems, and racial identities. The Creole city exists in a modern world of technology and economy, but more so than most other American cities, New Orleans continues to revere its unique traditions as part of the community's identity.

In this context, many residents desperately hold onto the attributes and customs that define the city as different from everywhere else in the United States. After Katrina the very evident effort to maintain, safeguard, and promote traditions is encouraging for those who appreciate the city's rich culture. Importantly, the culture bearers of New Orleans's unique customs continue to actively pass on their knowledge to succeeding generations.

One sees the process of knowledge sharing in family kitchens, at music performances, and on the streets where parades and maskers often represent generations of history and pride. The elders also impart the spiritual importance of their community role as keepers of the proverbial flame. Even though the processes of gentrification and Americanization continue, as long as the city can maintain and hold onto its precarious location near the mouth of the Mississippi River, the sinful, spiritual Isle of Orleans will continue to creolize newcomers and carry on.

Relevant Historic Sites

New Orleans Katrina Memorial, 5056 Canal Street: The sensitive memorial commemorates the unidentified victims of the catastrophic flood.

Historic Lower Ninth Ward/Industrial Canal Floodwall Marker, intersection of Jourdan Avenue and North Johnson Street: This historical marker commemorates the history of the surrounding neighborhood and the site of the devastating Hurricane Katrina levee breach that inundated the area.

Shell Beach Katrina Memorial, 1320 Yscloskey Highway, Shell Beach, St. Bernard: The granite memorial honors those lives lost in St. Bernard Parish during Hurricane Katrina.

Backstreet Cultural Museum, 1531 St. Philip Street, New Orleans: This museum in the historic Tremé neighborhood interprets New Orleans's unique and colorful African American costuming and masking traditions.

New Orleans African American Museum, 1417–1418 Governor Nicholls Street: This museum in the heart of the Tremé interprets the city's rich African American culture and history through a number of rotating exhibits and educational programs.

Epilogue

Where Will New Orleans Celebrate the Quadricentennial in 2118?

In the years after Katrina, numerous books were published on the subject of New Orleans history and culture. Two prominent authors, historian Lawrence Powell and former Tulane University president Scott Cowen, characterized New Orleans as the "Accidental City" and the "Inevitable City," respectively. Although the two assessments may appear contradictory, New Orleans is in many ways a manifestation of both views. Powell is correct that Bienville's hasty selection of the site on the bend of the Mississippi near the intersection of Lake Pontchartrain and Bayou St. John was accidental and improvised. And Cowen's claim for the city's inevitable rise and resilience in its current location is also appropriate.[1]

For an accidental, inevitable city, New Orleans's resilience over the past three centuries reflects its residents' historic commitment to both the geographic place and the creolized culture that emerged. We will likely never know why the Quinipissa abandoned their settlement in the late 1600s before Iberville observed their fallow fields at the future site of the Vieux Carré in December 1699. But since its French founding in 1718, New Orleans has remained occupied despite the environmental threats of storms and floods, as well as the challenges of fires, wars, and epidemics.

The geographical location close to the mouth of North America's largest river has led to the inevitable development of the site as a commercial crossroads. The Indigenous locale of Bulbancha appears to have been occupied intermittently and seasonally as a settlement and trading site before 1718. Ever since France established the village of La Nouvelle Orléans and Spain ruled the subsequent town of Nueva Orleans, the American city of New

Orleans continues as an international port and multilingual crossroads, expanding the functions it served historically before the arrival of Europeans and Africans.

The location surrounded by wetlands has always been vulnerable to environmental factors: both floods from the river and winds and tidal surges from hurricanes. History also shows us that intersections of rivers and seas always seem to attract settlements for trade. That phenomenon is certainly true of New Orleans. Despite the power of nature and the vulnerability of the location, people remain and continue to return after any environmental challenge or disaster.

Given the likelihood of continued coastal erosion in the wetlands surrounding the metro area, modern New Orleans will increasingly face more environmental challenges in the coming decades. The federally funded Coastal Protection and Restoration Authority, established after Katrina, has issued a plan called Coast 2050 that promotes initiatives to create a sustainable coast south of New Orleans, given the region's importance to trade and to the energy industry, in addition to the location's cultural significance.[2]

Coast 2050 has issued a map of the predicted land loss at the mid-twenty-first-century mark. The graphic depicts a dramatic loss of marshlands and swamp along the entire Louisiana coast. By 2050, the New Orleans area along the Mississippi River may only exist as a finger of land extending into the Gulf and on the edge of the coast, with no buffer to lessen the power of hurricane winds or tidal surges. This map raises these questions: How much environmental change will affect the city, and can New Orleans create a sustainable system that enables it to remain in its current location? If the map's predictions are realized, then what can we imagine for New Orleans in the future?

The Louisiana Folklife Program, under director Maida Owens, has initiated efforts to address the importance of place and culture and the challenges of "culture migration." The agency's Bayou Culture Collaborative organization offers workshops that help culture bearers in vulnerable communities across south Louisiana maintain their unique cultures and traditions while facing the reality of migrating inland to new locations.[3]

Given the exodus of some St. Bernard and Plaquemines Parish residents to higher ground after Katrina, one can expect the continuation of a gradual population shift toward the elevated north shore of Lake Pontchartrain.

Residents in flood-prone areas may be unable to find affordable home insurance. Those with less means will seek affordable housing outside New Orleans and perhaps commute to work in the city. Wealthier residents will likely continue to congregate on the higher ground because they can afford the rising costs of the inhabitable land.

One can imagine that New Orleans will likely evolve into the "Venice of America." In that city built on the marshes and deltas of the Brenta River in northeastern Italy, the canal-laced islands are one of the top sightseeing destinations in Europe. The economy largely depends on tourism, especially during the popular Carnival season. Housing is so costly that hospitality and tourism service workers commute from less-expensive communities on the nearby mainland. Residents in the city live with seasonal flooding called *acqua alta* (high water) that requires residents and visitors to wear high boots and walk on makeshift boardwalks in the streets.

New Orleans will, of course, need to take action to remain a livable city. After Katrina, the local architectural firm Waggonner and Ball issued a master plan for the city called "Living with Water." The proposal suggests ways to create a sustainable environment and housing designs for New Orleans, while acknowledging the threat of hurricane tidal surges and monsoon rains. The plan advocates such ideas as creating more water-retention ponds to maintain a healthy wetland soil base and prevent street flooding.

The multidisciplinary approach also encourages reuse of the city's canals for recreation, socializing, and gardening—not just for drainage. In this vision, the architects advocate the creation of the Lafitte Blueway—essentially re-creating the Carondelet Canal that connected the French Quarter to Bayou St. John—paralleling the Lafitte Greenway. Importantly, the plan calls for smart building techniques, in which housing design will be suited to and accommodate seasonal flooding. All these ideas come with a hefty price tag, which New Orleans can unlikely afford. Indeed, the city's antiquated drainage infrastructure struggles to meet current needs during heavy rains.[4]

Clearly, New Orleans and the entire metro area will have to face a future in which all these predicted scenarios and solutions are possible. Geographer Craig Colten, in his history of New Orleans water management, characterizes the city as the "unnatural metropolis."[5] New Orleans may owe its existence today to modern levees, Wood screw pumps, and water diversions, and so the city's future will need to continue to be shaped by innovative environmental engineering feats. The metro area was fortunate to receive the federally funded billion-dollar flood protection investment after Katrina. Developing upgraded systems will continue to rely on federal largesse in a generally low-tax, public-funds–deficient state.

Even if New Orleans can respond to environmental challenges, the issue of housing affordability may be one of the biggest barriers to the survival of the city's unique culture and traditions. Today, many families with deep local roots, along with the city's culture bearers, find life in New Orleans difficult in terms of housing, crime, environmental threats, affordable education, and opportunity. Some are moving to Baton Rouge, Lafayette, Houston, Dallas, or Atlanta, where they can earn a living and still be close to their hometown and able to visit relatives or attend important festivities on weekends.

But can New Orleans's unique traditions and culture survive through relocation to adjacent areas? In the French culinary concept of *terroir,* specific soil and weather conditions determine the taste of foods and wines. Can New Orleans's cultural guardians transfer their traditions to the different *terroir* of LaPlace, St. Tammany Parish, or Baton Rouge? Can Black Masking Indians or second-line parades be removed from the Isle of Orleans and perhaps find a new home north of Lake Pontchartrain? Or will the culture bearers live in these other locations and return to New Orleans to carry on their traditions when they are able? The latter scenario occurred in the immediate post-Katrina years, and still continues for some.

In light of the city's current environmental challenges and the recent commemoration of its tricentennial, one must ask this question: What will the city's quadricentennial celebration in 2118 look like? Will New Orleans exist on a slim finger of land along the natural ridge of the river, in which the French Quarter is the lowest settlement on the river? Will much of the city housing be in the form of raised homes on stilts or on high brick foundations to withstand even stronger winds, monsoon street flooding, and higher tidal surges?

One can only imagine. But given the native residents' and newcomers' commitment to maintaining the city's unique celebrations, costuming, and culinary traditions, the process of adaptation and creolization in the new era will continue. New Orleanians have always passed down their traditions to successive generations, with each younger generation transforming the specific traditions to give them new relevance. As New Orleans moves forward, the people will continue to adapt and creolize in the changing physical environment. And the unnatural, accidental, inevitable Isle of Orleans-Bulbancha will live on in some form of existence and memory. In reality and history, New Orleans will always exist as an incredible, exceptional Creole American city.

Notes

Introduction

1. Sublette, *The World That Made New Orleans,* 79; Bernard, "Creoles"; Kein, *Creole.*

2. Bernabé, "De La Negritude à la Créolité"; Glissant, "Creolization in the Making of the Americas"; Hall, "Créolité and the Process of Creolization"; Martineau, "Creolization: Beyond a Concept"; Dawdy, *Building the Devil's Empire,* 5–6.

3. Midlo Hall, *Africans in Colonial Louisiana,* 159.

4. Tregle, "Creoles and Americans," 156–59.

5. Tregle, "Creoles and Americans"; Logsdon and Bell, "The Americanization of Black New Orleans," 201–60.

6. See, for example, the Creole Heritage Center in Natchitoches, Louisiana: https://www.nsula.edu/creole/.

7. To reinforce this point, French president Charles de Gaulle once famously asked, "Comment voulez-vous gouverner un pays avec deux-cent quarante-six variétés de fromage" (How can one govern a nation with two hundred and forty-six varieties of cheese?).

8. For more information on the resurgent Baby Dolls masking tradition, see Vaz, *The "Baby Dolls."*

1. Bulbancha

1. D'Iberville, *Iberville's Gulf Journals,* 111–12.

2. Benedetto, "Bulbancha Is Still a Place"; Bentley, "Reviving Indigenous Histories with 'Bulbancha Is Still a Place.'"

3. Byington, *Dictionary of the Choctaw Language,* 85, 596.

4. Campanella, *Bienville's Dilemma,* 279.

5. D'Iberville, *Iberville's Gulf Journals,* 56.

6. D'Iberville, *Iberville's Gulf Journals,* 58–64.

7. D'Iberville, *Iberville's Gulf Journals,* 56.

8. The Army Corps of Engineers' Old River complex built north of Baton Rouge in the 1950s prevents the Mississippi River from diverting the river's dominant current toward the Atchafalaya River and Basin, as the river would do in the natural deltaic cycle. For a history of hydraulic

engineering in the Atchafalaya Basin, see Reuss, *Designing the Bayous;* Campanella, *Bienville's Dilemma,* 77–96.

9. Kniffen et al., *The Historic Indian Tribes of Louisiana,* 14–34.

10. McWilliams, *Fleur de Lys and Calumet,* 13. See also Le Page du Pratz, *The History of Louisiana,* 17.

11. D'Iberville, *Iberville's Gulf Journals,* 112–13.

12. Le Page du Pratz, *The History of Louisiana,* 295.

13. D'Iberville, *Iberville's Gulf Journals,* 45–48, 89.

14. D'Iberville, *Iberville's Gulf Journals,* 47–48, 65; Read, *Louisiana Place Names of Indian Origin,* 21. For a history of the Houma people and migrations, see Verdin, *Return to Yakni Chitto.*

15. Darensbourg, "Ishak Indigenous People."

16. McWilliams, *Fleur de Lys and Calumet,* 91; Kniffen et al., *The Historic Indian Tribes of Louisiana,* 257–59.

17. D'Iberville, *Iberville's Gulf Journals,* 55.

18. D'Iberville, *Iberville's Gulf Journals,* 39, 44, 46, 58–59, 61, 67, 78, 87, 122, 12; Le Page du Pratz, *The History of Louisiana,* 35–36; McWilliams, *Fleur de Lys and Calumet,* 5, 61, 159, 218.

19. D'Iberville, *Iberville's Gulf Journals,* 59

20. McWilliams, *Fleur de Lys and Calumet,* 4.

21. Kniffen et al., *The Historic Indian Tribes of Louisiana,* 124–25.

22. Byington, *Dictionary of the Choctaw Language,* 93, 107; Read, *Louisiana Place Names of Indian Origin,* 19–20.

23. Jacques Tanesse, *Plan of the City and Suburbs of New Orleans, from an Actual Survey Made in 1815,* Charles del Vecchio of New York and Pierre Maspero of New Orleans, 1817, Historic New Orleans Collection.

24. D'Iberville, *Iberville's Gulf Journals,* 111–12.

25. McWilliams, *Fleur de Lys and Calumet,* 8–9.

26. D'Iberville, *Iberville's Gulf Journals,* 43, 44, 46, 55, 64.

27. D'Iberville, *Iberville's Gulf Journals,* 64.

28. McWilliams, *Fleur de Lys and Calumet,* 109.

29. McWilliams, *Fleur de Lys and Calumet,* 109.

30. McWilliams, *Fleur de Lys and Calumet,* 109, 111.

31. Le Page du Pratz, *The History of Louisiana,* 204–15.

32. Byington, *Dictionary of the Choctaw Language,* 83; McWilliams, *Fleur de Lys and Calumet,* 111–12.

33. Byington, *Dictionary of the Choctaw Language,* 391.

34. D'Iberville, *Iberville's Gulf Journals,* 69; Usner, *Indians, Settlers, and Slaves,* 199.

35. Usner, *Indians, Settlers, and Slaves,* 205; Byington, *Dictionary of the Choctaw Language,* 419.

36. Le Page du Pratz, *The History of Louisiana,* 202–3.

37. For more information on Choctaw food traditions, see Thompson, *Choctaw Food.*

38. D'Iberville, *Iberville's Gulf Journals,* 44, 46, 59.

39. Kidder, "Making the City Inevitable," 9–21.

40. Usner, *American Indians in Early New Orleans,* 76–128.

41. Usner, *Weaving Alliances with Other Women;* Kniffen et al., *The Historic Indian Tribes of Louisiana;* Mueller, *Nations Within;* Schmelzer, "Bulbancha Forever, From NOLA to Minneapolis:" Duncan, "Decolonize This."

42. Baurick, "The Last Days of Isle de Jean Charles." For an account of Houma migrations, see Verdin, *Return to Yakni Chitto.*

2. La Nouvelle Orléans

1. Although Pénicault claimed the first buildings were constructed in the fall of 1717, geographer Richard Campanella argues that the carpenter's recollection was likely incorrect and that Bienville was correct that they were built during the winter of 1718. McWilliams, *Fleur de Lys and Calumet,* 208–9; Campanella, *Bienville's Dilemma,* 110.

2. Dawdy, *Building the Devil's Empire,* 150–51; Dejean, *Mutinous Women,* 243–84.

3. Powell, *The Accidental City,* 23–32. For a history of the Company of the Indies, see Greenwald, *Marc-Antoine Caillot and the Company of the Indies in Louisiana.*

4. Dejean, *Mutinous Women,* 42; Midlo Hall, *Africans in Colonial Louisiana,* 59–60; Powell, *The Accidental City,* 53; Usner, *Indians, Settlers, and Slaves,* 32; Greenwald, "John Law."

5. Powell, *The Accidental City,* 40–41.

6. Powell, *The Accidental City,* 34–40. For an exploration of the fur trade between Natchitoches and New Orleans during the French period, see Burton and Smith, *Colonial Natchitoches.*

7. McCash, "Wait, Bienville Had Tattoos?"

8. Campanella, *Bienville's Dilemma,* 109–14.

9. McWilliams, *Fleur de Lys and Calumet,* 208–9.

10. McWilliams, *Fleur de Lys and Calumet,* 210–11.

11. De la Harpe and de Beauvilliers, *Veue de la Nouvelle Orléans,* 1720.

12. Clark, *Voices from an Early American Convent,* 77, 87.

13. *Carte du cours du fleuve St. Louis* (1732?).

14. Powell, *The Accidental City,* 45–46.

15. Powell, *The Accidental City,* 81, 90, 123; Wilson, "The Plantation of the Company of the Indies." For a history of the colonial West Bank, see Campanella, *The West Bank of Greater New Orleans.*

16. *Carte du cours du fleuve St. Louis* (1732?).

17. Dawdy, *Building the Devil's Empire,* 63–98.

18. O'Neill, "The French Regency and the Colonial Engineers"; Chase, *Frenchmen Desire Good Children,* 27–38.

19. Lassus, "Vue et Perspective de la Nouvelle Orléans."

20. Powell, *The Accidental City,* 53–55.

21. McWilliams, *Fleur de Lys and Calumet,* 228–56.

22. Mills, "The Chauvin Brothers: Early Colonists of Louisiana"; Ingersoll, *Mammon and Manon in Early New Orleans,* 35–66.

23. Powell, *The Accidental City,* 46.

24. Dawdy, *Building the Devil's Empire,* 139–188; Dejean, *Mutinous Women,* 9–33.

25. Dawdy, *Building the Devil's Empire,* 99–137.

26. Dawdy, *Building the Devil's Empire,* 99–100.

27. Dawdy, *Building the Devil's Empire,* 92, 146–48, 161.

28. Saucier, "Carte particulière du cours du flueve St. Louis depuis le village sauvage jusqu'au dessous du Detour aux Angloix," 1749.

29. Houdaille, "Quelque Donneés sur Le Population de Saint-Domingue au le XVIII Siecle," 859–72.

30. Dawdy, *Building the Devil's Empire,* 189–91, 200; Midlo Hall, *Africans in Colonial Louisiana,* 131–32; Usner, *American Indians in Early New Orleans,* 15.

31. Midlo Hall, *Africans in Colonial Louisiana,* 99, 103–4; Usner, *American Indians in Early New Orleans,* 14–16.

32. D'Iberville, *Iberville's Gulf Journals,* 154; Midlo Hall, *Africans in Colonial Louisiana,* 115–18. For a history of maroons in the Americas, see Diouf, *Slavery's Exiles;* for an account of Afro-Indigenous creolization, see Prud'Homme-Cranford, Barthé, and Jolivétte, *Louisiana Creole Peoplehood.*

33. Nevilles and Ritz, *The Brothers Neville,* 244; Usner, *American Indians in Early New Orleans,* 117–18. For a recent history of Black Masking Indians, see Dewulf, *From the Kingdom of Kongo to Congo Square;* Sakakeeny, "Mardi Gras Indians."

34. Midlo Hall, *Africans in Colonial Louisiana,* 97–99; Usner, *American Indians in Early New Orleans,* 12–15.

35. Le Page du Pratz, *The History of Louisiana,* 18–20.

36. Dawdy, *Building the Devil's Empire,* 185–86.

37. For a history of the Ursulines in French colonial New Orleans, see Clark, *Masterless Mistresses;* Irvin, "The Ursuline Convent."

38. Clark, *Voices from an Early American Convent,* 20–91.

39. Clark, *Voices from an Early American Convent,* 89–90.

40. Clark, *Voices from an Early American Convent,* 78, 81, 82–83.

41. Clark, *Masterless Mistresses,* 41–57; Irvin, "Ursuline Convent."

42. Wegmann, "Government House: First Louisiana Supreme Court Location, 1813–1818."

43. Various recent histories of slavery and enslaved people in New Orleans and its environs can be found in Midlo Hall, *Africans in Colonial Louisiana;* Ingersoll, *Mammon and Manon in Early New Orleans;* Usner, *Indians, Settlers, and Slaves;* White, *Voices of the Enslaved;* Seck, *Bouki Fait Gombo.* A table of French slave-trade ships can be found in Midlo Hall, *Africans in Colonial Louisiana,* 60.

44. Midlo Hall, *Africans in Colonial Louisiana,* 28–55.

45. Usner, *Indians, Settlers, and Slaves,* 157–65.

46. For more information on the issue of humanity and morality among the enslaved in colonial New Orleans, see White, *Voices of the Enslaved.*

47. White, *Voices of the Enslaved.*

48. Le Page du Pratz, *The History of Louisiana,* 358, 366.

49. Midlo Hall, *Africans in Colonial Louisiana,* 157–200.

50. Le Page du Pratz, *The History of Louisiana,* 366.

51. McWilliams, *Fleur de Lys and Calumet,* 251; Le Page du Pratz, *The History of Louisiana,* 362–63; GhaneaBassiri, *A History of Islam in America,* 18–36.

52. Seck, *Bouki Fait Gombo,* 129–39.

53. McWilliams, *Fleur de Lys and Calumet,* 220; Usner, *Indians, Settlers, and Slaves,* 191–218.

54. McWilliams, *Fleur de Lys and Calumet,* 236.

55. Clark, *Voices from an Early American Convent,* 77.

56. Clark, *Voices from an Early American Convent,* 40, 80.

57. Le Page du Pratz, *The History of Louisiana,* 366.

58. Seck, *Bouki Fait Gombo*, 125–29.

59. Le Page du Pratz, *The History of Louisiana*, 201–208; Midlo Hall, *Africans in Colonial Louisiana*, 34–38.

60. Midlo Hall, *Africans in Colonial Louisiana*, 59; Powell, *The Accidental City*, 74; Seck, *Bouki Fait Gombo*, 125–29.

61. Flournoy, "In Senegal, a Return to Homegrown Rice."

62. Le Page du Pratz, *The History of Louisiana*, 165–66.

63. Midlo Hall, *Africans in Colonial Louisiana*, 59. For a history of rice in the Americas, see Carney, *Black Rice;* Tibbetts, "African Roots, Carolina Gold."

64. Le Page du Pratz, *The History of Louisiana*, 166.

65. Le Page du Pratz, *The History of Louisiana*, 166.

66. Laussat, *Memoirs of My Life*, 68.

67. Le Page du Pratz, *The History of Louisiana*, 76–77; Dart, "Early Episodes in Louisiana History," 205.

68. Powell, *The Accidental City*, 83–86; Ouchley, "Natchez Revolt of 1729."

69. Dawdy, *Building the Devil's Empire*, 189–218.

70. Powell, *The Accidental City*, 109–12.

71. For a history of Acadian settlement, see Brasseaux, *Acadiana*.

72. Bellin, *Plan de la Nouvelle Orléans*, 1764, Historic New Orleans Collection.

3. Nueva Orleans

1. Evans, *Congo Square*, 137.

2. Jefferys, *Plan of New Orleans, Capital of Louisiana*, 1768, Library of Congress; Trudeau, *Plano de la Ciudad de Nueva Orleans y las Habitationes Imediatas*, 1798, Louisiana State Museum, 11552.5.

3. Dawdy, *Building the Devil's Empire*, 219–46; Powell, *The Accidental City*, 129–63.

4. Powell, *The Accidental City*, 165–70, 216–17.

5. Blackbird, "'It Has Always Been Customary to Slaves of Savages,'" 525–58; Hangar, *Bounded Lives, Bounded Places*, 24–26, 42–51. For a history of Indigenous slavery in North America, see Rushforth, *The Bonds of Alliance*.

6. Sublette, *The World That Made New Orleans*, 96–97; Hangar, *Bounded Lives, Bounded Places*, 24–26, 42–51. For an account of free persons of color in New Orleans in the Spanish period, see Bell, *Revolution, Romanticism, and the Afro-Creole Protest Tradition in Louisiana*, and *Creole New Orleans in the Revolutionary Atlantic*.

7. Caughey, *Bernardo de Gálvez in Louisiana*.

8. Bishpam, "Fray Antonio de Sedella," 24–37; Gassler, "Pere Antoine," 59–63.

9. Bishpam, "Fray Antonio de Sedella."

10. Gassler "Pere Antoine."

11. Midlo Hall, *Africans in Colonial Louisiana*, 233.

12. For a history of the Monsantos in Spanish colonial New Orleans, see Ford and Stiefl, *The Jews of New Orleans and the Mississippi Delta*.

13. Ermus, "Reduced to Ashes," 292–331; 617 Chartres, Collins C. Diboll Vieux Carré Survey, The Historic New Orleans Collection; https://www.hnoc.org/vcs/property_info.php?lot=18489.

14. Ermus, "Reduced to Ashes," 300.

15. Bellin, *Plan de la Nouvelle Orléans.*

16. Powell, *The Accidental City,* 199–200.

17. Information on Guillemard provided by Robert Cangelosi, reviewing files of Samuel Wilson, January 21, 2024.

18. For a history of the Cabildo, see Wilson and Huber, *The Cabildo on Jackson Square.*

19. Tanesse, *Plan of the City and Suburbs of New Orleans,* 1817.

20. 617–621 Chartres St., Collins Diboll Vieux Carré Survey, Historic New Orleans Collection, https://www.hnoc.org/vcs/property_info.php?lot=18489.

21. 527–533 Royal St., Collins Diboll Vieux Carré Survey, Historic New Orleans Collection, https://www.hnoc.org/vcs/property_info.php?lot=18681.

22. For an early history of Almonester in New Orleans, see King, *New Orleans: The Place and the People.*

23. For a history of Faubourg Santa Maria (Ste. Marie), see Friends of the Cabildo, *New Orleans Architecture Vol. VII: The American Sector;* Powell, *The Accidental City,* 346–51; Campanella, "Urbanism at Its Best: An Historical Geography of Magazine Street."

24. Trudeau, *Plano de la Ciudad de Nueva Orleans y las Habitationes Imediatas,* 1798.

25. Maps depicting the original town plan vary in terms of the settlement footprint. For example, in the original plan (likely drawn up by Pierre Le Blond de La Tour) around 1722, the grid encompasses a depth of six blocks. Maps such as that of Jacques-Nicolas Bellin from 1764 show a depth of only four blocks, ending at Dauphine. Samuel Wilson Jr., "The Vieux Carré, New Orleans: Its Plan, Its Growth, Its Architecture," manuscript provided by Robert Cangelosi, September 3, 2024.

26. Dawdy, *Building the Devil's Empire,* 139–41.

27. *Plano de la Ciudad de la Nueva Orleans, Las Lineas Rojas manifiestan la parte destruida por el encindio del la 8 Deciembre 1794.*

28. Bishpam, "Fray Antonio de Sedella."

29. Beerman, "A Genealogical Study of Luis Peñalver y Cárdenas," 33–44; Powell, *The Accidental City,* 287; "Peñalver y Cardenas," *Catholic Encyclopedia,* vol. 11.

30. Powell, *The Accidental City,* 171.

31. Text message from musician Bruce Daigrepont, September 29, 2024.

32. For a history of the Isleño immigration in Louisiana, see Din, *The Canary Islanders of Louisiana.*

33. Din, *The Canary Islanders of Louisiana.*

34. Perez, "Isleños."

35. For information on the historical debates regarding Andalusian social and religious tolerance, see Menacal, *The Ornament of the World;* Fernández-Morera, *The Myth of Andalusian Paradise.*

36. Midlo Hall, *Africans in Colonial Louisiana,* 276–315, table on 279.

37. Sublette, *The World That Made New Orleans,* 106–15.

38. The Bantu-French word *gombe/gombo* evolved from the Bantu Angolan dialects of Umbundu (*ochinggômbo*) and Kimbundu (*kingombo*).

39. Nobles, "Gumbo," 98–115.

40. Sublette, *The World That Made New Orleans,* 283.

41. Johnson, "New Orleans' Congo Square," 117–57.

42. Sublette, *The World That Made New Orleans,* 123.

43. Davis-Kahina, "An Introduction to Bamboula."

44. Sublette, *The World That Made New Orleans,* 120–23.

45. Midlo Hall, *Africans in Colonial Louisiana,* 201–36.

46. Powell, *The Accidental City,* 257–58.

47. Bernard, "Gumbo in 1764?"; Nobles, "Gumbo"; DePriest, "Choctaw Gumbo."

48. Laussat, *Memoirs of My Life,* 86.

49. Hill, "The History of the Chayote (Mirliton) in the United States."

50. Bonner, "José Francisco Salazar y Mendoza."

4. American Boomtown

1. Laussat, *Memoirs of My Life,* 89, 92–95.

2. For an overview of the historic conflicts between Great Britain and France, see Clarke, *1,000 Years of Annoying the French.*

3. Laussat, *Memoirs of My Life,* 99, 103.

4. "To Jefferson from Claiborne, 30 August 1804."

5. "To Thomas Jefferson from William C. C. Claiborne, 30 August 1804." For more information on the context of the Angle-Creole divide, see Faber, *Building the Land of Dreams;* Dessens, *Creole City.*

6. *American State Papers: Documents, Legislative and Executive, of the Congress of the United States;* Vernet, "A Community of Resistance," 47–70.

7. Kelman, *A River and Its City,* 19–49.

8. "A History of the Codes of Louisiana: Civil Code."

9. "From Thomas Jefferson to the Ursuline Nuns of New Orleans, 13 July 1804."

10. O'Neil, "A Quarter Marked by Sundry Peculiarities," 235–77; Nolan, "Tricentennial Thursday: The Louisiana Purchase and New Orleans Catholics."

11. For more information on the legacy of Saint-Domingue immigrants in New Orleans, see Dessens, *Creole City;* Bell, *Creole New Orleans in the Revolutionary Atlantic.*

12. Dessens, *From Saint-Domingue to New Orleans,* 149–87.

13. Hankins, *Raised to the Trade,* 61–95; Vlach, "The Shotgun House," 47–56; Edwards "Shotgun," 62–96.

14. "Cousin Cottage, 1231 Marais Street, Faubourg Treme, Orleans Parish."

15. For more information on Jackson's contempt for the Baratarians, see Remini, *The Battle of New Orleans.*

16. For a history of the Baratarian military involvement in the battle, see De Grummond, *The Baratarians and the Battle of New Orleans;* de Grummond, *Renato Beluche;* Davis, *The Pirates Lafitte.*

17. Usner, *American Indians in Early New Orleans,* 48. For an overview of Choctaw relations with the United States during this period, see Carson, *Searching for the Bright Path;* O'Brien, *Choctaws in a Revolutionary Age.*

18. Campanella, "Neutral Ground."

19. For a detailed history of city politics during this period, see Kendall, *History of New Orleans,* chapter 43.

20. William Henry Brooke (artist) and J. M. Starling (printer), "Sale of Estates, Pictures and Slaves in the Rotunda, New Orleans," 1842, The Historic New Orleans Collection.

21. For more information on the history of opera in New Orleans, see Kmen, *Music in New Orleans.*

22. Norman, "Norman's Plans of New Orleans and Environs, 1845."

23. For more information on this American-Creole political division, see Kendall, *History of New Orleans,* chapter 8.

24. Samuel Augustus Mitchell, "Plan of New Orleans," Philadelphia, ca. 1867, Louisiana State Museum. 1989.002.002.

25. For information on Irish immigration and labor during this period, see Kelly, *The Irish in New Orleans.*

26. Northup, *Twelve Years a Slave,* 49

27. Hangar, *Bounded Lives, Bounded Places,* 164–165; "A History of the Black Codes of Louisiana: The Black Code."

28. Laussat, *Memoirs of My Life,* 51–52, 60–61.

29. Johnson, *Soul by Soul,* 1–18.

30. Bardes, "Antebellum Slavery in Urban Louisiana."

31. For more information on the Deslondes Revolt, see Rasmussen, *American Uprising.*

32. Wall et al., *Louisiana: A History,* 156–57.

33. For the history of Creoles in early American New Orleans, see Thompson, *Exiles at Home;* Bell, *Revolution, Romanticism, and the Afro-Creole Protest Tradition in Louisiana,* and *Creole New Orleans in the Revolutionary Atlantic.*

34. For a history of the Creole exodus, Gehman, *The Free People of Color in New Orleans;* Gehman, "Louisiana Creoles Who Immigrated to Mexico."

35. Sullivan, "Composers of Color of Nineteenth Century New Orleans," 51–82.

36. Porche-Frilot, "Propelled by Faith."

37. Brock, "Jordan Noble."

38. For the history of Marie Laveau, see Fandrich, *The Mysterious Voodoo Queen, Marie Laveau;* Ward, *Voodoo Queen;* Long, *A New Orleans Voudou Priestess.*

39. Clark, *The Strange History of the American Quadroon,* 38.

40. Cizek, "Free Women of Color in the Development of Faubourg Marigny."

41. Excerpt from Christian Schultz, *Travels on an Inland Voyage, 1808,* as found in Evans, *Congo Square,* 138.

42. Excerpt from *The Journal of Latrobe,* as found in Evans, *Congo Square,* 143–45; *Sublette, The World That Made New Orleans, 271–88.*

43. Edwards et al., "Bartélémey Lafon in New Orleans, 1792–1820."

44. For a history of the Marigny, see Friends of the Cabildo, *New Orleans Architecture Vol. IV: The Creole Faubourgs.*

45. Edwards et al., "Bartélémey Lafon in New Orleans."

46. Edwards et al., "Bartélémey Lafon in New Orleans."

47. For a history of the Tremé, see Friends of the Cabildo, *New Orleans Architecture Vol. IV: The Creole Faubourgs.*

48. Starr, *Southern Comfort,* 33–55.

49. For a history of the restaurant, see Guste, *Antoine's since 1840.*

50. Bégué, *Madame Bégué's Recipes of Old New Orleans Creole Cookery.*

51. Maylié, *Maylié's Table d'Hote Recipes.*

52. Armstrong, *Satchmo,* 85.

53. For a history of Pontalba, see Vella, *Intimate Enemies.*

54. For a history of the Pontalba buildings, see Huber and Wilson, *Baroness Pontalba's Buildings.*

55. For more information on the history of Tabasco pepper sauce, see Bernard, *Tabasco.*

56. D. Appleton, "Map of the United States, Mexico & C.," David Appleton and Co., New York, 1849, Louisiana State Museum.

57. Starr, *Bamboula!*, 32–45.

5. The Simmering Gumbo Pot

1. Lafcadio Hearn, "A Creole Type"; *The Selected Writings of Lafcadio Hearn*, 260–61.

2. For more information on the history and legacy of Hearn in New Orleans, see Starr, *Inventing New Orleans*.

3. Chamberlain, "Severed Heads to Statehouse," 79–96.

4. Pratt, "Unionism in Louisiana."

5. Sacher, "Civil War Louisiana."

6. "From the Diary of Clara Solomon, May 8th, 1862."

7. Berry, "Negro Troops in Blue and Gray," 165–190.

8. Glatthaar, "The Civil War through the Eyes of a Sixteen-Year-Old Black Officer," 201–16. For more information on the history of Cailloux, see Ochs, *A Black Patriot and a White Priest*.

9. Simpson, "Michael Hahn."

10. Paper Monuments, "Street Car Protests 1867."

11. Hogue, *Uncivil War*, 31–52.

12. Hogue, *Uncivil War*, 116–43.

13. Vella, "Edgar Degas."

14. Lindner, "The Boré Plantation"; Lindner and Dutra, "No Sugar-Coating: The Plantation History of Audubon Park."

15. Currier and Ives, *The City of New Orleans, the Mississippi River, Lake Pontchartrain in the Distance*, ca. 1880, Library of Congress, https://www.loc.gov/item/90715980/, based on John Bachman, *Bird's Eye View of New Orleans*, ca 1851, Library of Congress, https://www.loc.gov/item/93500720/.

16. Kelman, *A River and Its City*, 119–56

17. Chamberlain, "Severed Heads to Statehouse," 79–96.

18. Hardee, *Topographical Drainage Map of New Orleans and Surroundings*, 1878.

19. Colten, *Unnatural Metropolis*, 77–107.

20. See Medley, *We as Freemen*, chapters 1 and 7.

21. See Medley, *We as Freemen*, chapter 1.

22. Paper Monuments, "Comité des Citoyens."

23. Tregle, "Creoles and Americans," 181–85.

24. Desdunes, *Nos Hommes et Notre Histoire;* Desdunes, *Our People and Our History;* Lanusse, *Les Cenelles;* Bruce, "Les Cenelles."

25. Dorsey Abdul-Salaam, "Aristide Mary."

26. For a history of Storyville, see Long, *The Great Southern Babylon;* Landau, *Spectacular Wickedness*.

27. Armstrong, *Satchmo*, 94–95.

28. Long, *The Great Southern Babylon;* Arceneaux, "Storyville, Madams and Music."

29. Armstrong, *Satchmo*, 127. For a history of politics and race in relation to Mardi Gras, see Gill, *Lords of Misrule*.

30. Stewart, "The Mexican Band Legend," 1–14 and "The Mexican Band Legend, Part II," 1–17.

31. Ho, "Millaudon Chinese"; Campanella, "Chinatown."

32. Ho, "Shrimp Drying in Louisiana."

33. Gonzales, "Stories Told about the Nineteenth Century Filipino Settlement at St. Malo, Louisiana."

34. Tomlinson, "The History of the Raised Floor House in Louisiana."

35. Ware, "Croatians in Louisiana."

36. Saloom and Turner, "Roots of the Cedar: The Lebanese Heritage in Louisiana."

37. "History," Holy Trinity Greek Orthodox Church.

38. Nystrum, *Creole Italian,* 13–33, 59–84.

39. Scott, "The Seamy Tale of the Italian Mafia"; "Lanata and Giacona," *Historic BK House and Gardens.*

40. For an overview of the Robert Charles Riot, see Hair, *Carnival of Fury.*

41. Nystrum, *Creole Italian,* 159–81.

42. *Map of New Orleans Showing Streetcar Railways System of the New Orleans Railway Co., January 1904.*

43. For a history of Hearn in New Orleans, see Starr, *Inventing New Orleans.*

44. Desdunes, *Nos Hommes et Notre Histoire.*

45. Otto, "Dan Desdunes and the History of Omaha Jazz."

6. The Birthplace of Jazz

1. Poster from 1915 Panama Expo San Francisco.

2. Brothers, *Louis Armstrong in His Own Words,* 5.

3. Brothers, *Louis Armstrong in His Own Words,* 12.

4. Raeburn, "Stars of David and the Sons of Sicily," 123–52.

5. For more information on the historic evolution of Bourbon Street, see Campanella, *Bourbon Street.*

6. Ramsey and Smith, *Jazzmen.*

7. Armstrong, *Satchmo,* 120

8. Armstrong, *Satchmo,* 119–20.

9. Armstrong, *Satchmo,* 144.

10. World War I Draft Cards: Louis Armstrong, National Archives Records Administration, Atlanta, https://www.archives.gov/atlanta/wwi-draft/armstrong.html.

11. Ari Kelman, *A River and Its City,* 119–56.

12. Campanella, "Envisioned 'River District' Was the Cotton Press District of the 1800s."

13. Cohen, *The Fish That Ate the Whale.*

14. Armstrong, *Satchmo,* 116.

15. Lomax, *Mister Jelly Roll,* 6.

16. Lomax, *Mister Jelly Roll,* 62.

17. Barrett, "Louis Armstrong and Opera," 216–41.

18. White, "New Orleans Brass Bands," 69–96.

19. Brothers, *Louis Armstrong in His Own Words,* 31; Armstrong, *Satchmo,* 142–43.

20. Chamberlain, "Searching for the Gulf Coast Circuit," 1–18.

21. Chamberlain, "The Goodson Sisters," 1–9.

22. Raeburn, "Sicilian Jazzman."

23. For a history of tourism in the early twentieth century, see Stanonis, *Creating the Big Easy.*

24. Colten, *Unnatural Metropolis,* 71–107. For a history of New Orleans's hydrological challenges, see Campanella, *Draining New Orleans.*

25. Armstrong, *Satchmo,* 83.

26. Kelman, *A River and Its City,* 157–96. For a history of the 1927 flood, see Barry, *Rising Tide.*

27. Haas, "New Orleans on the Half-Shell," 283–310; Sorum, "Much Depends on Local Customs."

28. For more information on World War II mobilization in New Orleans, see Chamberlain, *Victory at Home.*

29. "The Story of Arnaud's," 1950.

30. Arnaud's menu (ca. 1950), Special Collections, Howard-Tilton Memorial Library, Tulane University, https://digitallibrary.tulane.edu/islandora/object/tulane%3A17500/datastream/PDF/view.

31. Original Fabacher's menu, Special Collections, Howard-Tilton Memorial Library, Tulane University, https://digitallibrary.tulane.edu/islandora/object/tulane%3A17950/datastream/PDF/view

32. Logsdon, "Muffuletta Sandwich."

33. Mizell-Nelson, "Po-Boy Sandwich"; Mizell-Nelson, "Po-Boy Sandwich."

34. Armstrong, *Satchmo,* 86.

35. Armstrong, *Satchmo,* 85.

36. Armstrong, *Satchmo,* 214.

37. Brothers, *Louis Armstrong in His Own Words,* 6–7.

38. Leathem and Nossiter, "Red Beans and Rice," 128–39; Beriss, "Red Beans and Rebuilding," 241–63.

39. Armstrong, "Pops' Favorite Dish—Creole Red Beans (Kidney) and Rice."

40. Raffray, "The Origins of the Vieux Carré Commission, 1920–1941," 283–304.

41. For more information on the 1920s-era French Quarter, see Reed, *Dixie Bohemia.*

42. Ramsey, *Jazzmen,* 250.

7. America's Most Interesting City

1. For more information on Armstrong's post–World War II tours with the U.S. State Department, see Von Eschen, *Satchmo Blows up the World;* Williams, *White Malice.*

2. Riccardi, "De-Satch-uration"; Bergreen, *Louis Armstrong,* 473.

3. For more information on women's political activism in the early twentieth century, see Tyler, *Silk Stockings and Ballot Boxes,* 122–68; Haas, *DeLesseps S. Morrison and the Image of Reform.*

4. Riccardi, "De-Satch-uration."

5. For an overview of Morrison's racial policies, see Haas, *DeLesseps S. Morrison and the Image of Reform.*

6. Devlin, *A Girl Stands at the Door;* Simmons, *Crescent City Girls.*

7. U.S. Census, 1960, https://www2.census.gov/library/publications/decennial/1960/pc-s1-supplementary-reports/pc-s1-52.pdf.

8. For a history of female civil rights activism in New Orleans, see Frystack, *Our Minds on Freedom.*

9. Carver and Smith, "Sit-Ins and Marches at City Hall."

10. Jasmin, "The Desegregation of a University."

11. Retz, "Integrating UNO: Legal and Political Actions."

12. For a history of early New Orleans rock 'n' roll, see Coleman, *Blue Monday.*

13. For more information on the history of the modern West Bank, see Campanella, *The West Bank of Greater New Orleans.*

14. Cripple and Jarret, "Dooky Chase's Restaurant." For a reflection on Leah Chase's life and cooking experiences, see Chase, *And Still I Cook,* and Chase, *The Dooky Chase Cookbook.*

15. Kaplan-Levinson, "'The Monster': Claiborne Avenue before and after the Interstate."

16. Gratz, "Remembering Bill Borah"; Baumbach and Borah, *The Second Battle of New Orleans;* Massa, "Fifty Years Later."

17. For a history of New Orleans tourism in the post–World War II era, see Souther, *New Orleans on Parade.*

18. For a history of African American political mobilization after World War II, see Germany, *New Orleans after the Promises,* and of African American activism after World War II, see Moore, *Black Rage in New Orleans.*

19. For an overview of the Black Panther movement in New Orleans, see Arend, *Showdown at Desire.*

20. Euraque, "Honduran Memories."

21. For a history of gay activism in New Orleans, see Perez and Palmquist, *In Exile.*

22. For more information on the Up Stairs Lounge fire, see Fieseler, *Tinderbox,* and for a history of the city's gay community in the 1960s, see Long, *Cruising for Conspirators.*

23. For more information on post-segregation social problems facing African Americans in New Orleans, see Broom, *The Yellow House;* Moore, *Black Rage in New Orleans.*

8. "Ain't Dere No More"

1. Matthews, *F'SURE!*; Duplantier, "Bunny Matthews' World View."

2. Champagne, *The Yat Dictionary;* Higgins, *The Joy of Y'at Catholicism;* Canatella, *The Yat Language of New Orleans;* Perkins, "How to Tawk Right."

3. Mann, "The Long, Strange Resurrection of New Orleans."

4. Ruffin, "New Orleans Expatriates Satchmo and Lil Wayne."

5. For a history of tourism and racism in New Orleans, see Thomas, *Desire and Disaster in New Orleans;* Miles, *Tales from the Haunted South.*

6. Spangler, "We All the Way Outside."

7. Ho, "Yakamein."

8. Ho, "Yakamein."

9. Beriss, "Red Beans and Rebuilding," 9–14.

10. For a history of the Tremé community, see Crutcher, *Tremé.* For a reflection on the uptown-downtown divide, see Young, "Canal Street Gets the Post-Mamboist Treatment."

Epilogue

1. Powell, *The Accidental City;* Cowen, *The Inevitable City.*

2. Coastal Protection and Restoration Authority, https://coastal.la.gov/funding/cwppra/; "Restoring the Wetlands of Coastal Louisiana since 1990," https://lacoast.gov/new/Default.aspx; Scott, "Louisiana 2050: Rising Seas Will Upend Life."

3. Office of Cultural Development, Division of the Arts, Louisiana Folklife Program, Bayou Cultural Collaborative, https://www.crt.state.la.us/cultural-development/arts/folklife/bayou-culture-collaborative/index; Verdin, *Return to Yakni Chitto;* Verdin, "In the Heart of the Yakni Chitto."

4. Waggonner and Ball, "Living with Water."

5. Colten, *The Unnatural Metropolis.*

Bibliography

American State Papers: Documents, Legislative and Executive, of the Congress of the United States. Part 10, vol. 1.

Arceneaux, Pamela. "Storyville, Madams and Music." Online exhibit, Historic New Orleans Collection. https://www.hnoc.org/virtual/storyville/fighting-racial-segregation.

Arend, Orissa. *Showdown at Desire: The Black Panthers Take a Stand in New Orleans.* Fayetteville: University of Arkansas Press, 2010.

Armstrong, Louis. *Satchmo: My Life in New Orleans.* New York: Da Capo Press, 1954 [1986].

Armstrong, Louis, and Lucille Armstrong. "Pops' Favorite Dish—Creole Red Beans (Kidney) and Rice." Louis Armstrong House Archives. https://www.camelliabrand.com/louis-armstrongs-creole-red-beans-kidney-and-rice/.

Bardes, John. "Antebellum Slavery in Urban Louisiana." *64 Parishes.* Last modified February 14, 2023. https://64parishes.org/entry/urban-slavery-in-antebellum-louisiana.

Barrett, Joshua. "Louis Armstrong and Opera." *Musical Quarterly* 76, no. 2 (Summer 1992): 216–41.

Barry, John. *Rising Tide: The Great Mississippi Flood of 1927 and How It Changed America.* New York: Simon & Schuster, 1997.

Baumbach, Richard O., and William Borah. *The Second Battle of New Orleans: A History of the Vieux Carré Riverfront Expressway Controversy.* Lafayette: University of Louisiana Lafayette Press, 1981.

Baurick, Tristan. "The Last Days of Isle Jean Charles: A Louisiana Tribe's Struggle to Escape the Rising Sea." NOLA.com. August 28, 2022. https://www.nola.com/news/environment/the-last-days-of-isle-de-jean-charles-a-louisiana-tribe-s-struggle-to-escape/article_70ac1746-1f22-11ed-bc68-3bde459eba68.html.

Beerman, Eric. "A Genealogical Study of Luis Peñalver y Cárdenas, Spain's First Bishop of Louisiana and Florida." *Records of the Catholic American Society of Philadelphia* 89, no. 1–4 (March–December 1978): 33–44.

Bégué, Elizabeth Ketterling. *Madame Bégué's Recipes of Old New Orleans Creole Cookery.* Gretna: Pelican Publishing, 2012.

Bell, Caryn Cossé. *Revolution, Romanticism, and the Afro-Creole Protest Tradition in Louisiana, 1718–1868.* Baton Rouge: Louisiana State University Press, 1997.

———. *Creole New Orleans in the Revolutionary Atlantic, 1775–1877.* Baton Rouge: Louisiana State University Press, 2023.

Benedetto, David. "Bulbancha Is Still a Place: Speaking with Editor-Who-Is-Not-a-Chief Jeffery Darensbourg." vienolavie.org, June 10, 2019. https://www.vianolavie.org/2019/01/10/bulbancha-is-still-a-place-speaking-with-editor-who-is-not-a-chief-jeffery-darensbourg/.

Bentley, Justin. "Reviving Indigenous Histories with 'Bulbancha Is Still a Place.'" antigravitymagazine.com, September 2018. https://antigravitymagazine.com/feature/reviving-indigenous-histories-with-bulbancha-is-still-a-place/.

Bergreen, Laurence. *Louis Armstrong: An Extravagant Life.* New York: Crown Publishing, 1998.

Bernabé, Jean. "De La Negritude à la Créolité: Elements pour une approche comparée." *Études Françaises* 28, nos. 2–3 (1992): 23–38.

Bernard, Shane. "Creoles." *64 Parishes.* Last modified March 10, 2022. https://64parishes.org/entry/creoles.

———. "Gumbo in 1764?" *Bayoublogspot,* October 3, 2011. https://bayoutechedispatches.blogspot.com/2011/10/gumbo-in-1764.html.

———. *Tabasco: An Illustrated History.* Oxford: University of Mississippi Press, 2007.

Beriss, David. "Red Beans and Rebuilding: An Iconic Dish, Memory, and Culture in New Orleans," in *Beans and Rice: A Unique Dish in a Hundred Places,* edited by Richard Wilk and Livia Barbosa, 241–63. London: Berg Publishers, 2012.

Berry, Mary F. "Negro Troops in Blue and Gray: The Louisiana Native Guards, 1861–1863." *Louisiana History* 8, no. 2 (Spring 1967): 165–90.

Bishpam, Clarence Wyatt. "Fray Antonio de Sedella: An Appreciation." *Louisiana Historical Quarterly* 2 (January 1919): 24–37.

Blackbird, Leila. "'It Has Always Been Customary to Slaves of Savages': The Problem of Indigenous Slavery in Spanish Louisiana Revisited, 1769–1803." *William and Mary Quarterly* 80, 3 (July 2023): 525–58.

Bonner, Judith H. "José Francisco Salazar y Mendoza." *64 Parishes.* Last modified August 11, 2016. https://64parishes.org/entry/jos-francisco-xavier-de-salazar-y-mendoza.

Brasseaux, Carl, with photographs by Philip A. Gould. *Acadiana: Louisiana's Historic Cajun Country.* Baton Rouge: Louisiana State University Press, 2011.

Brock, Jerry. "Jordan Noble: Drummer, Soldier, Statesman." *64 Parishes.* Last modified June 3, 2019. https://64parishes.org/jordan-noble.

Brooke, William Henry (artist), and J. M. Starling (printer). "Sale of Estates, Pictures and Slaves in the Rotunda, New Orleans," 1842. Historic New Orleans Collection.

Brothers, Thomas, ed. *Armstrong in His Own Words: Selected Writings.* Oxford: Oxford University Press, 1999.

Broom, Sarah M. *The Yellow House.* New York: Grove Press, 2019.

Bruce, Clint. "Les Cenelles." *64 Parishes.* Last modified September 11, 2023. https://64parishes.org/entry/les-cenelles.

Burton, Helen Sophie, and F. Todd Smith. *Colonial Natchitoches: A Creole Community on the Louisiana–Texas Frontier.* College Station: Texas A&M University Press, 2008.

Byington, Cyrus. *Dictionary of the Choctaw Language.* Washington, DC: Government Printing Office, 1915.

Campanella, Richard. *Bienville's Dilemma: An Historical Geography of New Orleans.* Lafayette: University of Louisiana Press, 2008.

———. *Bourbon Street: A History.* Baton Rouge: Louisiana State University Press, 2014.

———. "Chinatown." *64 Parishes.* Last modified January 31, 2019. https://64parishes.org/entry/chinatown.

———. *Draining New Orleans: The 300-Year Quest to Dewater the Crescent City.* Baton Rouge: Louisiana State University Press, 2023.

———. "Envisioned 'River District' Was the Cotton Press District of the 1800s." *New Orleans Times-Picayune/Advocate,* June 6, 2021. https://richcampanella.com/wp-content/uploads/2021/06/2021_06_Geographies-Campanella_Cotton-Press-District.pdf.

———. "Neutral Ground." *Louisiana Cultural Vistas,* February 2020. https://richcampanella.com/wpcontent/uploads/2020/02/article_Campanella_LCV_Autumn2015_NeutralGround-1.pdf.

———. *The West Bank of Greater New Orleans: A Historical Geography.* Baton Rouge: Louisiana State University Press, 2020.

———. "Urbanism at Its Best: An Historical Geography of Magazine Street." *Preservation in Print,* November 1, 2020. https://prcno.org/urbanism-best-historical-geography-magazine-street.

Canatella, Ray. *The Yat Language of New Orleans: "The Who Dat Nation"—The True Story—How It All Began.* iUniverse Publishing: 2007.

Carney, Judith. *Black Rice: The African Origins of Rice Cultivation in the Americas.* Cambridge, MA: Harvard University Press, 2001.

Carson, James Taylor. *Searching for the Bright Path: The Mississippi Choctaws from Prehistory to Removal.* Lincoln: University of Nebraska Press, 1999.

Carver, Courtney, and Lauren Smith. "Sit-Ins and Marches at City Hall." *New Orleans Historical,* accessed April 17, 2024. https://neworleanshistorical.org/items/show/1375?tour=90&index=6.

Caughey, John Walton. *Bernardo de Gálvez in Louisiana, 1776–1783.* Gretna: Pelican Publishing, 1998.

Chamberlain, Charles. "Severed Heads to Statehouse: The Political Landscape of the Sugar Coast." In *Charting the Political Landscape from Natchez to New Orleans*, edited by Laura Kilcer VanHuss, 79–96. Baton Rouge: Louisiana State University Press, 2021.

———. "The Goodson Sisters: Female Pianists and the Function of Gender in the Jazz Age." *Jazz Archivist* XV (2001): 1–9.

———. "Searching for 'the Gulf Coast Circuit': Mobility and Cultural Diffusion in the Age of Jim Crow, 1900–1930." *Jazz Archivist* XIV (2000): 1–18.

———. *Victory at Home: Manpower and Race in the American South during World War II*. Athens: University of Georgia Press, 2003.

Champagne, Christian. *The Yat Dictionary*. New Orleans: Lavender Ink, 2012.

Chase, John Churchill. *Frenchmen Desire Good Children: . . . and Other Streets of New Orleans!* Gretna: Pelican Publishing, 2001.

Chase, Leah. *And Still I Cook*. New Orleans: Pelican Publishing, 2011.

———. *The Dooky Chase Cookbook*. New Orleans: Pelican Publishing, 1990.

Cizek, Eugene. "Free Women of Color in the Development of Faubourg Marigny." *Preservation in Print*, April 17, 2018. https://prcno.org/free-women-color-development-faubourg-marigny/.

Clark, Emily. *Masterless Mistresses: The New Orleans Ursulines and the Development of a New World Society, 1727–1834*. Chapel Hill: Omohundro Institute and the University of North Carolina Press, 2007.

———. *The Strange History of an American Quadroon: Free Women of Color in the Revolutionary Atlantic World*. Chapel Hill: University of North Carolina Press, 2013.

———., ed. *Voices from an Early American Convent: Marie Madeleine Hachard and the New Orleans Ursulines, 1727–1760*. Baton Rouge: Louisiana State University Press, 2007.

Clarke, Stephen. *1,000 Years of Annoying the French*. London: Black Swan Press, 2010.

Cohen, Rich. *The Fish That Ate the Whale: The Life and Times of America's Banana King*. London: Picador, 2013.

Coleman, Rick. *Blue Monday: Fats Domino and the Lost Dawn of Rock 'n' Roll*. New York: DeCapo Press, 2007.

Colten, Craig E. *Unnatural Metropolis: Wresting New Orleans from Nature*. Baton Rouge: Louisiana State University Press, 2005.

———, ed. *Transforming New Orleans and Its Environs: Centuries of Change*. Pittsburgh: University of Pittsburgh Press, 2000.

"Cousin Cottage, 1231 Marais Street, Faubourg Treme, Orleans Parish." https://loc.getarchive.net/topics/cousin+cottage.

Cowen, Scott. *The Inevitable City: The Resurgence of New Orleans and the Future of Urban America*. New York: St. Martin's Press, 2014.

Cripple, Joseph, and Mindy Jarret. "Dooky Chase's Restaurant." *New Orleans Historical,* accessed April 17, 2024, https://neworleanshistorical.org/items/show/1354.

Crutcher, Michael. *Tremé: Race and Place in a New Orleans Neighborhood.* Athens: University of Georgia Press, 2010.

Darensbourg, Jeffrey U. "Ishak Indigenous People." *64 Parishes.* Last modified February 19, 2024. https://64parishes.org/entry/ishak-indigenous-people.

Dart, William Kernan. "Early Episodes in Louisiana History" *Louisiana Historical Quarterly* 1, no. 3 (1918): 190–209.

Davis, William C. *The Pirates Lafitte: The Treacherous World of the Corsairs of the Gulf.* Boston: Mariner Books, 2006.

Davis-Kahina, Chenzira. "An Introduction to Bamboula." Youtube.com, March 26, 2017. https://www.youtube.com/watch?v=s1SbQh9qKkk&t=188s.

Dawdy, Shannon. *Building the Devil's Empire: French Colonial New Orleans.* Chicago: University of Chicago Press, 2008.

De Grummond, Jane Lucas. *The Baratarians and the Battle of New Orleans.* Baton Rouge: Louisiana State University Press, 1961.

———. *Renato Beluche: Smuggler, Privateer, and Patriot, 1780 to 1860.* Baton Rouge: Louisiana State University Press, 1999.

Dejean, Joan. *Mutinous Women: How French Convicts Became Founding Mothers of the Gulf Coast.* New York: Basic Books, 2022.

DePriest, John. "Choctaw Gumbo." *64 Parishes.* Last modified February 29, 2024. https://64parishes.org/choctaw-gumbo.

De Saint-Aulaire, Felix Achille Beaupoil. *Vue d'une Rue du Faubourg Ste. Marie,* ca. 1821. Historic New Orleans Collection. 1937.2.3

———. *Vue d'une Rue du Faubourg Marigny,* ca. 1821. Historic New Orleans Collection. 1937.2.2.

Desdunes, Rodolphe Lucien. *Nos Hommes et Notre Histoire.* Montreal: 1911.

———. *Our People and Our History: Fifty Creole Portraits.* Translated and edited by Sister Dorthea Olga McCants. Baton Rouge: Louisiana State University Press, [1973] 2001.

Dessens, Nathalie. *Creole City: A Chronicle of Early American New Orleans.* Gainesville: University Press of Florida, 2016.

———. *From Saint-Domingue to New Orleans: Migrations and Influences.* Gainesville: University Press of Florida, 2010.

Devlin, Rachel. *A Girl Stands at the Door: The Generation of Young Women Who Desegregated America's Schools.* New York: Basic Books, 2018.

Dewulf, Jeroen. *From the Kingdom of Kongo to Congo Square: Kongo Dances and the Origins of the Mardi Gras Indians.* Lafayette: University of Louisiana Lafayette Press, 2017.

D'Iberville, Pierre LeMoyne. *Iberville's Gulf Journals.* Translated and edited by Richebourg Gaillard McWilliams. Tuscaloosa: University of Alabama Press, 1981.

Din, Gilbert. *The Canary Islanders of Louisiana.* Baton Rouge: Louisiana State University Press, 1999.

Diouf, Sylviane A. *Slavery's Exiles: The Story of the American Maroons.* New York: New York University Press, 2014.

Dorsey Abdul-Salaam, Connie. "Aristide Mary." Edited by Lauren Smith and Jessica Dauterive. *New Orleans Historical.* Accessed April 17, 2024. https://neworleanshistorical.org/items/show/1703.

Duncan, Tracey Anne. "Decolonize This: How to Decolonize Your Summer Travel." *MIC.* originally published June 6, 2022, updated February 20, 2024. https://www.mic.com/life/ethical-travel-activist-tours-chicago-new-orleans-nyc.

Duplantier, Aaron. "Bunny Matthews' World View: Race, Art, and Love for New Orleans." *Folklife in Louisiana,* 2012. https://www.louisianafolklife.org/lt/articles_essays/lfmbunny.html.

Edwards, Jay D. "Shotgun: The Most Contested House in America." *Buildings and Landscapes, Journal of the Vernacular Architecture Forum* 16, no. 1 (Spring 2009): 62–96.

Edwards, Jay, with Ina Fandrich and Gabriele Richardson. "Bartélémey Lafon in New Orleans, 1792–1820: A Report to the Louisiana Division of Historic Preservation." Edited by Jay Edwards. September 2019. https://www.crt.state.la.us/Assets/OCD/hp/grants/NPShistoricfunding-2019/Barthelemey%20Lafon%20in%20New%20Orleans_Final.pdf.

Ermus, Cindy. "Reduced to Ashes: The Good Friday Fire of 1788 in Spanish Colonial New Orleans." *Louisiana History* 54, no. 3 (Summer 2013): 292–331.

Euraque, Samantha. "Honduran Memories: Identity, Race, Place, and Memory in New Orleans, Louisiana." Master's thesis, Louisiana State University, 2004.

Evans, Freddi Williams. *Congo Square: African Roots in New Orleans.* Lafayette: University of Louisiana Lafayette, 2011.

Faber, Eberhard L. *Building the Land of Dreams: New Orleans and the Transformation of Early America.* Princeton, NJ: Princeton University Press, 2015.

Fandrich, Ina J. *The Mysterious Voodoo Queen, Marie Laveau: A Study in Powerful Female Leadership in Nineteenth Century New Orleans.* London: Routledge, 2005.

Fernández-Morera, Darío. *The Myth of Andalusian Paradise: Muslims, Christians, and Jews under Islamic Rule in Medieval Spain.* Wilmington, DE: Intercollegiate Studies Institute, 2016.

Fieseler, Robert W. *Tinderbox: The Untold Story of the Up Stairs Lounge Fire and the Rise of Gay Liberation.* New York: Liveright Publishing, 2018.

Flournoy, Angela. "In Senegal, A Return to Homegrown Rice." *New York Times Magazine,* November 11, 2021. https://www.nytimes.com/2021/11/11/t-magazine/senegal-homegrown-rice.html.

Ford, Emily and Barry Stiefel. *The Jews of New Orleans and the Mississippi Delta: A History of Life and Community along the Bayou.* Charleston: Arcadia Publishing, 2012.

Friends of the Cabildo. *New Orleans Architecture, Volume VII: The American Sector.* Gretna: Pelican Publishing, 1971.

———. *New Orleans Architecture, Volume IV: The Creole Faubourgs.* Gretna: Pelican Publishing, 1975.

"From the Diary of Clara Solomon, May 8th, 1862." https://dragoon1st.tripod.com/cw/files/look_solomon.html.

"From Thomas Jefferson to the Ursuline Nuns of New Orleans, 13 July 1804." Founders Online, National Archives. https://founders.archives.gov/documents/Jefferson/01-44-02-0064.

Frystack, Shannon. *Our Minds on Freedom: Women and the Struggle for Black Equality, 1924–1967.* Baton Rouge: Louisiana State University Press, 2009.

Gassler, F. L. "Pere Antoine: Supreme Officer of the Holy Inquisition of Cartagena, in Louisiana." *Catholic Historical Review* 8, no. 1 (April 1922): 59–63.

Gehman, Mary. *The Free People of Color in New Orleans: An Introduction.* Createspace, 2009.

———. "Louisiana Creoles Who Immigrated to Mexico." https://www.dvillepress.com/LCMC.php.

Germany, Kent. *New Orleans after the Promises: Race, Poverty, Citizenship, and the Search for the Great Society.* Athens: University of Georgia Press, 2007.

GhaneaBassiri, Kambiz. *A History of Islam in America: From the New World to the New World Order.* Cambridge: Cambridge University Press, 2010.

Gill, James. *Lords of Misrule: Mardi Gras and the Politics of Race in New Orleans.* Oxford: University of Mississippi Press, 1997.

Glatthaar, Joseph T. "The Civil War through the Eyes of a Sixteen-Year-Old Black Officer: The Letters of Lieutenant John H. Crowder of the 1st Louisiana Native Guards." *Louisiana History* 35, no. 2 (Spring 1994): 201–16.

Glissant, Eduard. "Creolization in the Making of the Americas." *Caribbean Quarterly* 54, nos. 1–2 (March–June 2008): 81–89.

Gonzales, Randy. "Stories Told about the Nineteenth Century Filipino Settlement at St. Malo, Louisiana." *Louisiana Folklife,* 2019. https://www.louisianafolklife.org/LT/Articles_Essays/lfmStMalo.html.

Goodman, Henry, ed. *The Selected Writings of Lafcadio Hearn.* New York: Citadel Press, 1949.

Gratz, Roberta Brandes. "Remembering Bill Borah: Killing a French Quarter Expressway Was only a Start." *The Lens,* October 10, 2017. https://thelensnola.org/2017/10/10/remembering-bill-killing-a-french-quarter-expressway-was-only-the-start/.

Greenwald, Erin. "John Law." *64 Parishes.* Last modified February 19, 2024. https://64parishes.org/entry/john-law-2.

———. *Marc-Antoine Caillot and the Company of the Indies in Louisiana: Trade in the French Atlantic World.* Baton Rouge: Louisiana State University Press, 2016.

Guste, Roy. *Antoine's since 1840: 175th Anniversary Celebration.* New Orleans: Roy Guste, 2014.

Haas, Edward N. *DeLesseps S. Morrison and the Image of Reform: New Orleans Politics, 1946–1961.* Baton Rouge: Louisiana State University Press, 1974.

———. "New Orleans on the Half-Shell: The Maestri Era, 1936–1946." *Louisiana History* 13, no. 3 (Summer 1972): 283–310.

Hair, William Ivy. *Carnival of Fury: Robert Charles and the New Orleans Riot of 1900.* Baton Rouge: Louisiana State University Press, 2008.

Hall, Stuart. "Créolité and the Process of Creolization." In *Creolizing Europe,* edited by Encarnación Gutiérrez Rodriguez and Shirley Anne Tate, 1–25. Liverpool: Liverpool University Press, 2015.

Hangar, Kimberly. *Bounded Lives, Bounded Places: Free Black Society in Colonial New Orleans, 1769–1803.* Durham, NC: Duke University Press, 1997.

Hankins, John Ethan. *Raised to the Trade: Creole Building Arts of New Orleans.* New Orleans: Arcadia Publishing, 2003.

Higgins, Earl J. *The Joy of Y'at Catholicism.* Gretna: Pelican Publishing, 2007.

Hill, Lance. "The History of Chayote (Mirliton) in the United States: One of the Noblest Gifts the Vegetable Kingdom Can Offer Man." Mirliton.org. https://www.mirliton.org/wp-content/uploads/2022/04/The-History-of-Chayote-Mirliton-in-the-United-States-final.pdf.

Hirsch, Arnold R., and Joseph Logsdon, eds. *Creole New Orleans: Race and Americanization.* Baton Rouge: Louisiana State University Press, 1992.

"History." Holy Trinity Greek Orthodox Church. http://holytrinitycathedral.org/history.html

"History of the Black Codes of Louisiana: The Black Code." Law Library of Louisiana. https://lasc.libguides.com/c.php?g=254608&p=1697981.

"A History of the Codes of Louisiana: Civil Code." Law Library of Louisiana. https://lasc.libguides.com/c.php?g=254608&p=1697972.

Ho, Winston. "Millaudon Chinese." Researching Chinese American History in New Orleans, March 9, 2016. https://nolachinese.wordpress.com/2016/03/09/the-millaudon-chinese/.

———. "Shrimp Drying in Louisiana." *64 Parishes.* Last modified March 22, 2023. https://64parishes.org/shrimp-drying-in-louisiana.

———. "Yakamein." Researching Chinese American History in New Orleans, February 28, 2020. https://nolachinese.wordpress.com/2020/02/28/yakamein/.

Hogue, James K. *Uncivil War: Five New Orleans Street Battles and the Rise and Fall of Radical Reconstruction.* Baton Rouge: Louisiana State University Press, 2011.

Houdaille, Jacques. "Quelque Donneés sur Le Population de Saint-Domingue au le XVIII Siecle." *Population* 28e, Nos. 4–5 (1973): 859–72. https://www.persee.fr/doc/pop_0032-4663_1973_num_28_4_15523.

Huber, Leonard, and Samuel Wilson Jr. *Baroness Pontalba's Buildings*. New Orleans: Friends of the Cabildo, 1964.

Ingersoll, Thomas N. *Mammon and Manon in Early New Orleans: The First Slave Society in the Deep South, 1718–1819*. Knoxville: University of Tennessee Press, 1999.

Irvin, Hilary. "The Ursuline Convent." *64 Parishes*. Last modified March 16, 2021. https://64parishes.org/entry/ursuline-convent-2.

Jasmin, Alecia Duplessis. "The Desegregation of a University." *Tulane Magazine* (September 2013): 14–19. https://sopa.tulane.edu/sites/default/files/The%20Desegregation%20of%20Tulane.pdf.

Johnson, Jerah. "New Orleans' Congo Square: An Urban Setting for Early Afro-American Cultural Formation." *Louisiana History* 32, no. 2 (Spring 1991): 117–57.

Johnson, Walter. *Soul by Soul: Life inside the Antebellum Slave Market*. Cambridge, MA: Harvard University Press, 1999.

Kaplan-Levinson, Laine. "'The Monster': Claiborne Avenue before and after the Interstate." *Tripod New Orleans*, May 5, 2016. https://www.wwno.org/podcast/tripod-new-orleans-at-300/2016-05-05/the-monster-claiborne-avenue-before-and-after-the-interstate.

Kein, Sybil, ed. *Creole: The History and Legacy of Louisiana's Free People of Color*. Baton Rouge: Louisiana State University Press, 2000.

Kelly, Laura. *The Irish in New Orleans*. Lafayette: University of Louisiana Lafayette, 2014.

Kelman, Ari. *A River and Its City: The Nature of Landscape in New Orleans*. Berkeley: University of California Press, 2004.

Kendall, John Smith. *History of New Orleans*. Chicago: Lewis Publishing, 1922.

Kidder, Tristan R. "Making the City Inevitable: Native Americans and the Geography of New Orleans." In *Transforming New Orleans and Its Environs: Centuries of Change*, edited by Craig E. Colten, 9–21. Pittsburgh: University of Pittsburgh Press, 2000.

King, Grace. *New Orleans: The Place and the People*. New York: McMillan Press, 1926.

Kmen, Henry A. *Music in New Orleans: The Formative Years, 1791–1841*. Baton Rouge: Louisiana State University Press, 1966.

Kniffen, Fred B., et al. *The Historic Indian Tribes of Louisiana, from 1542 to the Present*. Baton Rouge: Louisiana State University Press, 1987.

Landau, Emily Epstein. *Spectacular Wickedness: Sex, Race, and Memory in Storyville, New Orleans*. Baton Rouge: Louisiana State University Press, 2013.

Lanusse, Armand. *Les Cenelles*. Text established by Mia. D. Reamer. Shreveport: Les Cahiers de Tintamarre, 2003.

Lassus, Jean-Pierre. *Vue et Perspective de la Nouvelle Orléans*. C.A.O.M. Aix-en-Provence (France) DFC Louisiane 71 (pf6B).

Laussat, Pierre-Clément de. *Memoirs of My Life*. Translated by Sister Agnes-Josephine Pastwa, edited by Robert D. Bush. Baton Rouge: Louisiana State University Press, 1978.

Leathem, Karen Trahan, and Sharron Stalworth Nossiter. "Red Beans and Rice." In *New Orleans Cuisine: Fourteen Signature Dishes and Their Histories*, edited by Susan Tucker, 128–39. Oxford: University of Mississippi Press, 2009.

Le Page du Pratz, Antoine-Simon. *The History of Louisiana*. New Orleans: Pelican Press. Reprint of the original English translation, London, 1774.

Lindner, Taylor. "The Boré Plantation." Edited by Kalie A. Dutra and Kathryn O'Dwyer. *New Orleans Historical*. Accessed April 17, 2024. https://neworleanshistorical.org/items/show/1656.

Lindner, Taylor, and Kalie A. Dutra. "No Sugar-Coating: The Plantation History of Audubon Park." Edited by Kathryn O'Dwyer. *New Orleans Historical*. Accessed April 17, 2024. https://neworleanshistorical.org/tours/show/131.

Logsdon, Dana. "Muffuletta Sandwich." *64 Parishes*. Last modified June 29, 2023. https://64parishes.org/entry/muffuletta-sandwich.

Logsdon, Joseph, and Caryn Cossé Bell. "The Americanization of Black New Orleans." In *Creole New Orleans: Race and Americanization*, edited by Arnold R. Hirsch and Joseph Logsdon, 201–60. Baton Rouge: Louisiana State University Press, 1992.

Lomax, Alan. *Mister Jelly Roll*. Berkeley: University of California Press, 1950.

Long, Alecia. *Cruising for Conspirators: How a New Orleans DA Prosecuted the Kennedy Assassination as a Sex Crime*. Chapel Hill: University of North Carolina Press, 2021.

———. *The Great Southern Babylon: Sex, Race, and Respectability*. Baton Rouge: Louisiana State University Press, 2005.

Long, Carolyn. *A New Orleans Voudou Priestess: The Legend and Reality of Marie Laveau*. Gainesville: University Press of Florida, 2007.

Mann, Charles C. "The Long, Strange Resurrection of New Orleans." *CNN Money*, August 29, 2006. https://money.cnn.com/magazines/fortune/fortune_archive/2006/08/21/8383661/index.htm.

Martineau, Michelle Edwige Jeanne. "Creolization: Beyond a Concept, a Perpetual Construction of Identity." *érudit*, March 23, 2022. https://apropos.erudit.org/concepts-creolization/?lang=en.

Massa, Dominic. "Fifty Years Later: A Look back at the Fight to Stop the Vieux Carré Riverfront Expressway." Nola.com, July 3, 2019. https://www.nola.com/news/50-years-later-a-look-back-at-the-fight-that-stopped-the-vieux-carre-riverfront/article_51344a08-9dae-11e9-ba53-43de99fc6963.html.

Matthews, Bunny. *F'SURE! Actual Dialogue Heard on the Streets of New Orleans*. New Orleans: Neetof Press, 1978.

Maylié, Eugenie Lavedan. *Maylié's Table d'Hote Recipes.* 1951. Louisiana Research Collection, Howard-Tilton Memorial Library, Tulane University.

McCash, Doug. "Wait, Bienville Had Tattoos?" Nola.com, July 22, 2019. https://www.nola.com/entertainment_life/wait-bienville-had-tattoos-yep-the-founder-of-new-orleans-was-inked/article_3fb157c2-1136-5f52-9ee7-6b9db3923cf7.html.

McWilliams, Richebourg Gaillard, ed. *Fleur de Lys and Calumet: Being the Pénicaut Narrative of French Adventure in Louisiana.* Tuscaloosa: University of Alabama Press, 1988.

Medley, Keith. *We as Freemen: Plessy v Ferguson.* Gretna: Pelican Publishing, 2003.

Menacal, Maria Rosa. *The Ornament of the World: How Muslims, Jews, and Christians Created a Culture of Tolerance in Medieval Spain.* New York: Back Bay Books, 2003.

Midlo Hall, Gwendolyn. *Africans in Colonial Louisiana: The Development of Afro-Creole Culture in the Eighteenth Century.* Baton Rouge: Louisiana State University Press, 1992.

Miles, Tiya Alecia. *Tales from the Haunted South: Dark Tourism and Memories from the Civil War Era.* Chapel Hill: University of North Carolina Press, 2015.

Mills, Gary. "The Chauvin Brothers; Early Colonists of Louisiana." *Louisiana History* 15, no. 2 (Spring 1974): 117–31.

Mizell-Nelson, Michael. "Po-Boy Sandwich." *New Orleans Historical.* Accessed April 17, 2024. https://neworleanshistorical.org/items/show/480.

———. "Po-Boy Sandwich." *64 Parishes.* Last modified May 5. 2021. https://64parishes.org/entry/po-boy-sandwich.

Moore, Leonard. *Black Rage in New Orleans: Police Brutality and African American Activism from World War II to Hurricane Katrina.* Baton Rouge: Louisiana State University Press, 2010.

Mueller, Tim (photographs), with Risa Mueller and Sarah Sue Goldsmith (text). *Nations Within: The Four Sovereign Tribes of Louisiana.* Baton Rouge: Louisiana State University Press, 2004.

Neville, Art, Aaron Neville, Charles Neville, Cyril Neville, and David Ritz. *The Brothers Neville.* Cambridge, MA: Da Capo Press, 2000.

Nobles, Cynthia LeJeune. "Gumbo." In *New Orleans Cuisine: Fourteen Signature Dishes and Their Histories,* edited by Susan Tucker, 98–115. Oxford: University of Mississippi Press, 2009.

Nolan, Charles. "Tricentennial Thursday: The Louisiana Purchase and New Orleans Catholics." *Clarion Herald,* June 21, 2018.

Northup, Solomon. *Twelve Years a Slave.* New York: Penguin, 2013.

Nystrum, Justin. *Creole Italian: Sicilian Immigrants and the Shaping of New Orleans Food Culture.* Athens, University of Georgia Press, 2018.

O'Brien, Gregory. *Choctaws in a Revolutionary Age, 1750–1830.* Lincoln: University of Nebraska Press, 2005.

Ochs, Stephen J. *A Black Patriot and a White Priest: André Cailloux and Claude Paschal Maistre in Civil War New Orleans.* Baton Rouge: Louisiana State University Press, 2000.

O'Neil, Charles Edwards. "The French Regency and the Colonial Engineers: Street Names of Early New Orleans." *Louisiana History* 39, no. 2 (Spring 1998): 207–14.

———. "A Quarter Marked by Sundry Peculiarities: New Orleans, Lay Trustees, and Père Antoine." *Catholic Historical Review* 76, no. 2 (April 1990): 235–77.

Otto, Jesse J. "Dan Desdunes and the History of Omaha Jazz." *History Nebraska,* Fall 2011. https://history.nebraska.gov/dan-desdunes-and-the-birth-of-omaha-jazz/.

Ouchley, Kelby. "Natchez Revolt of 1729." *64 Parishes.* Last modified August 8, 2022. https://64parishes.org/entry/natchez-revolt-of-1729.

Paper Monuments. "Comité des Citoyens." Narrative by Lauren Lastrape and art by Rachel Cockrill. *New Orleans Historical.* Accessed April 17, 2024. https://neworleanshistorical.org/items/show/1405.

———. "Street Car Protests 1867." Narrative by Suzanne-Juliette Mobley and art and Jeremy Paten. *New Orleans Historical.* Accessed April 17, 2024. https://neworleanshistorical.org/items/show/1433.

Perez, Frank, and Jeffrey Palmquist. *In Exile: The History and Lore Surrounding New Orleans' Gay Culture and Oldest Gay Culture and Its Oldest Bar.* LL-Publications, 2012.

Perez, Samantha. "Isleños." *64 Parishes.* Last modified February 19, 2024. https://64parishes.org/entry/islenos.

Perkins, Chuck. "How to Tawk Right—A Lexicon of New Orleans Terminology and Speech." https://www.gumbopages.com/yatspeak.html.

Porche-Frilot, Donna Marie. "Propelled by Faith: Henriette Delille and the Literacy Practices of Black Women Religious in Antebellum New Orleans." PhD diss., Louisiana State University, Baton Rouge, 2005.

Powell, Lawrence N. *The Accidental City: Improvising New Orleans.* Cambridge, MA: Harvard University Press, 2012.

Pratt, Adam. "Unionism in Louisiana." *64 Parishes.* Last modified December 19, 2016. https://64parishes.org/entry/unionism-in-louisiana.

Prud'Homme-Cranford, Rain, Darryl Barthé, and Andrew J. Jolivétte, eds. *Louisiana Creole Peoplehood: Afro-Indigeneity and Community.* Seattle: University of Washington Press, 2022.

Raeburn, Bruce Boyd. "Sicilian Jazzman." *64 Parishes.* Last modified June 1, 2016. https://64parishes.org/sicilian-jazzman.

———. "Stars of David and the Sons of Sicily: Constellations beyond the Canon in Early New Orleans Jazz." *Jazz Perspectives* 3, no. 2 (August 2009): 123–52.

Raffray, Jeanette. "The Origins of the Vieux Carré Commission, 1920–1941." *Louisiana History* 40, no. 3 (Summer 1999): 283–304.

Ramsey, Frederick, Jr., and Charles Edward Smith, eds. *Jazzmen.* Armed Services edition. New York: Harcourt, Brace, and Co., 1939.

Rasmussen, Daniel. *American Uprising: The Untold Story of America's Largest Slave Revolt.* New York: Harper Collins, 2011.

Read, William A. *Louisiana Place Names of Indian Origin: A Collection of Words.* Tuscaloosa: University of Alabama Press, 2008.

Reed, John Shelton. *Dixie Bohemia: A French Quarter Circle in the 1920s.* Baton Rouge: Louisiana State University Press, 2012.

Remini, Robert V. *The Battle of New Orleans: Andrew Jackson and America's First Military Victory.* New York: Penguin Book, 2001.

"Restoring the Wetlands of Coastal Louisiana since 1990." https://lacoast.gov/new/Default.aspx.

Retz, Becky. "Integrating UNO: Political and Legal Actions." *New Orleans Historical.* Accessed April 17, 2024. https://neworleanshistorical.org/items/show/550.

Reuss, Martin, *Designing the Bayous: The Control of Water in the Atchafalaya Basin: 1800–1995.* College Station: Texas A&M University Press, 2004.

Riccardi, Ricky. "De-Satch-uration." *64 Parishes.* Last modified November 30, 2023. https://64parishes.org/de-satch-uration.

Ruffin, Maurice Carlos. "New Orleans Expatriates: Satchmo and Lil Wayne." *64 Parishes.* Last modified April 15, 2019. https://64parishes.org/new-orleans-expatriates-satchmo-and-lil-wayne.

Rushforth, Brett. *The Bonds of Alliance: Indigenous and Atlantic Slaveries in New France.* Chapel Hill: University of North Carolina Press, 2013.

Sacher, John M. "Civil War Louisiana." *64 Parishes.* Last modified November 6, 2022. https://64parishes.org/entry/civil-war-louisiana.

Sakakeeny, Matt. "Mardi Gras Indians." *64 Parishes.* Last modified February 21, 2020. https://64parishes.org/entry/mardi-gras-indians.

Saloom, Yvonne Nassar, and I. Bruce Turner. "Roots of the Cedar: The Lebanese Heritage in Louisiana." *Folklife in Louisiana,* 1994. https://www.louisianafolklife.org/lt/articles_essays/lebanese.html.

Schmelzer, Paul. "Bulbancha Forever: From NOLA to Minneapolis, a Movement to Revive Indigenous Names Grows," *The Ostracon,* January 4, 2021. https://theostracon.net/bulbancha-indigenous-naming-jeffery-darensbourg/.

Scott, Mike. "Louisiana 2050: Rising Seas Will Upend Life: Time is Running out to Limit the Impact." Nola.com, September 14, 2023. https://www.nola.com/news/environment/louisiana-2050-the-states-perilous-future-as-seas-rise/article_af75ba34–4dae-11ee-94cc-c7fe71b2b51d.html.

———. "The Seamy Tale of the Italian Mafia, Extortion, and a 1908 Bloody Showdown at the Beauregard-Keyes House." Nola.com, May 25, 2021. https://www.nola.com/entertainment_life/the-seamy-tale-of-the-italian-mafia-extortion-and-a-1908

-bloody-showdown-at-the/article_7ce3276e-bc1a-11eb-bbc5-cb1f9ff6734c.html.

Seck, Ibrahima. *Bouki Fait Gombo: A History of the Slave Community of Habitation Haydel (Whitney Plantation) Louisiana, 1750–1860*. New Orleans: University of New Orleans Press, 2014.

Simmons, LaKisha Michelle. *Crescent City Girls: The Lives of Young Black Women in Segregated New Orleans*. Chapel Hill: University of North Carolina Press, 2015.

Simpson, Amos E. "Michael Hahn." *64 Parishes*. Last modified August 10, 2021. https://64parishes.org/entry/michael-hahn-2.

Sorum, William A. "Much Depends on Local Customs: The WPA's New Deal for New Orleans, 1935–1940." Master's thesis, University of New Orleans, 2010.

Souther, J. Mark. *New Orleans on Parade: Tourism and the Transformation of the Crescent City*. Baton Rouge: Louisiana State University Press, 2013.

Spangler, Dalton. "We All the Way Outside: Flagboy Giz Tells His Mardi Gras Indian Story." *Offbeat Magazine*, January 25, 2023. https://www.offbeat.com/articles/we-all-the-way-outside-flagboy-giz-tells-his-mardi-gras-indian-story/.

Stanonis, Anthony. *Creating the Big Easy: New Orleans and the Emergence of Modern Tourism*. Athens: University of Georgia Press, 2006.

Starr, S. Frederick. *Bamboula! The Life and Times of Louis Moreau Gottschalk*. Oxford University Press, 1995.

———. *Inventing New Orleans: The Writings of Lafcadio Hearn*. Oxford: University of Mississippi Press, 2001.

———. *Southern Comfort: The Garden District of New Orleans, 1800–1900*. Princeton, NJ: Princeton University Press, 2005.

Stewart, Jack. "The Mexican Band Legend: Myth, Reality, and Musical Impact—Preliminary Investigation." *Jazz Archivist* 6, no. 2 (December 1991): 1–14.

———. "The Mexican Band Legend, Part II." *Jazz Archivist* 9, no. 1 (May 1994): 1–17.

"Story of Arnaud's." 1950. Special Collections, Howard-Tilton Memorial Library, Tulane University. https://digitallibrary.tulane.edu/islandora/object/tulane%3A18399/datastream/PDF/view.

Sublette, Ned. *The World That Made New Orleans: From Spanish Silver to Congo Square*. Chicago: Lawrence Hill Books, 2008.

Sullivan, Lester. "Composers of Color of Nineteenth Century New Orleans: The History behind the Music." *Black Music Research Journal* 8, no. 1 (1988): 51–82.

Thomas, Lynell. *Desire and Disaster in New Orleans: Tourism, Race, and Historical Memory*. Durham, NC: Duke University Press, 2014.

Thompson, Ian. *Choctaw Food: Remembering the Land, Rekindling Ancient Knowledge*. Durant, OK: Choctaw Nation Education Special Projects, 2019.

Thompson, Shirley Elizabeth. *Exiles at Home: The Struggle to Become American in Creole New Orleans*. Cambridge, MA: Harvard University Press, 2009.

Tibbetts, John H. "African Roots, Carolina Gold." *Coastal Heritage Magazine* 21, no. 1 (Summer 2006), 3–10.

"To Thomas Jefferson from William C. C. Claiborne, 30 August 1804." Founders Online, National Archives. https://founders.archives.gov/documents/Jefferson/01-44-02-0292.

Tomlinson, Elizabeth. "The History of the Raised Floor House in Louisiana." LSU Ag Center. https://www.lsuagcenter.com/topics/family_home/home/design_construction/design/the-history-of-the-raisedfloor-house-in-louisiana.

Tregle, Joseph G., Jr. "Creoles and Americans." In *Creole New Orleans: Race and Americanization,* edited by Arnold R. Hirsch and Joseph Logsdon, 131–85. Baton Rouge: Louisiana State University Press, 1992.

Tucker, Susan, ed. *New Orleans Cuisine: Fourteen Signature Dishes and Their Histories.* Oxford: University of Mississippi Press, 2009.

Tyler, Pamela. *Silk Stockings and Ballot Boxes: Women and Politics in New Orleans, 1920–1963.* Athens: University of Georgia Press, 1996.

Usner, Daniel H., Jr. *American Indians in Early New Orleans: From Calumet to Raquette.* Baton Rouge: Louisiana State University Press, 2018.

———. *Indians, Settlers, and Slaves in a Frontier Exchange Economy: The Lower Mississippi Valley before 1783.* Chapel Hill: University of North Carolina Press, 1992.

———. *Weaving Alliances with Other Women: Chitimacha Indian Work in the New South.* Athens: University of Georgia Press, 2015.

Vaz, Kim Marie. *The "Baby Dolls": Breaking the Race and Gender Barriers of the New Orleans Mardi Gras Tradition.* Baton Rouge: Louisiana State University Press, 2013.

Vella, Christina. "Edgar Degas." *64 Parishes.* Last modified February 13, 2019. https://64parishes.org/entry/edgar-degas.

———. *Intimate Enemies: The Two Worlds of the Baroness de Pontalba.* Baton Rouge: Louisiana State University Press, 1997.

Verdin, Monique. "In the Heart of the Yakni Chitto," *Issues in Science and Technology* 40, no. 2 (Winter 2024). https://issues.org/monique-verdin-art-yakni-chitto/.

———. *Return to Yakni Chitto: Houma Migrations.* New Orleans: University of New Orleans Press, 2020.

Vernet, Julian. "A Community of Resistance: The Organization of Protest in New Orleans against the U.S. Territorial Administration, 1803–1805." *French Colonial History* 11 (2010): 47–70.

Vlach, John Michael. "The Shotgun House: An African Architectural Legacy, Part 1." *Pioneer America* 8, no. 1 (January 1976): 47–56.

Von Eschen, Penny M. *Satchmo Blows up the World: Jazz Ambassadors Play the Cold War.* Cambridge, MD: Harvard University Press, 2006.

Waggonner and Ball Architecture and Environment. "Living with Water." https://wbae.com/living-with-water-2/.

Wall, Bennett H., et al., eds. *Louisiana: A History.* 3rd ed. Wheeling, IL: Harlan Davidson Press, 1997.

Ward, Martha. *Voodoo Queen: The Spirited Lives of Marie Laveau.* Oxford: University of Mississippi Press, 2004.

Ware, Carolyn. "Croatians in Southeastern Louisiana." *Folklife in Louisiana,* 1996. https://www.louisianafolklife.org/lt/articles_essays/main_misc_croatians_s_la.html#tab12.

Wegmann, Mary Ann, the Law Library of Louisiana, and the University of New Orleans History Department. "Government House: First Louisiana Supreme Court Location, 1813–1818." *New Orleans Historical.* Accessed April 17, 2024. https://neworleanshistorical.org/items/show/801.

White, Michael. "New Orleans Brass Bands: A Cultural Tradition." In *The Triumph of the Soul: Cultural and Psychological Elements of African American Music,* edited by Ferdinand Jones and Arthur C. Jones, 69–96. New York: Praeger Press, 2000.

White, Sophie. *Voices of the Enslaved: Love, Labor, and Longing in French Louisiana.* Chapel Hill: University of North Carolina Press, 2019.

Williams, Susan. *White Malice: The CIA and the Covert Recolonization of Africa.* New York: Public Affairs Books, 2021.

Wilson, Samuel, Jr. "The Plantation of the Company of the Indies." *Louisiana History* 31, no. 2 (Spring 1990): 161–90.

Wilson, Sam, Jr., and Leonard V. Huber. *The Cabildo on Jackson Square.* Gretna: Pelican Publishing, 1973.

World War I Draft Cards: Louis Armstrong. National Archives Records Administration, Atlanta, https://www.archives.gov/atlanta/wwi-draft/armstrong.html.

Young, Zachary. "Canal Street Gets the Post-Mamboist Treatment." *Offbeat Magazine,* October 4, 2010. https://www.offbeat.com/news/canal-street-gets-the-post mamboist-treatment/.

Index